INTERACTIVE
EVALUATION
PRACTICE

To our parents,
Florence and Robert King
and
Ellen and Leo Stevahn,
who taught us that people matter

INTERACTIVE

EVALUATION

PRACTICE

Mastering the Interpersonal Dynamics
of Program Evaluation

JEAN A. KING
University of Minnesota

LAURIE STEVAHN
Seattle University

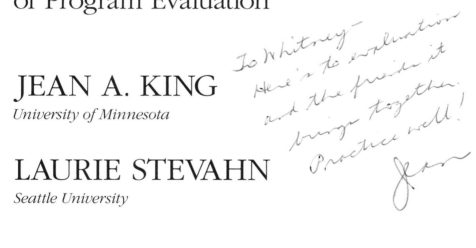

Los Angeles | London | New Delhi
Singapore | Washington DC

Los Angeles | London | New Delhi
Singapore | Washington DC

FOR INFORMATION:

SAGE Publications, Inc.
2455 Teller Road
Thousand Oaks, California 91320
E-mail: order@sagepub.com

SAGE Publications Ltd.
1 Oliver's Yard
55 City Road
London EC1Y 1SP
United Kingdom

SAGE Publications India Pvt. Ltd.
B 1/I 1 Mohan Cooperative Industrial Area
Mathura Road, New Delhi 110 044
India

SAGE Publications Asia-Pacific Pte. Ltd.
33 Church Street
#10-04 Samsung Hub
Singapore 049483

Acquisitions Editor: Vicki Knight
Associate Editor: Lauren Habib
Editorial Assistant: Kalie Koscielak
Production Editor: Laureen Gleason
Copy Editor: Megan Granger
Typesetter: C&M Digitals (P) Ltd.
Proofreader: Talia Greenberg
Indexer: Sheila Bodell
Cover Designer: Anupama Krishnan
Marketing Manager: Nicole Elliott
Permissions Editor: Adele Hutchinson

Printed in the United States of America

Library of Congress Cataloging-in-Publication Data

King, Jean A.

Interactive evaluation practice: Mastering the interpersonal dynamics of program evaluation / Jean A. King, Laurie Stevahn.

p. cm.
Includes bibliographical references and index.

ISBN 978-0-7619-2673-3 (pbk.)

1. Evaluation research (Social action programs) I. Stevahn, Laurie. II. Title.

H61.K5453 2013
001.4—dc23   2011049039

This book is printed on acid-free paper.

MIX
Paper from
responsible sources
FSC® C014174

12 13 14 15 16 10 9 8 7 6 5 4 3 2 1

BRIEF CONTENTS

Detailed Contents

ABOUT THE AUTHORS

Jean A. King, PhD, is professor and director of Graduate Studies in the Department of Organizational Leadership, Policy, and Development at the University of Minnesota, where she teaches in the Evaluation Studies program. With more than 30 years of experience conducting evaluations, she has taught evaluation courses and mentored graduate students for 20-plus years. Jean founded the Minnesota Evaluation Studies Institute in 1996 and currently serves as its director. She received her bachelor's, master's, and doctoral degrees from Cornell University and taught middle school English in upstate New York before moving to New Orleans, LA, to become a professor at Tulane University. In 1989 she moved upriver to the University of Minnesota as the founding director of the Center for Applied Research and Educational Improvement in the College of Education and Human Development, a position she held for 4 years before working collaboratively to revitalize program evaluation instruction in the college. She has received numerous awards for her work, including the Myrdal Award for Evaluation Practice and the Ingle Award for Extraordinary Service from the American Evaluation Association, three teaching awards, and three community service awards. A sought-after presenter and longtime writer on evaluation, she is the author of numerous articles, chapters, and reviews and retains an abiding interest in participatory evaluation and evaluation capacity building.

Laurie Stevahn, PhD, is associate professor in the College of Education at Seattle University and director of the Educational Leadership doctoral program, where she teaches graduate courses in educational research, social justice in professional practice, models of teaching, assessment for learning, and leadership for effective schools. She earned her doctorate in educational psychology from the University of Minnesota, her master's in curriculum and instruction from Seattle Pacific University, and her bachelor's in political science from Pacific Lutheran University. Prior to joining the academy, she taught high school social studies and mathematics in Washington State and founded Professional Development Associates, a consulting company specializing in human resource and organization development, program design and implementation, and participatory evaluation for capacity building. Laurie conducts research on conflict resolution training and essential competencies for program evaluators and has published on these topics in a variety of journals, including *American Educational Research Journal*, *American Journal of Evaluation*, and *Child Development*. She also is coauthor of three books for professionals: *Cooperative Learning: Where Heart Meets Mind*, *The Portfolio Organizer: Succeeding With Portfolios in Your Classroom*, and *Needs Assessment Phase III: Taking Action for Change*. Her honors include the National Staff Development Council's Best Non-Dissertation Research Award for examining the effectiveness of the Louisiana Center for Law and Civic Education's teen leadership program on conflict resolution and violence prevention. She is past chair of two American Educational Research Association Special Interest Groups (Cooperative Learning: Theory, Research, and Practice; Conflict Resolution and Violence Prevention) and currently serves on the executive board of directors for the International Association for the Study of Cooperation in Education. In addition to her work with organizations across the United States, Laurie's international work includes invited presentations in Australia, Canada, the Czech Republic, Greece, Italy, and the Netherlands.

PREFACE

"It always seems impossible until it's done."

—Nelson Mandela

To say that this book has been at least 10 years in the making is not an exaggeration. The two of us met in the late 1990s when Laurie was working on her doctorate in educational psychology at the University of Minnesota and registered for a colloquium on evaluator competencies. Very quickly, we realized that we shared common passions—rigorous research, interactive teaching, high-quality writing, and stimulating conversations, to say nothing of smoked salmon, fine wine, and Pearson's Nut Goodies. Within a year we became professional collaborators, merging evaluation practice and social psychology. We began coteaching a workshop that applied principles of social psychology to participatory evaluation, showing participants how to use the solid grounding of psychological research to frame interactions among people involved in evaluations. We became increasingly enthusiastic about our content, naming it "interactive evaluation practice." Encouraged by workshop attendees, after a couple of years we wrote a book proposal and were pleased to get a contract in fairly short order. And then life intervened.

Year by year, we remained keenly aware of the need to complete our manuscript. At the American Evaluation Association conference in Atlanta (2004), we visited the Margaret Mitchell House and Museum on Peachtree Street. A bookmark in the gift shop quoted Mitchell's answer as to why she had written *Gone With the Wind:* "In a weak moment I decided to write a book." Agreeing with the sentiment completely, we bought two bookmarks and went back to work on our outline. Six years later that chapter-by-chapter outline was thoroughly detailed, and we finally began to turn those years of bullet points into prose. In retrospect—and surely to our publisher's dismay—we think the delay was beneficial. We couldn't have written *this* book 10 years ago because we've learned a great deal in that time as we've interacted with people working on program evaluations in a variety of settings and content areas and continued to apply these ideas ourselves on evaluation projects.

Even as we suffered from obsessive outlining syndrome, our reasons for writing the book in the first place kept alive the hope that someday we would actually write it. First, we believe that interpersonal skills are vital to the practice of program evaluation and that the field to date has not adequately addressed their importance. In fact, it has barely acknowledged their existence. Second, we believe that program evaluators should ground the interpersonal elements of their practice in what research has told us about human interaction. *Not* to do so is a waste of accumulated knowledge. Third, we believe that people are genuinely able to develop effective interpersonal evaluation practice. Some individuals evidence a natural knack for things interpersonal, while others need to acquire skills more purposefully—but everyone can learn these skills. We've seen that happen on a regular basis.

Our goal, then, was to create a unique manuscript, an accessible, hands-on book rooted firmly in research, one that evaluators could use as a resource as they practiced and reflected on their interpersonal craft over time. We wanted it to be incredibly serviceable, including exhibits and templates for repeated use and multiple examples from different types of practice and content. The true measure of our success in writing the book would be the number of copies with extensive highlighting and marginalia, dog-eared pages, and sticky notes marking important sections. Let us be clear, though, about what this book is *not*.

First, it is not an introductory book on how to conduct program evaluations. There are many such books widely available, and our short list of recommendations would include Alkin (2011); Bamberger, Rugh, and Mabry (2011); Chen (2005); Davidson (2005); Fitzpatrick, Sanders, and Worthen (2010); Patton (2012); and Russ-Eft and Preskill (2009).

Second, it is not a book describing an approach to (or a model for) participatory evaluation. It is simply wrong to say that if you're thinking about things interpersonal, then you must be engaged in what the field labels "participatory evaluation." We would argue that interactive evaluation practice applies to *all* evaluation, not only to participatory evaluation. Program evaluation, at its core, is a human enterprise. Every evaluation, even one that is independently designed and implemented by an evaluator or evaluation team to guard against bias, requires that evaluators (or at least some members of an evaluation team) interact with a wide range of individuals and groups—clients, potential users, staff members, support personnel, data sources, and so on—before, during, and even after the study. Creative evaluators will use the skills and strategies presented in this book in every setting, whether or not a given evaluation features extensive stakeholder participation. So, while this book is not a general introduction to the process of designing and conducting a program evaluation, we would nevertheless argue, emphatically, that its content applies to all evaluation practice.

Third, let us state what to us is obvious: This is not a book about clever icebreakers. In our experience, some people assume, incorrectly, that attending to personal interaction and interactive strategies is important only at the beginning of projects, i.e., that they function well for introducing people and putting them (at least those who don't roll their eyes) at ease. On the contrary, we would argue that the content of the skill-building chapters in Part II, grounded as it is in a research base, is not only useful to every form of evaluation but, as we are often told, in interpersonal interactions in other realms as well—from amicably settling disagreements with a spouse to managing a supervisor's outsize ego, from successfully negotiating with a teenager over curfew expectations to addressing workplace conflict.

As we thought about how to describe the book's structure, an old Monty Python routine came to mind. For those of you old enough to remember, Anne ("That's A-n-n-e, Anne, not a-n") Elk's "theory" on Brontosauruses fits our book. Like Brontosauruses, it is thin at one end; much, much thicker in the middle; and thin again at the far end.

- The three chapters in Part I present interactive evaluation practice (IEP) by introducing the concept (Chapter 1), framing it (Chapter 2), and presenting its foundations in research, ending with a set of seven principles for IEP (Chapter 3).
- The much thicker Part II—two and a half times as long as the other parts—contains five chapters and multiple exhibits and templates to help you develop skills and strategies for IEP: holding evaluation conversations (Chapter 4), applying interactive strategies (Chapter 5), managing conflict (Chapter 6), creating a viable evaluation process (Chapter 7), and handling the unexpected (Chapter 8). A word of warning: Many of the topics addressed in these chapters (e.g., conflict management, culture, and organization development) themselves deserve to be—and indeed are—the subjects of entire books. What we have done is focus explicitly on how these issues affect interpersonal interactions during evaluations. Readers who are interested in more detailed coverage of specific content should use the reference list at the end of the book to identify additional sources.
- The three chapters in Part III each contain a teaching case that reflects a different type of practice: evaluator-directed, collaborative, and participant-directed. For each case, there are three sets of reflection questions about how the evaluation is going at different points in the process, a set of what we call

case study TIPS (exercises that ask readers to *think* about, *interact* with, *practice*, and *situate* the content), and a summary of how the IEP principles apply, both positively and negatively, to the case. The cases are not intended to be exemplary evaluation studies but, rather, studies that have interpersonal elements meriting discussion. Our hope is that applying Part II skills, strategies, and considerations to these cases will help readers make the transition from reflecting on these cases to reflecting on their own evaluation practice.

We think there are two likely ways that people will read this book. For many, including newcomers to program evaluation, it may make sense to start at the beginning and read straight through, ideally joining with a partner to work on and discuss the case chapters in Part III. Experienced practitioners may prefer to start with Part I to gain an understanding of how IEP is framed, then read the chapters in Part II in whatever order makes personal sense; our thought is that practicing professionals may want to choose specific content on an "as-needed" basis. Moving on to the TIPS exercises following each chapter in Part III may also prove useful to practitioners; the "Situate" activities, in particular, provide an opportunity to reflect on personal evaluation practice in relation to the cases. Evaluation instructors should note that the "Interact" activities are designed for use in a classroom, although they can also be done independently. Students may want to write up their own cases for group discussion, borrowing the structure from the chapters in Part III.

Three final details: First, we have purposefully alternated the gender of evaluators in our examples throughout the book to suggest the field's gender equity. We hope that is an accurate reflection of the field. Second, there is a glossary at the end of the text (pp. 382–387). Words that are boldfaced in the text appear in the glossary. Third, our evaluation practice is located primarily in the United States, so that is where our case examples are based. We believe, however, that the principles of interactive evaluation practice work internationally and look forward to discussing these ideas with colleagues who work in non-U.S. settings.

Now, together, let's begin to master the interpersonal side of program evaluation. Here's to successful interactive evaluation practice!

—Jean A. King and Laurie Stevahn
March 2012

ACKNOWLEDGMENTS

As collaborators and friends, we have always appreciated the challenge and privilege of bringing the ideas in this book to life and strive to do so in our practice on a daily basis. Truly, our ongoing professional partnership has only deepened our commitment to cooperative processes and the power of interactive evaluation practice. We remain grateful for opportunities to collaborate on evaluation projects and remain close friends, even after the 10-plus-year task of writing this book.

We sincerely want to thank those in our respective circles who continue to support and sustain us in wonderful ways. Jean thanks her family: "friend husband," Herr Mann, and editor *par excellence* Stuart Appelbaum; son Ben and daughter Hannah Appelbaum, who, thankfully, remind her on a regular basis what really matters in this life; brother Robert, who provides her helpful examples and zany props; and feline assistants Marvel Dawn (who sadly didn't live to see the manuscript completed) and Gustopher. She also thanks her student and community collaborators, who routinely provide new lessons, examples, and inspiration. A special thanks to her colleagues in Anoka-Hennepin Independent School District #11 (MN), especially Lelia Redin, Laurie Resch, Donna Studer, Michelle Langenfeld, Mary Clarkson, and Johnna Rohmer-Hirt; the collaborative evaluation process described in Chapter 10 was adapted in part from evaluation capacity building activities that Anoka-Hennepin staff have developed over the past decade. Finally, Jean wants to thank five colleagues who have long been part of her professional circle and a source of inspiration and hope these many years: Jason Millman and Dick Nunneley (of blessed memory), Marv Alkin, Dick Krueger, and Michael Quinn Patton. Laurie thanks her family: "mom," "dad," and "brother Mike" in California, whose unconditional love, constant caring, and unwavering support truly make "home" a place of the heart; and her Rowley and Galligan and Mund relatives in Minnesota, who continue to fill her life with inspiration and joy, especially when "reflection circles" at family gatherings sustain and honor what matters most. She also thanks her friends and colleagues near and far who are like family—Patty Noah and Ralph Graves; Linda Munger; Nancy Schultz and her husband, Ray (whose spirit lives on); Margit McGuire and Steve Milam; Tom and Brenda Kidd; Jindy and Dave Yantis—who listen, inspire, believe, and always seem to know when nothing could be better than a word of encouragement or an invitation to connect—savoring wine, telling stories, sharing life. Belonging to communities of faith also nourishes Laurie's soul and keeps her whole—she is grateful for the people of God at St. Luke's (Bellevue, WA), Gloria Dei (St. Paul, MN), St. Mark's (Pleasant Hill, CA), and First Lutheran (Bothell, WA). Finally, Laurie extends thanks to three scholars and friends whose theorizing, research, and practice in cooperation and constructive conflict resolution continue to illuminate and influence her professional and personal pathways profoundly: David W. Johnson, Roger T. Johnson, and Morton Deutsch.

We sincerely thank those at SAGE who have dedicated time and talent to this volume, including C. Deborah Laughton, who worked at SAGE when we signed this book's contract; the entire editorial, production, and marketing team for attending to every detail; and especially Vicki Knight, acquisitions editor, for providing thoughtful and insightful guidance and for getting us to this day. Finally, we and SAGE gratefully acknowledge the contributions of the following reviewers who took time during a busy academic year to provide helpful feedback: Chris L. S. Coryn, Western Michigan University; Douglas Klayman, Social Dynamics, LLC; George W. Noblit, University of North Carolina at Chapel Hill; Ladislaus Semali, Pennsylvania State University; Christopher Stream, University of Nevada, Las Vegas; Mangala Subramaniam, Purdue University; and Rose M. Ylimaki, University of Arizona.

PART I

AN INTRODUCTION TO INTERACTIVE EVALUATION PRACTICE

The three chapters in Part I provide an introduction to interactive evaluation practice (IEP). Chapter 1 begins the introduction by explaining the importance of interpersonal dynamics in program evaluation, distinguishing between Patton's (2008) *personal* factor and what we call the *interpersonal* factor, and providing basic definitions of program evaluation, IEP, and evaluator role. Chapter 2 structures a discussion of IEP by presenting three frameworks: basic inquiry tasks, the interpersonal participation quotient, and evaluation capacity building, demonstrating how these three can work together to explicate IEP. Chapter 3, the final chapter in Part I, presents IEP's foundations in social interdependence theory and research on evaluation use, culminating in seven principles that each chapter in Parts II and III will systematically apply: get personal, structure interaction, examine context, consider politics, expect conflict, respect culture, and take time.

1

INTRODUCING INTERACTIVE EVALUATION PRACTICE

Chapter Preview

- Explain why program evaluators should pay attention to interpersonal dynamics
- Distinguish between the personal and interpersonal factors in program evaluation
- Define program evaluation and interactive evaluation practice (IEP)
- Discuss the concept of evaluator role in IEP

INTRODUCTION

To be human is to engage in interpersonal dynamics. *Inter*: between. *Personal*: people. *Dynamics*: forces that produce activity and change. Combining these definitions, **interpersonal dynamics** are the forces between people that lead to activity and change. Whenever and wherever people interact, these dynamics are at work, whether managing a tense meeting between competitors for a contract, coming late to a party where you don't know a soul, leading a group of 7-year-olds in a boisterous game of hide-and-seek, buying a triple skinny cappuccino from a bleary-eyed barista, or conducting a program evaluation. Program evaluators must skillfully manage interpersonal dynamics as they engage others in the often challenging activities of evaluation, successfully applying the techniques of interactive evaluation practice to facilitate the process over time.

This chapter sets the stage for understanding interactive evaluation practice. It begins with a rationale for paying attention to interaction among people in program evaluations and then elucidates basic distinctions, definitions, and the key concept of the evaluator's role.

WHY IT PAYS TO PAY ATTENTION TO INTERPERSONAL DYNAMICS IN PROGRAM EVALUATION

The reality of evaluation practice demands interaction with people—clients, collaborators, stakeholders, and data sources, among others. What this interaction looks like, of course, can vary. Some evaluators meet with their clients at the beginning of a study and don't see them again until the final report is drafted. Other evaluators interact with clients routinely, working together to frame questions, to design data collection procedures, and, ultimately, to make judgments. Still others coach people as they evaluate their own programs or build their organizations' capacity to conduct evaluations. Regardless of how frequently or in what ways an evaluator chooses to interact with people, however, interpersonal skills matter. Consider the following true story, a cautionary tale about the unintended consequences of failing to attend to interpersonal dynamics.

The tension in the state senator's office was as oppressive as Louisiana humidity. He leaned back in his chair and launched the 2-pound evaluation report onto his desk. It landed with authority. "All I see in here are stories and descriptions. Lots of words but no numbers. Didn't you people ever think to check if students *learned* anything thanks to what you did?" The assembled state department staff, school personnel, and external evaluators grimaced, remembering the choice they had explicitly made 2 years earlier. The outcome of that collaborative planning session had been clear: To collect standardized test data would violate the spirit of the innovation. How could teachers and administrators reinvent public schooling within the confines of traditional standardized achievement tests?

And so the evaluators gathered no test scores. Instead, for 2 years, enormous amounts of qualitative data crammed file folders and bankers' boxes, morphing gradually into three-to-four-page, single-spaced baseline cases in 10-point font for each of 39 sites—almost 100 pages of cutting-edge, thick description that formed the baseline for a multimillion-dollar, 10-year statewide school change evaluation. But not if this legislator cut off funding to the state office that directed the program.

"If you want test scores for the 3 years, we can easily get them," a district administrator volunteered. The group quickly nodded in agreement. Was that a snarl on the legislator's lip before he spoke? "You're too late. I can't support this program in the next biennial budget." The result: Within months, the state office was dismantled, its staff fired or moved to other positions, and the participating districts statewide headed into a third year of major reform with no external funding. The legislator, incidentally, won reelection that November.

Although in many cases the consequences are less dire, clear risks exist when evaluators fail to pay attention to interpersonal dynamics in evaluation studies or, just as bad, when they try to and fail. As evident in the story, an evaluator may inadvertently ignore issues important to critical stakeholders. In this case, the evaluation team failed to consult the state legislator, a powerful stakeholder in the final analysis, to determine his information needs, and the proposed 10-year experiment died at the end of 2 years. The need for buy-in or ownership by key personnel in a political context, of course, is not news. But some evaluators fail to appreciate fully the interpersonal complexities and the subtle—and not-so-subtle—interplay of personality, ego, and politics inherent in any evaluation.

Consider these additional examples:

- A group of program directors in a statewide collaborative became key informants in the design of an evaluation system for the larger organization. Not truly supporting the system approach, they engaged in perfunctory interactions with the evaluator, smiling and minimally providing what they were asked to. Simultaneously, they met individually with key board members in an attempt to sabotage the study behind the evaluator's back, complaining that the evaluation procedures simply couldn't capture what took place in the programs they directed.

- A novice evaluator asked a group of urban Hmong parents to make suggestions for improving a poorly attended, culturally specific parent-education program, not knowing that Hmong culture deems it impolite to criticize authority in public. In the group setting, the parents all said they could think of no needed changes, which the evaluator happily reported to program staff and the funder.

- In a collaborative study that intentionally taught participants evaluation skills, a group of experienced teachers felt obligated to take on certain technical details, even though they privately questioned their ability to do so. Given the limited resources for the project, they feared that expressing any concerns might undermine the effort. Uncomfortable asking the evaluator for help, they constructed a survey and analyzed its results, learning only later that inadequacies in the survey limited the value of the information they collected.

As these examples show, the potential for interpersonal snags is common, and, unfortunately, many evaluators learn about them after the fact, when it is too late to respond.

THE PERSONAL AND INTERPERSONAL FACTORS

Interestingly, the field of program evaluation has acknowledged the importance of the personal factor—focusing evaluation activities and findings on people who care about them—for more than 30 years (Patton, 1978). **Utilization-focused evaluation,** "evaluation done for and with specific, intended primary users for specific, intended uses" (Patton, 2008, p. 37), brings the personal factor into evaluation practice. In discussing the research from which the idea emerged (Patton et al., 1977), Patton (2008) defines the **personal factor** and its value:

The personal factor is the presence of an identifiable individual or group of people who personally care about the evaluation and the findings it generates. Where such a person or group was present, evaluations were used; where the personal factor was absent, there was a correspondingly marked absence of evaluation impact. (p. 66; emphasis in original)

If evaluators want to increase the likelihood of use, then identifying and working closely with specific individuals or groups of people who are interested in the evaluation process and its results are of paramount importance, helping focus the study. "The personal factor represents the leadership, interest, enthusiasm, determination, commitment, assertiveness, and caring of specific individual people" (Patton, 2012, pp. 63–64). While evaluation influence—its capacity to produce changes in understanding or knowledge indirectly (Kirkhart, 2000)—may be important to evaluation's big picture in the long run, in the short term, the personal factor highlights the importance of one-on-one, face-to-face interactions between the evaluator and eventual users. In the words of Michael Patton (2012),

Evaluators need skills in building relationships, facilitating groups, managing conflict, walking political tight ropes, and effective interpersonal communications to capitalize on the importance of the personal factor. Technical skills and social science knowledge aren't sufficient to get evaluations used. People skills are critical. (p. 76)

As the following example demonstrates, an evaluator can directly apply the personal factor. During the evaluation of a staff development program in a national nonprofit organization, an evaluator might meet regularly with two primary intended users: the organization's director, who commissioned the study, and the head of the training program being studied. In the planning phases of the evaluation, she would solicit concerns and questions that each wanted addressed, then design the evaluation to ensure that those answers were available at the study's conclusion. As the evaluation developed, she would again touch base with these potential users to discuss what methods would be credible in their context and what might happen if results of one sort or another emerged. They would review data collection instruments together to make sure they made sense. At the reporting stage, she would develop reports that presented the evaluation outcomes clearly in light of their potential use both in the training program itself and in the organization more broadly. Acknowledging the personal factor—attending to the interests of two key intended users—enables the evaluator to target the evaluation, ensuring that the study will generate information they can use. Of course, given the multiple factors affecting decision making in any organization, there is no guarantee that they *will* use it.

While evaluation writings to date have given widespread attention to Patton's personal factor, by contrast, they have paid scant attention to what we call the *inter*personal factor. In an address to the American Evaluation Association almost 20 years ago, then-President Karen Kirkhart (1995) coined the term **interpersonal validity**—the extent to which an evaluator is able to relate meaningfully and effectively to individuals in the evaluation setting—but explicit attention to the concept has been slow in coming. The **interpersonal factor** highlights the unique ability of an evaluator to do two things: (a) interact with people constructively throughout the framing and implementation of evaluation studies and (b) create activities and conditions conducive to positive interactions among evaluation participants. The interpersonal factor is the mechanism that brings the personal factor to life and enables it to work. The *personal factor* is concerned with making evaluation useful by engaging key stakeholders; the *interpersonal factor* is concerned with creating, managing, and ultimately mastering the interpersonal dynamics that make the evaluation possible and inform its outcomes. One is concerned with eventual use, the other with establishing buy-in among participants and a valid evaluation process.

On the plus side, an evaluator's interpersonal skills may encourage people to examine their program honestly or to consider negative findings with a positive attitude. On the minus side, an evaluator who is unable to interact with people effectively places an evaluation study at great risk. He may fail to identify key issues for the inquiry or the political constraints that threaten it. He may antagonize important stakeholders and jeopardize the value of the data collected. Absent effective interpersonal interactions, program evaluation is like a machine without proper lubrication. At best, the machine works. Gears may grind and teeth sheer off cogs, but nothing breaks down. At worst, the entire evaluation enterprise grinds to a screeching halt amidst a cloud of steam.

If the interpersonal factor is so important, you may well ask why the field to date has largely ignored it. The development of program evaluation points to five likely reasons for the omission.

First, this inattention may stem from the presumption early on that what mattered in evaluation were the technical skills of research design and large-scale quantitative methodology. Experience fairly quickly pointed out that while such skills were surely necessary in some settings, they were certainly not sufficient if evaluations were going to make meaningful contributions to program improvement and social change. A growing awareness that decision makers did not necessarily act on evaluation results—the implosion of the Big Bang Theory of Use—led evaluators to study the multiple factors that affect evaluation use in organizations. As noted, the personal factor emerged from one such study, but issues related to the explicit skills required to interact effectively with people in evaluation settings—the "how to"—did not.

A second possible reason is also methodological but more contentious. For well over a decade (the late 1970s to the early 1990s), program evaluators engaged in a highly visible debate about the relative value of **quantitative methods**—the field's mainstay since its inception in the 1960s—and **qualitative methods**, which emerged as a helpful solution in responding to certain types of evaluation questions. The *either/or* nature of the conflict eventually yielded to a more inclusive *both/and* dialogue and, for most, to the widespread acceptance of mixed methods. The reascendance of the so-called gold standard of experimental design in the past few years has again focused attention on the intricacies of quantitative research design. The interpersonal skills required for effective evaluation, however, have remained an issue more pertinent to qualitative data collection, rather than to the general examination of the interpersonal skills required of evaluators in all settings.

A third reason the interpersonal factor has not gained currency relates to the minimal research to date on program evaluation using various social relations theories in psychology or sociology. Exhibit 1.1 lists the doctoral disciplines of 34 winners of professional awards related to evaluation theory: the Evaluation Research Society's Myrdal Award for Science, the Lazarsfeld Award for Evaluation Theory (1977–1982), and, following the creation of the American Evaluation Association (AEA), AEA's theory award (the continuation of the Lazarsfeld Award) that merged the two earlier awards (1983–2010). Of these 34 respected scholars in evaluation, 6 (18%) hold doctoral degrees related to measurement, inquiry, or statistics. Further, 14 (41%) completed advanced degrees in a discipline that studies interpersonal issues (i.e., psychology, social psychology, educational psychology, clinical psychology, anthropology, communications research, social work), and an additional 5 (15%) earned degrees in sociology—more than half, a total of 56%, hold degrees that provided a grounding in the interpersonal. Their primary contributions to evaluation theory, however, did not directly address social psychological or sociological issues, focusing instead on measurement, research design, methods, and the developing practice of evaluation.

Exhibit 1.1   Doctoral Disciplines of Recipients of Professional Theory Awards in Evaluation

Evaluation Research Society Alva and Gunnar Myrdal Science Award Recipients		
Award Winner	**Year[1]**	**Doctoral Discipline**
Donald Campbell	1977	Social psychology
Frederick Mosteller	1978	Mathematical statistics
Lee J. Cronbach	1979	Educational psychology
Carol Weiss	1980	Sociology
Peter Rossi	1981	Sociology
Thomas Cook	1982	Communications research
Evaluation Research Society/AEA Lazarsfeld Award for Evaluation Theory Recipients		
Award Winner	**Year[2]**	**Doctoral Discipline**
Angus Campbell	1977	Political science
Harold Watts	1980	Economics
Aaron Wildavsky	1981	Political science
Thomas Chalmers	1982	Medicine
James Coleman	1983	Sociology
Gene Glass	1984	Educational psychology
Daniel Stufflebeam	1985	Measurement and statistics
Michael Scriven	1986	Philosophy
Egon Guba Yvonna Lincoln	1987	Quantitative inquiry Higher education administration

[1]The Alva and Gunnar Myrdal Science Award existed separately from the Lazarsfeld Award from 1977 to 1982, when the AEA was created, and one theory award (the Lazarsfeld) continued.

[2]The Lazarsfeld Award has not been given every year, including 1978, 1979, 1998, 1999, 2001, 2004, 2006, and 2011.

Award Winner	Year[2]	Doctoral Discipline
Robert Stake	1988	Psychology
Richard Nathan	1989	Political economy and government
Ernest House	1990	Education
Richard Light	1991	Statistics
Rudolf Moos	1992	Psychology
Huey Tsyh-Chen	1993	Sociology
William Shadish	1994	Clinical psychology
Marvin Alkin	1995	Education
Mark Lipsey	1996	Psychology (social psychology and psycholinguistics)
Michael Quinn Patton	1997	Sociology
David Fetterman	2000	Educational and medical anthropology
Thomas Schwandt	2002	Educational inquiry methodology
Jennifer Greene	2003	Educational psychology
Werner W. Wittmann	2005	Psychology
Karen Kirkhart	2007	Social work and social science
J. Bradley Cousins	2008	Educational measurement and evaluation
Donna Mertens	2009	Educational psychology
Jonathan Morell	2010	Social psychology

A fourth reason for the inattention to the interpersonal factor is more practical. Interpersonal interactions are to evaluators as water is to fish, and evaluators—theorists and practitioners alike—have seemingly taken social interaction for granted in program evaluation. Evaluation textbooks routinely acknowledge the challenge of situational politics but rarely provide specific strategies or skill building for responding to them. By contrast, certain fields—for example, social work, clinical psychology, and special education—acknowledge the necessity of training practitioners in interpersonal skills. Clients in these fields require high-quality interaction because it is essential to effective practice. Providing practitioners with systematic training in interpersonal interaction increases the likelihood of their success, and *not* providing such training would seem a glaring omission. Such common sense has not been the case in program evaluation, perhaps because—interpersonal skills or not—in most cases the evaluative process simply moves forward, regardless of the quality of interpersonal interactions.

A fifth reason may relate to the rather basic fact that teaching people inter-personal skills is challenging. Many interpersonal skills are neither simple nor mechanical but, instead, are overwhelmingly complex. Even if someone is able and willing to learn, the fact that context affects the interpretation of interpersonal interactions—for example, an evaluator's attempt at objectivity in one context may be labeled a lack of cultural understanding in another—means that teaching them can require a great deal of time and practice. Consider an example borrowed from sociolinguistics: A man winks as an attractive young woman walks by. What sense can an evaluator make of this?

- Is he making a pass at her?
- Did his lunch disagree with him?
- Is he signaling a comrade?
- Does he have a twitch?
- Is he engaging in an obsessive-compulsive ritual?
- Is his contact lens bothering him?

Each explanation makes sense in a certain context, but knowing which is the correct interpretation requires understanding the man and young woman's relationship to each other in that context. If making sense of a simple interpersonal interaction like a wink is a challenge, how much more difficult, then, is understanding the multiple and continuing interactions among individuals in even a small program evaluation? The training challenge *is* daunting.

Yet even as we acknowledge the difficulty of teaching interpersonal skills, the good news is that these skills *can* be taught. In describing a seminar he formerly led, M. Q. Patton (personal communication, July 7, 2005) explained,

> Everybody had to go out and form a task force with an actual non-profit, negotiate an evaluation, come back, [and] share their experiences. We would role play them—the problems they ran into, the politics, the resistance. We would role play that, [then] they'd go back and try something different [and] bring it back in. We'd train people the way therapists get trained, the way that group facilitators get trained. . . . So it is learnable.

You *can* learn to foster successful interpersonal interactions in evaluation settings, and the purpose of this book is to teach exactly that.

We believe that the ability to interact skillfully with individuals and groups is one of the fundamental competencies of an evaluator, because the process of program evaluation is, finally, a series of human interactions and relationships over time. Hackneyed though the image may be, every evaluation study is like

notion of "assisted sensemaking" to the far broader imperative of improving social conditions generally.

Our definition of **program evaluation** borrows heavily from these earlier definitions. We define evaluation as follows:

> A process of systematic inquiry to provide sound information about the characteristics, activities, or outcomes of a program or policy for a valued purpose.

This definition differs from other definitions in two ways. First, acknowledging that people use evaluation for various purposes, our definition provides a category label, calling each of these potential uses "a valued purpose." In a given setting, evaluation clients and sponsors—the likely users of the evaluation—establish the study's purpose or purposes, and what they identify should then both guide the process and determine the extent to which it is ultimately labeled successful. Successfully identifying the valued purposes is one of the initial interpersonal challenges of any evaluation.

Second, to our minds it is an evaluator's job to provide not just *any* information but *sound* information about the object being studied. This feature distinguishes program evaluation from activities such as public relations or the manipulative efforts of project administrators who know in advance the answers they intend to find. Regardless of the process used, to be called evaluation an inquiry must demonstrate that the information collected results from transparent and mutually agreed-on procedures that ensure the data's quality. These will surely vary from situation to situation. The information gathered in a low-cost evaluation of a small social service program in a rural county will likely differ from that collected in a well-funded 50-state federal policy study. In every case, however, the evaluator must frame a systematic inquiry process that will generate the best information possible in that setting. Effective interpersonal interactions are essential to ensure that the data meet the field's standards of accuracy.

While the definitions in Exhibit 1.2 share commonalities, they also speak loudly and clearly to differences. One definition (Fitzpatrick et al., 2010), for example, references the criteria for making a judgment. Another (Weiss, 1998a) makes explicit the need for standards in an evaluation. In an earlier edition of a popular textbook, Posavac and Carey (2006) defined evaluation as a "collection of methods, skills, and sensitivities" needed to determine certain things about a human service, coming closest to identifying an evaluator as a person with specific knowledge and characteristics.

Because these definitions—our own included—speak to the general case, it is not surprising that they omit the fact that evaluators must interact with people to get the job of evaluation done. This leads us to the definition of interactive evaluation practice (IEP):

> **Interactive evaluation practice** is the intentional act of engaging people in making decisions, taking action, and reflecting while conducting an evaluation study.

We purposefully use the word *interactive* rather than *interpersonal* to describe this practice to highlight the fact that the evaluator and those involved in evaluations inevitably act on each other—the influence goes in both directions. IEP builds on what we know about structuring successful interpersonal dynamics in evaluation. In the best of times, people will make good decisions and take effective action as a result. We believe that attending to the interpersonal factor is an essential competency for evaluators as they develop relationships with their clients, program staff, and participants. The **Essential Competencies for Program Evaluators** (Stevahn, King, Ghere, & Minnema, 2005; see Appendix C) affirm this by identifying interpersonal competence as one broad category of competencies that includes six specific skills: "uses written communication skills, uses verbal/listening communication skills, uses negotiation skills, uses conflict resolution skills, facilitates constructive interpersonal interaction (teamwork, group facilitation, processing), and demonstrates cross-cultural competence" (p. 51).

An evaluator skilled in IEP will determine what interactions are needed to accomplish an evaluation's valued purpose, whether that is measuring the attainment of specific goals, making recommendations for program modification, or increasing the capacity of an organization to study itself. Effective interactions will also increase the likelihood that the study can generate sound information, regardless of the data collection method. The attention to reflection builds in a thoughtful interaction between and among the evaluator and program leaders, staff, and other stakeholders, a feedback loop to ensure that the study stays on track.

How does IEP relate to Patton's utilization-focused evaluation (UFE)? The message of UFE is straightforward: Focusing your evaluation on the concerns and questions of people who are intended to use its process and results increases the likelihood that they will use them. Taking a page from UFE, IEP also focuses on the intended users of evaluation studies but is broader and includes interactions with other people throughout the course of a study. Given the fear and resistance with which some people greet evaluation, a single thoughtless interaction—whether with a key stakeholder or with a client giving data—holds the potential to doom a study. As its definition suggests, the interpersonal factor has two components:

- First, the ability of an evaluator to interact constructively with a variety of players to further the success of an evaluation study
- Second, the ability to structure activities conducive to promoting mutual success among people who participate in the evaluation

Simply stated, the evaluator's interpersonal challenge is to create situations where people can meaningfully discuss issues related to the study and to engage people intentionally step by step throughout the evaluation process to envision its possibilities and use its results. Detailed explanation and examples of IEP form the content of this book, but before proceeding, we believe a brief digression into the metaphysics of evaluation is in order to address, in just a few pages, the enduring question of what it all might mean.

Evaluation Metaphysics

People, even evaluators, take comfort in the language of the familiar. On the one hand, a descriptive concept such as purpose can help you analyze evaluation practice. For example, a study that sets out to determine whether or not an early intervention program has attained explicit goals will surely differ from a formative evaluation of that program's development. These will both differ from a comparative multisite study of early intervention programs across the nation. Another helpful notion is the concept of role, which distinguishes, for example, between internal and external evaluators. Both internal and external evaluators are paid to work in an organization, but their relationships with staff differ because of the nature of their positions. **Internal evaluators** know the context well but may feel pressured to respond in certain ways. **External evaluators** may not know the setting well but may see aspects that people who live there no longer notice. These labels, then, allow us to discuss critical attributes that require attention in evaluation practice.

On the other hand, just as the definitions of evaluation suggest multiple possibilities for practice, so, too, do other evaluation terms. The clarity of theoretical categories can quickly become fuzzy in the light of evaluation reality, making an evaluator's job confusing. Consider the following examples.

- Stufflebeam and Shinkfield (2007) critique 26 approaches to program evaluation grouped into five categories: (1) pseudo-evaluations, (2) questions- and methods-oriented approaches (quasi-evaluation), (3) improvement- and accountability-oriented approaches, (4) social agenda and advocacy approaches, and (5) eclectic approaches. Although the many approaches are conceptually distinguishable, studies often, even typically, will use more than one, creating an overlap and interaction of approaches. Decision making, for example, is extremely common in evaluation contexts, and Stufflebeam and Shinkfield place UFE in its own category ("eclectic") because its portmanteau-like nature means it can effectively interact with any of the other approaches.

- The notion of **formative** and **summative evaluation** (Scriven, 1967) distinguishes between two types of evaluation studies: formative studies typically conducted for program staff to improve the program, and summative studies typically conducted for funders or significant others outside of the program for **accountability**. As useful as the distinction is, however, Scriven (1991a) notes that every formative evaluation is in a sense summative (i.e., outcomes of the program are documented up to that point) and every summative evaluation is in a sense formative (i.e., people may use the results to alter the program). To complicate matters further, consider two recent conceptual additions: Patton's (2011) **developmental evaluation** is similar to formative evaluation but applies to situations where formal summative evaluation is unlikely, and Scriven's (2005) **ascriptive evaluation** distinguishes situations where an evaluative judgment is made but no use is possible, e.g., the value of Hannibal's elephants in the ancient Punic Wars.

- The straightforward concept of **evaluator role** has witnessed a recent evolution (Ryan & Schwandt, 2002). Even the most basic distinction—so easily defined—between internal and external evaluators discussed above is not necessarily clean in practice (King & Stevahn, 2002). An internal evaluator in a large, multilayered organization is functionally an external evaluator for many, while an external evaluator who is regularly hired to conduct an evaluation task can quickly take on the attributes of an insider. The real issue in this role distinction is the potential for bias, and it is not always true that an insider is more likely to be at risk in this regard than an outsider, as the traditional definitions suggest. Skolits, Morrow, and Burr (2009) identify 10 roles that evaluators play at different times in the evaluation process: manager, detective, negotiator, designer, diplomat, researcher, judge, reporter, use advocate, and learner. The explicit expansion of the evaluator's role into the realm of empowerment, advocacy, and social improvement further increases its complexity as evaluators find active ways to address the AEA (1995) guiding principle that highlights "taking into account the diversity of interests and values that may be related to the general and public welfare."

Multiple evaluation approaches, multiple types of evaluation, multiple evaluator roles—the complexity of evaluation practice increases with each added distinction. So how, finally, does an evaluator know what to do with this multiplicity of ideas?

Our answer is straightforward: Regardless of your purpose, approach, or role, what ultimately matters is an evaluator's ability to engage people in framing and implementing an effective study. Interactions make or break any evaluation process. Yes, the field has many terms and category labels you can use to pigeonhole concepts and analyze particular situations, and, yes, it is often helpful to know them. You can even use them as a springboard for discussion in evaluation meetings.

But the intricacies of effective practice are not so easily captured. As Patton's (2008) sage Halcolm reminds us, "There are five key variables that are absolutely critical in evaluation use. They are, in order of importance: people, people, people, people, and people" (p. 59). We believe that Halcolm's key variables apply not just to evaluation use but to the entire evaluation enterprise. The targeted pursuit of high-quality interpersonal interactions will allow you to work collaboratively with clients to create shared understandings of whatever situations you find yourselves in and to make the best of them.

What is the meaning of it all, then? Metaphysical questions never have easy answers. The novice evaluator may well feel confusion and frustration learning on the job. Armed with a fairly empty tool kit, she may seek a way to understand or connect concepts and make sense of her evolving practice. So, too, the experienced evaluator who wants to improve the quality of her studies. To the extent that technical terms are helpful, we say, by all means, learn them and use them. But they may not provide ready solutions for every setting because evaluation is not a paint-by-numbers task but, rather, a blank sheet that people color in as a group activity. Knowing how to facilitate interactions, evaluators have at their fingertips procedures for moving the process forward, regardless of what is happening. Let us descend, then, from metaphysics to the world of practice, where IEP lives.

THREE ROLES OF THE EVALUATOR IN INTERACTIVE EVALUATION PRACTICE

Kermit the Frog, of Muppet fame, sometimes laments that it's not easy being green. Green evaluators—newcomers to the field—may well agree as they struggle to apply unfamiliar language and concepts. This experience can apply to individuals purposefully entering the field and also to those we call accidental evaluators, people without formal training who end up responsible for conducting evaluations in their organizations. The multiple definitions of evaluation shown in Exhibit 1.2, for example, contain conflicting implications for the activities of a program evaluator and raise various questions. At the most basic level, should an evaluator stop work once a judgment is made, or is it better to continue working until someone pays attention to the results? Can he do a study in a completely local context, or must he always view it in light of social improvement more broadly conceived? And how should he decide what to do in a specific evaluation setting?

In the midst of the complexity of an evaluation process, IEP acknowledges the challenging nature of the work and focuses on three roles that every evaluator must play regardless of the evaluation context or approach: decision maker, actor, and reflective practitioner.

Evaluator as Decision Maker

Given the multifaceted nature of the evaluation context and process, the first evaluator role in IEP is that of decision maker. Whatever the approach taken, it ultimately falls to the evaluator to decide what will be done during the course of a study. In fact, it is the evaluator's ethical responsibility to do so. The many menus that Patton (2008, 2012) created for *Utilization-Focused Evaluation* provide options for evaluation practice. Others will no doubt be added as time passes. The interactive nature of the evaluation decision making will vary depending on the type of evaluation. To borrow Patton's restaurant metaphor, in some cases the evaluator will be akin to a server at a restaurant, taking orders from clients or participants who have the menu in hand. In other cases she will be given carte blanche and simply asked to do the job. Regardless, decisions must be made to move the evaluation process forward. We believe that the choice making should be reasoned and purposeful and that, despite the multiple options that always exist, it requires neither the wisdom of King Solomon nor that of Patton's sage Halcolm to make good choices.

Evaluator as Actor

The second evaluator role in IEP—that of actor—has two parts. First, in an evaluation setting, the evaluator is the person responsible for getting things done. Once decisions are made, it falls to the evaluator to implement them by taking action, by *doing* something. Storybook images spring to mind: the little red hen, the little engine that could, Rumpelstiltskin weaving straw into gold, perhaps even Don Quixote. Regardless of constraints, the evaluation must go on, and it is the evaluator's job as prime mover to make that happen. The second component to the evaluator's role as actor is as a performer in the theatrical drama of the evaluation process. Other participants in the evaluation can freely speak their minds, disrupt meetings unproductively, gossip, and engage in subversive activities, but not the evaluator. In this sense, the evaluator plays a challenging role that is part leader, part manager, and part wise counselor. He provides leadership at each stage of the process, manages and troubleshoots activities, and, throughout, listens carefully to people's concerns and addresses their needs both individually and as groups.

Evaluator as Reflective Practitioner

The third role is essential to implementing the other two roles effectively. To make good decisions and act wisely during an evaluation, this role demands periodic examination of ongoing activities and a thoughtful assessment of what is going well and what may need adjustment. The evaluator asks, "How are things going? What changes—large or small—might improve this study? To what extent are interpersonal interactions fostering or hindering the study's progress?" Fortunately, the field has developed documents for assessing high-quality evaluation practice. The **Program Evaluation Standards** (Yarbrough et al., 2011; see Appendix A), AEA's (1995) **Guiding Principles for Evaluators** (see Appendix B), **Essential Skills Series in Evaluation** endorsed by the Canadian Evaluation Society (1999), and **Essential Competencies for Program Evaluators** (Stevahn et al., 2005; see Appendix C) all provide evaluators content for reflective practice. Standards and guidelines from other professional evaluation organizations literally from around the world provide additional frameworks for reflection.

Reflection is especially important at key transition points in the study (e.g., immediately prior to data collection or after data analysis during report development) and whenever a situation arises that demands immediate attention (e.g., a survey response rate that is unacceptably low or any meeting that goes poorly). Intuitively, the **action research** cycle—plan, act, observe, and reflect—provides a simple heuristic for reflective practice, and the process can be more or less formal depending on the nature of the reflection. Field notes written during the study become grist for the reflection mill and, ultimately, for personal metaevaluation at the end of the study. The more serious the situation under consideration, the more formal the reflection process should be.

CHAPTER REVIEW

This chapter introduced the concept of interactive evaluation practice. Effective interpersonal dynamics can make or break an evaluation study, which is why program evaluators should pay careful attention to them.

1. For several reasons the field of evaluation has not, to date, paid much attention to the interpersonal nature of evaluation practice.

2. The *personal factor,* which originated in utilization-focused evaluation (Patton, 2008), is concerned with making evaluation useful by engaging the key people who will eventually use its process and/or results; the *interpersonal factor* is concerned with creating and managing the interpersonal dynamics that make evaluations possible and inform their outcomes.

3. The *interpersonal factor* has two components: (a) an evaluator's ability to interact constructively with a variety of players to further the success of an evaluation study and (b) the ability to structure activities conducive to promoting mutual success among evaluation participants.

4. *Interactive evaluation practice* involves an evaluator's intentional commitment to play three roles while conducting an evaluation study: (a) decision maker, (b) actor, and (c) reflective practitioner.

2

FRAMING INTERACTIVE
EVALUATION PRACTICE

Chapter Preview

- Present a primer on *basic inquiry tasks* (BIT)
- Explain the *interpersonal participation quotient* (IPQ), which details who is involved in the evaluation, in what ways, and to what degree
- Describe *evaluation capacity building* (ECB) for thinking about the ultimate outcomes of an evaluation
- Illustrate how these three frameworks (BIT, IPQ, and ECB) work together to frame effective interactive evaluation practice

---

INTRODUCTION

You may remember the story about the visitor lost in New York City who asks a bustling New Yorker for directions: "How do I get to Carnegie Hall?" Without missing a step, the New Yorker calls back over his shoulder: "Practice."

Practice is the story of every evaluator's life. Even the most meticulously planned program evaluation will contain unpredictable moments and challenges that may make a once seemingly clear path uncertain and missteps likely. In reality, evaluations are messy for novice and well-seasoned evaluators alike, despite the step-by-step, linear portrayal commonly presented in program evaluation textbooks. Part of the messy nature of an evaluation study lies in its interpersonal dimensions—the interactions between the evaluator and those who take part in the evaluation, as well as among the people in the organizations where it takes place. Interactive evaluation practice (IEP), the ability of an evaluator both to interact with people constructively throughout the evaluation and to create activities that lead to positive interactions, acknowledges the centrality of human interaction and relationships in conducting program evaluations. In some studies evaluators seek to keep their distance and maintain as much objectivity as possible. Some evaluators even go so far as to say they don't engage in IEP or that IEP doesn't apply to their practice. Such comments ignore an important reality of program evaluation. Even in situations where potential bias is a concern, evaluators must still interact directly with a variety of people—clients, individuals with access to potential data sources, and other stakeholders—to identify critical issues related to both planning and implementing the many details of an evaluation study. So, to greater or lesser degrees, IEP applies to all evaluation practice.

In this chapter we present three frameworks for thinking about the roles and relationships of those involved, each with an acronym for easy reference. The first is a primer that outlines seven **basic inquiry tasks (BIT)**—i.e., framing evaluation questions, designing the study, identifying sources of information, collecting and analyzing data, and interpreting and reporting results. The second is the **interpersonal participation quotient (IPQ)**, which specifies varying degrees of evaluator and stakeholder involvement in making and enacting decisions throughout an evaluation study. The third is **evaluation capacity building (ECB)**, which considers the evaluator's role in supporting an organization's ability to engage in continuous improvement. Together, these frameworks for IEP can clarify who will participate in an evaluation study, in which ways, and for what reasons.

A PRIMER ON SEVEN BASIC INQUIRY TASKS

Theoretical research, applied research, action research, program evaluation—all are forms of inquiry. Despite the unique features of each and the numerous ways in which each can be conducted—in laboratory or field settings; under natural or manipulated conditions; with convenience, purposive, or randomized samples; for sponsors, clients, or those who seek to build knowledge or engage in self-study; on a large or small scale—inquiry, most broadly framed, encompasses seven basic tasks. Those tasks include the following:

1. Framing questions

2. Determining an appropriate design

3. Identifying samples or data sources

4. Collecting data

5. Analyzing data (organizing results)

6. Interpreting results, including drawing implications or making recommendations

7. Reporting and disseminating the findings

Although we recognize that this list of seven basic tasks greatly oversimplifies the complexity of most evaluation studies, it essentially describes the fundamentals of what "doing" evaluation entails—and thereby serves as a useful heuristic for thinking about the role of the evaluator as a decision maker, actor, and reflective practitioner. Exhibit 2.1 shows how these tasks translate into evaluation practice. Framing questions enables evaluators to address the underlying purpose or rationale of the study. These questions guide other aspects of the study, including choices about the overall approach, evaluation model, or particular design employed. The questions also point to needed sources of information—from people or existing databases—which requires choices about sampling. Collecting these data—for example, through interviews, surveys, observations, tests, or preexisting documents—and analyzing them to determine results also depend on the original guiding questions. Choosing appropriate methods for data collection and analysis may greatly enhance the credibility of the study and, in all likelihood, the usefulness of its results. Interpreting those results—making sense of what the findings mean and determining their implications—paves the way for making recommendations for the future of the

Exhibit 2.1   Seven Basic Inquiry Tasks (BIT)

Basic Inquiry Tasks	Conducting an Evaluation Study
1. Questions	Clarify the evaluation study:
2. Design	• Purpose, questions, approach, design, information needs, and sources • Budget, resources, timeline, grant requirements • Situational analysis—context, politics, interpersonal relationships
3. Sample/sources	• Involvement of sponsors, program leaders, staff, other stakeholders, primary intended users
4. Data collection	Collect data from targeted sources
5. Data analysis	Analyze data to determine results
6. Interpretation	Interpret results and (perhaps) develop recommendations
7. Report	Present findings and recommendations

SOURCE: © 2000 Laurie Stevahn.

program or policy evaluated. Reporting the study's findings and recommendations to interested parties completes the inquiry process.

Practical considerations such as the evaluation budget, time constraints, quality demands, the political context, and the nature of relationships among those within the program surely influence the specifics of these seven basic tasks, and the tasks realistically expand to incorporate other needed components as defined by the unique nature, aims, or circumstances of any particular evaluation. Nevertheless, the seven tasks of inquiry provide a useful outline for focusing evaluators on what doing evaluation requires. In light of IEP, keeping the BIT framework in mind from the start will remind evaluators where they are ultimately headed when engaging in initial as well as ongoing conversations with clients. Consider the scenario in Exhibit 2.2, in which members of a local garden club want to study the feasibility of involving people who receive food from a nonprofit organization in community vegetable gardens to fill the agency's shelves. If you were the evaluator in this situation, how would you respond?

Exhibit 2.2   BIT Scenario: Let's Conduct a Study

The Community Garden Project

During a long, cold winter the leaders of a garden club made plans for an exciting new project: community garden plots to grow fresh produce for the local nonprofit food shelf. Club members envisioned recruiting families who received food from the nonprofit to participate in planting, tending, and harvesting. This seemed like a "win–win" situation—participants would expand their knowledge of nutrition from participating and experience the pride that comes from growing one's own food. Several businesses and organizations in the area had agreed to donate property for planting, and a well-known local gardener with ties to the community had agreed to teach a series of workshops on how to nurture a vegetable garden. Best of all, the county government was providing an evaluator to study the program as it developed.

One concern was that no one knew whether the families who used the food shelf would be willing or able to work in the gardens. Some club members felt strongly that such work might teach people skills they could use in planting their own gardens in coming years and might even enable them to have higher-quality food and more of it, at least during the summer months. The extra help would certainly make the project more doable. Others doubted if struggling families would be interested in getting their hands dirty—literally—for a period of several months, especially since their children would be out of school and in need of child care.

"I know," said a gardener who had experience with community-based projects and knew something about gathering data from participants. "Let's do focus groups. I've used them before. They're group interviews where people bounce ideas back and forth. If we can get different groups of food-shelf users together and have them talk, we'll find out if our ideas make any sense." Those in the planning session agreed enthusiastically and immediately started writing questions for the interviews. As the discussion continued, the head of the club turned to the evaluator and asked, "What focus group interview questions would you suggest?"

How would you—the evaluator—respond?

    A. "Give me a minute and I'll generate a list of possible focus group questions; club members can add theirs as well."

    B. "Whoa! Let's first determine if we have the technical ability to record, transcribe, and analyze all the input that focus groups will produce."

    C. "Let's back up and start at the beginning. First we need to agree on the overall purpose of the study, then decide if focus groups will be the best way to get information for that purpose."

    D. "You've got to be kidding. It's impossible to get food-shelf participants to show up for anything."

The garden project scenario illustrates what often takes place at the start of an evaluation study: The excitement of people envisioning project possibilities quickly leads to brainstorming ideas for collecting data from various sources without first clarifying purpose. The four responses represent different levels of awareness on the part of the evaluator about important steps in the process of inquiry.

- *Response A* is from an evaluator caught up in the enthusiasm of the moment, jumping in to craft interview questions, but without a clear purpose. Eager to apply focus group expertise, this evaluator not only fails to consider a range of useful data collection methods and sources, but also fails to realize that specifying the purpose of a study is prerequisite to making sound methodological choices.
- *Response B* reveals an evaluator who at least recognizes that more thought should be given to the ramifications of gathering data from focus groups, but still fails to see the futility of making decisions about data collection without clear evaluation questions to guide the methods chosen.
- *Response C* shows a thoughtful evaluator who understands the importance of first clarifying purpose and framing questions because doing so guides all other inquiry decisions in the evaluation. If garden club members proceed without a clear focus, they risk wasting precious time, energy, and resources on evaluation tasks that may not yield useful information. Planning how to collect data, and from whom, first requires targeting evaluation questions. For example, consider these: (a) Will the garden project be feasible for the

food-shelf agency? (b) What agency procedures or policies will enable or impede the success of the project? (c) What foods are currently sought, needed, or desired by food-shelf clients? (d) Will these vegetables be desirable and/or culturally appropriate for clients? (e) Will clients be willing and able to work in the garden? Only the last question requires input from those who receive food from the agency, and a simple survey may be the most efficient and effective method for obtaining that information. The agency most likely will be able to provide accurate information on all the other questions—and must be the source for information on organization or program structures apt to support or hinder success.

- *Response D* reminds us that personal prejudices are unwarranted in evaluation practice; evaluators with biases toward programs or participants should not conduct studies. The ethical evaluator always strives to uphold **evaluation standards** and apply professional competencies, which means paying attention to personal proclivities and, when necessary, removing oneself from conducting studies.

Although the seven inquiry tasks of evaluation can take many forms and are not as linear in actual practice as listed in Exhibit 2.1, we would argue that evaluators should first focus a study by establishing purpose and framing questions. Clarity on what will be examined signals sound decision making and critique throughout. For example, questions will specify information needs that, in turn, will point to (a) evaluation approaches and designs capable of addressing those needs, (b) samples/sources and data collection techniques needed to answer the questions, and (c) appropriate quantitative or qualitative analyses to produce valid/reliable/trustworthy results. Likewise, clearly defined evaluations also enable evaluators and other participants to deal adequately with logistical considerations, including budgets, timelines, resource allocations, and how best to disseminate results and recommendations. Essentially, the way evaluators frame and conduct studies will strengthen or limit the credibility—and, therefore, usefulness—of evaluation findings. Keeping the BIT framework in mind while planning and implementing evaluations can help those involved successfully move along productive pathways.

THE INTERPERSONAL PARTICIPATION QUOTIENT

The IPQ, the second framework of this book, shown in Exhibit 2.3, emphasizes three fundamental realities of every evaluation context. First, a relationship exists among the evaluator and her clients, the program staff, and other evaluation stakeholders for the purpose of evaluation decision making and implementation. Second, the primary responsibility for making and implementing evaluation decisions may lie in three places: with the evaluator, with someone else in the setting (e.g., program administrators, staff, participants, or community members), or jointly with both. Third, the evaluation decision-making and implementation relationship may shift during the course of the study. The basic question this framework addresses is, "Who directs the evaluation?"

The idea that various dimensions of evaluation practice can be placed on a continuum is not new. Several evaluation writers (e.g., Cousins, Donohue, & Bloom, 1996; Cousins & Whitmore, 1998; King & Stevahn, 2002; Krueger & King, 1997; Weiss, 1998a) have presented such conceptualizations. Based on Krueger and King's (1997) chart, the IPQ emphasizes the "relationship possibilities" between evaluator and evaluation participants. The framework in Exhibit 2.3 creates a range of possibilities and three major categories of evaluation studies: evaluator-directed, collaborative, and participant-directed. Anchored by what we call **evaluator-directed evaluation** studies at one end and **participant-directed evaluation** studies at the other, it depicts the extent to which the evaluator and those involved in the study—potentially, the sponsor, clients, program leaders, staff, and other stakeholders—are involved in evaluation decision making, implementation, and reflection.

Exhibit 2.3   Interpersonal Participation Quotient (IPQ)

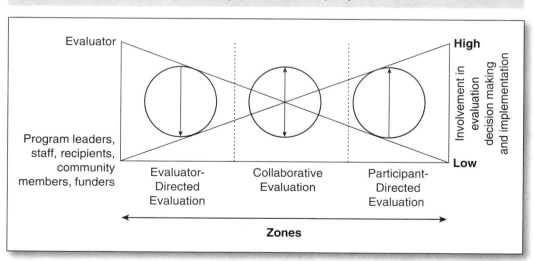

SOURCE: Adapted from King and Stevahn (2002, p. 5). Used with permission.

Why a quotient? The quotient emphasizes the two-part nature of interaction. You can think of the relationship between an evaluator (or evaluation team) and study participants as a division problem, where the numerator is the evaluator's efforts and the denominator is those of everyone else. In an evaluator-directed study, the bulk of the activities fall to the evaluator. In a collaborative study, these efforts are roughly equal. In a participant-directed study, the bulk of the activities falls not to the evaluator but to those involved on-site. Each of these types is described in the following sections.

Evaluator-Directed Studies

In evaluator-directed program evaluations, the evaluator acts as the master craftsperson who designs, produces, and delivers the evaluation product. As such, the evaluator plays a central role in all seven of the BIT, including shaping the purpose of the evaluation; determining the evaluation questions; choosing the design and sample; collecting, analyzing, and interpreting data; and reporting the findings. Although the evaluator interacts with the evaluation sponsor and/or clients (which may include program staff, service recipients, and other stakeholders), the interaction typically occurs at the study's onset to discuss needs and options, establish purposes and questions, clarify expectations and actions, and finalize timelines and contracts. Thereafter, the evaluator as expert shoulders responsibility for nearly all evaluation decisions and tasks, including sampling, data collection, data analysis, interpretation of results, recommendations, and reporting. Of course, the wise evaluator will pay attention to the primary intended users of the evaluation throughout (Patton, 2008), but it is primarily the evaluator who initiates communication regarding the evaluation. This is illustrated on the framework by the one-way arrow from high evaluation control of the evaluator to low evaluation participation of others.

What might such an evaluation look like in practice? Consider the case of the evaluation of a major civic engagement initiative at a large, well-funded foundation. After several years, the board of directors commissioned a formal study on the extent to which projects funded under the initiative were successful in achieving the initiative's major intent: increasing the civic involvement of people from lower income levels. The foundation's lead evaluator developed a request for proposals (RFP) and a competitive bidding process, and a research organization with a sizeable staff and impressive track record eventually won the contract. Evaluators from this organization met with foundation staff to finalize evaluation questions and frame a design and sampling plan. They then conducted the evaluation—developing instruments, making extensive site visits to collect data, compiling data in electronic form, analyzing the databases and interpreting results, and so on. The evaluation's final report pointed to minimal impact at best, despite the millions of foundation dollars invested in the initiative.

Although disappointed by the results, foundation members found them credible and accepted the report. They thanked the external evaluators for sharing the sampling and data collection strategies, tools, and protocols before enacting them, all clearly designed to hear the voices of those most closely connected to impact. The evaluators took primary responsibility for the study's conduct but wisely kept key foundation staff (the primary intended users of the study) informed of evaluation decisions at key junctures throughout. Evaluator-directed studies still require certain types of interactions with clients—often more infrequent than not—but it is typically the evaluator who makes the contacts and leads the inquiry.

Collaborative Studies

In what we have labeled **collaborative evaluation**, the evaluator becomes a co-investigator with the evaluation client and others in a collaborative process of joint decision making and doing (e.g., see Weiss, 1998a, pp. 99–100). Please note that a number of terms and labels describe such approaches to program evaluation (see Exhibit 2.4). In some sense, all evaluation is "participatory" in that at least one client must interact with an evaluator to begin the process, but to label an evaluation participatory signals the active engagement of nonevaluators in the evaluation process. Because authors have used the term *participatory* in many different ways over the years, we have chosen the label *collaborative* for the category encompassing the middle zone of evaluation practice in Exhibit 2.3. What we are calling collaborative evaluation reflects a commitment to coplanning and "colaboring"—hence, col-*labor*-ative.

In this zone, the evaluator and a select group of program staff and participants ideally interact throughout the course of the evaluation to develop and refine all its aspects—purpose, approach, methods, processes, products, and dissemination. Democratic decision making and mutual participation in completing evaluation tasks become paramount, based on the belief that direct involvement of participants will foster shared ownership and, therefore, increase commitment to using the evaluation results. Here, structures and norms typically exist that support ongoing communication between the evaluator and others involved in the evaluation. Through frequent meetings, for example, both

Exhibit 2.4 Forms of Collaborative and Participatory Evaluation

Term	Definition
Action research	"The scientific process whereby in a given problem area, where one wishes to improve practice or personal understanding, inquiry is carried out by the practitioner" (McKernan, 1988, p. 174); "trying out ideas in practice as a means of improvement and as a means of increasing knowledge" (Kemmis & McTaggart, 1988, p. 6).
Collaborative evaluation	Collaborative evaluations involve six interactive components: "identify the situation, clarify the expectations, establish a shared commitment, ensure open communication, encourage best practices, and follow specific guidelines" (Rodriguez-Campos, 2005, p. 2).
Communicative evaluation	"A complementary evaluation approach that may be used along with the primary methods of school accountability to provide a more comprehensive picture of the school environment" (Brooks-LaRaviere, Ryan, Miron, & Samuels, 2009, p. 372).
Community-based research (CBR)	"CBR is a partnership of students, faculty, and community members who collaboratively engage in research with the purpose of solving a pressing community problem or effecting social change" (Strand, Maruloo, Cutforth, Stoecker, & Donohue, 2003, p. 3).
Deliberative democratic evaluation	"In our opinion, there are three requirements for deliberative democratic evaluation: inclusion of all relevant interests; the evaluation is dialogical, in order to be able to identify the real interests of the relevant parties; and the evaluation is deliberative, in the sense that results are discussed by the relevant parties" (House & Howe, 2000, p. 5).
Empowerment evaluation	*"An evaluation approach that aims to increase the probability of achieving program success by (1) providing program stakeholders with tools for assessing the planning, implementation, and self-evaluation of their program, and (2) mainstreaming evaluation as part of the planning and management of the program/organization"* (Fetterman & Wandersman, 2005, p. 28, emphasis in original).
Inclusive evaluation	"Inclusive evaluation involves a systematic investigation of the merit or worth of a program or system, for the purpose of reducing uncertainty in decision making, and to facilitate positive social change for the least advantaged. . . . It . . . explicitly recognize[s] that certain voices have been absent, misrepresented, or marginalized, and that inclusion of these voices is necessary for a rigorous evaluation" (Mertens, 1999, p. 5).
Organizational learning	A continuous process of growth and improvement that uses information or feedback about both processes and outcomes (i.e., evaluation findings) to make changes; is integrated with work activities and within the organization's infrastructure (e.g., its culture, systems and structures, leadership, and communication mechanisms); and invokes the alignment of values, attitudes, and perceptions among organizational members (Preskill & Torres, 1999).

Term	Definition
Practical participatory evaluation (P-PE)	"The core premise of P-PE is that stakeholder participation will enhance evaluation relevance, ownership, and thus utilization" (Cousins & Whitmore, 1998, p. 6).
Responsive evaluation	An evaluation approach in which the evaluator seeks to understand and address stakeholders' concerns and information needs without "[creating] a consensus that does not exist" (Stake, 1975, p. 26).
	"I [Robert Stake] make strong distinctions between self-study and external responsive evaluation. . . . For me, the inquiry belongs to the evaluator" (Abma & Stake, 2001, p. 9).
Transformative participatory evaluation (T-PE)	"[T-PE] invokes participatory principles and actions in order to democratize social change" (Cousins & Whitmore, 1998, p. 7).
Value-engaged evaluation	"*A value-engaged approach to evaluation emphasizes responsiveness to the particularities of the context, inclusion of and engagement with multiple stakeholder perspectives and experiences, and attention to the social and relational dimensions of evaluation practice*" (Greene, 2005, p. 27; emphasis in original).

the evaluator and those involved can discuss concerns, contribute expertise, negotiate solutions, plan actions, and monitor the evaluation's effectiveness. This is illustrated in the framework by the two-way arrow between the evaluator and program staff, participants, and other stakeholders, where their evaluation involvement intersects.

In practice, collaborative evaluations often reinforce the value of the old adage that two heads (or more) are better than one. Consider the evaluation of a charter school's curriculum and programming that involved teachers and administrators, parents, central office staff, and, for certain components, students. The evaluation committee consisted of about two dozen adults who met monthly for more than a year and a group of students who conducted a study of their experiences at school. The school's internal evaluator facilitated both groups, beginning with discussions of which issues to address. People had competing perceptions of the key issues. For the adults, these included the mandatory field-experience supervision added to full-time teaching assignments, the lack of meaningful options for gifted and talented students, and a grading scheme that allowed no failure. For students, these included the quality of the school lunch, the so-called elective classes that were in reality assigned, and the lack of interesting extracurricular activities. Working together, both groups framed evaluation questions, worked on instruments to collect data, helped with data collection and analysis, and then used what was learned to prepare recommendations for the school's governing board. The effort was a true collaboration.

Participant-Directed Studies

The larger the role that participants play in an evaluation, the more the study becomes participant-directed. At the extreme, participant-directed studies assign no role to a professional evaluator because they constitute organizational or programmatic "business as usual." In participant-directed evaluation studies the evaluator acts as a coach. She serves as a sounding board, providing feedback, consultation, or advice to program staff or participants who are in charge of their own evaluation. In this zone, those on-site function as "communities of learners" in an ongoing process of inquiry to answer self-determined questions deemed important to their program. The evaluator, therefore, becomes a consultant who periodically provides evaluation expertise—technical assistance and quality control—when sought by those who are actively conducting their own inquiry. This is illustrated on the IPQ by the one-way arrow from low evaluation involvement of the evaluator to high evaluation involvement of evaluation participants. Participant-directed evaluation is not a new idea, and several of the approaches included in Exhibit 2.4—deliberative democratic evaluation, empowerment evaluation, transformative participatory evaluation, and certain forms of action research—build on a desire to study community issues collectively. There are, on the one hand, limitations to participant-directed evaluation, including in many cases a lack of knowledge of how to conduct evaluations on the part of participants, scarce resources to support the process, and the political challenges of knowing who should participate in all phases of the study.

On the other hand, participant-directed evaluation holds the potential to engage individuals in meaningful studies of issues in their organization or community while simultaneously teaching them evaluative knowledge and skills. Consider, for example, a group of American Indian teenagers who, with the support of a native evaluator, conducted an evaluation of the perceived outcomes of their reservation's health programming. The evaluator was responsible for teaching the teenagers how to develop an interview protocol, how to conduct interviews, and how to record and analyze qualitative data. The teenagers then interviewed every one of the community's elders. After analyzing the data, the young people made a formal presentation to the tribal council. The council received good information about the elders' perspectives; the youth learned the skills of an evaluator.

In sum, the IPQ places role in a relational context. Whether internal or external, evaluators can play the strong "take-charge" leadership role typical of evaluator-directed evaluations, a collaborative shared-responsibility role with evaluation participants, or a consultative role that uses indirect influence to support an existing group's own study. Making that role explicit can clarify people's expectations for both the evaluator and those from the program who actively participate in the study. Without such clarity, an evaluator may be less certain about how to proceed. For example, consider the scenario in Exhibit 2.5, in which a client unexpectedly shortens a deadline for completing an evaluation task. If you were the evaluator in this situation, how would you respond?

Exhibit 2.5   IPQ Scenario: Who Does What, When?

The Evaluation Timeline Crunch

People were surprised when a meeting to discuss the upcoming program evaluation turned out to be fun. By the end of the first hour, small group discussions of potential study topics had generated more than two dozen possibilities. It wasn't often that the entire agency staff—including the Spanish-speaking child-care workers—got together in one room, but the project had adopted a collaborative process to build evaluation capacity, and the director wanted everyone there. When asked to come up with questions they'd like an evaluation to answer, everyone had ideas: how to help clients become truly self-sufficient, how to increase school attendance for teenage members of the youth group, how to make sure that preschool children enter kindergarten ready to learn, how to get funding to support young immigrant parents. The list grew by the minute.

Within 2 hours, the group had prioritized topics for study by voting on those concerns perceived to be most urgent. They also had identified an upcoming community meeting where a survey could quickly collect information to jump-start the evaluation process. Everything seemed to be falling into place, until the evaluator realized that the community meeting was scheduled to take place next week. The agency director turned, smiled, and said, "You'll be able to develop a good survey in time for that meeting, won't you?"

How would you—the evaluator—respond?

   A. "Of course—I'll take on that responsibility. I'll bring you a draft of the survey tomorrow morning."

   B. "Let's form a task force with some of your staff members. I'll meet with them over the next few days and together we'll design the survey."

   C. "I won't be able to create a questionnaire on such short notice this time—but if you and your staff can draft the survey, I'll read it over and provide feedback for fine-tuning."

   D. "You've got to be kidding. That's not in my contract."

The timeline crunch describes a common scenario in evaluation practice. As studies evolve, good ideas and opportunities for data collection may emerge suddenly, and the evaluator faces a dilemma. Is it better to rush ahead and get the data or, moving more slowly, miss one opportunity but perhaps develop a better instrument? The four responses suggest different expectations on the part of the evaluator and the evaluation participants.

- *Response A* is that of an evaluator taking personal responsibility for the data collection at all costs, even though events have compressed the timeline.
- *Response B* documents a more collaborative approach. Working together, the evaluator and representatives from the program will make the data collection possible within the new timeline.
- *Response C* places responsibility for the revised schedule on program staff. If they can do the work in time, then the survey will be administered; if not, it won't.
- *Response D* is a reminder that rudeness on the part of the evaluator during interpersonal interactions is never acceptable.

Is there a best response for the evaluator in this scenario? One could argue that because the client originally envisioned the evaluation study as a collaborative venture aimed at building the evaluation capacity of program staff, solutions that involve the staff in partnership with the evaluator constructing the survey within the new timeline would best advance the original intent of the evaluation. The program director may favorably perceive a joint effort (*Response B*) if previous discussions about options on the IPQ have occurred and expectations have been established—especially if everyone systematically revisits the continuum to discuss how the roles and responsibilities of all players are unfolding and to suggest appropriate adjustments.

If such discussions have not occurred or been reconfirmed through continuous processing, the program director may expect the evaluator to say, "I'll do it" (*Response A*), then feel slighted or indignant if that is not the evaluator's response. So, too, an eager evaluator may automatically say, "I'll do it," without considering the missed opportunity to train program staff further in how to develop well-constructed surveys or the personal toll that likely will result from solely shouldering the responsibility for developing the survey in such short order. Resentment can quickly replace enthusiasm. In both instances, the IPQ can be a useful tool for helping evaluators and evaluation participants discuss and clarify their evaluation decision-making and implementation roles—and for staying on track when, as often happens, unexpected circumstances arise.

THE EVALUATION CAPACITY BUILDING FRAMEWORK

Unlike the IPQ, which looks at the relationship between the evaluator and those who take an active part in the evaluation, the third framework—ECB, depicted as a continuum in Exhibit 2.6—addresses the relationship between the evaluator and the organization in which the study occurs. Specifically, ECB examines the evaluator's commitment to building the continuing capacity of organization members to conduct evaluation studies within their organization, which may ultimately promote organizational change over time.

Exhibit 2.6 Evaluation Capacity Building (ECB)

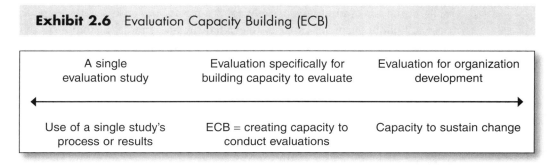

SOURCE: Adapted from King and Stevahn (2002, p. 8). Used with permission.

The ECB framework stems from three related concepts: process use (King & Thompson, 1983; Patton, 1994, 2008), organizational learning (Preskill & Torres, 1999), and evaluation capacity building (Baizerman, Compton, & Stockdill, 2002; McDonald, Rogers, & Kefford, 2003). For the first time, in Patton's 1997 edition of *Utilization-Focused Evaluation,* a separate chapter on the use of the evaluation process itself—as opposed to the use of evaluation findings—suggested that people can learn through participating in an evaluation and that an evaluator can take advantage of this fact. Organizational learning highlights an organization's conscious commitment to "using all of its members' capabilities. . . . Organizational learning is dependent on individuals and teams sharing their learning in an ongoing, systemic way" (Preskill & Torres, 1999, p. 43). Linking these ideas, Compton, Glover-Kudon, Smith, and Avery (2002) distinguish between evaluation practice and ECB practice: For "the ECB practitioner . . . the focus . . . [is] on responding to requests for evaluation services while simultaneously considering how today's work will contribute to sustaining the unit in the longer term" (p. 55).

At one end of the ECB continuum is traditional **evaluation use**—the use of an individual study's process or results for developmental, formative, or summative evaluation. This includes the various roles of evaluation presented by Scriven (1967). Research has documented factors that affect use, including the presence of interested people or supportive political conditions. As previously mentioned, Patton (2008) lists explicit strategies that the utilization-focused evaluator can select from in working with primary intended users to increase the likelihood that people will attend to results—for example, determining what information primary intended users want and what methods are credible in the context, engaging people in scenarios related to possible use, and reviewing and interpreting data collectively.

ECB—using an evaluation not only for its results but also for the explicit purpose of building people's capacity to evaluate again—marks the middle of the continuum. This is the evaluation equivalent of teaching people to fish rather than giving them fish to eat. In many cases, ECB is a highly appropriate evaluation outcome for collaborative evaluators, where process use serves an important and measurable function. Case descriptions in a volume of *New Directions for Evaluation* (Compton, Baizerman, & Stockdill, 2002) describe the process through which evaluators in four organizations—a school district, the American Cancer Society, the Centers for Disease Control, and the World Bank—worked more or less successfully to build infrastructure and institutionalize evaluation processes. Preskill and Boyle's (2008) multidisciplinary model of ECB encompasses the complexity of capacity building efforts in organizations, detailing the evaluation knowledge, skills, and attitudes that, in the right culture and sustained by the right resources, can lead to sustainable evaluation practice over time.

Anchoring the other end of the continuum, the use of evaluation to support change in an organization is an even broader commitment that an evaluator may take. This is a commitment not only to building the capacity to conduct evaluations but to building an organization's capacity to *use* these evaluations to improve over time—whether called organization development, total quality management, or continuous improvement. This is evaluation in service of the change process within the context of an organization, moving the evaluator well beyond a traditional evaluation role and into that of change agent.

Not all evaluators will choose to incorporate the ECB framework into their practice. Some reject this continuum as unrelated to the evaluator's role and distinguish capacity building and organizational change from the practice of program evaluation (as opposed to evaluation facilitation). But for those who include these activities among their potential roles, making them explicit will help clarify people's expectations. For example, consider the scenario in Exhibit 2.7, in

Exhibit 2.7   ECB Scenario: Creating Conditions for Change

We Did *Our* Part

The district's internal evaluator was pleased to be included on an assessment team planning the highly visible curriculum review of a controversial basic skills program, now in its third year of implementation. The evaluator had been hired in part to create a system of ongoing data collection that would provide evidence for a continuous improvement change effort in the district, and this was one of the first studies to spearhead that effort. As the planning team examined student data and listed potential stakeholders, there was a long pause. To its dismay, the percentage of students of color served in the program was 2 times greater than their total percentage in the district population, and African American boys, in particular, were present in high numbers. The superintendent had charged the team with building strong ties with the growing communities of color in the district to ensure that all students, regardless of background, received an excellent education.

The evaluator explained that having solid representation from parents of color in every aspect of the evaluation was essential, both for the study's validity and for political reasons. But the planning group also knew that involving parents of color would not be easy since they represented a small percentage of the district population and, for a variety of reasons, were rarely active in school affairs. The deputy superintendent who was on the committee convinced the superintendent to send a carefully crafted letter to all parents of color whose children were involved in the program, inviting them to join the formal assessment team for monthly evening meetings, offering child care, a meal, and transportation. Three weeks went by, and only one parent of color returned the sign-up slip agreeing to take part.

At the next planning meeting, the head of the curriculum study sighed and said, "Well, we did our part. I just can't figure out why those parents aren't willing to take the time to help. I can't understand why they aren't interested in their children's education. At least we can say that we gave them the opportunity to get involved, but now we need to move on to meet our evaluation deadlines."

How would you—the evaluator—respond?

    A. "I'm concerned about the usefulness of this study. Without participation from parents of color, the results won't be credible."

    B. "There may be better ways to recruit parents of color. Let me explain a variety of techniques, then let's decide which are most feasible."

    C. "Let's revisit our long-term objectives. What can we do to build solid ongoing relationships with parents of color to involve them fully and continuously in district change over time?"

    D. "You've got to be kidding. We might as well cancel this study right now since you obviously don't know how to work with communities of color."

which a school district strives for organizational change through ongoing study of curricular programs. If you were the evaluator in this situation, how would you respond?

The "we-did-our-part" scenario deals with the issue of representation—the need for a critically important segment of the population to take part in the evaluation study. The four responses reveal different expectations regarding the evaluator's relationship to the organization in which the study is being conducted.

- *Response A* represents a traditional approach to evaluation use. The focus is on the study itself and ensuring that evaluation decisions, data, analyses, and interpretations will be useful and technically adequate.
- *Response B* suggests a different orientation, a commitment to ECB by using the study to teach team members evaluation skills for this and future studies.
- *Response C* goes even further, suggesting a serious effort to facilitate ongoing organizational change in the district by building community connections.
- *Response D,* once again, reminds us that interpersonal interactions require sensitivity and diplomacy and that accusatory statements rarely make successful evaluation studies possible.

The overall focus of the curriculum review study in this scenario is to equip school district employees and parents with the skills to engage collaboratively in continuous evaluation for district-wide improvement. In this light, *Response C* is most aligned with the organization development focus. Any serious discussion on how to foster organizational change, therefore, will necessarily include conversations on how to recruit successfully and connect meaningfully those individuals who must engage in the endeavor for it to be successful. When organization development is the overall goal, both immediate success (i.e., the study's usefulness) and future success (i.e., its capacity to effect and sustain change) can and most probably should be part of the evaluation decision making.

IEP recognizes the centrality of human interaction in conducting all program evaluation studies, regardless of whether the interaction takes place between evaluator and client in the more directive sense or between evaluator and program leaders/workers who participate in the evaluation in a more collaborative sense (see Exhibit 2.3). When organization development is also the goal, the evaluator must additionally be concerned with framing interactions that will increase the capacity of organizational members to engage continuously in conducting and using the results of their own studies, thereby focusing on ECB (see Exhibit 2.6). Essentially, commitment to continuous improvement through ongoing evaluation involves developing an organizational culture characterized by continuous evaluation and the use of results. Therefore, the more organization development is the target of an evaluation, the more the dynamics between evaluator and stakeholders should be positive and supportive, both in evaluation decision making and implementation.

APPLYING THE FRAMEWORKS TO EVALUATION PRACTICE

In practice, evaluators can intentionally apply the BIT, IPQ, and ECB frameworks in combination to plan and conduct effective studies from start to finish. The following scenarios briefly illustrate what this might look like in three different contexts.

Scenario 1: Accreditation for a Health Clinic

Health professionals operating a small, private, inner-city clinic for families with low incomes needed program accreditation to be eligible for government funding that could expand their programs and services. The director of the clinic hired a team of external evaluators with accreditation experience to conduct the study. The team met with the director at the onset to review the published accreditation standards that set the entire focus for the study. At the meeting, the team also reviewed the mandatory data collection instruments and scoring rubrics the accrediting body had provided and then developed a feasible sampling plan, with director input, that would not disrupt patient care during the study. After establishing a budget and a timeline, the evaluators reconfirmed the agreement to conduct the study independently and to provide a final report upon completion. Essentially, this meant that once the contract was signed, the evaluators would collect and analyze all data according to accreditation protocols and would not discuss the evaluation processes or findings with clinic personnel—including the director—until the study had ended to help ensure a fair and unbiased assessment. By first focusing on purpose (BIT), the team realized that the intent of the evaluation was summative (the use end of ECB), the results to be used solely for accreditation qualification. Therefore, an evaluator-directed study was necessary (IPQ).

In this case, the evaluators, the director, and the health professionals who worked at the clinic all understood why it was important for the evaluation team to carry out all the tasks (BIT) without the involvement of any personnel. Sharing copies of the three IEP frameworks with the director at the initial meeting facilitated the conversation as they worked through various evaluation issues, understandings, and agreements. The team and the director signed the evaluation contract, and the accreditation study began.

Scenario 2: Customer Satisfaction in the Hospitality Industry

The owners of a chain of family restaurants wanted to know how satisfied customers were with their dining experiences. Over the years, they had periodically hired independent evaluators to conduct short-term studies but now saw the value of engaging their managers in such evaluations. After all, it makes good sense to develop intentionally the capacity of managers to conduct simple periodic evaluations on the likes and dislikes of diners, because they supervise staff who directly provide service. The owners asked an experienced evaluator who worked at company headquarters to lead the next customer satisfaction evaluation, but with the explicit purpose of involving general managers (GMs) and eventually all front- and back-of-house managers to build their capacity to conduct future evaluations. The internal evaluator obtained the owners' approval to use a two-tiered "train-the-trainer" model, which first would entail working directly with GMs to build their capacity to conduct evaluations at each establishment. The GMs, in turn, would eventually involve their front- and back-of-house managers in assessments to develop a larger capacity network. GMs were willing to participate in this endeavor, in part, because their biannual bonuses were dependent on quarterly revenue, which they knew was closely linked to sales and, therefore, to customer satisfaction.

At the initial meeting with the GMs, the owner of the company and the internal evaluator, the lead on this project, distributed copies of the IEP frameworks as references while explaining the goal of this new endeavor. The purpose was clear: to assess customer satisfaction (BIT). In doing so, this evaluation would also be designed intentionally to build the capacity of the managers to conduct evaluations (ECB), the ultimate future goal being to involve other managers. The roles of "lead evaluator" and "GMs" would be collaborative (IPQ); together, they would "colabor" to complete the inquiry tasks. After developing a timeline for the evaluation and setting regular meeting dates, the lead evaluator and GMs got to work. Everyone mutually decided that they should adapt an existing satisfaction survey, so small groups brainstormed various dimensions of customer experience that might be important to include on a questionnaire. One GM went online and compiled sample questionnaires from other restaurants.

Over the next month, the survey was piloted, refined, and printed; managers then distributed it to all diners over the same 1-week time period, and the data were entered into an Excel spreadsheet. The lead evaluator computed descriptive statistics for the Likert-scale items and then involved the GMs in qualitative analysis for the open-ended items. By doing so, managers developed/refined their skills in data analysis. Together, the managers and evaluator discussed findings and interpretations, then developed short-term action plans for continuing practices associated with diners' "kudos" and improving areas in which customers expressed dissatisfaction. Eventually, the GMs were able to conduct their own studies by involving other managers at each restaurant.

Scenario 3: Organization Development in an Educational Institution

Each year, an innovative high school received national awards for its excellence in preparing students to succeed in the 21st century, whether its graduates were college or vocation bound. From the time it opened to the present, this public school focused on the four cornerstones of its mission: "We continuously strive to (a) capitalize on technology for innovative teaching, learning, and assessment; (b) nurture cooperative/collaborative processes for support, development, and continuous improvement of all; (c) exercise social responsibility by engaging in the community; and (d) honor and respect each other and all of humanity." Administrators and staff were strategically hired to work at this school for their commitment to and experience with implementing and sustaining continuous improvement assessment programs for organization development. A team of specialists in the research and evaluation office at the school managed these efforts, which took the form of ongoing self-studies. Each academic department in the school was involved in a 4-year process of improvement aligned with the experiential learning cycle paradigm: "plan, act, reflect, refine." People in each department would "plan" the first year, "act" the second, "reflect" the third, and "refine" the fourth. Everyone participated in this process—administrators, teachers, students, parents—which resulted in uniformly high levels of sophistication with evaluation. The self-studies were always aimed at enabling the school to live its mission, broadly framed by the four cornerstones noted above.

One day the chair of the interdisciplinary studies department phoned a private consultant, well known for evaluation expertise, to seek advice on options for using mixed methods in the next self-study cycle of data collection, to occur during the "act" component of the paradigm. The evaluator suggested a face-to-face meeting and brought copies of the IEP frameworks, along with some overview materials on mixed-methods evaluation. At the start of the meeting, the consultant wanted to check perceptions and assumptions, so he used the frameworks as talking points to confirm that members of the department (a) continuously carried out the seven inquiry tasks (BIT)—or variations—during each self-study cycle, (b) embraced the self-study paradigm strategically to promote capacity to sustain effective school change for organization development (the organization development end of ECB), and (c) autonomously conducted each assessment as a participant-directed endeavor (IPQ). These assumptions were correct, so the consultant indicated that on that day he would listen to questions and concerns, share some information about mixed methods, and be willing to assist future applications, with the understanding that his role would be one of providing support materials or training for using mixed methods—he would not actually participate in conducting the study—and would bill the school at an hourly rate whenever they desired his input or guidance.

The agreement was formally written and signed, and, thereafter, the consultant looked forward to those times throughout the year (infrequent as they were) when calls for assistance came from the school. The frameworks kept the boundaries clear; the external evaluator played the role of "sounding board," "feedback provider," or "resource supplier" only when asked—after all, it was the school's study conducted by department members and needed to stay that way. This working relationship proved fruitful for all involved.

CHAPTER REVIEW

This chapter presented three frameworks for conceptualizing and grounding interactive evaluation practice. Each is useful for establishing expectations and reflecting on important interpersonal dimensions of evaluation projects. Illustrations throughout show how these frameworks are useful in real-world practice.

1. The *basic inquiry tasks* (BIT), presented in Exhibit 2.1, outline seven broad steps for conducting an evaluation study. Evaluators across diverse contexts and fields of practice can use them to plan what needs to be done as well as to think about where involving others makes sense.

2. The *interpersonal participation quotient* (IPQ), presented in Exhibit 2.3, depicts the relationship between an evaluator and evaluation participants on a continuum of practice, from evaluator-directed to collaborative to participant-directed studies. It reminds everyone that the mix can vary—and should, depending on different purposes for different studies—when it comes to determining who to involve in evaluation decision making and implementation. Agreeing what to pursue up front sets helpful parameters and expectations.

3. The *evaluation capacity building* (ECB) framework, presented in Exhibit 2.6, examines the relationship between an evaluator and the organization in which the evaluation takes place. It highlights the potential of evaluations to increase capacity for (a) use of a single study's findings, (b) evaluation skill development of participants, and (c) ongoing organizational change over time.

4. Together, the BIT, IPQ, and ECB frameworks help evaluators determine (a) who should be involved in the tasks of inquiry (e.g., evaluators, clients/stakeholders, program leaders/providers, and so on), (b) to what degree (e.g., decision making only, implementation only, or both), and (c) for what organizational purposes (e.g., use of a single study's findings, capacity building, or continuous improvement).

3

THEORETICAL FOUNDATIONS FOR INTERACTIVE EVALUATION PRACTICE

Chapter Preview

- Explain why the field of program evaluation lacks the theory-building tradition of the social sciences
- Detail two theoretical foundations that inform interactive evaluation practice (IEP): *social interdependence theory* and research on *evaluation use*
- Present principles for IEP derived from these empirically supported foundations

INTRODUCTION

Social psychologist Kurt Lewin (1951) once wrote, "There is nothing so practical as a good theory" (p. 169). Fifty years later, educational change expert Michael Fullan (2001) responded, "There is nothing so theoretical as good practice" (p. xiii). Theory and practice go hand in hand, each strengthening the other. What could be more practical than a well-formulated theory consistently useful for systematically solving real-world problems? Practice risks futility if based solely on what we think works rather than on well-validated theory. The reverse is also true. What could be more theoretical than effective practice based on implicit, cohesive, underlying conceptual structures? As the ivory-tower, higher-education stereotype suggests, theory isolated from real-life practice will rarely provide useful guidance for action.

This chapter brings theory and research to the forefront of interactive evaluation practice (IEP). First, we discuss why practical rather than theoretical concerns have dominated the field of program evaluation throughout its evolution. Next, we present two empirically supported theoretical foundations—*social interdependence theory* and *evaluation use*—to guide effective IEP. Finally, we present a set of principles derived from these foundations for evaluator decision making, implementation, and reflection in IEP.

WHERE'S THE THEORY?

In a television commercial popular during the 1980s, a small but feisty old woman stood with eyes fixed intently on what appeared to be a larger-than-life-sized hamburger. Upon opening the enormous bun, she found a meat patty so miniscule that she blurted out, "Where's the beef?" We could ask a similar question when it comes to finding substantive theoretical foundations for practice within the field of program evaluation. Where's the theory? Just as we typically expect beef to play a defining role in what constitutes a first-rate hamburger, we also might reasonably expect theory to play a central role in guiding effective program evaluation practice. Yet it's difficult to find theory in evaluation as you traditionally would in the social sciences. In contrast to many social science disciplines, developing and testing theories to inform evaluation practice—conducting research on program evaluation itself—has not to date been a primary concern in the field. Instead, methods-oriented issues, often philosophical in nature and difficult to research, have dominated the field of program evaluation since its inception, fueling passionate and prolonged discussions on such controversial topics as

- whether social science experiments can adequately address the practical dimensions of evaluation, highlighting the tension between seeking "truth" through rigorous experimental research design (like randomized control trials) versus attending to the highly pragmatic political realities and situational needs of stakeholders and decision makers;
- whether qualitative methods have a legitimate place in program evaluation practice, revealing deep divisions between the epistemological values of the quantitative and qualitative paradigms; and
- whether participatory evaluation approaches that involve stakeholders in the processes of designing and implementing studies even qualify as evaluation. Empowerment evaluation (Fetterman, 2001), for example, has been accused of "giving evaluation away" because evaluators become facilitators in the process of conducting such program evaluations (Stufflebeam & Shinkfield, 2007), rather than focusing solely on judging a program's merit, worth, and value.

Factors Impeding Research on Evaluation Practice

We believe that evaluation professionals and scholars largely have not conducted social science research on program evaluation—that is, formulating, testing, and refining theories to guide practice in real-world contexts—for six reasons.

1. *Lack of conceptual consensus.* Coherent conceptualization is the hallmark of theory building in any discipline, yet many in the field of evaluation disagree on the meaning of terms. For example, as noted in Chapter 1 (see Exhibit 1.2), *program evaluation* means different things to different people. Theory, too, can be construed in many ways; "no single understanding of the term is widely accepted" (Shadish, Cook, & Leviton, 1991, p. 30). Ambiguity and confusion can result. Without precisely defined terms or consensus on the meaning of key concepts, it becomes difficult to construct evaluation theories or validate them. The transdisciplinary nature of evaluation itself (Scriven, 1994, 2003) may have inhibited theory building. Thinkers as well as practitioners in evaluation come from diverse backgrounds, make different ontological and epistemological assumptions, focus on diverse purposes, conduct evaluations in diverse areas, and embrace diverse research traditions (Stufflebeam & Shinkfield, 2007).

2. *A relatively young field.* Because program evaluation is a relatively recent addition to academic settings, it has been evolving toward disciplinary status for decades but remains less well defined than other disciplines (Fitzpatrick, Sanders, & Worthen, 2010; Worthen, Sanders, & Fitzpatrick, 1997). Likening it to putting the cart before the horse, some would argue that it makes little sense to conduct research on theories of program evaluation before the field reaches some maturity. Just as you would avoid conducting a summative evaluation of a program that is not fully operational, neither would you devote energy to conducting research on evaluation before developing models or theoretical conceptualizations that warrant study. The fact that the field of program evaluation only began in the last half of the 20th century may have implications for its ability to develop and empirically validate underlying theories. Stufflebeam and Shinkfield (2007) offer a similar perspective:

   The relatively young evaluation profession has advanced substantially in conceptualizing the program evaluation enterprise but has far to go in developing overarching, validated theories to guide the study and practice of program evaluation. The program evaluation literature's references to program evaluation theories are numerous, but these references are often pretentious. (p. 68)

3. *Lack of financial support for evaluation research.* Theory building in academic disciplines, which necessitates research, tends to be centered in institutions of higher education that support such activity. Although a number of universities (and a few government offices) in the United States, Canada, and Australia offer evaluation training programs (e.g., see Altschuld, Engle, Cullen, Kim, & Macce, 1994; LaVelle & Donaldson, 2010), these programs tend to be embedded in departments that are relevant but not exclusively devoted to program evaluation, such as psychology, public administration, educational research, educational psychology, educational administration, sociology, human resources, and measurement and statistics. Academic departments of program evaluation are rare, unlike the situation in other disciplines that have their own departmental homes. And even though program evaluation studies and graduate degrees are offered in university-based programs, doctoral candidates often conduct research on their respective areas of interest (such as education, social work, and public health), rather than on program evaluation itself. This may be the case in part because little funding exists for research on evaluation. Grants from foundations or funds from organizations that sponsor social programs tend to be earmarked for program evaluation studies, not for research on program evaluation theory.

4. *Focus on program theory.* Attention to theory in program evaluation has focused predominantly on *program theory*—the causal links between a program's activities (that is, its operations, procedures, services, interventions) and its intended outcomes, both short- and long-term. Sometimes called program logic, program theory attempts to make explicit the implicit assumptions (logic) on which the effectiveness of a program is based. Theories of change are similar but provide an explanation for program design by specifying causal mechanisms (Patton, 2012, p. 235). Attending to such theories can provide helpful direction for determining the purpose of an evaluation, identifying important evaluation questions, designing the study, and so on. Although evaluators initially tended to neglect program theory (e.g., see Chen, 1990, 2005), most evaluators today recognize its practical value and often attend to it in designing evaluation studies (Donaldson, 2007; Frechtling, 2007; Funnell & Rogers, 2011). Comprehensively explicating and testing evaluation theory, however, has not garnered the same attention.

5. *Practical focus.* Program evaluation is a highly pragmatic field, and evaluators tend to concentrate on conducting studies for clients rather than validating the theoretical assumptions underlying various evaluation models. Like pilots in midair whose immediate priority must be to fly their airplanes successfully, evaluators in "midair" must concentrate on doing what is necessary to complete evaluation studies effectively. They constantly face pressure to "do" evaluation expediently, inexpensively, and excellently—hence, the development of a comprehensive set of standards (Yarbrough, Shula, Hopson, & Caruthers, 2011) to guide professional practice rather than a focus on traditional theory building, as in the academic disciplines. To most clients, validating evaluation theory is not cost effective. Why should they pay to develop theory for the field?

6. *Continuing focus on evaluation models and methods.* Program evaluation became a national concern in the 1950s and 1960s when the U.S. government mandated large-scale social programs. The notion of a funded mandate for accountability created an immediate need to conduct large-scale, deadline-driven evaluation studies in highly visible political contexts. Again, the compelling priority was to "do" evaluation, not theorize about it or conduct research on it. As noted in Chapter 1, the issues that emerged from those early evaluations revealed the limitations of traditional experimental research applied to evaluation problems. Randomized quantitative experiments often could not fully address the site-specific concerns or situational decision-making needs of stakeholders. Thereafter, the quest for program evaluation approaches that could address highly contextual and political issues began, as did a related debate over the legitimacy of qualitative versus quantitative methods. Developing alternative models of evaluation continues to be a priority in the field as evaluators seek to address persistent situational challenges. Research to validate theoretical assumptions on which models are based, however, largely has not been conducted. Stufflebeam and Shinkfield (2007) concur:

> While evaluation theorists have advanced creative and influential models and approaches for conducting program evaluations, these constructions have not been accompanied by a substantial amount of empirical research. Thus, no substantial body of evidence exists on the functioning of different evaluation approaches. (pp. 58–59)

They continue by noting that "overall, the program evaluation field has far to go in quests to develop and present research-based theories whose predictions hold true" (pp. 76–77).

We agree with those who call for program evaluation research toward developing and validating generalizable theories useful for enhancing practice (e.g., Campbell & McGrath, 2011; Mark, 2003; Mark, Donaldson, & Campbell, 2011; Mark & Henry, 2004; Stufflebeam & Shinkfield, 2007). Doing so will require intentional focus and sustained effort as we move into the future, especially given these six reasons that tend to work against such aspirations (King, 2003). In the meantime, however, useful theoretical foundations are available to support IEP, including the two we shall now discuss.

THEORIES TO USE IN INTERACTIVE EVALUATION PRACTICE

IEP signals evaluators to focus strategically on the human dimensions of evaluation efforts. As defined in Chapter 1, IEP intentionally directs evaluators to (a) interact constructively with stakeholders throughout in ways that foster use of results and (b) create conditions and structure activities that promote positive interactions among evaluation participants. Doing so speaks directly to *process* and *use* issues that have become prominent across diverse evaluation contexts over the past several decades. Relevant concerns include:

- Who should be involved in program evaluation, and what roles should they play?
- What are appropriate responsibilities, activities, and interactions for evaluators, sponsors/funders, stakeholders, and intended users before, during, and after an evaluation study?
- Who will use the results of evaluation in what ways, and how can use of findings be promoted and supported?
- How do roles and relationships among various participants in the evaluation process facilitate or frustrate the use of results?
- How do organizational structures enhance or inhibit use?
- What competencies are essential for program evaluators to conduct evaluation studies aimed at organizational change?

Two empirically supported theoretical frameworks—one from social psychology, the other from program evaluation itself—provide guidance for action. First, *social interdependence theory* helps us understand how to structure evaluation goals and tasks in ways that will foster cooperative interaction among participants for success in conducting evaluation studies. Second, theoretical conceptualizations of *evaluation use* help us determine whom to engage in evaluation planning and implementation, as well as the types of conversations and planning tasks most likely to promote actual application of findings. We chose these two theoretical foundations for IEP because both are research supported, relevant to the interpersonal dynamics of evaluation practice, and directly applicable to evaluations spanning diverse purposes, contexts, and designs. These theoretical foundations differ, however. Social interdependence theory comes from the psychological sciences and has been rigorously researched for decades. Its concepts and outcomes are clear and can be explained in short order. By contrast, researchers have conducted studies on the conceptual framework of evaluation use for more than four decades, but as yet, there is no formal social science theory to test and, sadly, its research grounding is not entirely solid (Brandon & Singh, 2009). Nevertheless, the existing research does provide a helpful basis for thinking about IEP, which is why we include it here. In the sections that follow, we explicate these two theoretical frameworks.

Social Interdependence Theory

Social interdependence theory (see Deutsch, 1949a, 1949b, 1973, 2006; Johnson & Johnson, 1989, 2005a, 2009; Johnson, Johnson, & Stevahn, 2011) provides a powerful theoretical foundation for both explaining and influencing human interaction in any profession. Originating in the field of social psychology, this theory has a solid base of empirical support that emerged over the past century through social science inquiry conducted by hundreds of independent researchers across numerous settings, populations, and contexts (see Johnson & Johnson, 2005a, 2009; Johnson, Johnson, & Stevahn, 2011). The theory specifies how individuals can be in relationship with each other (cooperatively or competitively), the type of interaction characteristic of each relationship (promotive or oppositional), and the likely subsequent outcome (mutually or exclusively beneficial). Understanding the theory starts with distinguishing between social interdependence (i.e., needing the participation of oneself and others to accomplish a goal) and social independence (i.e., operating alone to accomplish a goal)—and recognizing that interdependent relationships may be either cooperative (producing win–win outcomes) or competitive (producing win–lose outcomes).

Social interdependence exists when the actions of individuals affect other individuals' outcomes (see Johnson & Johnson, 2009). When your actions, for example, facilitate or hinder the success of another and that person's actions also affect the extent to which you succeed, social interdependence defines the relationship. In contrast, *social independence* exists when individuals stand alone—i.e., the actions of others do not affect your outcome and vice versa. Whether or not you are linked to others—as well as how you are linked—largely depends on the goals you pursue and the structure of those goals. Individualistic goals, for example, can be accomplished successfully without the participation of others, as in the simple case of recreational fishing. You can launch your rowboat, bait your hook, cast your line, and secure (or lose) your catch without needing anyone else to participate in the venture. Your success (or failure) largely lies with you and the skill, patience, and determination you bring to the task.

Many goals, however, can be achieved only when others participate in the pursuit. The question is, how will those involved participate? What types of interaction will occur? Will mutually enhancing "helping" behaviors prevail, or will individuals try to outdo each other? Once again, the answer lies largely in the structure of the goals.

A competitive goal requires not only the participation of others because you cannot win or be first, best, fastest, and so on without others who also are in the game trying to attain that goal; competing requires surpassing all others to succeed. The goal itself links you to others in oppositional ways, which means that you can succeed only if all others fail (i.e., a negative correlation exists between you and others in achieving the goal). In a fishing derby, for example, the person who reels in the largest or heaviest fish wins the prize and related prestige. If you are participating in that derby, you know that your actions will affect both your outcomes and the outcomes of the other competitors, either helping or hurting your—or their—chances of winning. To increase your chances of winning, you may purchase costly lures prior to the event, secure state-of-the-art tackle, research the feeding habits of certain fish species, arrive early to secure the best location on the lake, withhold useful knowledge from other participants, and refuse to share equipment.

A cooperative goal also requires the participation of others, but in mutually enhancing ways. To achieve a cooperative goal, all participants must succeed. The most compelling cooperative goals are those that establish clear and strong *positive interdependence* among participants—meaning that the success of every individual is necessary for the success of the group, and vice versa (i.e., a positive correlation exists between oneself and others in achieving the goal). Cooperative goals, therefore, create relationships among participants that emphasize the importance of promoting mutual success. A commercial fishing expedition, for example, involves participants in achieving the cooperative goal of safely and efficiently filling the hold of the vessel with fish, thereby establishing cooperative links among all on board. Everyone—including the captain, engineer, crew, and cook—must successfully contribute and coordinate needed (and often specialized) skills, knowledge, resources, energy, and muscle to achieve the goal successfully. One person cannot succeed alone. Furthermore, any group member not successfully contributing to the accomplishment of the goal would make the overall outcome for every other member less than what it could have been with full and effective participation. Cooperative goals, therefore, create a sense of both need and responsibility—no one person has all the skill, muscle, or know-how to succeed, which motivates participants to team up and pitch in to promote mutual success. The group is only as productive as its weakest contributor.

Social interdependence theory (Deutsch, 1949b) posits that the type of goal structured among individuals (cooperative vs. competitive) determines the type of interaction that occurs (promotive vs. oppositional), which, in turn, influences outcomes (mutually vs. exclusively beneficial). This theory, depicted in Exhibit 3.1, has a substantial base of empirical research support rarely found in the social sciences (see Johnson & Johnson, 1989, 2005a, 2009). Hundreds of studies—primarily experimental and correlational—were conducted throughout the 20th century and first decade of the 21st century by diverse researchers from different disciplines (e.g., psychology, counseling, education, business, organization development), in different settings (e.g., education, business, health, government), across diverse populations (children, adolescents, adults), in diverse cultural contexts and geographic locations (North America, South America, Europe, Australia, Asia). Findings across a range of measures consistently demonstrate that cooperative goal structures (compared to competitive or individualistic) result in (a) increased productivity and effort to achieve, (b) enhanced peer relations, and (c) greater psychological health and social competence (Johnson & Johnson, 2009).

Exhibit 3.1   Social Interdependence Theory (Deutsch, 1949b)

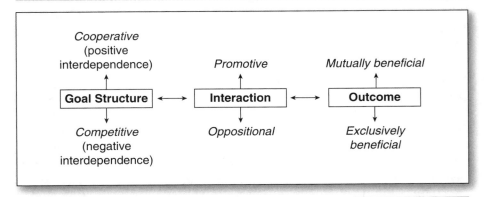

SOURCE: © 1995 Laurie Stevahn.

Evaluators who understand *social interdependence theory* can use it in several ways. First, it becomes a lens through which to assess the situational context of the organization that houses the program to be evaluated, or the program itself. Determining the extent to which a cooperative or competitive culture exists within the evaluation setting, for example, may be crucial for pursuing, clarifying, framing, or declining to conduct a study. Trying to conduct a collaborative study in a competitive environment will present serious challenges to evaluators and organizational members alike; it may be unwise to pursue such a pathway. The theory also may help evaluators identify key players in the organization and reveal underlying political agendas, be they cooperative, competitive, or individualistic, which can become the substance of questions to explore the evaluation context (see Chapter 4).

Second, when conducting collaborative studies, evaluators can use *social interdependence theory* to foster constructive participation among participants by structuring positive interdependence into program evaluation tasks. Clearly establishing cooperative goals by defining joint products or outcomes, dividing tasks, designating distinct yet interconnected jobs, sharing or jigsawing one set of materials, arranging workspace to facilitate interpersonal access and communication—all of these become factors that can strengthen the extent to which participants feel interconnected, motivated to work together, and committed to mutual success.

Ultimately, *social interdependence theory* becomes a tool for thinking about and enacting interactive dimensions of program evaluation studies across the basic inquiry tasks, interpersonal participation quotient, and evaluation capacity building frameworks presented in Chapter 2. Evaluators put this theory into practice each time they intentionally structure evaluation tasks as cooperative goals for mutual accomplishment. Knowing the power of positive interdependence and applying it strategically to facilitate collaborative studies better enables those involved to build evaluation capacity and foster continuous organizational learning. This also becomes foundational to resolving conflicts constructively.

Theoretical Conceptions of Evaluation Use

Hofstetter and Alkin (2003) once wrote, "For as long as modern-day evaluations have existed, so too have questions about evaluation use" (p. 219). Questions about use have indeed permeated the evaluation literature since its inception. Do decision makers and other evaluation participants *do* anything with the results of an evaluation? If so, *what?* And how can evaluators foster meaningful and appropriate use? Roughly 40 years ago Weiss (1972) identified the need for empirical research on people's use of evaluations, noting the clear cost in failing to do so. Spending money on processes or findings that remain unused wastes limited resources and benefits no one. Fortunately, researchers responded to Weiss's call, engaging in a steady stream of research and conceptual development examining the factors that affect evaluation use or utilization (the terms are used interchangeably). Now Christie (2007) can note that "evaluation utilization is arguably the most researched area of evaluation, and it also receives substantial attention in the theoretical literature" (p. 8). Before discussing what research has taught us about evaluation use, a review of the framework that has structured this research since the mid-1970s is in order.

Studying Evaluation Use

In the 1970s, scholars interested in the topic borrowed a typology from knowledge utilization to generate a set of categories for analyzing users' actions. Exhibit 3.2 outlines three long-standing types of evaluation use: (a) **instrumental use,** in which people take direct action based on evaluation findings; (b) **conceptual use,** or **enlightenment,** in which people learn something from an evaluation report even if they do not immediately apply it; and (c) **political, persuasive,** or **symbolic use,** in which people take advantage of evaluation findings for perceived personal gain. At one point, a scholarly argument pitted Michael Quinn Patton and instrumental use against Carol Weiss and enlightenment, resulting finally in the awareness that evaluation use is not a question of *either* instrumental use *or* enlightenment but, rather, *both/and.* In other words, instrumental and conceptual uses are both important concepts in understanding how decision makers act on and with evaluation results. In given settings, political or symbolic use can also be critically important, at its worst leading to evaluation misuse or abuse.

In the past decade or so, the use typology has expanded, adding two additional types of use and an additional category of instrumental use. As mentioned earlier, Patton (1994, 1997) named the concept of *process use,* recognizing that use can arise not just from the results of an evaluation but also from the evaluation process itself. **Process use** (or *evaluation learning use;* Ottoson & Martinez, 2010) refers to the influence of the evaluation process on people and systems being evaluated. When people participate in evaluation discussions, for example, they may learn how to frame questions, develop questionnaire items, or interpret data. This is important because, in contrast to results-based use, process use lies more directly in an evaluator's hands.

Exhibit 3.2   Types of Evaluation Findings Use

Type	Use For	Definition	Examples
Instrumental	Action	The use of evaluation findings for making decisions	An administrator reads the results of a study that document a program that fails to meet its intended goals and cuts the program from the budget the following year.
Conceptual or enlightenment*	Understanding	The use of evaluation findings to better understand a program or policy	An executive director considers the results of a study but lacks the resources to act on them. In the process she comes to understand a certain kind of program in a different way.
Political, persuasive, or symbolic	Justification	The use of evaluation findings to support a decision someone has already made or to persuade others to hold a specific opinion	A manager finds data to support his belief about the best type of program for certain clientele and uses it to convince other administrators of its merit.
			A leader hires an evaluator to conduct a study only because she wants to tell a superior that an evaluation has been conducted. The results do not matter.

*Fleischer and Christie (2009) distinguish between conceptual use, which refers to changes in program staff and others directly involved in the evaluation, and enlightenment, which refers more broadly to influence in the field.

Evaluators can develop and enhance evaluation activities in hopes of facilitating purposeful engagement and, with it, possible process use. A second newly named type of use is **valuing use**, "use of the core work of evaluation to place value on a program or policy; use of the totality of the evaluation, not solely its process and/or outcomes" (Ottoson & Martinez, 2010, p. 10).

Finally, a study of the evaluations of the Drug Abuse Resistance Education (DARE) program contributed an additional refinement to the categories of use (Weiss, Murphy-Graham, & Birkeland, 2005). **Imposed** or **carrot-and-stick use** occurs when program managers with the power to do so mandate a particular form of evaluation use. Analytically, this is a unique category of instrumental use—people are "using" the results of an evaluation, which qualifies as instrumental use—but in an unconventional, indirect way, and the fact that they *must* do so makes it a special case (p. 26). Indeed, in contrast to earlier concerns about non-use or underuse, M. Q. Patton (personal communication, March 23, 2006) now labels *overuse* as a concern for evaluators whose political and bureaucratic colleagues are legislating action when certain data points (e.g., achievement test scores or a prespecified number of felony convictions) are reached.

Moving beyond the inaugural quarter century of use conceptualizing, the early decade of the new millennium has, in addition, brought a burst of theoretical activity that has reconceived the field's attempts to understand its impact. While this is not an entirely new idea (Weiss, 1972, 1998b), scholars are now emphasizing possibilities that the focus on direct use of either evaluation results or processes has not adequately captured. Their interest is instead on the indirect, intangible influence that evaluation studies may have on individuals, programs, and communities. What has emerged from this thinking is a spotlight on an integrated understanding of evaluation's consequences using the concept of **evaluation influence** (Alkin & Taut, 2003; Henry & Mark, 2003; Kirkhart, 2000; Mark & Henry, 2004) as a unifying construct. Ottoson and Martinez (2010) call this **leveraged use.** This development, while of theoretical interest, does not affect our discussion of IEP, of course, because IEP seeks to enhance evaluation practice directly, not indirectly.

Analytically, the evaluation use typology may be a helpful tool, but it is not a validated theory. Although some have articulated theoretical models of evaluation use or influence (e.g., Johnson, 1998; Kirkhart, 2000; Ottoson & Martinez, 2010), evaluation scholars—as discussed previously in this chapter—have not, by and large, engaged in the systematic pursuit of validated social science theory, even regarding this commonly studied topic (Stufflebeam & Shinkfield, 2007). In contrast to the distinguished history of empirical research on social interdependence with literally hundreds of studies, the formal research base on evaluation use is far thinner. Indeed, a review of the methodological warrants for the findings of this research comes to a grim conclusion:

> As a body of evidence for a scientific understanding of the use of evaluation findings . . . the results of the studies on use are currently of questionable quality. . . . Standing alone as a body of results about evaluation use . . . the findings of the studies examined here do not as a whole have sufficient scientific credibility. (Brandon & Singh, 2009, p. 135)

In their critique of the empirical use research, Brandon and Singh (2009) identified 52 studies—16 surveys (31%), 16 "narrative reflections" (31%), 11 case studies (21%), and 9 simulations (17%)—and concluded that overall the set met one criterion of soundness, a "mix of quantitative and qualitative approaches and various kinds of study designs" (p. 133), but that it failed on a second and perhaps more important criterion, content validity. Setting validity issues aside, a summary from a review of empirical research on evaluation use concludes with the following statement: "It is impossible, finally, to answer the question of which characteristics are most related to increasing the use of evaluations in a straightforward manner" (Johnson et al., 2009, p. 388).

It is perhaps a comment on the youth of this field that even for a topic that has been studied fairly extensively, practitioners must be advised to use these scholarly results with caution. Future research that takes a systems perspective and attends to the complexity of evaluation processes in organizations over time may ultimately provide better guidance for practice. In the meantime, though, the results of the existing research taken as a whole do ring true, making them appropriate grounding for IEP as we await further theoretical developments.

What Research Says About Evaluation Use

Accepting the limitations previously noted, then, what exactly do we know about evaluation use? Initial research in response to Weiss's (1972) call suggested that evaluation's version of the Big Bang Theory, i.e., that people await formal evaluation reports and then directly use the results to make changes, is, in many cases, just not so (King & Pechman, 1984; Preskill & Caracelli, 1997; Weiss, 1998b). Decision makers are often unwilling or unable to apply findings in light of the conflicting demands of the political context in which they work. In addition, evaluation results are frequently contradictory or inconclusive, offering unclear implications for action. Nevertheless, people do routinely use evaluation results, but not necessarily in "go/no-go" ways. Research indicated that "instrumental" use—the direct application of evaluation results—was perhaps less remarkable than scholars once expected, occurring with regularity and often relying on information learned prior to the drafting of the final report (Alkin, Daillak, & White, 1979).

During the late 1970s and early 1980s, scholars conducted both naturalistic and simulation studies to identify key factors affecting the use of evaluations (King & Thompson, 1983), and by the mid-1980s, they produced summary sets of factors shown to affect evaluation use. Alkin (1985) and his colleagues at UCLA identified three broad categories affecting use: human factors, context factors, and evaluation factors. Reviewing 65 use studies, Cousins and Leithwood (1986) divided the meaningful factors into two sets: (a) those related to evaluation implementation (evaluation quality, credibility, relevance, communication quality, findings, and timeliness) and (b) those related to the decision or policy setting (information needs, decision characteristics, political climate, competing information, personal characteristics, and commitment and/or receptiveness to evaluation).

The Cousins and Leithwood (1986) review identified two factors, one each from the implementation and decision-setting sets, as being most important in leading to use: evaluation quality and the characteristics of the decisions being made. Quality included the features of the process, such as methods sophistication, choice of model, and rigor; the characteristics of the decisions being made included their significance, type, and the novelty of the program. The picture that emerged from this early synthesis suggested that evaluators need to design and implement high-quality studies that would provide rigorous and relevant information for important decisions facing decision makers.

More recent syntheses bring Cousins and Leithwood's (1986) initial findings up to date. In the first update, Shula and Cousins (1997) reviewed empirical and theoretical literature that analyzed writings from 1986 to 1996, identifying two new learnings from that decade's research: the significance of evaluation context and the positive use of the evaluation process. They noted that newer research documented the importance of the organizational context, along with an understanding of the uses resulting from the evaluation process, also known as process use. Studies examining the effects of collaboration between the evaluator and stakeholders pointed to the value of such efforts (Ayers, 1987; Cousins, 1996; Greene, 1987, 1988). This review, then, added two additional evidence-based considerations for evaluators: first, the value of paying close attention to the organizational context in which evaluations occur and, second, the potential of taking advantage of the effects that may develop when people are active participants in a study.

In a more recent review, Johnson et al. (2009) conducted an extensive analysis of empirical studies of evaluation use from 1987 to 2005, 20 years after the original Cousins and Leithwood (1986) study, but applying a quality criterion for including studies. Somewhat surprisingly, 25 of the 41 studies reviewed (61%) examined elements not covered by the 1986 framework, confirming the additions noted by Shula and Cousins (1997). The review generated two additions to the original framework:

1. Apart from the processes used, a new characteristic emerged in the implementation category: evaluator competence (e.g., time spent, reputation, political acuity).

2. An entirely new factor category—stakeholder involvement—emerged to accommodate the outcomes of the 25 studies that examined aspects of evaluation use not represented in the original framework, perhaps reflecting an increase in the practice of participatory evaluation.

The review also provided support for five of the original factors: (a) the importance of effective communication, (b) the relevance of information from the implementation factors, (c) potential users' commitment or receptiveness to evaluation, (d) the political climate, and (e) decision characteristics from the decision or policy-setting factors. In sum, the review's findings highlighted the importance of stakeholder involvement in facilitating evaluation use. As Johnson et al. (2009) put it,

> Stakeholder involvement is a mechanism that facilitates those aspects of an evaluation's process or setting that lead to greater use. More than just involvement by stakeholders or decision makers alone, however, the findings from this literature review suggest that engagement, interaction, and communication between evaluation clients and evaluators is key to maximizing the use of the evaluation in the long run. (p. 389)

In other words, by engaging, interacting, and communicating effectively with people in a given context—the interpersonal factor—an evaluator can actually work to increase use.

An additional literature synthesis (Cousins, Goh, Clark, & Lee, 2004) addressed a topic closely related to use, with implications for evaluation capacity building. This review of empirical studies and reflective case narratives examined the integration of evaluative inquiry into organizational culture. Based on the synthesis, their conceptual framework placed three aspects of evaluation (inquiry, capacity, and consequences) within a broader organizational context that included support structures, learning capacity, and consequences. They named the overlap between evaluation capacity and organizational learning capacity "organizational readiness for evaluation" (p. 103) and argued that evaluation capacity building was an example of conceptual evaluation use. The implications for evaluators committed to building evaluation capacity are to think organizationally, thoughtfully building the infrastructure and data collection systems to create, document, and support an organization's ongoing learning.

A recent survey of more than 1,000 members of the American Evaluation Association's Topical Interest Group on Evaluation Use documented people's strong perspectives about the evaluator's role. At least 85% of respondents agreed or strongly agreed that the evaluator's role includes the following: involving stakeholders in the evaluation process (98%), facilitating organizational learning (89%), and maximizing intended use by intended users (86%). When asked their perspectives about stakeholder involvement, more than three-quarters (78%) agreed or strongly agreed that involving multiple stakeholders increases the use of evaluation findings (Fleischer & Christie, 2009). This basically aligns with research findings in social psychology that indicate people are more committed to implementing decisions when they have been involved in making those decisions (Johnson & Johnson, 2009)—another reason to pay attention to interpersonal processes when conducting program evaluation studies.

What, finally, does research tell us about evaluation use? Even as we acknowledge the relative limitations of the existing research base, taken together these syntheses provide direction for program evaluators who want their use-oriented practice to be evidence-based. First, research suggests that evaluators need to be highly competent (or at least perceived to be) and able to design rigorous studies that will provide potential users—those who are committed or receptive to evaluations—targeted information related to the decisions they face. Second, research suggests that it makes good sense to actively engage stakeholders during the evaluation process, taking advantage of people's involvement to help them learn about the evaluation process as they go. Regardless of the roles people play, communication about the evaluation process and its results matters. Remember the personal and interpersonal factors? There is an empirical basis documenting the importance of effective interaction with both intended users and other participants in evaluations. Finally, research suggests that evaluators—especially those seeking to build evaluation capacity—may benefit by paying attention to the contexts in which they work, striving to understand organization politics and the broader systems within which the evaluation process and its results exist.

THEORY-BASED PRINCIPLES FOR INTERACTIVE EVALUATION PRACTICE

IEP recognizes the imperative of human interaction in program evaluation and focuses on attending to the interpersonal factor throughout. As we have noted previously, this means two things: (a) constructively interacting with a variety of players to promote success along the way and (b) intentionally structuring activities to promote the accomplishment of evaluation tasks. Whether studies are evaluator-directed, collaborative, or participant-directed, effective interaction with those involved will be essential. Sometimes interactions will be with one or several individuals, such as a funder or program leader to frame a study at the start, or with primary intended users at key junctures as the study is conducted. Other times interaction will be continuous with a host of organizational and community members, all collaboratively involved in the evaluation, or periodic when people conducting their own self-study seek consultative input or training from the evaluator.

Regardless of which approach is pursued, or for what purpose, the principles for IEP presented in Exhibit 3.3 underscore the importance of interpersonal interaction in evaluation practice and provide direction for bringing the interpersonal factor to life. These principles are derived from the conceptual definition of IEP presented in Chapter 1, the frameworks for envisioning IEP presented in Chapter 2, and the theoretical foundations for IEP presented in Chapter 3.

Exhibit 3.3 Principles for Interactive Evaluation Practice

IEP Principle	What This Means
1. Get personal.	• Find people who care about the evaluation and its results, especially primary intended users. • Know your leaders; they make a difference. • Involve people in evaluation planning, decision making, and implementation to increase their commitment to using results.
2. Structure interaction.	• Not all interactive participation is good; it may be helpful or not. • Goal structures influence whether interpersonal interaction will be constructive or destructive. • Structure positive interdependence for cooperative interaction likely to produce mutually beneficial outcomes and positive interpersonal relations.
3. Examine context.	• Always analyze the evaluation context. • Know that mixed motives are always in play in social situations; cooperative people may have competitive motives. • Consider context from a variety of perspectives; both macro and micro views provide valuable information—consider the forest as well as its trees.
4. Consider politics.	• Understand that evaluation processes and results are not the only factors that inform decisions; political forces are also at play.
5. Expect conflict.	• Conflict is not inherently bad; recognize its virtue. • Conflict will occur; manage it constructively.
6. Respect culture.	• Appreciate the power of culture; different cultural foundations greatly influence perspective. • Seek and engage multiple and diverse voices. • Value differences, clarify assumptions, and create mutual meaning.
7. Take time.	• Interpersonal processes take time; be ready to devote time to what matters for successful IEP. • Positive interpersonal relationships develop progressively; persevere. • Think of IEP as a journey that involves shared decision making and constructive conflict resolution; it's a step-by-step process that will in all likelihood provide new insights along the way.

SOURCE: © 2010 Jean A. King & Laurie Stevahn.

1. *Get personal* because, perhaps most fundamentally, successful evaluation practice is about relationships. Those who are organization or program leaders, those who will use evaluation results, those who will be instrumental in conducting various evaluation tasks, those who will be asked to provide input, those who have the power to block processes or pave smooth pathways—all these people matter. Relationships developed with and among them are apt to be instrumental to the overall success of a study.

2. *Structure interaction* because this provides a nuanced way to think about participation. Evaluators should not automatically assume people's participation means helping or collaborating. Those involved could just as well interact in unhelpful ways or compete for personal gain in obstructive ways—and evaluators should realize this. Structuring cooperative interaction supports the type of relationships that will result in productive and constructive working relationships.

3. *Examine context* because of the importance of situation analysis. Evaluators need to know the lay of the land and its inhabitants. Whether internal or external, all evaluators would do well to consider the evaluation context as comprehensively as appropriate and possible. We encourage evaluators to look through different lenses—e.g., use the cooperative lens to determine if teamwork is the norm, use the capacity building lens to determine if organization development is alive and healthy, and use the many other lenses available in this book and other resources. The point is that most organizations are complex. Trying to understand that complexity should help evaluators as they make evaluation decisions, take action, and reflect on effectiveness.

4. *Consider politics* because political concerns are interwoven into the fabric of every organization or program and therefore affect evaluation practice. In a perfect world, framing and conducting evaluation studies would occur without limited budgets or resources, changes in legislative policies, restraints on timetables or schedules, and the like, but these, and numerous other examples, are a constant reality—and evaluators must deal with them. Conducting effective studies means always keeping an eye on the political landscape and what that might mean for evaluation implementations.

5. *Expect conflict* because it will occur—guaranteed. However, don't let "fight-or-flight" tendencies get the upper hand. Instead, recognize that conflict has value and can be leveraged for good. Every disagreement or

dispute signals possibilities for change—and positive change will be more likely when conflict is managed constructively.

6. *Respect culture* because it greatly influences perspective. Each person brings unique life experiences, identities, values, traditions, languages, assumptions, and expectations to the evaluation process. Evaluators should appreciate how multiple voices can enrich that process and systematically seek pluralistic views, always aware that diversity takes many forms—ethnic/racial background being one among many. Culturally competent evaluators will honor culture always and work with others to forge shared meaning.

7. *Take time* because time is of the essence to attend to each of these principles. What matters will take time. Although we assume that nearly all evaluators wish for more time, we suggest focusing on how best to use the time available. Trade-offs will be necessary, but always consider the value of devoting time to those activities that will strengthen the interpersonal interactions and relationships ultimately needed to get the job done well.

CHAPTER REVIEW

This chapter presented the theoretical foundations for interactive evaluation practice (IEP). IEP builds on two empirically supported theoretical foundations: *social interdependence theory* and *evaluation use.*

1. For several reasons the field of program evaluation to date has not developed the research and validated theory common to other social sciences.

2. *Social interdependence theory* (see Johnson & Johnson, 2009) provides an empirically grounded foundation for explaining and influencing human interaction by specifying how individuals can be in relationship with each other, the type of interaction characteristic of each relationship, and the likely subsequent outcome. Originating in social psychology, this theory posits that goal structures (cooperative or competitive) determine interpersonal interaction (promotive/responsive or oppositional/obstructive), which, in turn, influences outcomes (mutual or exclusive).

3. Evaluators can apply *social interdependence theory* in practical ways: (a) as a lens through which to assess an evaluation's context, (b) as a way to foster constructive participation among participants in collaborative studies, and (c) as a tool for thinking about and enacting interactive dimensions of evaluation studies.

4. *Evaluation use* is possibly the most highly studied research topic in the field. An evolving typology has identified six forms of use: (a) instrumental, (b) conceptual/enlightenment, (c) political/persuasive/symbolic, (d) process, (e) valuing, and (f) imposed/carrot-and-stick (a special form of instrumental). The additional concept of *evaluation influence* focuses on the indirect, intangible consequences that evaluation studies may have over time.

5. A review of the rigor of evaluation use research found that the results of use studies to date are of questionable quality and lack scientific credibility. Nevertheless, taken as a whole, the results reveal consistent patterns, making them an appropriate grounding for IEP.

6. Existing research on evaluation use suggests three things: (a) Evaluators need to be highly competent (or at least perceived to be) and able to design rigorous studies to provide users information, (b) actively engaging stakeholders during the evaluation process is a good idea and can help them learn about the evaluation process, and (c) evaluators should pay attention to the contexts in which they work, striving to understand organization politics and broader systems.

7. The seven principles for IEP derived from the theoretical foundations of *social interdependence theory* and *evaluation use* are (1) get personal, (2) structure participation, (3) examine context, (4) consider politics, (5) expect conflict, (6) respect culture, and (7) take time.

PART II

Skills and Strategies for Interactive Evaluation Practice

As its title states, Part II addresses skills and strategies for interactive evaluation practice (IEP) and includes many charts and templates for easy use. The order of the five chapters is purposeful. Chapters 4, 5, and 6 detail the basic building blocks for IEP. Chapter 4 begins by discussing the role and goals of conversations in evaluation practice, distinguishing them from other types of conversations, and provides conversation starters and questions for effectively engaging people in evaluation conversations. Chapter 5 provides a rationale for using **interactive evaluation strategies**, followed by detailed instructions for 13 interactive strategies and examples of how evaluators can use the strategies for a variety of purposes. Chapter 6 presents a definition of conflict and theoretical frameworks for thinking about it in evaluations, including specific skills and competencies that evaluators can use to manage conflict constructively when it occurs.

With these basics established, the final two chapters in Part II discuss how to create a viable interactive evaluation process and what to do when that process breaks down. Chapter 7 identifies the foundations and components that affect the viability of IEP, then outlines specific planning and actions for developing an effective process. It continues with a description of evaluation capacity building and the importance of ongoing reflection during IEP. Chapter 8 deals with handling the unexpected in program evaluation, providing potential responses, both specific and general, and discussing how to resolve trade-offs in evaluation decision making. Each chapter in Part II ends with a chart that applies the IEP principles to the skills or strategies that are the subject of that chapter (see Appendix D for a summary of these IEP principle applications).

4

THE NUTS AND BOLTS OF EVALUATION CONVERSATIONS

Chapter Preview

- Examine the role of conversations in evaluation practice
- Distinguish evaluation conversations from other conversations
- Introduce seven overarching goals for evaluation conversations
- Provide evaluation conversation starters and detailed questions for engaging people
- Apply the interactive evaluation practice principles to evaluation conversations

INTRODUCTION

An old saying reminds us that talk is cheap, but, cheap or not, talk is the currency of a successful evaluation process. Conversations enable evaluators to stay connected with clients, intended users, and other stakeholders throughout an evaluation, and, if things get rocky—when, for example, an evaluator inadvertently offends a key participant, the response rate to a critical survey is unacceptably low, or a data-laden report draft proves incomprehensible—conversations keep the evaluation moving forward. Of course, the content of the conversations varies as the process unfolds. Sometimes it can include an urgent heads-up about an unanticipated problem threatening to derail the evaluation; other times a conversation brings happy news, such as a finding that affirms what program leaders believed to be true. At any time, however, meaningful dialogue between evaluators and participants in the evaluation is central to the process.

We therefore begin the skill development section of this book by underscoring something an evaluator *can* control—or at least actively pursue and shape—throughout the evaluation. Given an evaluation's interactive nature, evaluators must engage both potential and continuing clients in substantive conversations. They do so for three important reasons: to find out what clients want them to do, to facilitate the evaluation process, and to monitor how well it is going. Although not all evaluators view interaction as critical, we believe that the imperative to communicate is inviolate regardless of where the study sits on the interpersonal participation quotient (IPQ, shown in Exhibit 2.3). It may be especially important in the evaluator-directed zone, where contact between evaluator and client is often less regular or routine.

This chapter first highlights the role of conversations in evaluation practice, distinguishing what makes them different, and then suggests seven overarching goals for such conversations throughout the evaluation, including conversation starters and sample questions for each. The chapter concludes by explaining how you can use the IEP principles presented in Chapter 3 to guide and ground evaluation conversations.

THE ROLE OF CONVERSATIONS IN EVALUATION PRACTICE

If this chapter were a language course, we would call it Conversational Evaluation 101. A conversation is an informal talk with someone, and hundreds of such interactions will occur during a program evaluation. Our point is straightforward: Effective evaluators know how to talk with people, and they have conversations repeatedly throughout the course of an evaluation study. Their ability to interact constructively with a variety of people and their ability to structure meaningful activities are hallmarks of interactive evaluation practice (IEP).

- At an evaluation's inception, clients explain what they want, and evaluators listen attentively and ask questions: Who are the program's stakeholders, and what are their concerns? Who might use the evaluation results, and how will they participate in the study? Who in the organization can and will take part? Who holds power in this setting? Are cultural issues likely to make a difference? What are the resources for the project? What are the funder's evaluation requirements? Are there external constraints that may influence timing and report formats?
- As a study is framed, conversations continue to shape the process as evaluators continue to ask: What questions will the evaluation seek to answer? What is the **logic model** or program theory staff are using? What

are the most effective designs and methods that will answer the questions? What reports will meet the information needs of various audiences? Who will prepare or deliver them?

- Throughout the process, reflective evaluators keep talking and listening—to clients, intended users, and other stakeholders—for any number of reasons: to find out how things are going, to identify changes that might improve the study, to make sense of what they are hearing.

Evaluation conversations occur in many venues: formal meeting rooms, staff offices, and hallways on the way to lunch. They are often interconnected and overlapping, and many stakeholders will add their voices. People may offer strongly held ideas that conflict—for example, when administrators focus on the bottom line of an expensive program, while staff touts its impressive outcomes—or they may present a unified view. Whether owing to context, culture, or personality, some individuals may be uncomfortable expressing their thoughts openly, while others are more than pleased to state their opinions—loudly—in any forum to anyone who will listen. And therein lies the challenge. Whatever an evaluator's approach, the conversations surrounding her practice and skill as the manager of those conversations are essential to moving the process forward. An evaluator's ability to converse effectively with people in an evaluation setting may well be a predictor of the eventual quality of the study that results. An inability to do so—for example, the evaluator who dominates discussions without listening to others or who fails to identify ongoing tensions between key stakeholders—may result in an evaluation that, while in some sense technically adequate, fails to provide intended users accurate information they can act on.

The need to converse effectively is essential even for evaluations that are not highly collaborative. Every evaluation requires a certain level of participation, at the very minimum a client who initially tells the evaluator what he wants done and some form of reporting to the client at the study's conclusion. Consider two examples, one negative and the other positive.

- One example of the importance of evaluation conversations—a negative one—is evident in the first situation described in Chapter 1. Recall in that study the evaluation team purposefully and even with pride chose not to collect test score data, responding to the wishes of the planning group that feared the potentially limiting effects of doing so in the first 2 years of program implementation. Sadly, had the evaluators taken the time to hold even one conversation with the state legislators ultimately responsible for funding the program, they might have quickly come to understand the importance of test scores—any test scores—in the policy arena in which the legislators functioned. Despite the many detailed qualitative case studies, absent test scores, the credibility of the entire evaluation was questioned, and the legislator with the potential to affect the program used his clout to cut its funding. To quote *Cool Hand Luke,* what they had there was a "failure to communicate," and the effect in both cases was grim.

- A second and positive example is the case of a university professor hired to evaluate a large, federally funded training program for health professionals operating in hundreds of community and technical colleges across the country. Once the evaluator had won the evaluation contract, he held initial conversations with agency officials to determine exactly what they wanted to know and the data needed to answer their questions. He then assembled an evaluation team that finalized the design and sample, developed and piloted data collection instruments, and began to collect data. Although he and his team made virtually every decision in planning and conducting the study, he communicated frequently with his contact, seeking input from an agency perspective, asking questions about specific concerns (e.g., how long a survey staff would be willing to complete), and generally ensuring that each step of the evaluation process met with approval. Knowing that the response rate to one survey was critical to the design, he elicited help from higher-ups at the agency, who sent the letter inviting participation. Even though the evaluator was conducting an evaluator-directed study—that is, making decisions and implementing the evaluation plan—he had numerous conversations with his client throughout the course of the study. The final evaluation report, posted on the agency website, was the culmination of these conversations over the study's 3 years.

Without frequent conversations, then, evaluators would be unable to do their job. But what distinguishes a program evaluation conversation from the many similar interactions people have each day? By appearance, evaluation conversations look like any other conversation. Imagine two people sitting across a table from each other, engaged in a face-to-face conversation. Can you tell by looking if they are engaged in an evaluation conversation, as opposed to some other type? Unless you are able to hear what they are saying, the answer is probably not. So what makes an evaluation conversation distinct?

HOW PROGRAM EVALUATION CONVERSATIONS DIFFER FROM OTHER CONVERSATIONS

Evaluation conversations come in many forms. As noted earlier, settings can differ, as can interpersonal dynamics. There are phone calls; informal meetings at an evaluator's office, a coffee shop, or a restaurant; formal meetings around conference tables; and chats during visits to program sites. "In hallway conversations, over coffee, before and after meetings, over the telephone, and through informal networks, the word gets passed along when something useful and important has been found" (Patton, 2012, p. 365). Exhibit 4.1 defines the terms frequently used to describe people who participate in an evaluation. Although the evaluation client and the primary intended user may be different, they are often one and the same, and for this reason we use the terms *client* and *primary intended user* interchangeably.

Exhibit 4.1 Participant Roles for Evaluation Conversations

Term	Definition
Stakeholders	Individuals who have a vested interest in a program or its evaluation
Audience	The individuals or groups who receive evaluation reports
Sponsors/ funders	The people who provide resources to conduct an evaluation
Clients	The people who hire an evaluator and typically help shape and monitor the evaluation study
Primary intended users	"Those *specific* stakeholders selected to work with the evaluator throughout the evaluation" (Patton, 2008, p. 72; emphasis in original)
Program participants	Individuals who receive services from or take part in a program
Evaluation participants	Individuals who take part in a program evaluation in one of two ways: (1) participating in making decisions about the evaluation or in implementing it, or (2) providing data in one form or another

NOTE: In evaluation settings people often play multiple roles. A funder, for example, may also be a primary intended user and an active participant in the study, both by helping make decisions and by providing data. Even with this potential for overlap, the different named roles allow evaluators to distinguish among people in an evaluation context.

Based on Schwab's commonplaces of learning, the commonplaces of evaluation point to four components of every evaluation conversation: (1) a context in which the discussion occurs, (2) a client or intended user, (3) the content of the evaluation process or its results, and (4) an evaluator (King, 1988). In an evaluation setting each of these contributes to a conversation that begins as the evaluation is conceived and may continue well past the time that the evaluator delivers a final report. Each necessarily affects the conversations that will follow. What makes evaluation conversations unique is the setting in which the program and its evaluation occur, the people involved—an evaluator and client—and the content of their conversations.

Context

Students in introductory classes quickly learn that a safe answer to virtually any question about program evaluation is, "It depends" (Trochim, 2008). Evaluations are highly situational, grounded in specific times and places, each of them unique. An important part of evaluation conversations must therefore seek to understand this uniqueness. Questions such as the following become useful: What is the history of this particular program in this particular setting? What conditions or features in this milieu are critical to understanding how the program works? Do people tend to work together in a collaborative fashion, or are they basically on their own? How do culture and politics, large and small, affect the program? How has evaluation played out in this context in the past? In what ways might this evaluation project be supported or at risk?

The Client/Primary Intended User

A key participant in any evaluation conversation is the person who initiates the process to begin with—the evaluator's customer, typically called the client, who may be an individual or a group of people. As the process begins, clients are trying to determine what the proposed evaluation might look like, and they may not have a clue, even when they think they do. Among clients new to the field, there is the distinct possibility that they won't know what evaluation is or can be, what they want or need, or how they're going to use the process or its results. They may have a misconception about the possibilities, hold negative attitudes, or even, on rare occasions, harbor the desire to predetermine the results.

The practice of utilization-focused evaluation focuses attention on the role of *primary intended user* in addition to that of client. Patton (2008) indicates,

> Primary intended users of an evaluation are those *specific* stakeholders selected to work with the evaluator throughout the evaluation to focus the evaluation, participate in making design and methods decisions, and interpret results to assure that the evaluation is useful, meaningful, relevant, and credible. (p. 72; emphasis in original)

This means that the primary intended users are the key individuals with and for whom the evaluator works in a setting. Their information needs and concerns guide the study from inception to conclusion, and they are actively engaged throughout: in its framing, in identifying credible data collection methods, and in making sense of the results.

Conversation Content

Now that there is a context and someone to talk to, it is time to identify the topics specific to an evaluation conversation. Evaluators hold technical power, guide conversations, and ensure the appropriateness of each study. At its most basic, an evaluator and a client will meet to discuss the prospects for beginning an evaluation. There is an unavoidable power dynamic in these conversations in that clients can choose to hire or fire external evaluators, while internal evaluators have to worry similarly about their future, although in a different way. Negotiating explicit and fair contracts results from important conversations held prior to starting an evaluation. As Stufflebeam (1999) puts it, "Without such agreements the evaluation process is constantly subject to misunderstanding, disputes, efforts to compromise the findings, attack, and/or withdrawal—by the client—of cooperation and funds" (p. 1). O'Sullivan (2004) writes, "How evaluators respond to evaluation requests determines whether they will be employed to conduct the proposed evaluations" (p. 41). She identifies three topics for these clarification conversations: "gathering information about the program's nature and scope, determining the purpose of the evaluation, and probing the resources available to conduct the evaluation" (p. 41).

Evaluators would do well to develop specific questions in advance to get at these topics. Stufflebeam (1999, p. 1) developed a helpful resource to prepare for negotiations: a checklist for use by evaluators and clients during evaluation contract negotiations so that key issues will be surfaced, discussed, agreed on, and recorded prior to the study's launch. The checklist includes the following categories:

- Basic considerations, including the object and purpose of the evaluation, the client and other audiences, the values that will guide the study, etc.
- Types of information that the contract could include, e.g., what is required, data collection procedures, instruments, follow-up, etc.
- Two kinds of analytical procedures, one for quantitative data and one for qualitative
- Report details, including deliverables and their due dates; formats, contents, lengths, audiences, and delivery methods for both interim and final reports; and any restrictions/permissions required
- Reporting safeguards, e.g., issues of anonymity/confidentiality, who will have editorial authority and final authority to release reports
- Protocol specifics: (a) contact people, (b) rules for contacting program staff, and (c) communication channels
- Evaluation management issues: (a) the timeline for the evaluation work of both clients and evaluators and (b) assignment of responsibilities for the evaluation
- Possible client responsibilities, e.g., access to information, equipment and materials, workspace, etc.
- Evaluation budget elements, e.g., amounts and dates, conditions for payment, limits/restrictions, etc.
- Provisions regarding review and control of the study: (a) for amending and canceling the contract, (b) for modifying the evaluation design if necessary, and (c) for metaevaluation

From the initial negotiations and over the course of an evaluation, evaluators may work with many people, and, while not everyone is a client in the formal sense of that word, all will have conversations with the potential to affect an evaluation's course. This is a reminder, if we needed one, of why an evaluator's ability to manage interpersonal dynamics is a critical skill. Typically, evaluators and clients/primary intended users share a common commitment to wanting the study done well, so together they make decisions about the process as it unfolds. Among others, topics often include the following:

- *Technical concerns.* The evaluator is responsible for two things: first, ensuring that the design and data are the best possible given the constraints of the context and, second, that the technical quality of the study meets the accuracy standards of the Program Evaluation Standards (Yarbrough, Shula, Hopson, & Caruthers, 2011). Although some may feel insecure around or threatened by evaluators' technical expertise, it is our job to ensure high-quality evaluation. Technical matters can therefore become critically important topics for conversation. Consider, for example, clients who feel pressure from funders to "prove" that their program leads directly to desired outcomes even in short periods of time. It falls to evaluators to shine the light of measurement reality on desired causal claims, collecting data that come as close as technically possible to demonstrating potential causal relations. When pressured on any technical issue, evaluators must stay the course and adhere to professional standards.

- *Political issues.* If technical issues are the evaluator's bailiwick, the reality of the context's politics belongs to the client. Both at its inception and over time, evaluators need to discuss the realities of interpersonal interactions that may affect the evaluation. Context uniquely affects the study as participants engage in evaluation activities. When, for example, the newly appointed interim director of a department in a large county agency attended a meeting about a previously negotiated evaluation contract and made clear his desire to change expectations for the work, the external evaluator, confused by the sudden modification, contacted another staff member to understand what was going on. Since internal evaluators live in an organizational setting, they may be better able to navigate its political waters, creating evaluation processes that are as practical as they can be.

- *Resource questions.* Years ago mothers advised their daughters not to talk about money on the first date, but evaluators, of necessity, should ask about money and other resources as soon as possible after an evaluation is conceived and every time questions arise about a study's funding. For external evaluators, this means determining the expected expenses for evaluation tasks and discussing them with clients; for internal evaluators, this means identifying time and other needed resources and ensuring that organizational funding or personnel are available. How many times has an evaluator spoken with potential clients and designed a study to address their issues, only to find out later that the available budget for the study is woefully inadequate? The $5,000 that is a large sum of money to a small aerobics or teen-parenting program unfortunately doesn't go far in many evaluation settings. As tasks change over the course of an evaluation, it often makes sense to negotiate additional resources or to cut back on what will be done with existing funds.

The Evaluator

Ideally, the evaluator brings a variety of knowledge and skills to the table—technical knowledge related to systematic inquiry and the practice of program evaluation, along with competencies in situational analysis, project management, reflection, and interpersonal skills, including cultural competence (Stevahn, King, Ghere, & Minnema, 2005). Because many clients initially find evaluation to be a foreign language, the evaluator typically leads the conversation, discussing what the client wants evaluated and why and considering the feasibility of a study in light of available resources and other constraints. The evaluator's technical expertise is key. Although everyone is an intuitive evaluator—people are constantly making value judgments—the evaluator wears the mantle of social science inquiry, wielding its power and, for the uninitiated, explicating its mysteries. Werner Heisenberg, one of the 20th century's great physicists, once wrote, "Science is rooted in conversation"—and it falls to evaluators in conversations to make the evaluation process and its technical components comprehensible and to do so in a nonthreatening manner.

The conversations of external evaluators may differ from those of internal evaluators. External consultants can choose whether or not to take a contract and may use initial conversations to make the determination, whereas internal evaluation staff may be required to take on a study regardless of their feelings about it. But internal evaluators also have choices to make. These relate to the practicality of shaping the evaluation so that a useful study will result in a context they probably understand well.

Regardless of placement, it is incumbent on all evaluators to get evaluation conversations right for at least two reasons. First, as evaluation professionals, evaluators hold responsibility for their own professional practice (American Evaluation Association, 2004; see Appendix B) and for the ethical conduct of evaluation studies (Yarbrough et al., 2011). Second, external and internal evaluators alike may suffer later for bad decisions early on. If, as sometimes happens, an evaluator agrees to conduct extensive interviews but doesn't build in sufficient budget support for transcription and qualitative analysis, the team may find itself doing challenging intellectual work for minimum wage.

What, then, distinguishes an evaluation conversation from other conversations? First, as noted earlier, evaluation conversations engage two individuals or groups of individuals in a given context in a single-minded focus on the evaluation process and its results, working together to make sure that the evaluation will be as useful and sound as conditions allow. Second, even if there are only two people in the room, evaluation conversations never involve only two people. Standing on the shoulders of colleagues past and present, evaluators bring their current versions of evaluator competencies, an awareness of the field of program evaluation with its guiding principles and standards, and the practical knowledge gleaned from previous studies. Clients bring the ghosts of evaluations past and present, an awareness of the complexity and political challenges of their organization, and ongoing relationships with multiple people in the evaluation context. Third, evaluation conversations are not one-time affairs. To be effective, evaluators and clients need to talk throughout the evaluation. And what exactly do they talk about? With the groundwork laid, let's get to the actual nuts and bolts of evaluation conversations.

OVERARCHING GOALS AND SAMPLE QUESTIONS FOR EVALUATION CONVERSATIONS

The phrase *nuts and bolts* brings to mind basement workshops, hardware stores, and renovation sites. For people unskilled at carpentry, it may also signal intense frustration. But this image is an apt one for discussing evaluation conversations because, just as nuts and bolts connect basic components in a construction project, the questions that follow will join evaluators and evaluation participants in important conversations to strengthen evaluations. We prescribe a set of seven broad goals for conversation that evaluators can use to engage clients, primary intended users, and other appropriate people/stakeholders in planning and implementing an evaluation.

Initial evaluation conversations take place when entering an evaluation context, before a project actually begins. Three goals frame these conversations:

1. Understand the client's and participants' perceptions of evaluation and establish positive relationships.

2. Determine what the client/primary intended user wants/needs.

3. Determine whether the context is a viable setting for a program evaluation.

The next three goals for conversation, not surprisingly, overlap with the basic inquiry tasks (BIT) introduced in Chapter 2 and should be pursued once the evaluator is committed to a study. In fact, conversations to achieve these goals realistically will take place in a repeated fashion throughout its duration:

4. Determine how the study will be conducted.

5. Determine how best to collect and analyze information.

6. Determine what the data mean and how best to present them.

Throughout the process and especially at its conclusion, the seventh and final goal for evaluation conversations encourages evaluators to reflect with their clients on the evaluation process.

7. Reflect on how the evaluation is going and what has been learned.

Two exhibits provide detailed information to enable evaluators to shape conversations throughout the evaluation. Exhibit 4.2 links the seven overarching conversation goals to issues evaluators may consider at specific stages in an evaluation and potential pitfalls signaling concerns that could require special attention. Exhibit 4.3 starts with the same overarching goals, then, for each, provides conversation starters to initiate an evaluation conversation, along with a sample of more detailed questions that evaluators can select from, adapt, or add to in preparing for conversations in specific contexts. You'll see that a few of these questions assume more knowledge of evaluation than a typical client might have (e.g., knowledge of different approaches and designs or of measurement). For those questions, the evaluator would outline sufficient content for the conversation, explaining throughout to ensure that the answer to the question sufficiently addresses the issue.

Exhibit 4.2   Goals for Evaluation Conversation, Issues to Consider, and Potential Pitfalls

Conversation Goals	Issues to Consider	Potential Pitfalls
Before agreeing to conduct a study . . .		
1. Understand the client's and participants' perceptions of evaluation and establish positive relationships.	• Setting and atmosphere in which the conversation is held (formal, constrained, open, friendly, well documented, etc.) • Preexisting relationships with key participants • Prior knowledge of and reputation of the individuals • Cultural issues to attend to in the setting • Level of people's evaluation knowledge/experience • People's attitudes toward program evaluation	• There is an evident hostility or lack of trust between/among people involved in the evaluation. • Participants hold negative attitudes toward evaluation. • Evaluator lacks familiarity with the cultures involved.

(Continued)

Exhibit 4.2   (Continued)

Conversation Goals	Issues to Consider	Potential Pitfalls
2. Determine what the client/primary intended user wants/needs.	• The reason for the evaluation at this time, including the source of initiation • Specific requirements of the study (e.g., accountability data or reports required, deadlines) from funders/sponsors • Extent of existing program documentation (rationale, goals, activities, etc.) • Clarification or development of logic model, program theory, or theory of change (as appropriate) • Primary intended users for the evaluation • Extent to which clients have thought through the study, including (a) specific information about what clients want from the proposed study (e.g., its purposes, who will use the results) and (b) clarity of decisions that may result (e.g., programmatic "go/no-go," staffing, improvement processes)	• Clients are unaware of or unclear about what they want. • The funders' expectations for the program or its evaluation are unrealistic. • The program theory is incomplete or overly idealistic. • Clients want to commission a pseudoevaluation (i.e., they already know the desired results of the evaluation). • Cultural issues/assumptions or conflicts of interest are likely to affect the evaluation negatively.
3. Determine whether the context is a viable setting for a program evaluation.	• Understanding the organizational environment in which this study will take place • Existence of underlying needs or conflicts that might affect the evaluation • An inclusive list of stakeholders and their likely concerns • Potential resistance to evaluation or to change • Resources available for the study, including budget and in-kind commitments	• There is evident hostility or a lack of trust between/among people involved in the evaluation. • Clients are unwilling to participate in key decisions related to the evaluation. • Leaders who are gatekeepers are not actively involved. • There are no clear intended users or uses for the study. • Limited resources are available for the study. • Available time is unlikely to support a viable study.

Conversation Goals	Issues to Consider	Potential Pitfalls
	• Timeline for the evaluation and its components • Potential ethical, legal, or cultural considerations • Other feasibility issues, including likely constraints (e.g., political issues in the organization, staff interest, personnel turnover)	• Cultural issues/assumptions may limit the study's outcomes. • The evaluator is unable to develop a strong design.
After agreeing to conduct the study and throughout . . .		
4. Determine how the study will be conducted.	• The overall approach to the evaluation, including purposes and potential uses • Broad, overarching questions the evaluation will answer • The information required to answer these questions • A feasible design and credible methods for collecting necessary data • Instrumentation plans • A sampling plan	• Clients are unaware of or unclear about what they want. • Clients are unwilling to participate in key decisions related to the evaluation. • Available time or other resources are unlikely to support a viable study. • The chosen design and methods are not credible in the given context. • Cultural issues/assumptions may limit the study's outcomes.
5. Determine how best to collect and analyze information.	• Identifying and recruiting appropriate samples • Developing or locating instruments and implementing the data collection plan • Checking the data for accuracy • Compiling and storing the data • Establishing who owns the results and who will have access • Determining the need for confidentiality • Analyzing the data, both quantitative and qualitative • Preparing appropriate data summaries	• Parts of the data collection plan prove to be unrealistic (e.g., the sample ultimately available differs from that needed; response rates are low). • The study costs more than expected. • The timeline is too short to meet the client's needs. • There is a lack of support from staff. • The data appear to have problems (validity, reliability). • Data get lost. • Analysts conduct inappropriate analyses. • Data summaries are confusing or unclear to primary intended users.

(Continued)

Exhibit 4.2   (Continued)

Conversation Goals	Issues to Consider	Potential Pitfalls
6. Determine what the data mean and how best to present them.	• Interpreting data in light of the context and drawing appropriate implications • Structuring and enhancing potential use • Whether or not to make judgments explicit and the criteria and standards with which to do so • Whether or not to develop commendations or recommendations • Structuring reports that will communicate clearly • Disseminating the results in various forms	• People draw incorrect interpretations from the data. • Intended users ignore the evaluator's statement of limitations. • Intended users want a simplistic version of the results. • Reports don't meet the needs of the primary intended users. • People run with parts of the analysis they like and disregard the rest. • Results are disseminated, but no one uses them.
During and after the study . . .		
7. Reflect on how the evaluation is going and what has been learned.	• Tracking the evaluation from beginning to end, tackling challenges as they arise • The eventual learnings that result from this study • What went well during the study and what didn't • Things to do differently next time	• Clients are unwilling to participate in routine reflection about the evaluation. • Problems arise but are not addressed. • Evaluators see no possibility for improvement in the evaluation process.

SOURCE: © 2010 Jean A. King & Laurie Stevahn.

Exhibit 4.3   Evaluation Conversation Starters and Sample Questions

Conversation Starters	Sample Questions
1. Understand the client's and participants' perceptions of evaluation and establish positive relationships.	
How do people in this organization feel about program evaluation?	• When you think about program evaluation, what word comes to mind? Why? • What was the best program evaluation you ever participated in? What made it good? What happened as a result?

Conversation Starters	Sample Questions
	• How do others in the organization feel about evaluation? On what do you base your comments? • What previous evaluation experiences have you had? • How has evaluation played out in this context in the past? • To what extent has staff received training in program evaluation, whether formal or informal? • How much experience has staff had with program evaluation? • How would you characterize their experiences? • Who are the evaluation champions in your organization?
Tell me about the organization's culture.	• How would you describe the culture of this organization? • How do people generally get along in this organization? • What previous involvement has your organization had with evaluation? • What is the organizational structure for program evaluation? • Is this an organization where evaluation is routinely part of ongoing work? • Who holds power in this setting? • To what extent might cultural issues, assumptions, or expectations affect the evaluation? • To what extent is there potential resistance to this evaluation or to change more generally? • To what extent are people likely to be eager participants in the evaluation process? • To what extent do people routinely use data as part of their ongoing activities?
2. Determine what the client/primary intended user wants/needs.	
What program is being evaluated?	• Tell me about the program you want evaluated. • How long has the program been in operation? Describe its development over time. • What is the history of this particular program in this particular setting? • What do you see as essential aspects and key characteristics of the program? • To what extent are the program's goals and objectives clearly specified? Are the program outcomes specified? • What are the program's activities? What do participants do? What does staff do? • Are there explicit criteria and standards for this program or others like it? • Has staff developed a logic model, program theory, or theory of change? What logic model or program theory is staff using? • Is the program being implemented as planned? If not, why not? • Do you have documentation or archival records for the program? • What have been the results of previous program evaluations (if any)?

(Continued)

Exhibit 4.3 (Continued)

Conversation Starters	Sample Questions
	• What are some of the problems, frustrations, joys, and positive activities that people report about this program?
	• What do people like most and least about this program?
	• What concerns have people expressed about this program?
	• What conditions or features in this setting are critical to understanding how the program works?
	• How do culture and politics, large and small, affect the program?
What is the purpose of this evaluation?	• Can you tell me how this evaluation came to be?
	• Why are you planning to conduct an evaluation at this time?
	• Is this a formative, summative, or developmental evaluation?
	• To what extent is accountability a factor in conducting the evaluation?
	• What are people most concerned about regarding this program and its evaluation?
	• What kind of information would be helpful?
	• Who might be interested in the results of this study?
	• Who will actually use the results of the evaluation? What are their concerns and questions?
	• Are there judgments or decisions that may be linked to the results?
	• What are expectations for the study?
	• Who are the stakeholders for this program, and what are their concerns?
	• Do you hope to teach people about the evaluation process through this study (i.e., build their evaluation capacity)?
	• Is this evaluation part of ongoing data collection in the organization?
	• To what extent is this part of a larger organization development process?
	• Are there any ethical, legal, or cultural considerations to keep in mind as we move forward with the evaluation?
What are the requirements for this evaluation?	• Is this evaluation in response to a mandate or a grant requirement?
	• Are there external constraints that may influence timing and report formats?
	• Who are the funders, and what are their expectations for the study?
	• Who is in charge of this evaluation?
	• Are there expectations about who should participate in the evaluation?
	• Are there any required data elements?
	• How many times is the evaluator expected to meet with the contractor? (O'Sullivan, 2004, p. 51)
	• Are there program events that the evaluator is expected to attend? (O'Sullivan, 2004, p. 51)
	• What are the reporting requirements?
	• What is the timeline for the evaluation? How fixed is it?

Conversation Starters	Sample Questions
3. Determine whether the context is a viable setting for a program evaluation.	
Help me understand the organizational setting where this evaluation will take place.	• What is the organizational hierarchy? Is there an organizational chart? • What is the organization's mission? Is there a strategic plan in place? How might these relate to the proposed evaluation? • In general, how do people get along in this organization? • How are tasks typically structured in this organization? • What kinds of opportunities exist for teamwork? • What structures already exist for people to discuss the evaluation? • What underlying organizational needs or conflicts might affect the evaluation? • To what extent do cultural issues, traditions, or expectations affect the organization? • Are there topics that are simply off-limits for discussion in this organization? • What other major initiatives are taking place in the organization that might compete with evaluation activities? • Has the organization engaged in evaluation capacity building or continuous improvement processes?
Who cares about this evaluation? How might they use the results?	• Who in the organization might be interested in engaging in the evaluation process? • Who in the organization can and will participate in the evaluation process? • Who might use the evaluation results, and how will they participate in the study? • If this evaluation is conducted to meet funding requirements, how can it also be useful to other people? • Who has demonstrated interest in this program in the past? In its evaluation? • Who has decision-making authority for the program being evaluated? • How will primary decision makers be involved in the evaluation? • Is there any sort of advisory structure (formal or informal) for the program? For the evaluation? • What structure exists for processing the evaluation results? • Is this a meaningful evaluation? Does the possibility exist that it has been created for political or symbolic reasons? • Imagine different outcomes for this evaluation. How might these affect the management and continued work of the program?
What support exists for this evaluation?	• What funding or other resources are available for this evaluation? • What role do you see for the evaluator in this project? • What are your expectations for stakeholder involvement?

(Continued)

Exhibit 4.3 (Continued)

Conversation Starters	Sample Questions
	• Are there staff members who will engage in this study? • Are there individuals who may oppose the study and work against it? • Are there any significant funding issues that may affect the evaluation? • Does the organization pay for overhead? (O'Sullivan, 2004, p. 51) • In what ways might this evaluation project be supported or at risk?
4. Determine how the study will be conducted.	
What overarching questions will frame this evaluation?	• Who will determine the overarching questions for the evaluation? Should a broad range of participants be involved? • To what extent do people know the evaluation questions they want answered? • Do these questions focus on important issues that will make a difference to the program? From whose perspective? • Will this evaluation result in judgments? About what? • Will this evaluation lead to decisions? Which? • From a measurement perspective, can these questions be answered well? • Is it feasible to answer these questions with the resources available? • Are there any ethical concerns about seeking to answer these questions? • Are there cultural issues or traditions to attend to in choosing the questions? • Who is going to use the information generated by these questions? • Do the intended users of results want to know the answers to these specific questions?
What overall approach and design for this evaluation make sense?	• There are many approaches to program evaluation. Of those available, which will work best for this evaluation? • Are there cultural issues or expectations to attend to in choosing the approach? • To what extent will this be an evaluator-directed, collaborative, or participant-directed study? • Do you hope to teach people about the evaluation process through this study (i.e., build their evaluation capacity)? • What design fits best for this evaluation? Does the context meet all required conditions for using the desired design? • Is the design selected feasible in this setting? Will it be credible to key participants? Will it adequately address the evaluation questions?

Conversation Starters	Sample Questions
5. Determine how best to collect and analyze information.	
What data collection methods will work well for this evaluation?	• What methods will be most credible to the intended users of the evaluation? • How will we ensure that the data are accurate, credible, and trustworthy? • What cultural issues require attention during data collection? • What is our sampling plan? • How will we ensure that all important voices are heard during the data collection process? • Are we creating our own or using existing instruments? • How will we ensure the quality of the instruments we use? • Who will actually collect the data? Will they receive training? • To what extent will budget issues affect data collection? • Is the data collection plan realistic? • Who will monitor the data collection process internally? • How will data be compiled and stored securely? • Is it possible that someone will attack the methods used in the evaluation? • What is the potential for conflict if we use these methods?
What analysis makes sense?	• How will we ensure that the analysis is accurate, credible, and trustworthy? • What analytical techniques are appropriate for the data collected? • Which types of analyses will best address the evaluation questions? • Will the primary intended users find the analysis credible? • Would different types of analyses conducted on the same data set provide a fuller picture of results? • Who has the expertise and/or skills necessary for the analyses deemed most appropriate? • Will special resources be required, such as qualitative analysis or statistical software packages? • Will special training be required for those participating in data analysis?
6. Determine what the data mean and how best to present them.	
What do the results mean?	• In general do the findings make sense from an organizational perspective? • What are the implications of these results for policy, practice, and future assessments? • What do the results mean in light of the strengths and limitations of the evaluation design? • Who should be involved in grappling with what the findings mean?

(Continued)

Exhibit 4.3   (Continued)

Conversation Starters	Sample Questions
	• Should standards or criteria be established for interpreting evaluation findings? • What do the results imply for commendations and recommendations? • Who will be involved in developing recommendations—evaluators, clients, both, or other stakeholders likely to be affected by the outcomes? • Do quantitative and qualitative findings align in mixed-methods studies? • Should guidelines for interpreting mixed-methods findings be established before drawing conclusions?
What reporting formats are likely to work well in this context?	• What are the internal or external requirements for reports? • Is there a need for a formal written report, and, if so, in what form? • How are primary intended users getting the information they need? • What reports will meet the information needs of various audiences? • Who will prepare or deliver reports?
7. Reflect on how the evaluation is going and what has been learned.	
What are the strengths and limitations of the evaluation at this point?	• What's going right with the evaluation? • What changes would you suggest? • Are samples/sources representative enough to address the evaluation questions adequately? • Are adequate, accurate, and credible data being collected capable of addressing the study's questions? • What are your people telling you about the evaluation process? • Should we stay on course at this point or revise procedures? • What lessons have we learned from being involved in evaluation tasks?
Now that the evaluation is complete, what lessons have been learned?	• If you were going to do this evaluation again, what would you do the same? Differently? Why? • What are the biggest lessons you've learned from this study's outcomes? • What do you think people learned from participating in this evaluation? • How can we apply lessons learned to future evaluation projects? • If capacity building was a goal, what did people learn about the evaluation process?

SOURCE: © 2010 Jean A. King & Laurie Stevahn.

Evaluators should keep two things in mind. First, some conversations will be held in written form as drafts are shared and edited or as people exchange e-mails or other forms of electronic communication. A "conversation" won't always involve two individuals talking face-to-face, although the dangers of miscommunication present in electronic interactions in many cases highlight the value of taking time to meet in person. No one can forward or blind copy the content of a face-to-face meeting. Second, the questions listed will not necessarily be asked outright or directly. Often an evaluator will need to finesse a challenging conversation or a tense situation, and asking a question outright may risk scuttling the interaction. Evaluators may want to consider these questions as topics around which to engage people in discussion. By having a conversation about a topic, you may get the information needed to move forward, even though you never ask the exact question directly.

How might an evaluator use these ideas to shape conversations? Take the example of a director at a small natural history museum who created a new exhibit and, using grant money, hired an evaluator to collect information. What she, the director, needed to know in the 6 months before the exhibit went on the road to museums around the country was straightforward: what worked for visitors ranging in age from early childhood to retirees, and what ought to be changed. In an e-mail, the director—the potential client—arranged for the evaluator to come to the museum to view the exhibit as it was being installed and to chat briefly about the study. She sent him a copy of the successful grant proposal, which included details about the exhibit and its evaluation requirements.

During this initial face-to-face conversation, the evaluator, who had worked with the director tangentially on an earlier study, built on an existing relationship with both her and her supervisor, who also came to the first informal meeting. He already knew that they and the museum's culture more broadly valued evaluation processes and paid serious attention to data. Because it was a natural history museum with numerous scientists on staff, methodological rigor was an important criterion, especially for qualitative methods; some staff members—although not the client and her boss—questioned the validity of so-called "soft" methods even though perceptual data were important indicators of visitor satisfaction. The evaluation budget totaled $10,000. Held while the director and evaluator stood in the exhibit gallery, this opening discussion primarily concerned the second, third, and fourth overarching evaluation conversation goals. Exhibit 4.4 outlines specific questions pertinent to these goals that the evaluator asked and summarizes the answers discovered.

Several additional conversations and related e-mail exchanges led within a month to a draft design that the director quickly approved and to an observation form and separate interview protocols for parents and teachers (adapted from other studies at the museum), which the director also reviewed and approved.

Exhibit 4.4 The Museum Evaluation: Questions and Answers From an Initial Evaluation Conversation

Conversation Goals	Questions	Answers
2. Determine what the client/ primary intended user wants/needs.	What are the expectations for the evaluation?	The grant requirements explicitly state that a formative evaluation will gather information for improving the exhibit before it begins traveling.
	Are any data required?	Nothing is specified in the grant.
	What is the timeline for the evaluation? Is it fixed?	The exhibit is scheduled to move to another site in 6 months. The evaluation needs to be completed in 4 months to allow time for any changes to be made in the exhibit. There is no flexibility in this timeline.
	What are the reporting requirements?	Given the short timeline, the director wants updates from the evaluator and his team on an ongoing basis and monthly meetings to discuss progress. The final report needs to be written for inclusion in a report to the funder.
	To what extent will this be an evaluator-directed, collaborative, or participant-directed study?	Although the director is interested in the evaluation, she is hiring the evaluator to handle both the planning and the implementation of the evaluation. She definitely wants an evaluator-directed study, as she is busy with other projects and has the funding to hire out.
	Are the exhibit's outcomes clearly specified?	The grant proposal states the exhibit's outcomes clearly.
	Who will use the results of the evaluation? What are their concerns?	The director and her superior are responsible for using the results of the study and are eager to do so. The director wants to know three things: (a) what people enjoy most about the exhibit, (b) their travel pattern through it (how they move from element to element; how long they stay at different elements), and (c) what they learn as a result of seeing the exhibit. Her superior is especially interested in the extent to which family versus school groups have different experiences.
	What decisions might be linked to the results?	Decisions about how to alter the exhibit so that enjoyable and popular elements are highlighted or enhanced and visitors' learning increased will be made based on the evaluation.

Conversation Goals	Questions	Answers
	Are there any special ethical, legal, or cultural considerations to keep in mind?	Many of the visitors to the exhibit will be children under the age of 18, so human subjects issues require attention. Parents may be willing to give permission for their children to be interviewed. It will be harder to get permission for children in school groups. If the evaluation relies on public behavior (e.g., tracking people in the public space of the exhibit), there will be less to worry about. Another issue concerns the potentially different responses of various cultural groups, so the evaluator needs to think about how to collect data to address that.
3. Determine whether the context is a viable setting for a program evaluation.	Does the exhibit have any type of advisory structure?	This exhibit does not have its own advisory structure, but the museum does have a citizens' committee that reviews the overall exhibit plan on an annual basis. They are not expected to review this evaluation's plans or results.
4. Determine how the study will be conducted.	Who will determine the overarching questions for the evaluation?	Because this will be evaluator-directed, the evaluator and his team will frame the overarching questions as well as everything else related to the study in consultation with the director.
	Is it feasible to answer these questions with the resources available?	The evaluator will plan the evaluation within the constraints of the existing budget. There may be some support available from museum volunteers, who may be able to collect certain data.

NOTE: This exhibit presents a portion of a much longer conversation held at the beginning of the museum evaluation. In this segment the evaluator focused on the second, third, and fourth conversation goals to find out more about the framing of the study and its implementation.

The evaluator hired two people to work on the project with him. Together they collected and analyzed data, interpreted results, and prepared brief summary reports for the director each month. These reports were the subject of monthly conversations with the director about how the evaluation was going and the extent to which the information gathered was useful to her. When an early analysis of the observation data suggested that boys' patterns of movement through the exhibit differed from those of girls, the director invited the evaluation team to a meeting with the exhibit's staff to discuss what these unexpected results might mean.

Author and Nobel Prize winner Naguib Mahfouz once noted, "You can tell whether an individual is clever by his answers. You can tell whether an individual is wise by his questions." So, too, the evaluator. The numerous questions listed in Exhibit 4.3 provide many options—although, admittedly, there are many more—for evaluators to frame evaluation conversations as a study begins, as it runs its course, and when it is finished. Evaluators who are able to frame conversations and effectively use the information gained are likely to increase ongoing support and feedback for the evaluation process from start to finish.

CONVERSATIONS AND THE INTERACTIVE EVALUATION PRACTICE FRAMEWORKS

This chapter has presented seven overarching goals for evaluation conversations, broadly framed conversation starters, and specific sample questions. Let's now briefly discuss each of the overarching conversation goals in light of the BIT (Exhibit 2.1), IPQ (Exhibit 2.3), and evaluation capacity building (ECB; Exhibit 2.6) frameworks presented in Chapter 2.

1. *How can the evaluation process reveal the client's/participants' perceptions of evaluation and foster positive relationships?* In early stages of the evaluation, the evaluator's primary role is that of actor, establishing connections with key individuals—clients and primary intended users— who will guide and support the process and understanding the organizational setting in which the evaluation will take place. Patton's (2008) personal factor emphasizes the importance of identifying those people who care about the evaluation and want to participate actively. By examining relationships and working to respect cultural concerns, an evaluator can come to understand how people in the context interact with one another, including their past experiences with program evaluation and the issues that are important to them. The IPQ may prove a helpful heuristic, as it makes the evaluator's role and related relationship with people explicit. If ECB is one of the evaluation's intentions, it is especially important to identify people's attitudes toward program evaluation and the organization's current culture to determine the baseline on which the ECB process will build.

2. *What does the client/primary intended user want or need?* This focus, related to framing questions, the first of the BIT, seeks to clarify the

client's evaluation needs by describing the program to be studied, the overall purpose and specific requirements of the study, and the existing resources for its conduct. The evaluator serves primarily as a decision maker, paying attention both to the concerns of key individuals and to cultural factors that may shape the study. Specific evaluation requirements may direct this initial framing of the study, and both the IPQ and the ECB frameworks can help clients choose situation-specific roles with varying levels of engagement for themselves and the evaluator.

3. *Is this context a viable setting for a program evaluation?* This concern zeroes in on the specifics that may affect the proposed evaluation. How might the reality of this organization affect the evaluation process, and who, exactly, might be the primary intended users engaged throughout? Again, the evaluator is first and foremost a decision maker, thinking about relationships, political factors, the potential for conflict, and cultural issues that will necessarily shape future activities. At this point reflecting on the BIT will push the evaluator to consider how the study might play out in this setting, and the IPQ and ECB may suggest possibilities for who on-site should engage in specific evaluative tasks.

4. *How will the study be conducted?* This points to technical issues related to the final evaluation questions the study will address and the general approach the evaluation will take. Here the evaluator's role as decision maker is critical to framing the study's overarching questions and developing a design and sampling plan—the first three of the BIT. It remains important to connect personally with the client and to identify possible political and cultural concerns that may affect the study's conduct. This is also the time to structure participation in the evaluation purposefully so people will interact meaningfully within the process. Collaborative or participant-directed studies will require special types of activities to engage people, as will those that seek to build evaluation capacity as a desired outcome.

5. *How can information best be collected and analyzed?* Now the evaluator becomes an actor, engaged in the quintessential technical activities of collecting and analyzing data, the fourth and fifth of the BIT. In collaborative or participant-directed studies, the evaluator will structure tasks that allow others to participate in collecting or analyzing data, paying ongoing attention to the quality of their work. If the study seeks to build people's capacity to evaluate, the data collection and analysis processes need to be instructional so people will learn by engaging in these two

activities. Although the emphasis at this stage is technical, evaluators should attend to issues of potential credibility of the data and their analysis to key users.

6. *What do the data mean, and how can they best be presented?* Once again the evaluator becomes an actor performing vital evaluation activities, the sixth and seventh of the BIT. The interpretation and reporting process needs to address the concerns of clients/primary intended users, and, depending where on the IPQ the study falls, the evaluator should carefully structure their participation with special attention to cultural details that may be at work. Evaluators engaged in collaborative studies and coaches for participant-directed studies must ensure the technical accuracy of the final interpretations and reports. Again, if ECB is a goal, this step must be shaped as instruction so people learn how to interpret and report evaluation results. As existing relationships and politics may affect both these activities, conflicts may arise as people see the end of the evaluation in view.

7. *How is this evaluation going, and what has been learned?* Ideally, the evaluator and clients have been answering these questions throughout the course of the evaluation, building on a commitment to attend to the issues that affect the primary intended users. At the end of the study comes a pause when the evaluator dons her reflection cap and engages her client in determining lessons learned across all the stages of the evaluation. The BIT, IPQ, and ECB frameworks may prove helpful in shaping a conversation about what worked well and when other options might have made better sense. Circling back to reflect on relationships may help people see how the interpersonal factor worked in their setting, or not.

Although never displayed in a gallery, effective evaluation conversations are surely an art form. The six interpersonal competencies in the Essential Competencies for Program Evaluators (Stevahn et al., 2005; see Appendix C) can all play a part in successful conversations during the course of an evaluation. Holding evaluation conversations requires continuing intentionality on the part of the evaluator and a commitment to both hearing and using people's input. In general, it is helpful to put people at ease as much as possible, to listen actively and take notes, and to continue asking questions. Playing the role of interviewer may elicit detailed responses from those being interviewed, and summarizing what the evaluator understands to be points of agreement may allow people to either agree or make corrections. Nonverbal cues often help tell a story, so evaluators need to use their interpersonal "antennae" to intuit when people have a different opinion or have more to say. In those situations it is important to follow up by asking for clarification or additional information.

In one sense, engaging in evaluation conversations is fairly straightforward. Most people love to talk, especially about themselves and things they find important. However, the next step, making decisions based on the information gleaned from the conversations, may prove more difficult. After all, not all talk is helpful, and some participants may hope to sabotage the evaluation rather than move it forward. The three IEP frameworks (BIT, IPQ, and ECB) provide a way to consider that next step—making decisions—with the potential for decisions well made.

APPLYING INTERACTIVE EVALUATION PRACTICE PRINCIPLES TO EVALUATION CONVERSATIONS

Regardless of where they are held or how formal they are, conversations are the lifeblood of the evaluation process. The ability to interact with people constructively is a hallmark of effective IEP, and conversations enable evaluators to engage in such interactions. Sometimes two people are engaged in the conversation; other times many people, including perhaps an evaluation team and a program team, crowd the room. Sometimes the people with the power to make key decisions are present; other times they are notably absent. Some conversations involve strong emotions vented as outbursts; others are business-like or even, on occasion, mind-numbing.

Exhibit 4.5 highlights how the IEP principles apply to evaluation conversations. "Get personal" reminds us that in using conversations to connect with primary intended users and others, evaluators can learn about how they interact and what matters to them. Evaluators should strive to structure conversations intentionally, systematically, and with thoughtful attention to cultural concerns. As people talk, the setting's context and political issues will unfold, and evaluators can build relationships that will carry them through the study. Conflict may well emerge through conversations, but conflict revealed can then become the topic of additional discussion. Please note that the admonition to "take time" applies across the board. In our opinion it is imperative that evaluators *make* time at every stage of a study for conversations that engage people in meaningful interactions for planning and conducting the evaluation.

Exhibit 4.5   Applying IEP Principles to Evaluation Conversations

IEP Principle	Applied to Evaluation Conversations
1. Get personal.	• Strategically engage primary intended users in evaluation conversations. Learn what matters to them; determine their priorities and agendas. • Pay attention to the ways in which people interact during evaluation conversations; identify personal interactive styles. • Be personally present in evaluation conversations; listen intently. • Strive to establish cooperative relationships in evaluation conversations.
2. Structure interaction.	• Intentionally interact with appropriate others to seek answers to the overarching goals of evaluation conversations. • Be systematic about structuring positive interdependence among conversation participants, to the extent possible. • Interact with primary intended users to create cooperative norms for the evaluation and, as possible and appropriate, within the organization.
3. Examine context.	• Engage in evaluation conversations with appropriate others to examine and better understand the context of the evaluation setting.
4. Consider politics.	• Engage in evaluation conversations with appropriate others to better understand political considerations, issues, and agendas that will likely affect the success of the evaluation study.
5. Expect conflict.	• Know that each person will bring diverse interests and perspectives to evaluation conversations; listen carefully and communicate understanding. • Frame conflicts and disagreements that may emerge in evaluation conversations as mutual problems to be solved rather than as contests to be won.
6. Respect culture.	• Apply cultural competence and cross-cultural communication skills in evaluation conversations. • Attend to cultural values, customs, norms, or traditions for respectful and constructive communication. • Value voice and inclusion in evaluation conversations.
7. Take time.	• Meaningful conversations take time; don't rush the process of obtaining important information that will be needed to shape an effective evaluation. • Systematically take time to reflect on what has been learned from evaluation conversations; use that information to determine future decisions and actions.

SOURCE: © 2010 Jean A. King & Laurie Stevahn.

CHAPTER REVIEW

Visiting the section of a hardware store where nuts and bolts are stored reveals how many different types exist. This is also true of the nuts and bolts of evaluation conversations. Evaluators need to consider multiple concerns in planning and conducting ongoing exchanges with clients.

1. Without frequent conversations, evaluators would be unable to do their job.

2. Evaluation conversations engage a client/primary intended user and an evaluator in a specific context discussing issues related to the evaluation, including (a) technical concerns, (b) political issues, and (c) resource questions. They occur throughout the evaluation process.

3. There are seven overarching goals for evaluation conversations: (a) Understand the client's and participants' perceptions of evaluation and establish positive relationships, (b) determine what the client/primary intended user wants/needs, (c) determine whether the context is a viable setting for a program evaluation, (d) determine how the study will be conducted, (e) determine how best to collect and analyze information, (f) determine what the data mean and how best to present them, and (g) reflect on how the evaluation is going and what has been learned. Evaluators can use these to guide and focus conversations.

4. This chapter provides detailed lists of potential issues, pitfalls, conversation starters, and more detailed questions for evaluation conversations. Exhibit 4.2 links the seven overarching goals to issues evaluators may consider at specific stages in an evaluation and to potential pitfalls that signal concerns. Exhibit 4.3 also starts with the overarching goals, then provides conversation starters to initiate an evaluation conversation and specific questions that evaluators can use in particular contexts.

5. The three interactive evaluation practice frameworks presented in Chapter 2 (basic inquiry tasks, interpersonal participation quotient, and evaluation capacity building) can help evaluators think more broadly about evaluation conversations.

5

AN EVALUATOR'S DOZEN OF INTERACTIVE STRATEGIES

Chapter Preview

- Revisit the interpersonal participation quotient and its implications for stakeholder involvement
- Review the rationale for the use of interactive evaluation strategies: Why? Where? When? How?
- Present, explain, and illustrate 13 interactive strategies for involving people in program evaluation processes
- Discuss how evaluators can use these strategies to accomplish four broad interactive purposes, carry out the basic inquiry tasks, and facilitate three levels of involvement in evaluation studies
- Illustrate how the strategies can be used in an evaluation scenario
- Discuss practical considerations in using these strategies successfully
- Apply the interactive evaluation practice principles to interactive strategies

INTRODUCTION

We continue the skill development section of this book by focusing on participants' interactions, a second feature evaluators can control—or at least influence by structuring activities—during the evaluation process. Just as all studies require conversations, so, too, do all require ongoing interactions. The conversations discussed in Chapter 4 are a verbal form of interaction. This chapter will discuss a broader range of possibilities, applicable from an evaluation's beginning to its end and often helpful in teaching people about the evaluation process as they learn through their active engagement.

Successful practice in any profession, discipline, or vocation requires appropriate sets of tools and the know-how to use them. Sometimes those tools are tangible—the saw, hammer, sander, leveler, or lathe in carpentry; the butcher block, cleaver, measuring cup, mixing bowl, or stockpot in cooking; the electronic hardware and software for graphic design in advertising. Other times the tools are intangible, yet just as necessary for doing a job well—communication skills for social advocacy, nurturing skills for effective parenting, leadership skills for organizational excellence. The same is true for the practice of program evaluation, which necessarily requires that people interact with one another. Regardless of where the study falls on the interpersonal participation quotient (IPQ), skilled evaluators need tools to engage others effectively in conducting evaluations.

- At the evaluator-directed end of the IPQ, evaluators are in charge of studies but initially involve clients and primary intended users in structuring both conversations and other interactions about purpose and desired outcomes. Even evaluators who work hard not to engage people in order to avoid potential bias have to interact with someone to set up data collection procedures and to collect data. At the study's end, they again engage people in making sense of the findings.
- Midrange on the IPQ, collaborative evaluators work directly with clients and others in the setting. As noted in Chapter 2, collaborative evaluations lie between evaluator-directed and participant-directed alternatives on the IPQ continuum. In collaborative practice, evaluators and clients work together actively to structure evaluation interactions.
- At the participant-directed end of the IPQ, evaluators support program leaders, whether staff or participants, in planning and implementing evaluations, typically by providing technical consultation and coaching throughout the process. The evaluator's role as coach means that she may teach people on-site the skills they need to conduct a study or minimally to ensure that whatever is done conforms to the standards of high-quality program evaluation.

In this chapter we present an evaluator's dozen of interactive strategies—13 in all—for engaging stakeholders throughout evaluation studies. In fact, we intentionally call these procedures *strategies* because we believe they can (and should) be applied strategically when conducting evaluations. First, we briefly revisit four grounding aspects of interactive evaluation practice (IEP): Why pursue it? Where will it work best? When should it be enacted? How can it be accomplished? We then present the 13 strategies that illustrate how evaluators can facilitate stakeholder involvement, each potentially a useful tool in interactive evaluation practice. We begin by listing each strategy, then systematically describe its applications across three types of outcomes:

- Major interactive purposes for facilitation: (a) promoting positive interpersonal relations, (b) developing shared understandings, (c) prioritizing and finalizing decisions, and (d) assessing evaluation progress
- The broadly framed basic inquiry tasks (BIT) of evaluation
- Levels of involvement in evaluations: (a) responding or reacting to existing information, (b) generating new information, and (c) organizing or synthesizing information for future use

After detailing all strategies, an overall chart summarizes each strategy's outcomes, advantages, disadvantages, and most useful applications. The chapter concludes by explaining how the IEP principles presented in Chapter 3 apply to using the interactive strategies for optimal outcomes.

GROUNDING INTERACTIVE EVALUATION STRATEGIES

Fundamentally, evaluation practice is about greater or lesser amounts of interaction—enabling evaluators and clients, primary intended users, and other stakeholders to work together constructively to focus, conduct, understand, present, and use the results of an evaluation study for its targeted purposes. At one extreme of the IPQ, an evaluator may initially meet with his clients to clarify the evaluation assignment and next see them to present a final report; at the other extreme, the evaluator may help clients conduct an evaluation of their own, serving as technical consultant, problem solver, and, in all likelihood, cheerleader throughout the process. Before describing various strategies that evaluators can employ to accomplish such work, let's revisit the rationale for engaging primary intended users and other key stakeholders in these ways, summarized in Exhibit 5.1: Why? Where? When? How?

Why Use Interactive Strategies in Evaluation?

Evaluators interact with clients and other stakeholders because such interactions help promote people's ownership of the evaluation process and its outcomes and increase the likelihood that they will use its results. We have already noted that all evaluations are at least minimally participatory because clients engage evaluators, internal and external alike, to conduct studies for them. Even in an evaluator-directed study, there will be interactions around the evaluation both as it is proposed and as it is conducted. Consider the community organizer in a small NGO

Exhibit 5.1   Grounding Interactive Evaluation Strategies

Interactive Evaluation			Foundations
Why	➡	*Why facilitate?*	To promote broad stakeholder ownership of • commitment to evaluation processes and outcomes • use of results for change • evaluation capacity building • data-driven continuous improvement • organization development
Where	➡	*What contexts?*	Cooperative contexts/environments/operations/conditions are most supportive, characterized by positive interdependence (mutual goals and joint rewards routinely structured into the setting)
When	➡	*When to conduct?*	• *Before* the evaluation begins (planning) • *During* the evaluation (conducting) • *After* the evaluation (reflecting/assessing) • *Ongoing* (continuous improvement or development)
How	➡	*How to facilitate?*	Interactive strategies (see *Strategies 1–13* and Exhibits 5.2–5.7)

SOURCE: © 2005 Laurie Stevahn & Jean A. King.

(nongovernmental organization) who was new to evaluation—and somewhat wary, having heard bad things about it from her more experienced colleagues. The foundation grant that funded her project to protect homeowners from foreclosure required a formal external evaluation. She was surprised at the initial meeting when the evaluation team asked her and her colleagues to generate and rank order things they wanted to know about the project and pleased when the study design included data collection around those issues. The evaluators later consulted with her about how to collect meaningful data from members of the immigrant communities that were important stakeholders for the project. Although she and other staff from the NGO did not actively frame the study or participate in data collection and analysis, the eventual recommendations from the evaluation provided them with specific data-based actions for shaping project activities in more productive ways. Having been part of the process, the organizer became committed to using its results. In general, if evaluation capacity building (ECB), continuous improvement, or organization development is a focal goal in conducting evaluation studies, then evaluators must create conditions for mutual stakeholder involvement (see Chapter 2, Exhibit 2.6). Quite simply, organizational leaders, program providers, and program recipients cannot acquire evaluation competence without actually practicing those skills. Meaningful participation becomes critical.

Where Will Interactive Evaluation Strategies Work Best?

While it is true that all evaluations are at least minimally participatory, not all actively engage primary intended users in extensive interactions. Wise evaluators will take situation analysis to heart before proposing the widespread use of interactive evaluation strategies. Organizations with environments, operations, conditions, or cultures characterized by cooperative goals and reward systems will typically experience greater success in conducting interactive activities. These are the places where positive interdependence among organizational or program members is visible and where mutual problem solving is both valued and rewarded. Although evaluators can use interactive evaluation strategies in organizations or programs exhibiting less-than-optimal conditions—sometimes with the hopeful intent to transform such places into models of excellence—evaluators should consider the real possibility of failure without key leaders on board or foundational structures, policies, and accountability systems altered to support such interactions. Evaluators sometimes ask what they can do in such a context, usually because they are working in one. The answer, practically, is to work on developing trust by structuring collaborative goals and joint rewards into the setting while acknowledging that the evaluator is rarely in a position to exert much influence on this process.

When Should Evaluators Use Interactive Evaluation Strategies?

Initial evaluation agreements between evaluators and organizational leaders may call for mutual involvement before, during, and after the study. Noted previously, meaningful involvement tends to increase commitment to implementation of proposed changes, so appropriately involving organizational/program staff—as well as those with stakeholder interests beyond the organization—makes sense from the onset. This may be especially important if continuous improvement or ongoing innovation is a primary goal in conducting an evaluation. Organization or program staff who ultimately must "be the change" by enacting it have vested interests in involvement throughout. For example, when the head of a state employment agency requested an evaluation of the unemployment application process at the local offices that handled such claims, he did not involve his busy staff in framing the study. This resulted in the omission of a critical factor affecting the offices, that those who were unemployed long-term lacked the computer skills that became essential in the application process when the offices were dramatically downsized. The staff, already frazzled from the overwhelming number of stressed individuals coming into their offices every day, viewed the evaluation's results with dismay and its suggestions for increased efficiency as unworkable. In general, even if ongoing involvement is not practical or feasible in certain situations (which it often is not), those contemplating interactive approaches to evaluation practice should consider when feedback from constituents would be helpful or prudent and at least provide opportunities for feedback or input whenever possible.

How Can Interactive Strategies Be Facilitated?

A host of participant-centered, interactive, cooperative procedures exists and can be employed to involve others meaningfully in IEP. Some are validated by a wealth of empirical research; others are deemed best practice by long histories of effective use (e.g., see Bennett & Rolheiser, 2001; Johnson & Johnson, 2009; Joyce, Weil, & Calhoun, 2009; Stevahn & King, 2010). Preskill and Russ-Eft (2005), for example, detail 72 activities for teaching people about program evaluation, divided into categories such as focusing the evaluation, issues of validity and sampling, and building and sustaining support for evaluation. In the sections that follow, we present an evaluator's dozen of interactive strategies—those we find especially applicable and adaptable across a wide array of evaluation aims, approaches, contexts, settings, and circumstances. First, we consider three broad sets of outcomes for which the strategies can be employed. We then elaborate on each of the 13 strategies by providing facilitation directions, examples, and possible uses.

FACILITATING INTERACTIVE EVALUATION STRATEGIES

For an evaluator committed to IEP, there is nothing better than people's active engagement—small groups excitedly generating ideas, intent discussions as people pore over data, numerous sheets of flip-chart paper covered with colorful writing, the smiles that frequently surround these conversations. Those who understand the basics grounding IEP summarized in the previous section intentionally seek facilitation strategies that will engage stakeholders in meaningful ways throughout the process. Although numerous possibilities exist—many originating in disciplines such as education (teaching), business (leadership, management, human resource development), and nonprofit work (skills training)—here we present an evaluator's dozen strategically useful in making evaluation studies more interactive. These interactive strategies become tools that evaluators and organizational leaders can use to engage others in successfully framing and accomplishing evaluation aims.

Before presenting the details of each strategy—directions, sample materials, facilitation tips, and so on—we introduce all 13 in general by considering three sets of broadly framed outcomes for which they can be employed. The first set pertains to four broad facilitation purposes important in evaluation practice (see Exhibit 5.2). The strategies noted in Column A deliberately promote positive interpersonal relations among those coming together to do the work of evaluation. Those in Column B develop shared understandings that ground subsequent evaluation decisions and implementations. Those in Column C deal directly with decision making by engaging participants in prioritizing and finalizing choices. Those in Column D—essentially all the strategies—may be used to assess how well the evaluation study is progressing both during its implementation and after its completion. Establishing and maintaining positive working relationships through which constructive problem solving can occur; forging shared understandings of assumptions, needs, goals, procedures, information, findings, and so on; making evaluation decisions for implementation; and assessing evaluation progress through reflection and processing—these are four areas of continuing concern in moving evaluations forward constructively. In identifying which strategies to use, evaluators can focus on a specific collaborative purpose and know which strategies may be appropriate.

Another essential set of outcomes pertains to the BIT of evaluation initially presented in Chapter 2 (see Exhibit 2.1). These tasks form the bedrock of conducting evaluation studies. Evaluators must frame questions from which evaluation designs, samples/sources, data collection, and analysis can be planned and implemented. With results in hand, they must interpret them and report findings. All these tasks hold potential for interactive involvement of stakeholders—and certain strategies are particularly useful for accomplishing each (see Exhibit 5.3). Some of the strategies are especially adaptable across the seven tasks, whereas others are more applicable for one or two specific tasks. For example, all the strategies can be used to collect data—the resulting product of each activity conceivably constitutes credible input for informing a study's questions. By contrast, one strategy—jigsaw—is particularly useful for preparing an evaluation report. Once a report is conceptualized, component parts are assigned to various individuals on an evaluation team; completed parts eventually are recombined like interlocking puzzle pieces to create one coherent and smoothly flowing document. Remember, however, that many of the strategies can be usefully employed to involve people in grappling with the information reported—by engaging stakeholders in making meaning of findings, developing shared understandings of results, or formulating feasible ways to enact recommendations (e.g., see Exhibit 5.2, Column B).

Exhibit 5.2   Interactive Strategies and Interactive Purposes

Interactive Strategies \ Interactive Purposes	A — Promote positive interpersonal relations for interactive evaluation practice	B — Develop shared understandings of evaluation assumptions, tasks, procedures, information, or results	C — Prioritize and finalize evaluation decisions	D — Assess evaluation progress
1. Voicing Variables	X			X
2. Voicing Viewpoints/Beliefs	X	X		X
3. Choosing Corners	X	X		X
4. Cooperative Interviews	X	X		X
5. Round-Robin Check-In		X		X
6. Making Metaphors		X	·	X
7. Data Dialogue		X		X
8. Jigsaw		X		X
9. Graffiti/Carousel		X		X
10. Concept Formation/Cluster Maps		X		X
11. Cooperative Rank Order			X	X
12. Fist to Five			X	X
13. Dot Votes/Bar Graphs			X	X

SOURCE: Stevahn and King (2010, Table 3.1).

As evaluators develop an evaluation plan, Exhibit 5.3 will point them to appropriate strategies to use to accomplish certain tasks in the evaluation process.

A final set of outcomes deals with various levels of stakeholder involvement (see Exhibit 5.4). Each strategy typically places different demands for engagement

Exhibit 5.3   Interactive Strategies and Basic Inquiry Tasks

Basic Inquiry Tasks / Interactive Strategies	1 Questions	2 Design	3 Sample/ sources	4 Data collection	5 Data analysis	6 Interpretation	7 Report
1. Voicing Variables	X			X		X	
2. Voicing Viewpoints/Beliefs	X	X		X		X	
3. Choosing Corners	X	X		X		X	
4. Cooperative Interviews	X			X		X	
5. Round-Robin Check-In	X	X		X		X	
6. Making Metaphors				X		X	
7. Data Dialogue		X		X			
8. Jigsaw	X		X	X	X		X
9. Graffiti/Carousel	X		X	X	X		
10. Concept Formation/Cluster Maps	X		X	X	X		
11. Cooperative Rank Order	X	X	X	X		X	
12. Fist to Five	X	X	X	X		X	
13. Dot Votes/Bar Graphs	X	X	X	X		X	

SOURCE: © 2001 Laurie Stevahn & Jean A. King.

on those participating. For example, those noted in Level I involve people in responding or reacting to set content or information. Those in Level II involve them in generating new information or input. Those in Level III involve groups in organizing, synthesizing, or interpreting information. Whether involving others to accomplish any of the four major interactive purposes or seven inquiry tasks of evaluation practice, evaluators should consider which types of involvement will best accomplish an evaluation's overall aims. When ECB or organization development is desired, then participants should be more rigorously involved, beyond simply responding or reacting to given options. For example, when the head of a small clinic sought to increase his staff's ability to conduct their own evaluations, he worked with an evaluator to employ

Exhibit 5.4   Interactive Strategies and Levels of Involvement

Levels of Involvement / Interactive Strategies	Level I Respond to set content/ information (obtain feedback/ reactions to closed-ended options)	Level II Generate content/ information (obtain substance/input to open-ended prompts)	Level III Organize or share content/information (analyze, categorize, interpret, or sequence/ order given information)
1. Voicing Variables	X		
2. Voicing Viewpoints/Beliefs	X		
3. Choosing Corners	X		
4. Cooperative Interviews		X	
5. Round-Robin Check-In		X	
6. Making Metaphors		X	
7. Data Dialogue		X	
8. Jigsaw	X	X	X
9. Graffiti/Carousel		X	
10. Concept Formation/Cluster Maps	X		X
11. Cooperative Rank Order	X		X
12. Fist to Five	X		X
13. Dot Votes/Bar Graphs	X		X

SOURCE: © 2001 Laurie Stevahn & Jean A. King.

strategies that would systematically engage them in asking evaluative questions, collecting, analyzing, and interpreting data, and making recommendations the data supported. Capacity building demands that stakeholders engage in the behaviors that are evaluation practice, thereby allowing participants to learn, refine, and internalize skills. Engagement in such rigor, however, must be weighed against other pragmatic considerations—both macro and micro— such as the overall evaluation timeline, budget, scope of use, and so forth;

individual participants' work responsibilities, schedules, and locations; the feasibility of regularly meeting face-to-face or through electronic platforms; amounts of time available for meetings related to the evaluation; skill sets that participants bring to the work versus training needed; and so on. Together, Exhibits 5.2 through 5.4 can assist evaluators in choosing appropriate strategies that will make sense in different situations.

What follows is an example of how evaluators can use these exhibits to identify potential strategies for an evaluation. Suppose an evaluator wants people mutually to comprehend a data set's analysis. Exhibit 5.2 identifies nine possible strategies (*Strategies 2–10*) to develop shared understandings. Exhibit 5.3 suggests that three strategies—*Strategies 8, 9,* and *10 (Jigsaw, Graffiti/ Carousel,* and *Concept Formation/Cluster Maps)*—are particularly helpful for data analysis. Exhibit 5.4 indicates that *Strategy 8: Jigsaw* is especially versatile because the evaluator can potentially use it three different ways—to involve participants in responding to set content, generating content, or organizing content. Participants could review and jigsaw different parts of a completed analysis; they could analyze different portions of the data and then jigsaw the collective results; or they could organize, sequence, and jigsaw sections of an analysis. *Strategy 9: Graffiti/Carousel* will require participants to respond quickly to open-ended prompts about the analysis (e.g., surprises, next steps, who needs to know), then *Strategy 10: Concept Formation/Cluster Maps* can involve people in making sense of the responses. Multiple options exist, and it is important to remember that the content of Exhibits 5.2 through 5.4 consists of suggestions based on years of practice using the strategies. Creative evaluators may well find alternative ways to use the strategies and new ones also well suited to accomplishing any of the four broad interactive purposes, seven inquiry tasks, or three levels of involvement in evaluation practice (e.g., see Stevahn & King, 2010).

INTERACTIVE EVALUATION STRATEGIES

We now present in detail the evaluator's dozen—12 plus 1—of interactive strategies. Each description begins by noting the various outcomes for which the strategy is particularly well suited. We then provide information on the approximate time and materials needed, step-by-step directions, facilitation tips, and possible variations. Each context will provide unique opportunities for applying and adapting these strategies to bring IEP to life. In different settings some will work better than others, and it is the evaluator's task to determine which make sense where.

STRATEGY 1: VOICING VARIABLES

Targeted outcomes: (shaded boxes)

Interactive Purposes	A Promote positive relations		B Develop shared understandings		C Prioritize and finalize decisions		D Assess evaluation progress	
Basic Inquiry Tasks	1 Question	2 Design	3 Sample/ sources	4 Collect data	5 Analyze data	6 Interpret results	7 Report	
Levels of Involvement	I Respond/react to set content/information		II Generate content/input			III Organize/share content/information		

Time: 5 to 10 minutes

Materials:

- A list of variables and a range of response options for each (see examples below)

Variables	Response Options
Birthplace/hometown	(USA) Northeast, Midwest, Southeast, South/Texas, Pacific Northwest, Southwest/California, Alaska/Hawaii; (non-USA) name continents, then ask what country
Job/role/position	Administrator, service provider, clerical/support staff, evaluator/researcher, HRD/trainer, public relations, client, other
Joined the organization/program	Within the past 5 years, 10 years, 15 years, 20 years, 25 years, beyond a quarter century (or in the first decade of the 21st century, 1990s, 1980s, 1970s, earlier)
Favorite task/skill	Designing projects, leading initiatives, teaching/mentoring, working with technology, analyzing issues, synthesizing information, collaborating, assessing progress
Favorite book/film	Comedy, mystery, romance, science fiction, action/drama, biography/history, sports
Evaluation experience	Entry/novice, proficient/skilled, mastery/expert; consider metaphor responses such as walker (beginner), jogger (some experience), marathon runner (solid experience), triathlon athlete (seasoned expert across diverse contexts)

(Continued)

(Continued)

Variables	Response Options
Evaluation question/focus (specify one)	Not important, somewhat important, definitely important, extremely important
Evaluation recommendation (specify one)	Strongly agree, agree, disagree, strongly disagree
Evaluation plan/ implementation (present one aspect)	Not feasible (not working well; stop/rethink), somewhat feasible (revise/refine before continuing), totally feasible (working well; proceed as planned)

Directions:

1. Welcome participants and explain the purpose of this activity—i.e., to share individual characteristics, make interpersonal connections, establish community for evaluation, address the question: "Who are we?"

2. Present one variable (e.g., birthplace) and its response options (e.g., North America, South America, Europe, Africa, Middle East, Asia, Australia, Pacific Islands).

3. Ask individuals to stand (or raise hands) for the response option that personally applies.

4. Facilitate reflection:

   a. Ask participants to estimate the percentage of people who respond to each option.

   b. Debrief similarities (mutual characteristics), differences (that become strengths when combined), and/or trends (notable response patterns) that exist overall.

   c. Highlight variables/responses that support interactive evaluation practice (such as core values, past experiences, diverse skills, unique perspectives, and so on).

Facilitation tips:

- Prepare four to eight key variables tailored to the context.
- Target variables that enable facilitators to learn about participant characteristics relevant to successful interactive evaluation practice.
- Target variables that enable participants to identify with one another (common qualities), admire uniqueness (contrasts), and focus on important aspects of program evaluation.

- Visually display or post variables and response options while verbally presenting them.
- Keep response options to a reasonable number (typically four or five per variable); too many alternative responses become confusing and cumbersome.
- Preview all the response options for a given variable (when the list is short) before asking participants to respond so everyone knows the entire slate of alternatives at the onset.
- Decide whether to allow participants to respond to all options that apply or to select only one.
- Keep the pace moving; avoid lengthy discussions on any of the variables or responses.
- Vary (or omit) follow-up reflection activities (estimating, debriefing, or highlighting responses) as appropriate to sustain interest, pique curiosity, enhance engagement, or accomplish goals.

Variations:

- Provide one set of Likert-scale response options that participants can apply repeatedly to a list of variables. The list of variables might entail potential evaluation questions (to elicit participant input on framing the study), possible recommendations (to obtain participant feedback on future actions), or evaluation implementations (to seek participant opinions on progress or effectiveness).
- Collect data by tallying responses (keep a written record). Arrange for observers to assist.
- Ask the entire group to stand. Instruct people to sit down as applicable items are called. The goal is to end with one or two people standing. For example, "Sit down if you . . . (were born in this city/town/community, are a twin, have five or more children, exercise daily, play a musical instrument, speak more than one language, volunteer regularly, prefer movies to sitcoms, have ridden a camel, eat ethnic food several times each week [e.g., Chinese, Mexican, Greek, Italian, Polish, Ethiopian], do celebrity impersonations, have a pet, tend a vegetable garden, like crossword puzzles, etc.)."

SOURCE: Stevahn and King (2010, Figure 3.1).

STRATEGY 2: VOICING VIEWPOINTS/BELIEFS

Targeted outcomes: (shaded boxes)

Interactive Purposes	A Promote positive relations		B Develop shared understandings		C Prioritize and finalize decisions		D Assess evaluation progress	
Basic Inquiry Tasks	1 Question	2 Design	3 Sample/ sources	4 Collect data	5 Analyze data	6 Interpret results	7 Report	
Levels of Involvement	I Respond/react to set content/information		II Generate content/input		III Organize/share content/information			

Time: 5 to 15 minutes for each belief statement

Materials:

- "Voicing Viewpoints Belief Sheet" (one per participant; each contains several statements with Likert-scale response options on topics relevant to program evaluation; see the example below)

Voicing Viewpoints Belief Sheet
A. Good evaluators share control of the evaluation study with clients from start to finish.
(circle one)　　　*strongly agree*　　　*agree*　　　*disagree*　　　*strongly disagree*
B. Program providers will bias an evaluation study if they are involved.
(circle one)　　　*strongly agree*　　　*agree*　　　*disagree*　　　*strongly disagree*
C. The people evaluating a program should be neutral toward it.
(circle one)　　　*strongly agree*　　　*agree*　　　*disagree*　　　*strongly disagree*
D. The most critical element in fostering commitment to use evaluation results is to involve at the onset as many people as possible in framing the evaluation study.
(circle one)　　　*strongly agree*　　　*agree*　　　*disagree*　　　*strongly disagree*

Directions:

1. Distribute a belief sheet to each participant.

2. Ask participants to read each statement and circle the response option that personally applies.

3. Facilitate whole-session discussion on each statement by asking participants to

   a. reveal responses by raising hands for each option;

   b. estimate response percentages for each option;

   c. share reasons underlying varied responses, then compare and contrast;

   d. consider what the reasons reveal about people's backgrounds, experiences, and assumptions relevant to program evaluation studies;

   e. revise each statement to make it one with which everyone can/will agree;

   f. discuss what the revised statements mean for successful interactive evaluation practice.

Facilitation tips:

- Prepare belief statements using language likely to produce varying responses among participants. Ideally, individual responses will be distributed across all the options. Testing statements in advance may suggest changes that will improve the distribution.

- Unlike valid and reliable Likert-scale survey items, belief statements for this activity should be crafted on a topic to include key words that likely will be interpreted differently by individuals. Ambiguous and undefined terms prompt rich follow-up discussion.

- The heart of this activity is discussing the reasons underlying various choices (which represent different perspectives) and what these reveal about individual assumptions.

- Prompt participants to articulate positions clearly and to listen carefully by communicating understanding of diverse perspectives. Such comparing and contrasting of reasons not only enables individual participants to engage in social perspective taking, but allows participants collectively to clarify, formulate, and agree to a set of mutual working assumptions.

- Lead participants in as many rounds of revising a statement as it takes to develop one with which everyone can agree. Allow adequate time, especially if participants are grappling with more than one belief statement.

- The well-articulated mutual beliefs that become the end product of this activity may be recorded and used as working group norms, periodically revisited for reflection and/or revision, especially in collaborative evaluations.

Variations:

- Post each Likert-scale option in separate corners of the room; ask participants to physically move to the corner that best represents personal proclivity and discuss reasons with others in the same corner (see *Strategy 3: Choosing Corners*).
- Distribute valid and reliable Likert-scale survey instruments. Collect data on responses by asking participants to submit their individual sheets; to ensure confidentiality, do not engage in discussion. If open discussion is appropriate, arrange for observers to record qualitative reasons that surface, and collect those data at the end of the discussion.
- Provide belief statements on various basic inquiry tasks. For example, (a) provide a set of possible purposes/focuses/questions and ask participants the extent to which they believe each is important to pursue, (b) craft belief statements that will reveal assumptions (or biases) on the value of quantitative versus qualitative versus mixed-methods studies, or (c) present a list of data-based recommendations and ask participants which they believe are most urgent for action.

SOURCE: Stevahn and King (2010, Figure 3.2).

STRATEGY 3: CHOOSING CORNERS

Targeted outcomes: (shaded boxes)

Interactive Purposes	A Promote positive relations		B Develop shared understandings		C Prioritize and finalize decisions		D Assess evaluation progress	
Basic Inquiry Tasks	1 Question	2 Design	3 Sample/ sources	4 Collect data	5 Analyze data	6 Interpret results	7 Report	
Levels of Involvement	I Respond/react to set content/information		II Generate content/input			III Organize/share content/information		

Time: 10 to 20 minutes

Materials:

- Question/statement (one or several) with four responses (post each response in a separate corner of the room; see examples below)
- "Choosing Corners" handout (one per participant; see the example provided)

Questions/Statements	Response Options (post one per corner)
Education: Which practice will most enhance student achievement?	1. Standardized testing 2. Professional development 3. School leadership 4. Parent involvement
Nonprofit: Which policy is most essential to program success?	1. Constantly revisiting mission 2. Systematically obtaining client input 3. Ongoing training for program staff 4. Data-based decision making
Government: Which criterion is most important for funding programs?	1. Clear organizational mission/vision 2. Evidence of ongoing success 3. Logic models to guide the program 4. Systemic program evaluation practice

(Continued)

(Continued)

Questions/Statements	Response Options (post one per corner)
Health: Public health initiatives should focus primarily on youth.	1. Strongly agree 2. Agree 3. Disagree 4. Strongly disagree
Business: Innovation can best be supported by . . .	1. Structuring teamwork in departments 2. Staying "tuned in" to market forces 3. Visionary leaders who enact change 4. Continuously listening to customers

Choosing Corners (one per participant)

Directions:
- Listen to the question and consider various responses posted in corners of the room.
- Move to the corner that matches your personal response.
- Greet and introduce yourself to one or two others in your corner.
- Exchange reasons for choosing that corner. Compare and contrast reasons; notice similarities and differences.

Question	The corner I chose and my reasons why	The person I met (name)	His/her reasons for choosing this corner
1			
2			
3			

Directions:

1. Present a question (or statement) on a relevant topic and four alternative responses.

2. Point to the corners in the room where the various responses are posted.

3. Instruct participants to choose individually the response that best reflects personal proclivity.

4. Ask participants to move to the corner chosen and

   a. pair up with another person in that corner,

   b. greet and introduce one another,

   c. exchange reasons for choosing that corner,

   d. compare and contrast reasons.

5. Facilitate whole-session sharing by systematically following up on each response option; move from corner to corner, asking several individuals within each to summarize key reasons for choices.

6. Discuss what the responses/reasons reveal about the group as a whole and implications for working together on evaluation tasks.

7. Present the next question and repeat the process.

Facilitation tips:

- Consider questions/statements relevant to (a) the organization/program, (b) its situational context, or (c) program evaluation decisions/implementations.
- After presenting the question/statement and alternative responses, provide time for participants to think privately before asking them to move to their chosen corner.
- If a question (or statement) has scaled response options (such as *strongly agree*, *agree*, *disagree*, *strongly disagree*; *excellent*, *good*, *fair*, *poor*; *essential*, *useful*, *marginal*, *unnecessary*), ask participants to revise the original statement to make it one that everyone can embrace (agree with, view as favorable, deem necessary) based on the issues/considerations that surfaced as people shared reasons for their responses. After each revision, participants can again choose the corner that best represents their response.
- People may well request an option such as *it depends*, preferring to stand in the middle of the room rather than choosing a corner. The facilitator can decide whether or not this should be an option.
- Use the "Choosing Corners" handout.

Variations:

- Frame an evaluation study by posting different evaluation questions in separate corners. Ask participants to move to the corner that contains the question or focus they deem most important.
- Explore evaluation recommendations by posting each in separate corners. Ask participants to move to the corner that contains the recommendation most (a) immediately

feasible, (b) important to enact first, (c) needed for program transformation, (d) foundational to organizational change, (e) likely to make an immediate impact, or (f) likely to require training and resources, etc.

- Assess evaluation progress by asking relevant reflection questions and posting possible responses in separate corners. For example: (a) How well is communication working in this evaluation (*excellent, good, fair, poor*)? (b) To what extent have we obtained adequate samples to address the study's questions (*excellent representation, good representation, fair representation, poor representation*)? (c) To what extent has data collection been a smooth process (*extremely smooth, mostly smooth, somewhat problematic, extremely problematic*)?

- Collect data by tallying the number of people in each corner (keep a written record). Arrange for observers to assist.

- Present a quotation relevant to some aspect of the evaluation and post different responses to it in separate corners. For example, consider whether you *strongly agree, agree, disagree,* or *strongly disagree* with each of the following quotations:

  - "It does not matter how slowly you go so long as you do not stop."—Confucius
  - "Imagination is more important than knowledge."—Albert Einstein
  - "Truth is rarely pure and never simple."—Oscar Wilde
  - "The highest result of education is tolerance."—Helen Keller
  - "I don't know the key to success, but the key to failure is trying to please everybody."—Bill Cosby

- Consider posting different word or picture metaphors in separate corners as responses to questions or sentence starters relevant to conducting an evaluation study (see *Strategy 6: Making Metaphors*). For example, "An effective participatory evaluation is like a . . . (*hiking expedition, theatrical production, skydiving adventure, tropical cruise*)"; "Which picture best illustrates the rewards of conducting a successful program evaluation?" Corner 1 displays a large heart-shaped box of chocolates; Corner 2 a tribal elder leading villagers in dance; Corner 3 people from diverse cultures walking arm in arm; Corner 4 smiling children using microscopes, telescopes, and magnifying glasses.

- One possibility when using a Likert-scale response is to have people line up on a continuum in order from, for example, *strongly agree* to *strongly disagree*. During the discussion, people may choose to move closer to one end or the other.

SOURCE: Stevahn and King (2010, Figures 3.3, 3.3a).

STRATEGY 4: COOPERATIVE INTERVIEWS

Targeted outcomes: (shaded boxes)

Interactive Purposes	A Promote positive relations		B Develop shared understandings		C Prioritize and finalize decisions		D Assess evaluation progress	
Basic Inquiry Tasks	1 Question	2 Design	3 Sample/ sources	4 Collect data	5 Analyze data	6 Interpret results	7 Report	
Levels of Involvement	I Respond/react to set content/information			II Generate content/input			III Organize/share content/information	

Time: 10 to 20 minutes

Materials:

- Interview topic/question (see examples below)
- "Interview Response Sheet" (one per team; see the example provided)

Interview Topics/Questions

- Think of a time when you successfully made a positive change in your professional practice. What was the change? Why did you make it? What influenced you to stick with it? What types of support were especially helpful in the transition?
- What is your most cherished professional accomplishment? Why? When did it happen? Where? What was it about? Who was involved?
- What are you especially proud of about your program or organization? Why?
- What's the one "wish" that you have for your program or organization? Why?
- What concerns you most about your program or organization? Why?
- Think of a time when you were asked to try something new. What was it? How did you feel? Did you actually try it? Why or why not? What influenced your decisions and the steps you took?
- Think of a time when you received feedback or information that motivated you to make a change. What was it about the feedback that was particularly helpful? Explain.
- Look over this list of evaluation recommendations. Which do you believe will be personally most challenging? Why? What types of support would you find especially helpful?
- Are the evaluation results being used to make positive impact? How can you tell? What's different now compared to before? What still needs to be accomplished?

Interview Response Sheet	
Interview topic/question:	
Name (one per box)	Response
1.	
2.	
3.	
Key group ideas Similarities, themes, insights, predictions, conclusions	

Directions:

1. Arrange participants in teams of three.

2. Announce that the team goal is to gather input on the interview topic/question from all members, then synthesize and use it to address relevant issues.

3. Distribute the "Interview Response Sheet" (one per team).

4. Assign the following roles (one per teammate):

   a. Interviewer (seeks input)

   b. Responder (provides input)

   c. Recorder (writes input on the "Interview Response Sheet").

5. Provide the interview topic/question and post probing questions; teammates rotate roles three times so each will take a turn at interviewing, responding, and recording (use the same interview topic/question for each rotation).

6. Monitor time and instruct teams to rotate roles at designated intervals (e.g., every 3 minutes).

7. Instruct each team to look at its "Interview Response Sheet." Identify similarities or common characteristics/qualities/themes threaded across the responses. Notice outlier responses that provide insight on the topic. Make predictions and/or draw conclusions about the topic.

8. Discuss what this information means for successful evaluation practice, use of results, organizational policy, or program implementation.

Facilitation tips:

- Make sure that the interview question/topic is (a) relevant to the situation/context, (b) open-ended and answerable, (c) linked to participants' personal backgrounds/ experiences, (d) meaningful and thought provoking, (e) safe and nonthreatening, and (f) useful for obtaining information. Be sure that each person will have a unique response to the question/topic.
- Model what an interview sounds and looks like if participants are new to this procedure.
- Post prompts useful for probing during the interview: *What? Why? Where? When? Who? How?*
- Model the rotation of roles by having one team demonstrate how it works.
- Use a timer to pace rotation to ensure equal intervals in each round of interviewing.
- If an opportunity presents itself to use this strategy "on the spot" without prepared response sheets, distribute one blank sheet of paper to each team. Instruct the team to fold the sheet into thirds (which produces three boxes). Each recorder writes the response of the person being interviewed in one of the boxes for each of the three interview rounds. Participants record common insights on the back of the sheet.

Variations:

- Facilitate pair interviews. Teammates record each other's responses on separate interview sheets. The person who interviews simultaneously records while the responder tells his/her story. After each has interviewed the other, each gives to the other a written copy of his/her personal response/story (as a gift).
- Facilitate four-square interviews. A group of four subdivides into two pairs. Each pair conducts a two-way interview on the same topic/question. The four teammates then reconnect; each shares the response/story of the person interviewed with the entire team.
- Frame an evaluation study by asking participants to focus on interview questions likely to reveal perspectives on (a) valued aspects of the organization/program, (b) what is working well, (c) what is not working well, (d) action theories underlying program policies or operations, and so on.
- Interpret evaluation results by asking participants to focus on interview questions relevant to (a) making sense of findings or (b) eliciting input on recommendations.
- Collect all "Interview Response Sheets"; use qualitative data analysis procedures/ techniques to summarize all responses/stories.
- If working with the same people repeatedly, organize them into base groups whose members will always start together. Begin each session with a cooperative interview. Provide a topic that will elicit personal stories pointed toward the major content to be presented or discussed that day. Each base group will complete its adapted "Interview Response Sheet" over time, column by column, as each new question is provided (see the adapted interview sheet that follows).

Base Group Interview Response Sheet				
Names	Session #1 Question A	Session #2 Question B	Session #3 Question C	Session #4 Question D
1.				
2.				
3.				

SOURCE: Stevahn and King (2010, Figures 3.5, 3.5a).

STRATEGY 5: ROUND-ROBIN CHECK-IN

Targeted outcomes: (shaded boxes)

Interactive Purposes	A Promote positive relations		B Develop shared understandings		C Prioritize and finalize decisions		D Assess evaluation progress	
Basic Inquiry Tasks	1 Question	2 Design	3 Sample/ sources	4 Collect data	5 Analyze data	6 Interpret results	7 Report	
Levels of Involvement	I Respond/react to set content/information			II Generate content/input		III Organize/share content/information		

Time: 5 to 10 minutes

Materials:

- Check-in question (relevant to the evaluation; see examples below)
- Chart paper (or alternative means to record/document input)

Check-In Questions

Opening sessions

- What is your current understanding of our purpose?
- What experience do you bring to today's topic/task?
- What word best describes your emotional reaction to the topic/task?
- What points/ideas have you thought more about since our last session?

Transitions within sessions

- What is your biggest "Ah-ha!"? What are you seeing more clearly now?
- What is the most useful idea/information presented so far?
- What is an important connection that you have made?
- What question would you like answered before we move on?

Closing sessions

- What did you especially value in this session?
- What was most personally relevant to you in this session?
- What was your most important lesson learned from this session?
- What insight from this session will you carry away and act on?

Directions:

1. Present the check-in question.

2. Provide private think time.

3. Emphasize the importance of keeping responses short (model a sound-bite response).

4. Systematically ask each participant to provide a brief response.

5. Document all responses on chart paper or electronically if appropriate.

6. Summarize input and clarify implications for evaluation practice.

Facilitation tips:

- Use this strategy to open or close a meeting or when transitioning from one topic/ activity to another within a meeting.
- Seek input from participants systematically, moving from person to person around the room.
- Allow people to pass. Before debriefing the entire collection of responses, return to those who passed to invite them once more to contribute (sometimes ideas come to people as they are listening to the contributions of others).
- Keep the pace moving; avoid commenting on responses until everyone has contributed.
- Discuss input by considering similarities and differences among all responses.
- Further analyze responses by applying *Strategy 10: Concept Formation/Cluster Maps*.
- Record/archive the input and/or analysis so the group can access/revisit it in the future. Consider documenting the input/analysis in the official meeting minutes.

Variations:

- Instruct small groups to engage in round-robin check-in (rather than everyone at large) to enable teammates to touch base with one another by systematically and briefly sharing perspectives on a given topic.
- Facilitate round-robin check-in by asking participants to form a community circle for responding. First, everyone silently thinks of a word or phrase to address the question provided. Second, everyone forms a circle by arranging themselves alphabetically according to their word or phrase. The facilitator is the alphabet anchor in the circle and says: "I have the letter *A* on my left shoulder and the letter *Z* on my right shoulder. Form a circle from *A* to *Z* according to the first letter in your word or phrase. Talk to each other to place yourself correctly in the circle." Once the circle is formed, each participant then shares aloud his/her response clockwise, person by person.

- Consider asking participants to respond randomly around the room (rather than systematically).
- Provide questions that elicit input relevant to framing evaluation questions or establishing the purpose of the study.
- Provide questions that elicit input relevant to interpreting evaluation results.
- Ask participants to first record their sound-bite responses with felt markers on half sheets or large cards before sharing aloud while showing the card. Collect all sheets and analyze the input qualitatively.
- Ask participants to respond by crafting metaphors (see *Strategy 6: Making Metaphors*).
- Assess progress by asking participants their perceptions of "pluses/wishes" relevant to the session, various evaluation tasks, or other pertinent issues (doing this aloud requires trust and a climate of safety). Discuss possibilities for taking action on the wishes; assign responsibility for follow-up.

SOURCE: Stevahn and King (2010, Figures 3.6, 3.6a, 3.7).

STRATEGY 6: MAKING METAPHORS

Targeted outcomes: (shaded boxes)

Interactive Purposes	A Promote positive relations		B Develop shared understandings		C Prioritize and finalize decisions		D Assess evaluation progress	
Basic Inquiry Tasks	1 Question	2 Design	3 Sample/ sources	4 Collect data	5 Analyze data	6 Interpret results	7 Report	
Levels of Involvement	I Respond/react to set content/information		II Generate content/input			III Organize/share content/information		

Time: 5 to 10 minutes per metaphor

Materials:

- Metaphor stem (an open-ended sentence starter; see examples below)
- Set of words/phrases, pictures/illustrations, or tangible objects that can be used to complete the metaphor stem (see examples below)

Metaphor Stems	Possible Responses
1. *A successful evaluation project is like a symphony because . . .* 2. *Implementing collaborative evaluation is like a roller coaster because . . .* 3. *Organizational change feels like . . . when . . .* 4. *Pitfalls while conducting an evaluation are like . . . because . . .*	Participants respond on their own (sets of words/phrases, visual images, or tangible objects are not provided by the facilitator)
5. *Successful evaluators are most like . . .* (*songbirds, giraffes, roosters, elephants, lizards, monkeys, eagles, armadillos, rabbits, goldfish, etc.*) *because . . .*	Set of words/phrases provided by the facilitator

Metaphor Stems	Possible Responses
6. *Organizational commitment to use evaluation results occurs when* . . . (postcards, paintings, drawings, photographs, magazine art, etc.) *because* . . .	Set of visual images provided by the facilitator
7. *Conflict in an evaluation study is like a* . . . (clothespin, tennis ball, flashlight, compass, gavel, feather, wooden spoon, stuffed animal, box of crayons, bow tie, deck of cards, key chain, chocolate bar, etc.) *because* . . .	Set of tangible objects provided by the facilitator

Directions:

1. Present an open-ended metaphor or simile (using the word *like*) stem.

2. Ask participants to complete the metaphor by either creating a response or selecting a response from a set of words, pictures, or objects.

3. Systematically ask participants to share their metaphors aloud; record and post responses.

4. Identify patterns, similar qualities, and/or unique outliers across the metaphor responses.

5. Discuss new insights revealed and their relevance to evaluation practice.

Facilitation tips:

- Sets of words or phrases can be provided in a wide variety of ways (e.g., a handout sheet, transparency or PowerPoint slide, chalkboard or whiteboard, poster chart, and so on). Choose an option that will be most efficient and effective in your situation.

- Display sets of visual images or tangible objects on a designated table in the room. Participants gather around the table to look at the items and select one to complete the metaphor.

- Each set of words, images, or objects should contain at least 10 to 15 items more than the total number of people participating (e.g., if 25 people participate, then the set should contain about 35–40 items).

- Sets of visual images can be collections of pictures, art cards, photos, postcards, magazine illustrations, etc.

- Sets of tangible objects can be collections of "odds and ends"—unusual gadgets or novelty items (such as a bobblehead doll, small wind-up toy, giant clown sunglasses, flashlight keychain, judge's gavel, artificial Hawaiian lei, rhinestone gloves, etc.), ordinary household items (such as various types of kitchen utensils, toiletries, garden tools, etc.), or office equipment (such as an ink blotter, stamp dispenser, rubber band, ruler, stapler, etc.). Store the collection of items in a plastic box, tote bag, or other easily transportable container.

Variations:

- Ask participants to make metaphors by using items in their pockets, billfolds, handbags, briefcases, or things they are wearing.
- Ask participants to make metaphors by using items they see in the room (this works best when the space contains a variety of interesting items and/or if the decor is colorful).
- Ask participants to generate diverse reasons for the "because" part of a metaphor/simile stem that designates one object, for example: "An evaluation plan is like a washing machine because. . . ."
- Record on posted chart paper metaphors that participants generate on their own (i.e., no props provided). Analyze by identifying common qualities or characteristics across all the metaphors listed (see *Strategy 10: Concept Formation/Cluster Maps*). Collect as data and findings when appropriate.

SOURCE: Stevahn and King (2010, Figure 3.4).

STRATEGY 7: DATA DIALOGUE

Targeted outcomes: (shaded boxes)

Interactive Purposes	A Promote positive relations		B Develop shared understandings		C Prioritize and finalize decisions		D Assess evaluation progress	
Basic Inquiry Tasks	1 Question	2 Design	3 Sample/ sources	4 Collect data	5 Analyze data	6 Interpret results	7 Report	
Levels of Involvement	I Respond/react to set content/information		II Generate content/input			III Organize/share content/information		

Time: 1 to 1.5 hours (depending on the total number of dialogue items)

- Opening: 10 to 15 minutes (welcome, introductions, agenda, purpose)
- Directions: 10 to 15 minutes (explain procedures, obtain consent, form groups)
- Dialogues: 10 to 15 minutes per dialogue item/sheet (3 items x 15 minutes = 45 minutes)
- Closing: 10 to 15 minutes (debrief, summarize, thank contributors for their input)

Materials:

- Topics (for data collection; see examples provided)
- "Data Dialogue Sheet" (one for each topic/question per group; see the example provided)

Data Dialogue Topics

- Communication within the organization/department/program
- Program delivery
- Program resources
- Program access for clients
- Professional development for service providers
- Leadership within the organization/program
- Evaluation sampling techniques
- Evaluation data collection methods
- Collaborative evaluation processes/tasks/practices

Data Dialogue Sheet	
Topic:	
Positives/benefits: What is working well?	Negatives/concerns: What is problematic?

Directions:

1. Arrange participants in teams of three or four.

2. Announce that the team goal is to gather input on given topics from all members.

3. Distribute the "Data Dialogue Sheet" (one per team).

4. Assign one person in each team to write/document input from all members.

5. Emphasize that the goal of this activity is to seek divergent viewpoints, not to sway others to change their views or to reach agreement/consensus within the group (write *all* contributions).

6. Debrief by asking each team to present one or two key points that surfaced during the dialogue.

7. Collect sheets for qualitative data analysis (see *Strategy 10: Concept Formation/ Cluster Maps*).

Facilitation tips:

- If input is sought on more than one topic, prepare a "Data Dialogue" packet containing
  a. a cover sheet with directions and space for participant consent signatures and
  b. a separate, color-coded dialogue sheet for each topic (different color per topic/sheet).

- Emphasize that this activity seeks all voices and diverse opinions on each topic; therefore, instruct participants to document all contributions (the goal is *not* to reach consensus or agreement within the group but, rather, to document individuals' divergent perspectives on the topic).

- Suggest that people take turns serving as the recorder (share this role). If only one person writes, he may not feel able to discuss fully, and his hand may get tired.
- Allow 10 to 15 minutes per topic/question for dialogue; we suggest no more than three topics/questions at any one sitting, each on a different-colored sheet of paper.
- Participants typically want to know what was discussed in other groups. Quickly debrief the activity by asking each group to share one or two key points that surfaced during the dialogue (these can be posted on chart paper so participants can quickly scan across the key points from each group).

Variations:

- Assess progress by asking participants their perceptions of "pluses/wishes" relevant to the session, various evaluation tasks, or other pertinent issues. Prepare the "Data Dialogue Sheet" by labeling the left column "Pluses" (positives) and the right column "Wishes" (issues, concerns, questions, suggestions). When working with the same people repeatedly, close each session by collecting responses, analyze for themes between sessions, then open the next session by sharing results and addressing wishes. A certain degree of trust and safety is required for sharing assessments aloud in small groups; therefore, when appropriate, adapt the activity by providing each participant with his/her own sheet for private and confidential responding.

SOURCE: © 2000 Laurie Stevahn & Jean A. King.

STRATEGY 8: JIGSAW

Targeted outcomes: (shaded boxes)

Interactive Purposes	A Promote positive relations		B Develop shared understandings		C Prioritize and finalize decisions		D Assess evaluation progress	
Basic Inquiry Tasks	1 Question	2 Design	3 Sample/ sources	4 Collect data	5 Analyze data	6 Interpret results	7 Report	
Levels of Involvement	I Respond/react to set content/information			II Generate content/input			III Organize/share content/information	

Time: 1 to 2 hours

- Less time for simple or concise information divided into a few segments
- More time for complex or voluminous information divided into numerous segments

Materials:

- Information packet (one packet per team; divide information into separate yet related segments like a jigsaw puzzle [color-code each segment if possible]; each packet contains one complete set of segments; arrange teams according to the number of segments in the packet—for example, arrange teams of three for a packet containing three segments, teams of four for four segments, teams of five for five segments, etc.; see the example below)

Information Packets *(each contains three different information sheets represented by ● ■ ◆)*	*Jigsaw Teams* *(each teammate in groups of three is responsible for a different information sheet)*
● = input from program administrators	Jigsaw teams: ●■◆ ●■◆ ●■◆ ●■◆
■ = input from program service providers	⬇ ⬆
◆ = input from program recipients	Expert pairs: ●● ●● ■■ ■■ ◆◆ ◆◆

Directions:

1. Prepare information packets prior to the meeting/session.

2. Arrange participants in teams according to the number of jigsaw segments in the packet (e.g., teams of three people for three segments).

3. Announce that the team goal is for all members to understand and use the entire body of information in the packet. Each member is responsible for a different segment of information, studies/learns it, and then presents it to the team.

4. Ask participants to read their own segment silently and note key points (allow appropriate time given the size/complexity of the segments).

5. Instruct individuals to form *expert pairs* by linking up with someone who has the same segment from another jigsaw team.

6. Expert pairs compare key points, discuss the information, and plan how to present it to their original jigsaw team (allow appropriate time given the size/complexity of the segments).

7. Individuals return to their original teams and then present segments in turn (akin to putting pieces of a jigsaw puzzle together to form a whole).

8. Ask teams to apply the whole body of information to evaluation such as determining next steps, evaluating effectiveness, or adjusting implementations.

9. Facilitate whole-session sharing by asking each team to report conclusions and then reach consensus on how to proceed.

Facilitation tips:

- Start with manageable segments of information that can be easily understood and explained.
- Provide a visual diagram (such as the example above) to show how the activity works (i.e., participants start in a jigsaw team and divide the information in the packet, form expert pairs to grapple with their distinct information segments, then return to their original jigsaw team to present their component).
- Keep jigsaw teams small whenever possible (ideally, three to four people per team).
- Sometimes larger teams may be appropriate, especially if the entire body of information naturally divides into six to eight segments (then arrange six to eight people per team) *and* if participants are experienced with the strategy (if not, then keep teams small—e.g., arrange teams of four, with each participant responsible for two of the eight information components, rather than eight people in a team each responsible for one component).

- Provide a follow-up activity that will require the team to apply the entire body of information toward some meaningful task. For example, after jigsawing and presenting findings from three different samples (managers, service providers, and clients), the team then applies the entire set of findings toward suggesting recommendations.

Variations:

- This strategy may be facilitated to provide teams with *set content/information* to understand (such as analyzed evaluation results that teammates subdivide, study, then present to one another toward comprehending the whole) or to ask teams to *generate input* (teammates subdivide and respond to different aspects of an overarching topic, such as a set of questions on organizational effectiveness relevant to communications, resources, policies) or to involve teams in *data or information analysis* (teammates subdivide and analyze data sets from different samples such as students, parents, teachers, administrators).
- If the information, material, or issue to be addressed is complex, consider forming teams of four or six. Subdivide teammates into pairs within each team; assign each pair a different segment of the information. The expert pair procedure (connecting with individuals from other teams who have similar parts) could be pursued (time permitting) or eliminated (because pairs already exist within each team). The point is that forming pairs within teams at the onset provides participants with built-in support for grappling with complex information, thereby promoting success.
- Use jigsaw to prepare an evaluation report. The team conceptualizes components that will form the report, then subdivides those components for writing. Once written, all components are presented to all members of the team, discussed, revised/edited, then combined into one complete report.

SOURCE: Stevahn and King (2010, Figure 3.10).

STRATEGY 9: GRAFFITI/CAROUSEL

Targeted outcomes: (shaded boxes)

Interactive Purposes	A Promote positive relations		B Develop shared understandings		C Prioritize and finalize decisions		D Assess evaluation progress	
Basic Inquiry Tasks	1 Question	2 Design	3 Sample/ sources	4 Collect data	5 Analyze data	6 Interpret results	7 Report	
Levels of Involvement	I Respond/react to set content/information		II Generate content/input			III Organize/share content/information		

Time: 50 to 60 minutes total (less time for few topics; more time for numerous topics)

- Generate graffiti: 5 to 10 minutes
- Analyze/synthesize graffiti: 45 to 50 minutes

Materials:

- Topics (different for each team; see examples below)
- Graffiti sheets (chart paper, one per topic/team)
- Sticky notes (different color per topic/team)
- Tables (one per topic/team)

Topics	Topic/Table/Team Rotation
Topic 1: *I feel supported in my work when . . .*	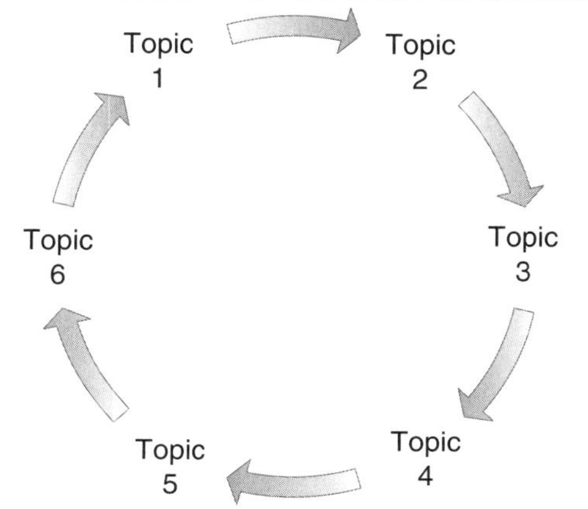
Topic 2: *I feel frustrated in my work when . . .*	
Topic 3: *Evaluations work best when . . .*	
Topic 4: *Evaluations are problematic when . . .*	
Topic 5: *People embrace change when . . .*	
Topic 6: *People struggle with change when . . .*	

Topic/Table/Team Rotation diagram showing Topic 1 → Topic 2 → Topic 3 → Topic 4 → Topic 5 → Topic 6 in a circular rotation.

Directions:

1. Arrange teams; provide a separate topic and table for each (three or four participants per team).

2. Announce that the team goal is to obtain input on a designated topic from all session participants, then analyze, synthesize, and report conclusions to the entire session.

3. Give each team one graffiti sheet (chart paper), each containing a different topic.

4. Provide each team with sticky notes (a different color per team).

5. Explain and facilitate the graffiti activity:

   a. All individuals silently/simultaneously write graffiti on their team topic for 1 to 2 minutes using sticky notes (one idea per sticky note, as many ideas as possible).

   b. Each team then passes its sheet clockwise to the next team (assign someone to carry the sheet to the next table).

   c. All participants write graffiti on this new topic.

   d. Sheets continue to rotate clockwise until each team's original topic returns home.

   e. Teams analyze and synthesize the graffiti on the topic/sheet by grouping similar items/ideas (see *Strategy 10: Concept Formation/Cluster Maps*).

Facilitation tips:

- Keep the activity moving by appropriately pacing rotations. Use a timer and display it for all to see (if possible).

- Typically, 60 seconds provides ample time for participants to contribute input on any given topic. Extend time for input to 2 minutes if topics require more elaborate thinking or detailed responses.

- Designate one person in each team who will be responsible for taking the sheet to the next team.

- Give directions for synthesizing the graffiti before the last rotation (i.e., before each team's original topic/sheet is returned in the rotation)—or post directions or provide each team with a direction sheet before the last rotation begins. Graffiti sticky notes tend to capture the interest of participants, so make sure they know what to do before receiving their graffiti sheet for analysis. Giving directions while teams have their graffiti sheet at their tables is futile (people will be focused on the graffiti, not on the facilitator's directions).

- Sticky notes can be color-coded by team (i.e., each team has a different color), to make it easy for a liaison to determine which team provided the graffiti that needs clarification. If a graffiti contribution is not understood, instruct each team to send the liaison to the team that provided the contribution to ask for clarification.

Variations:

- Post graffiti sheets on the wall in various places around the room. Direct teams to rotate physically by walking to each sheet (rather than passing the sheets to each team).
- Post graffiti sheets on the wall in various places around the room or place each sheet at a separate designated table. Facilitate one 5-minute round of "free for all"— individuals may visit and contribute to any or all posted graffiti sheets within the time allotted. Arrange and assign teams to analyze/organize the graffiti/information (one team per sheet).
- Use felt markers instead of sticky notes. Distribute one set of markers to each team (one marker for every teammate). Color-code markers by team (i.e., one color per team but different colors across teams—one team has blue markers, another red, another purple, another orange, another green, another brown).
- When facilitating large numbers of people, divide those participating into two session subgroups, then provide the same graffiti topics to teams within the two subgroups (see the diagram below). Compare and contrast themes/findings across teams with the same topic.

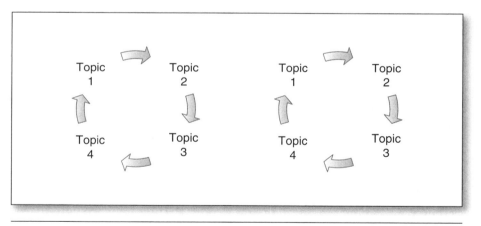

SOURCE: Stevahn and King (2010, Figure 3.11).

Targeted outcomes: (shaded boxes)

Interactive Purposes	A Promote positive relations		B Develop shared understandings		C Prioritize and finalize decisions		D Assess evaluation progress	
Basic Inquiry Tasks	1 Question	2 Design	3 Sample/ sources	4 Collect data	5 Analyze data	6 Interpret results	7 Report	
Levels of Involvement	I Respond/react to set content/information		II Generate content/input		III Organize/share content/information			

Time: 40 to 60 minutes (depending on the number of items in the data set and length of debriefing)

Materials:

- Data sets (one set per team containing 20–50 items; each item is on a separate card, paper strip, or sticky note; see the abbreviated example below)

Data Set: Helpful Resources	Clusters/Themes/Categories (name each category after grouping similar items)		
	Training	Technology	Data Management
1. Assistance with technology	3	1	2
2. Clerks to file/organize findings	8	4	5
3. Training for new procedures	9	10	6
4. Set up a website for clients		12	7
5. People to collect and analyze data			11
6. Data analysis/management help			
7. People to maintain databases			
8. Mentoring for new needed skills			
9. Ongoing staff development			
10. Experts to troubleshoot IT issues			
11. People to monitor progress and disseminate results			
12. Laptop computers for portable use at site visits			

Directions:

1. Arrange participants in teams of two, three, or four.

2. The team goal is to summarize a set of data using qualitative analysis.

3. Give each team one data set containing a collection of items.

4. Instruct teammates to cluster/categorize/group items that are alike (similar defining attributes).

5. Assign a specific role to each teammate (if helpful), for example:

   a. Card mover—clusters cards based on team discussion/consensus

   b. Scribe—takes notes on team discussion/reasoning

   c. Theme recorder—writes agreed-on labels/names for clusters based on defining attributes

   d. Time keeper—keeps team on task and alerts teammates to time deadlines

6. Label or name each group/category/cluster (create a label/name that reflects the underlying attribute among items in the cluster; each cluster represents a major theme).

7. Facilitate whole-session sharing by asking each team to present and post themes; identify repeated themes across teams; describe relationships/connections among themes.

8. Apply the major themes to evaluation concerns/issues/decisions.

Facilitation tips:

- Make sure items within the set are numbered or lettered for easy reference and discussion.
- Demonstrate how to identify common attributes for clustering items prior to teamwork (especially if this type of task is new to participants).
- Coach participants to avoid small numbers of clusters containing large numbers of items (e.g., two clusters each containing 20 items). Typically, this means participants have named broad categories first and then placed all items into those categories without zeroing in on the *core* attribute that binds items together. When this happens, people have typically made one of two common errors: (a) naming a category first, then trying to put items into it (e.g., office items, many of which have nothing to do with one another) or (b) identifying sequential links among items (e.g., linking a map, car, and highway [that do not have common defining attributes] instead of clustering items into distinct categories, each defined by the alike attributes/functions of the items, such as a map, GPS system, and road sign [navigation tools]; a car, airplane, and boat [transportation vehicles]; or a road, river, and footpath [thoroughfares].

Variations:

- Ask participants to generate information by writing ideas briefly with felt markers on half sheets. Spread the half sheets on the floor so everyone can see. Together, look for items that belong together based on core attributes and create columns for each category. For example, in a data set containing 50 challenging issues relevant to conducting participatory program evaluations, the following five can be grouped into one category because they all deal with framing an evaluation study: meaningful questions, narrowing focus, sponsor interests, clear targets, stakeholder concerns. Once category columns have been formed, name each. Collect the sheets in categories so each can be typed for future reference. For immediate reference, run tape across the half sheets in each column, then post on the wall.
- Use categories to create cluster maps that illustrate key themes (see the example below).

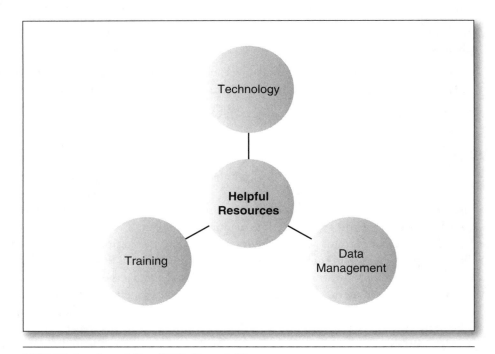

SOURCE: Stevahn and King (2010, Figure 3.12).

STRATEGY 11: COOPERATIVE RANK ORDER

Targeted outcomes: (shaded boxes)

Interactive Purposes	A Promote positive relations		B Develop shared understandings		C Prioritize and finalize decisions		D Assess evaluation progress	
Basic Inquiry Tasks	1 Question	2 Design	3 Sample/ sources	4 Collect data	5 Analyze data	6 Interpret results	7 Report	
Levels of Involvement	I Respond/react to set content/information			II Generate content/input		III Organize/share content/information		

Time: 60 minutes

- Less time for smaller data sets
- More time for larger data sets

Materials:

- Set of items (to rank/order/sequence; one set per team; each set contains 6–12 items, each item is on a separate card or paper strip; see the example below)

Set of Items

Evaluation Recommendation
Increase knowledge of and commitment to the organization's mission.

- Rank order the ideas below from most to least feasible for enacting the above evaluation recommendation.
- Next, sequence the same set of ideas from greatest to least potential for positive impact.

A. Post the mission statement prominently in every room and hallway.

B. Designate 1 day each month to focus on and celebrate mission.

C. Provide time for staff members to share ways they live the mission.

D. Distribute mission bookmarks, magnets, pens, water bottles, etc.

E. Write the mission on all documents such as agendas, announcements, meeting minutes, etc.

F. Review and discuss the mission at the start of each meeting.

Directions:

1. Arrange participants in teams of two, three, or four.

2. The team goal is to reach consensus on a rank, order, or sequence for a collection of items.

3. Give each team one set of items.

4. Instruct teams to rank the items according to an established criterion (such as importance, desirability, feasibility, level of difficulty, amount of training required, probable benefits, likelihood of success, etc.). Place cards or paper strips in an order that reflects "most to least" using the criterion specified. Items that describe actions or behaviors can be sequenced according to which should come first, second, third, and so on, to best accomplish a targeted goal.

5. Assign a specific role to each teammate if helpful, for example:

   a. Card mover—arranges cards in order based on team discussion/consensus

   b. Scribe—takes notes on team discussion/reasoning

   c. Timekeeper—keeps team on task and alerts teammates to time deadlines

   d. Reporter—presents the team's final product to everyone in the session

6. Facilitate whole-session sharing by asking each team to present and post rankings; identify which items repeatedly are ranked highest or lowest across teams, and discuss implications for overall conclusions and future actions.

7. Apply the results to evaluation concerns/issues/decisions.

Facilitation tips:

- Keep the number of items to be ranked reasonable (ideally, 6 to 12). Too few items tend to truncate meaningful interaction; long lists of items tend to overwhelm participants and produce frustration.
- Label each item with a number or letter for easy identification during discussion and debriefing.
- If time for preparing materials is short, items to be ranked may be listed and distributed on a single sheet of paper for discussion.
- Whenever possible, prepare items on tactile paper strips that physically can be ordered and rearranged by participants as their discussion and decision making unfolds.
- Color-code items for easy identification (i.e., each item has its own colored paper strip).
- Provide tape or glue so each team can secure paper strips to display its final ranking.

- Post rankings on the wall. Discuss similarities and differences across teams. Focus on the issues that emerged during the ranking and the rationales on which final rankings are based.
- Focus on items that rank highly across all (or most) teams. Facilitate whole-session discussion on those items to reach consensus for future action.

Variations:

- Frame an evaluation study by asking participants to rank the importance of (a) organizational/program issues or concerns or (b) a set of possible evaluation questions or purposes.
- Explore possible samples/sources by ranking which are most (a) crucial to addressing the evaluation questions and (b) feasible given available resources (time, money, assistance, etc.).
- Determine which evaluation recommendation priorities to pursue by ranking from *most* to *least* important, feasible, or essential for organizational or program change.
- Assess evaluation progress by ranking a list of actions from *most* to *least* successful, problematic, in need of revision, etc.
- Rank themes that emerge from *Strategy 10: Concept Formation/Cluster Maps* according to which are most important for success or should be pursued first, second, third, and so on.
- Rank force-field analysis data—i.e., lists of factors that enable or block organizational/program success or effectiveness—from *most* to *least* critical (see Stevahn & King, 2010).

SOURCE: Stevahn and King (2010, Figure 3.21).

STRATEGY 12: FIST TO FIVE

Targeted outcomes: (shaded boxes)

Interactive Purposes	A Promote positive relations		B Develop shared understandings		C Prioritize and finalize decisions		D Assess evaluation progress	
Basic Inquiry Tasks	1 Question	2 Design	3 Sample/ sources	4 Collect data	5 Analyze data	6 Interpret results	7 Report	
Levels of Involvement	I Respond/react to set content/information		II Generate content/input			III Organize/share content/information		

Time: 5 to 10 minutes (depending on the number of items presented and length of debriefing)

Materials:

- List of items (each to be rated/scaled/prioritized; see examples below)

List of Items *(with rating scale anchors)*

Interview options (undesirable/unworkable to highly desirable/workable)

- Face-to-face structured interviews
- Focus-group interviews
- Telephone interviews
- Interactive electronic interviews

Data collection options (useless to essential for addressing evaluation questions)

- Inspect existing documents
- Conduct on-site observations
- Survey clients
- Interview program staff
- Interview organizational leaders
- Survey community stakeholders

Evaluator experience (none to lots)

- Experience in framing evaluation questions
- Expertise in qualitative data analysis
- Expertise in quantitative data analysis
- Familiarity with managing databases
- Knowledge of organizational change

Personal characteristics (that's not me to that's totally me)
- Always dreamed of working in this profession/discipline
- Came to this profession/discipline by accident
- Have worked in every department in the organization

Directions:

1. Present the first item on the list.

2. Ask participants to rate/prioritize the item on a scale from 0 to 5 (*low* represented by a fist to *high* represented by five fingers).

3. Specifically designate the low/fist to high/five scale, such as from most to least important, needed, essential, effective, representative, knowledgeable, useful, doable, preferred, valued, etc.

4. Ask participants to estimate an average for each item by looking across everyone's ratings; document/record results.

5. Review ratings across the entire list of items; discuss implications and determine priorities.

Facilitation tips:

- Prepare a list of items relevant to a central topic or organizing theme (see examples above).
- Note that this procedure allows quick assessment of priorities but requires public disclosure, which eliminates confidentiality.

Variations:

- Use to determine quickly a sense of priorities regarding (a) questions or purposes for the evaluation, (b) sampling strategies or important sources of information to pursue, (c) strategies for collecting data or obtaining sources, (d) interpretations of evaluation results, or (e) recommendations for action.
- Use frequently to assess progress during the evaluation study. For example, close each meeting by quickly processing its effectiveness or the extent to which certain aspects of the evaluation are working well (five fingers) versus not (fist).
- Use in focus-group interview sessions as a springboard for further conversation on topics presented.
- Promote relationship building through appropriate self-disclosure by crafting a list of items relevant to personal characteristics, preferences, life experiences, and so on.

Focus on qualities that people likely will find interesting, admire, honor, identify with, marvel at, feel positive about, etc.

- Facilitate a "fist to three" version (the scale ranges from *zero/low* to *three/high*). Apply *Strategy 3: Choosing Corners* (label four corners of the room: 0, 1, 2, 3). Ask participants to move to the corner that corresponds to their response and share/discuss their stories with others in their corner. Whip around the corners, asking participants to share briefly with everyone. Collect data by tallying the number of people in each corner (keep a written record). Arrange for observers to assist.
- Use thumbs up, thumbs sideways, and thumbs down for a quick take on people's reactions.

SOURCE: Stevahn and King (2010, Figure 3.18).

STRATEGY 13: DOT VOTES/BAR GRAPHS

Targeted outcomes: (shaded boxes)

Collaborative Purposes	A Promote positive relations		B Develop shared understandings		C Prioritize and finalize decisions		D Assess evaluation progress	
Basic Inquiry Tasks	1 Question	2 Design	3 Sample/ sources	4 Collect data	5 Analyze data	6 Interpret results	7 Report	
Levels of Involvement	I Respond/react to set content/information			II Generate content/input		III Organize/share content/information		

Time: 10 to 20 minutes (depending on the number of items presented and length of debriefing)

Materials:

- Items/alternatives/options (post each on a separate chart sheet *or* prepare a bar graph chart, placing all options across the bottom of the horizontal axis; see examples below)
- Sticky notes, sticky dots, or stickers (uniform in size/shape for bar graphs)

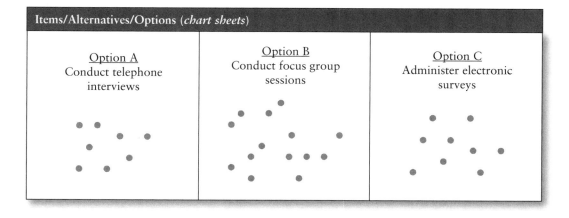

Items/Alternatives/Options (*chart sheets*)

Option A
Conduct telephone interviews

Option B
Conduct focus group sessions

Option C
Administer electronic surveys

Items/Alternatives/Options *(bar graph chart)*						
Provide descriptions of the alternative plans, then ask, *Which plan will best provide program staff with continuous professional development? Indicate which three plans would work best for you by placing your three sticky notes in the corresponding columns to create bar graphs.*						

		■				
		■				
		■				
		■	■			
■		■	■		■	
■	■	■	■		■	
■	■	■	■	■	■	■
■	■	■	■	■	■	■
■	■	■	■	■	■	■
Plan #1	Plan #2	Plan #3	Plan #4	Plan #5	Plan #6	Plan #7

Directions:

1. Post a chart sheet for each alternative *or* post one bar graph chart showing all options.

2. Give each participant sticky dots (one or several, equal in number, uniform in size and shape if creating a bar graph).

3. Ask participants to indicate which items/alternatives are most desired (preferred, important, valued, attainable, feasible, etc.) by placing dots on the corresponding chart sheets *or* by placing sticky notes in the column on the bar graph that corresponds to the desired item/alternative.

4. Explain the rules before asking people to make choices, especially when individuals have multiple dots or stickers. For example, indicate whether all or several dots/ stickers can be devoted to a single option or whether each dot/sticker must be devoted to different options.

5. Tally totals and record results for each option.

6. Apply the results (priorities/decisions) to conducting the evaluation or implementing the results.

Facilitation tips:

- Post and review the rules prior to voting. Explain the rationale underlying the rules.
- Make sure participants understand how the results will be used—e.g., as research data to be collected and analyzed, as a "dipstick" assessment to capture people's inclinations (but not for actual decision making), to finalize decisions about future actions, etc.
- Provide each participant with an equal number of dots/stickers—more if many alternatives exist, less for fewer alternatives. For example, if voting on 10 items, provide three dots/stickers if each must be devoted to different options, or five if multiple dots/stickers can be devoted to a single option.
- Demonstrate how to place sticky notes uniformly on the bar graph so accurate numeric comparisons can be made by glancing across options/bars.

Variations:

- Use to determine quickly a sense of priorities regarding (a) questions or purposes for the evaluation, (b) sampling strategies or important sources of information to pursue, (c) strategies for collecting data or obtaining sources, (d) interpretations of evaluation results, or (e) recommendations for action.
- Use at appropriate intervals during the evaluation to assess perceptions of progress on various aspects of the study.
- Collect data by recording, analyzing, and archiving responses.
- Ask participants to generate lists of organizational/program practices, policies, or resources that either promote or inhibit success or effectiveness (instead of providing set content/information). Post items generated on chart paper, and then invite participants to indicate through dot voting which items they deem most critical for future action.
- Draw a target for one option; have people place their dots closer to or farther away from the center to indicate preference for or commitment to that option. If you want people to provide input on several options, create a separate target for each.

SOURCE: Stevahn and King (2010, Figures 3.19, 3.20).

AN EXAMPLE OF THE STRATEGIES IN ACTION

Detailing directions for the interactive strategies will enable people to use them one at a time, a wise way novice facilitators can begin to expand their repertoires. In the flow of an actual evaluation, however, evaluators will often use several different strategies at a single meeting or over the course of a study. They may also insert a strategy on the fly when it becomes clear that people need to interact around a topic and an opportunity presents itself. The example that follows documents how the strategies can work in context. It highlights a major commitment by the deputy superintendent of a large suburban school district to use a collaborative evaluation to trigger an extensive review of the middle school program, which she headed. Knowing the importance of engaging a broad range of stakeholders, she asked the district's internal evaluator to organize an evaluation team to guide the yearlong study and to structure interactions among a variety of stakeholders using as many strategies as made sense. The evaluator began by organizing the extensive middle school data already in the district's database: the results of an annual parent satisfaction survey, the results of a comparable student survey, and criterion-referenced achievement test results at all middle school grade levels.

The Middle School Evaluation Advisory Committee was a group of 10 that included representation from important stakeholder groups: three teachers of different grades and subject areas, two teachers of students with special needs, a representative from the teachers' union, two central-office administrators, and two parents. Following introductions at the first meeting, the deputy superintendent commissioned the group, which then brainstormed what they believed were the critical issues for the study, including what electives to offer, the functioning of advisory classes, and the middle school components critical to keep in light of a possible budget cut. Because the deputy superintendent wanted to engage many people in conversations around these issues, the committee planned two daylong meetings, one to launch the study in October and the other to process its results in June. At the end of the initial meeting and every meeting thereafter, the evaluator used *Strategy 5: Round-Robin Check-In* to have each person describe his or her personal highlights of the discussion.

A month later the evaluation began with a daylong summit, a gathering of more than 50 people, each of whom represented at least one middle school stakeholder group—teachers and paraeducators from various grades, subject areas, and specializations (e.g., supplemental services and special education); building and central-office administrators; parents; state department representatives; teacher education faculty from nearby universities; student council members; community representatives; and so on. The deputy superintendent explained that the day's goal was to complete the first step of the BIT by identifying evaluation questions the group wanted answered. In collaboration with members of the Advisory Committee, the internal evaluator structured a day of small-group interactions and large-group debriefings. The day began with a welcome from the district superintendent and a review of the agenda. Throughout the rest of the day the evaluator used a variety of strategies, including the following:

- *Strategy 1: Voicing Variables.* When the superintendent finished, the evaluator asked people to stand in response to several variables: place of birth (most, it turned out, had grown up in the community), role in the district, length of time in the district (some were surprised at the number of years certain individuals had served), and evaluation experience (ranging from novice to well practiced, with most somewhere in the middle).

- *Strategy 4: Cooperative Interviews.* Next the evaluator formed groups of three, and they conducted cooperative interviews on the following topic: *What is your most positive memory of your junior high/middle school experience?* Each group did a quick analysis of the commonalities among teammates' interview responses; most mentioned a caring adult, an innovative lesson, or success as part of a team. These were briefly discussed in the large group. Reminded of what it felt like to attend middle school, people felt connected through their stories.

- *Strategy 2: Voicing Viewpoints/Beliefs.* To encourage people to reflect on their attitudes toward middle school programming, the evaluator asked them to respond individually in writing to three statements using a Likert scale (*strongly agree* to *strongly disagree*): (a) *Students learn best when they control their own learning activities,* (b) *All students should remain in middle school until they can read and do math at grade level,* and (c) *In middle school discipline and order are more important than learning.*

- *Strategy 3: Choosing Corners.* The evaluator chose the corners strategy to debrief the beliefs sheet statements. He posted each of four response options in a separate corner of the room (*strongly agree, agree, disagree, strongly disagree*), then asked participants to look at their response to the first statement, move to the corner that matched it, introduce themselves to one or two others, and discuss why they chose the response in that corner. After some large-group debriefing of the first statement, he repeated the process for the second and third statements. The group was encouraged to meet new people for each item. Through the small- and large-group discussion, certain dilemmas facing the middle school educators became clear—for example, the tensions between creative instructional activities and students' need to learn "the basics" and the need for both good behavior and learning.

- *Strategy 8: Jigsaw.* The evaluator had prepared easy-to-read summaries of the previous year's parent and student satisfaction survey results and of middle grades test results for the previous 3 years. He divided people into groups that included a mix of roles and content. People then counted off and regrouped into like-numbered groups that became expert on one type of data. Their task was to develop claims from whichever data their group had. With consultation as needed by the evaluator, the base groups reassembled after 40 minutes and compared claims from the different types of data. The base groups wrote their top five data-based claims about middle school education in the district on flip-chart sheets, which were then posted on the wall.

- *Strategy 7: Data Dialogue.* All the day's previous strategies led to this culminating discussion. Again in groups of three or four, people were handed two sheets. One sheet had the question, *What are the most important issues this middle school evaluation should examine?* The other had two boxes and asked people to discuss their perception of (a) the current status of the middle school electives and (b) the advisory classes. One of the group members took notes and, at the end of 15 minutes, turned the sheets in to the evaluator, who would type up and analyze the outcomes of the discussions.

- *Strategy 6: Making Metaphors.* For the final activity of the day, the evaluator asked participants to pick a magazine photograph that captured for them the middle school experience. People chose many different images—mountain climbing, a marching band, a bicycle race, a snowy owl, and so on. Each person described why he or she had chosen that particular picture and then taped it on the wall to create a gallery of middle school metaphors. The evaluator took a picture of the wall of photographs.

The summit generated a great deal of good will as well as many ideas for the evaluation to investigate. The Middle School Evaluation Advisory Committee processed the results with the evaluator's help, using *Strategy 11: Cooperative Rank Order* to determine the topics that would focus the evaluation. With their input, the evaluator then designed and conducted the study, asking the committee to review decisions (e.g., the instruments, samples) at monthly meetings. At these meetings, the group routinely used *Strategy 12: Fist to Five* to take informal votes on the extent to which committee members supported specific ideas.

Much of the data collection involved straightforward surveys and individual and focus-group interviews. The evaluator did, however, use strategies at a special half-day session with the student leaders of the district's six middle schools. The morning began, after quick introductions, with *Strategy 6: Making Metaphors*. Like the participants at the summit, each student was asked to identify the image that for him or her captured the middle school experience. Once the reasons for the picture selections were given and the pictures taped on the wall, the overwhelming negativity of the images became clear. The wall was covered with scenes of destruction, conflict, and darkness, and the contrast with the adults' gallery was evident. Students easily provided reasons—advisories were inconsistent and mostly, to them, a waste of time; some students were forced into double sections of reading and math and missed all the "fun stuff"; and the grading system was overly competitive from their perspective. Thankfully, the next activity was *Strategy 9: Graffiti/Carousel*, and students were able to brainstorm on topics such as *I feel supported at school when . . . , I feel frustrated at school when . . . , advisory works best when . . . ,* and *the most important extracurricular activities are. . . .* When each group received its original topic sheet back, covered with graffiti sticky notes, students were asked to engage in *Strategy 10: Concept Formation/ Cluster Maps*. Working together and moving the notes around, they created and named categories.

The evaluator took the student input to the Middle School Evaluation Advisory Committee, and, sensing people's immediate concern about negative input from student leaders across the district, he helped the group spontaneously engage in *Strategy 8: Jigsaw* to analyze the content of the different graffiti sheets. He divided them up so that two or three people became well versed in each of the topics. After about 15 minutes, he rearranged them so each group had all the content represented. The committee continued in these groups until they were confident they understood the students' concerns and hopes, and then they reconvened as a whole. The content on the sticky notes was not as negative as the metaphors might have suggested. The Advisory Committee did, however, decide to invite one student leader from each school to attend the end-of-year summit, where the group would discuss the evaluation's recommendations.

In preparation for that final summit, the evaluator created packets that contained all the data collected throughout the course of the study, including the data-based claims from the first summit, the two sets of metaphors, and the students' graffiti summaries, along with the compiled results of other data he had gathered. He asked the Advisory Committee to review recommendations he had developed (and had asked the deputy superintendent to review) that built explicitly on the evaluation's results.

Participants seemed to enjoy the final summit and stayed far beyond the official end time. Hosted by the Middle School Evaluation Advisory Committee members, the meeting included the following strategies:

- *Strategy 5: Round-Robin Check-In.* People went around the room with sound-bite introductions that included their names and year's best experience.
- *Strategy 8: Jigsaw.* This process was identical to that used in the fall but with new data. At the second summit, people knew exactly what to do and, within 90 minutes, were familiar with all the middle school data.
- *Strategy 11: Cooperative Rank Order.* The evaluator had prepared slips of different-colored paper for the eight different recommendations that came from the data. Working in small groups with glue sticks, the summit participants put the recommendations in order from most to least important to act on immediately. A note taker recorded people's reasons for the ordering. Each group posted its summary sheet on the wall with the recommendation slips glued in order. Even at a distance, people could see the colors of those at the top of the lists and those at the bottom. The summit participants created a decision rule for those recommendations that would be considered in the next step: Items had to be in the first, second, or third slot for at least half the small groups.
- *Strategy 13: Dot Votes/Bar Graphs.* Once these recommendations were identified, the evaluator wrote each one on a flip-chart sheet and posted them on the wall. He gave everyone three dots and asked them to place their dots on the recommendations they still thought were the most important to act on immediately. They could place all their dots on one recommendation or divide them between two or three. Once people had voted with their dots, the group discussed the recommendations that received the most dots, moving to considering actions for change.

By the end of the day, the deputy superintendent and evaluator were both pleased with the process that had structured activities that led to participants' feelings of mutual success. The bookend summit meetings had successfully engaged people in framing the evaluation and determining what to do with its results.

PRACTICAL CONSIDERATIONS
FOR USING INTERACTIVE STRATEGIES

We now turn to three practical issues relevant to facilitating the evaluator's dozen of strategies presented in this chapter. First, although these strategies can be applied in numerous ways across diverse approaches for a variety of evaluation aims, making choices about when and how to use each is both science and art. The science of determining which to apply in any given situation requires knowing how and why each works and being able to enact each with technical skill. The art of deciding which strategies to apply, however, requires considering the uniqueness of each evaluation situation, setting, culture, and context—dealing with the structural realities that will tend to either support or frustrate success. Science and art come together as those conducting evaluations recognize what each strategy can accomplish, the strengths and limitations of each, and possibilities for flexibly adapting or creatively linking/integrating them to deal with particular circumstances effectively.

When making choices, always consider available time in light of the time required to implement any given strategy (see Exhibit 5.5). Some can be facilitated quickly with relative ease; others require longer periods of time to explain directions, model procedures, engage participants meaningfully, document interactions, and debrief conclusions. Even when more complicated strategies can accomplish a targeted purpose or task well (such as *Strategy 8: Jigsaw* to develop shared understandings or *Strategy 10: Concept Formation/Cluster Maps* to analyze qualitative data) or create broader involvement (such as *Strategy 9: Graffiti/Carousel* to gather input for continuous data-driven assessment in ECB), they ultimately will fail if the time needed for facilitation falls short. In such cases, simpler strategies that take less time may be better options, even if they require people to react to set information rather than actually generating, analyzing, or interpreting it. You should also consider the culture of the group or organization you are planning to engage. Interactive strategies are less viable in certain instances—for example, when a group of high-powered professionals (sometimes physicians or attorneys) will participate or when the group will involve people who don't share a common language. Some individuals label these types of interactions "touchy-feely" and either refuse to participate or do so grudgingly, affecting the process. Better not to use the strategies than to try them and not succeed.

Second, consider the necessary resources and preparation for any given strategy. Some require few (if any) materials and little preparation; others

Exhibit 5.5 Facilitation Time

Time	Strategies												
	1	2	3	4	5	6	7	8	9	10	11	12	13
	Voicing Variables	Voicing Viewpoints/Beliefs	Choosing Corners	Cooperative Interviews	Round-Robin Check-In	Making Metaphors	Data Dialogue	Jigsaw	Graffiti/Carousel	Concept Formation	Cooperative Rank Order	Fist to Five	Dot Votes/Bar Graphs
Shorter 5–20 minutes	X	X	X	X	X	X			X			X	X
Moderate 30–60 minutes		X							X	X	X		
Longer 1–2 hours							X	X			X		

SOURCE: Stevahn and King (2010, Table 3.2).

require numerous materials carefully organized. Some can be easily managed by one person in almost every situation; others may require additional human resources such as cofacilitators or observers to monitor progress, offer assistance, or document/collect input when large numbers of people are involved. Again, certain strategies will be more or less feasible in any situation depending on the extent to which needed resources can be supplied and adequately prepared. Similar to the issue of time noted previously, a viable strategy for any task or purpose will be tenable and successful only if its resource needs can be met. To enhance flexibility in facilitating various strategies on the spot, we suggest preparing and always carrying a materials toolkit. Evaluators should store items in an easily transportable container and replenish supplies after each session to be ready for the next. There is nothing more frustrating than not having the needed resources—not enough half sheets or dots, or glue sticks that are no longer sticky—when you identify a strategy that is perfect for moving a group interaction forward. Items we recommend appear in Exhibit 5.6.

Third, consider facilitator skills relevant to the strategies. Repertoire entails knowing and being able to skillfully execute each in any given context with varied content. Developing fluency in applying strategies across diverse domains—what some call *executive control* (e.g., see Joyce & Showers, 1988; Joyce, Weil, & Calhoun, 2009), *automaticity* (e.g., see Bloom, 1986a; Moors & De Houwer, 2006), *expert performance* (e.g., see van Gog, Ericsson, Rikers, & Paas, 2005), or *mastery* (e.g., see Arredondo & Block, 1990; Block, 1980; Bloom, 1986b)—requires repeated practice, reflection, and

Exhibit 5.6 Facilitation Materials for Interactive Evaluation

Facilitator Materials

- PC and/or projector
- PowerPoint (to show slides and record participant input "on the spot")
- Blank transparencies and transparency markers (if using a projector)
- File cards (3 x 5)
- Chart paper/newsprint
- Felt markers
- Whiteboard markers
- Sticky notes (square or rectangular, in varying sizes and colors)
- Dots (or other stickers)
- Colored paper (8 1/2" x 11")
- Glue sticks
- Transparent tape
- Masking tape
- Scissors
- Sets of visual images (art cards, magazine pictures, postcards, photos, clip art, etc.)
- Likert-scale options on separate cards for posting in corners (*SA, A, D, SD*)
- Timer (visible to all, if possible)
- Cartoons (or funny transparencies)
- Noisemaker to signal attention from participants (gong, whistle, flute, dinger, etc.)
- Working norms poster ("rules" for group participation)
- Sense of humor

SOURCE: © 2001 Laurie Stevahn & Jean A. King.

refinement. People facilitating these strategies should consider their own mastery levels when making choices about use, especially in relation to existing contextual factors that may be challenging. Sometimes evaluators will facilitate various strategies to engage people in framing or carrying out evaluations, especially if collaborative approaches are adopted. At other times organizational leaders, administrators, or managers may use the strategies to engage program people in ECB or in using results for change-based initiatives. Other stakeholders with interests in the organization or program may also find themselves in situations where applying the interactive strategies will make sense.

Regardless of who facilitates the strategies, successful applications will require the ability to adapt each flexibly—sometimes unexpectedly in the midst of facilitation—to meet unique conditions, anticipated or not. We suggest cofacilitation as a viable way to hone facilitation skills and develop mastery, especially if using a complex strategy for the first time or when conditions are extremely challenging (such as environments fraught with instability or conflict). The point is to think about facilitator expertise in relation to likely circumstances when deciding which strategies to employ. It may be wiser to employ a simpler strategy with which one has fluency than a more complicated strategy in a mechanistic way, unsure how to make "on-the-spot" modifications crucial for success.

In summary, we present Exhibit 5.7 to assist evaluators and others involved in conducting or using the results of evaluation studies in making choices about which strategies to employ. Skill in effectively transferring them across contexts (such as government, health, education, business, community development work), circumstances (small to large numbers of people in single or multiple locations operating for profit or not with generous or meager budgets, providing goods or services), and content (public parks or library programs, exercise or nutrition programs, social studies or English programs, manufacturing or retail operations, food bank or immigrant language-training programs) involves recognizing opportunities and making appropriate adaptations. That means carefully considering what conditions exist in the organization or program (realizing they are innumerable, ever changing, systems-oriented, and never fully known) and how best to deal with those circumstances given the advantages and disadvantages of each strategy, some of which include facilitation time, resources, preparation, and facilitator mastery. Choosing and adapting strategies ultimately requires all three of the evaluator's roles—decision maker, actor, and reflector—as evaluators gain skill in facilitating interactions as part of their IEP.

Exhibit 5.7   Strategy Outcomes, Advantages, Disadvantages, and Useful Applications

Strategy	Outcome/ Product/Result (What You Get)	Advantages	Disadvantages	Useful Applications
1. Voicing Variables	• Frequency counts of participants' characteristics (similarities, differences) • Nominal variables	• Visual • Quick • Flexible • Engaging • Inexpensive; no extra materials needed • Can estimate percentages • Connects people around important characteristics • Works easily with large groups	• Focuses on surface attributes; no depth • Public display may make some feel uncomfortable; no hiding • Closed-ended items limit people's responses	• Introductory sessions • First-time meetings • When new participants are added to an existing group • As a quick change of pace
2. Voicing Viewpoints/ Beliefs	• Explicit beliefs or value orientations on a specific topic	• Catalyst for grounding conversations around beliefs, values, biases • Gives people an opportunity to speak about things that really matter to them • Reveals areas of agreement and disagreement in a group • Illuminates alternative perspectives	• Vague or ambiguous statements can annoy participants • Can be higher risk • Value-laden words may trigger negative reactions • Items must be carefully crafted for this strategy to work	• Establishing a set of common understandings • Examining program assumptions and purpose
3. Choosing Corners	• Frequency count (similarities, differences) of participants on the variables posted in the corners	• Illuminates and explicates people's positions or responses to a question or statement	• Movement can be distracting • Some participants may have physical challenges that make moving difficult	• Whenever there is a range of responses to a question or statement • Articulating dimensions of

(Continued)

Exhibit 5.7   (Continued)

Strategy	Outcome/ Product/Result (What You Get)	Advantages	Disadvantages	Useful Applications
	• Connecting people with similar answers • Rationales for each corner's response • Can be nominal or ordinal	• Visual • Kinesthetic; requires participant movement • Quick • Energizing and fun • Works for large groups • Can be used to reach consensus	• Can do only a few rounds at one time • Items must be carefully crafted for this strategy to work	mission statements, program purposes or assumptions, recommendations, etc. • Introductory sessions • First-time meetings • When new participants join an existing group
4. Cooperative Interviews	• Written self-disclosure around a targeted topic	• Fosters positive interpersonal relationships and interdependent roles • Immediately connects people around a relevant topic • Provides more in-depth discussion • Allows people to see similarities and differences • Engages people (leaning into the conversation) • Generates pertinent information in a relatively short time • Open-ended nature can allow exploration of reasons • Inclusive; all voices are sought and heard	• Assumes that people can adequately capture what others say in writing • Participants need interviewing skills to draw stories out • Open-ended nature of questions may allow people to go off on tangents	• Introductory sessions • First-time meetings • When new participants are added to an existing group • Explicating program theory • Telling anecdotes and stories

Strategy	Outcome/ Product/Result (What You Get)	Advantages	Disadvantages	Useful Applications
5. Round-Robin Check-In	• Sound-bite-length statement from each participant in response to a pertinent question • Not for introductions; need to have worked as a group	• Enables everyone to touch base quickly; a dipstick • Round-robin procedure gives everyone a voice and an opportunity to participate easily • Gets everyone actively involved immediately • Moves quickly • Open-ended	• If people opt out, you may have gaps • People may talk too long; answers need to stay short • People may become emotional and want to emote • Problematic in groups with more than 20–25	• Opening sessions • Making transitions between topics/ activities within one session • Closing sessions • Whenever it is helpful to know individual reactions or feelings
6. Making Metaphors	• Images in the form of words, pictures, or objects that participants connect to a targeted topic • Explanations that accompany each image presented	• Flexible; can use words, objects, pictures • Creative; allows people to use their imaginations • Expands understanding; promotes greater clarity of the image • Fun and energizing • Quick • Open-ended • Story quality that reveals what people are experiencing	• Some people struggle to come up with an image • Some people make unusual or even absurd connections • Has the potential to take the group off topic • May not be appropriate for serious or volatile contexts • Can be higher risk	• Introductory sessions • First-time meetings • Opening subsequent sessions • Making transitions between topics/ activities within one session • Closing a session
7. Data Dialogue	• Self-recorded written information around targeted topics generated through small-group conversation	• Cost-effective • Generates a lot of information in a short period of time • Balanced input from many participants	• People may be uncomfortable or unable to record responses • Recorder can limit what is written down	• Qualitative data collection when focus groups are not a viable option • Allowing all participants to voice their opinions

(Continued)

Exhibit 5.7 (Continued)

Strategy	Outcome/ Product/Result (What You Get)	Advantages	Disadvantages	Useful Applications
		• Inclusive; all voices are sought and heard • Participants often enjoy the dialogue process	• Participants typically don't record full sentences or lengthy ideas; details or complexities may be lost • Written answers may be confusing or unclear	
8. Jigsaw	• Participants understand all aspects of a body of information	• Efficient use of time • Allows people to be expert in one area/ domain and learn all content from other participants • Participants have specific roles and may feel good because of that • Allows illumination of similarities and differences	• Materials must be carefully prepared and arranged ahead of time (i.e., each team receives one complete set of jigsaw pieces that together make a whole) • The process can be complex to manage • The jigsaw is as good as the weakest participant	• Covering large amounts of content in a short time (e.g., input from different stakeholders that needs to be summarized) • Data analysis and reduction
9. Graffiti/ Carousel	• Many ideas (unedited information) on various targeted topics	• Energizing and fun; group energizer • An alternative to traditional brainstorming • Fast paced • Generates abundant information in a short time • Promotes high involvement • Fairly quick way to see repetitions and patterns	• Participants may interfere with the process • Handwriting issues • Responses may be too brief and may not make sense • Tend to get first responses, word associations, gut reactions; not deep or elaborate	• Giving participants an energy boost • Large-group generation of information • Qualitative data collection

Strategy	Outcome/Product/Result (What You Get)	Advantages	Disadvantages	Useful Applications
10. Concept Formation/ Cluster Maps	• Labeled clusters of like items (concepts) grouped from unedited ideas	• Satisfying cognitive task • Allows participants to determine directly similarities and differences • Challenges participants to think deeply about common attributes or reasons for groupings • May encourage people to identify assumptions	• Items may not group easily • People may struggle to create meaningful category labels • Participants may create inappropriate or odd groupings/ clusters • People try to force items into categories • Domineering person may take over; others withdraw	• Identifying common themes in information • Explicating program theory
11. Cooperative Rank Order	• Rank order of a series of items with the rationale for the ordering	• Thorough discussion and critical reasoning (why) • Aimed at true consensus • Social focus; everyone participates • Requires people to identify assumptions	• Time-consuming • Ranking too many items becomes cumbersome • Participants need interviewing/ probing skills to draw out reasons • Participants must be open to listening to others' positions	• Prioritizing options or preferences before a decision (e.g., evaluation questions, data sources, or recommendations) • Articulating the rationale underpinning a rank order
12. Fist to Five	• Participants' degrees of experience with, knowledge of, or preferences for certain variables/ qualities/factors • Ordinal variables	• Visual • Can be done in a more private way (only the facilitator sees the results) • Quick • Flexible • Engaging • Inexpensive; no extra materials needed	• Public display may make some feel uncomfortable; no confidentiality • Relies on people's own estimates and perceptions • People may not use the top or bottom end of the scale	• Situations where the facilitator needs to understand the range of skill in the room • Barometer check on whether a group is ready to move on

(Continued)

Exhibit 5.7   (Continued)

Strategy	Outcome/ Product/Result (What You Get)	Advantages	Disadvantages	Useful Applications
		• Can estimate the average • Works easily with large groups	• Doesn't work if people don't have experience with the variable in question • Closed-ended items limit people's responses	
13. Dot Votes/ Bar Graphs	• Group preferences identified from a list of alternatives	• Visual • Quick • Kinesthetic; requires participant movement • Energizing and fun • Works for large groups • Everyone can see the process and results • Can structure dot data in different ways (scattered, bar graph, target)	• Not true consensus; some people feel like losers • May not get at complexities or subtleties of issues • Only works for issues that can be categorized nominally • Public context so people may be influenced by others' votes	• Identifying value orientations (with belief statements) • Prioritizing options or preferences before a decision (e.g., evaluation questions, recommendations)

SOURCE: © 2001 Laurie Stevahn & Jean A. King.

APPLYING INTERACTIVE EVALUATION PRACTICE PRINCIPLES TO INTERACTIVE STRATEGIES

Interactive strategies are the tools that evaluators can use to engage others productively in evaluation efforts. Whether used to get input or feedback from stakeholders on set content, to generate new information, to analyze data, or to organize and share findings or recommendations, these strategies enable evaluators to connect participants in developing shared understandings of the evaluation, prioritizing and finalizing evaluation decisions, and assessing evaluation progress. Some of them are easy to facilitate and take little preparation; others are more elaborate and need detailed planning. All of them, however, keep the importance of building positive relationships at the forefront of evaluation practice and throughout. Engaging people meaningfully matters, not only for the quality of a study but also for using its results and building capacity for future evaluation practice.

The IEP principles in Exhibit 5.8 highlight the usefulness of applying interactive strategies in evaluation practice. When applied appropriately across various tasks of an evaluation study—especially studies framed as

Exhibit 5.8   IEP Principles Applied to Interactive Strategies

IEP Principle	Applied to Interactive Strategies
1. Get personal.	• Strategically use interactive strategies with appropriate others to engage them personally and meaningfully in cooperative work for successful evaluation practice. • Recognize how positive interdependence is structured into the interactive strategies and its potential for fostering positive relations and building trust among those participating.
2. Structure interaction.	• Apply the evaluator's dozen of interactive strategies to structure productive interaction and participation in evaluation studies.
3. Examine context.	• Apply interactive strategies with appropriate others to examine the context and setting of the evaluation study for effective decision making.
4. Consider politics.	• Apply interactive strategies with appropriate others to examine the political landscape, anticipate challenges, and problem solve issues.
5. Expect conflict.	• Systematically apply cooperative interactive strategies to establish the social foundation for dealing with conflict constructively when it occurs. • Recognize that cooperative interactive strategies invite diverse perspectives that may create tension; trust the power of positive interdependence for creating conditions for constructive outcomes. • Cooperation and conflict are not exclusive; although the interactive strategies purposely structure cooperation, individuals will bring divergent views to the process.
6. Respect culture.	• Appreciate how cooperative interactive strategies structure inclusion, value all voices, and capitalize on diversity for optimal decision making. • Recognize cultural/ethnic values and/or norms that support (or frustrate) the underlying cooperative intent of the interactive strategies.
7. Take time.	• Consider time needed to facilitate interactive strategies; some demand more time than others. Apply strategies thoughtfully in light of what each can accomplish and the time needed for success. • Recognize and appreciate the "strategy-versus-time" trade-off; interactive strategies may take time but can produce big payoffs for effective evaluation decision making, implementation, capacity building, and commitment to using results.

SOURCE: © 2010 Jean A. King & Laurie Stevahn.

collaborative endeavors—the 13 strategies get participants personally involved, with the substance of evaluation and with one another. Here positive interdependence plays a pivotal role as conversations and tasks are specifically structured as common goals to be accomplished, reinforced when roles and resources are arranged in interconnected ways. Jointly examining context and considering politics becomes part of that shared work. When conflict occurs, as it will, these strategies intentionally create the infrastructure to deal with it cooperatively. Remember that cooperative relationships likely to result from consistent use of these strategies will tend to influence those with disagreements to want to problem solve mutually rather than "win" at the expense of others. Respecting culture also requires seeking and valuing all voices, a hallmark of these strategies. Finally, although facilitating interactive strategies does take time—and we acknowledge the trade-offs inherent in deciding to devote time to using them—we encourage evaluators to make those decisions in light of other valued outcomes, such as commitment to using a study's results that becomes more probable when people have been involved in various aspects of evaluation practice. Again, in our opinion, it is essential that evaluators *make* time to engage stakeholders appropriately in planning and conducting evaluations. The interactive strategies in this chapter are vehicles for doing just that.

CHAPTER REVIEW

This chapter began by briefly reviewing the rationale for interactive practice, detailed in Exhibit 5.1. We then introduced directions for 13 interactive strategies—facilitation techniques—that evaluators can use to involve stakeholders in the evaluation process. The chapter includes a detailed example to demonstrate how one evaluator used some of the strategies over the course of a yearlong study.

1. The reason evaluators should interact with clients and other stakeholders is that such interactions help promote ownership of the evaluation process and its outcomes and increase the likelihood that those involved will use its results. Initial agreements between evaluators and clients/primary intended users may require mutual engagement before, during, and even after a study.

2. Exhibit 5.2 presents four broad purposes for the use of interactive strategies: (a) promoting positive interpersonal relations, (b) developing shared understandings, (c) prioritizing and finalizing decisions, and (d) assessing evaluation progress.

3. Evaluators can use the interactive strategies at every stage of an evaluation study, beginning to end. Exhibit 5.3 notes those that are especially useful and adaptable across the basic inquiry tasks.

4. There are three levels of possible involvement in evaluations: (a) responding or reacting to existing information, (b) generating new information, and (c) organizing or synthesizing information for future use. Exhibit 5.4 highlights which interactive strategies are useful for each level.

5. There are three practical considerations for using the facilitation strategies: (a) time available (see Exhibit 5.5), (b) essential resources and preparation (see Exhibit 5.6), and (c) required level of facilitation skill.

6. Each of the strategies has likely outcomes, advantages, disadvantages, and most useful applications, which are summarized in Exhibit 5.7.

6

MANAGING CONFLICT CONSTRUCTIVELY IN EVALUATION SETTINGS

Chapter Preview

- Define conflict and learn to recognize it in evaluation practice
- Introduce two theoretical frameworks to guide strategic choices in conflict situations: *conflict strategies theory* and *constructive conflict resolution theory*
- Discuss the importance of establishing cooperative relationships for dealing with conflict
- Describe integrative negotiation and how to apply it in evaluation settings
- Present and illustrate conflict competencies and how evaluators can use them in practice
- Apply the interactive evaluation practice principles to managing conflict constructively

INTRODUCTION

What comes to mind when you think of conflict in evaluation practice? Perhaps you remember a prolonged argument with a colleague—stemming from deeply ingrained philosophical differences—over the best methods to use in a large-scale, high-stakes project. Maybe you recall the anger you felt when a program director failed to communicate organizational policy changes in a timely manner, putting original data collection plans in jeopardy. Or possibly you are reminded of a collaborative evaluation in which project staff consistently failed to follow through with their tasks, each time assuming that you, as evaluator, could and would do whatever was necessary to get the job done. Sometimes organizational structures unexpectedly shift or individuals block evaluation progress, creating conflict for those involved. Change also creates conditions ripe for interpersonal or intergroup conflict in evaluation settings, as when administrators unexpectedly assign new tasks that disrupt familiar or comfortable staff routines, program providers eager for continuous improvement collide with less enthusiastic coworkers, or departments clash when resources reallocated for evaluations threaten to affect cherished programs or services. Regardless of people's good intentions, conflict inevitably will occur, and evaluators should be ready.

In this chapter we discuss ways evaluators can manage conflict constructively. We begin by defining conflict. We then briefly present two theoretical frameworks that underpin positive approaches to resolving conflict: *conflict strategies theory* (Johnson & Johnson, 2009) and *constructive conflict resolution theory* (Deutsch, 1973, 2006). Each of these reinforces the foundational significance of *social interdependence theory* presented in Chapter 3 by highlighting the positive role of cooperative relationships in conflict. These theories also reveal two sets of skills useful for managing conflict constructively. These skill sets involve (a) structuring cooperative goals among those carrying out evaluation tasks and (b) negotiating for mutual problem solving when conflict occurs. From these theories and skill sets, we then present five competencies evaluators and organizational leaders can master to proactively and productively weather the interpersonal storms that routinely surface as evaluations unfold. We conclude by discussing how the interactive evaluation practice (IEP) principles apply to handling conflict in evaluation settings.

RECOGNIZING CONFLICT IN EVALUATION PRACTICE

Deutsch's (1973) classic definition of **conflict** has stood the test of time: "A *conflict* exists whenever *incompatible* activities occur" (p. 10; emphasis in original). Incompatible activities are those that block, delay, or prevent the accomplishment of goals. Such activities often hinder effective evaluation practice. Consider the following scenarios:

- A key leader who is the driving force behind a collaborative evaluation for continuous improvement gets a new job and leaves the organization; the director of the organization then assigns others to spearhead the process, whether or not they are equipped to take on evaluation responsibilities.

- Members of a community of color whose voices are essential to assessing the effectiveness of a multisite program feel uncomfortable coming to the administrative office where focus-group sessions are scheduled; so, by and large, they don't participate. This dismays those conducting the evaluation and compromises the quality of results.
- An external evaluator fails to discuss a change in the sampling plan with the organization's lead internal evaluator prior to launching a major survey to determine the future of one of the organization's long-standing, yet recently struggling, programs; anger erupts and mistrust ensues.
- Line staff, feeling overwhelmed with what is already on their professional plates, do not respond to phone or electronic messages from evaluators and department leaders because they fear more tasks will be added to their heavy workloads; this obstructs progress and annoys evaluation steering committee members who are being pressured by sponsors to produce results.

Conflicts are inevitable in human interaction, which makes them unavoidable in evaluation practice. Conflicts such as those above are merely representations of wide-ranging possibilities that can fluctuate over time. For example, people enthusiastic about evaluation efforts at one point may lose interest when they discover plans have been altered or if the timeline stretches too far into the future. Others, seeing prospects for better meeting clients' needs, may get fired up as a study progresses.

Regardless of the issue or who takes part, every conflict holds the potential to disrupt, derail, or abruptly halt evaluation efforts. Whether that happens depends on how those involved respond. Fear, anger, and frustration can trigger defensive reactions that lead to win–lose outcomes, destructive actions, and the potential for long-term bitterness. Working to understand diverse perspectives, appreciate underlying interests, and develop mutually favorable solutions, however, can lead to win–win outcomes that enhance evaluation efforts and support positive relationships.

Evaluators who manage conflict constructively do so with intention. They create a climate conducive to positive conflict—yes, there is such a thing—by structuring cooperative relations whenever people meet to engage in evaluation conversations or work on evaluation tasks. They observe the interpersonal dynamics that unfold and recognize, name, and appropriately confront conflicts that occur. They understand alternative responses to conflict and the likely effects of each. They apply and model integrative negotiation skills to resolve problems mutually. They also assist coworkers and clients in using these skills so everyone can benefit.

THEORETICAL FRAMEWORKS FOR
CONSTRUCTIVE CONFLICT RESOLUTION

Two theories from social psychology, each solidly supported by empirical research (see Deutsch, 1973, 2006; Johnson & Johnson, 2009; Pruitt & Carnevale, 1993), provide insights into the dynamics of conflict. Both theories emphasize the importance of relationships in determining the course of interpersonal conflict and especially how that course either enables or impedes evaluation efforts.

Conflict Strategies Theory

When conflict occurs, how do those involved respond? Do they demand their way? Flee to avoid thorny issues and aggravated opponents? Appease in the interest of harmony? Strike a deal to get part of what they want? Problem solve to satisfy everyone? **Conflict strategies theory** (Johnson & Johnson, 2009) outlines these five responses (see Exhibit 6.1). Basically, people face two types of concerns in conflict situations: (a) achieving desired goals/interests and (b) maintaining positive working relationships. Placing these dual concerns on intersecting continua from *low* to *high* importance suggests five strategies for addressing conflict.

Forcing means achieving one's own goals at the expense of others'. Relationships don't matter; self-interest does. Like opponents struggling against each other during a chess match, one person's winning requires another's defeat. Someone loses, and relationships often suffer. A department leader, for example, who suddenly mandates an evaluation in the interest of program improvement, regardless of its likely effect on staff and clients, may create organizational dysfunction as angry people focus their energy on circumventing the study.

Withdrawing means giving up one's personal goals and positive relationships with others. It is a natural reaction to forcing. The person's actions say, literally, "I'm out of here." Neither self-interest in the goal nor relationships matter. Hiding or running away to avoid conflict resolves nothing, making everyone a loser. An evaluation team member, for example, who repeatedly misses meetings and refuses to respond to voice mail, text messages, or e-mail simultaneously blocks progress and creates mistrust.

Smoothing means giving up one's personal goals to maintain positive relationships with others at the highest level possible. Appeasing may satisfy others, but it requires sacrificing self-interest. In an evaluation context, an evaluator

Exhibit 6.1   Conflict Strategies Theory (see Johnson & Johnson, 2009)

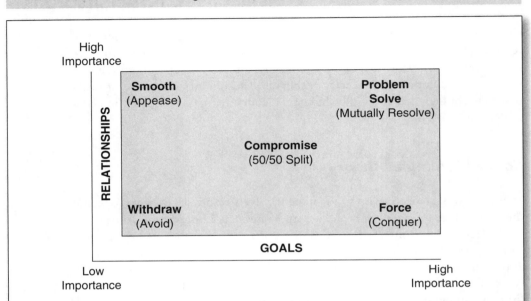

SOURCE: Adapted from Johnson and Johnson (2005b, p. 4:2). Used with permission.

may smile and willingly agree to requests from the sponsor, not expressing misgivings or desired alternatives. This concern about the tension or discomfort of expressing objections and different strategies, however, may ultimately result in insufficient funding for the proposed study.

Compromising means using give-and-take to create a 50/50 split when someone's personal goals and relationships with others are both moderately important. Seeing the benefits of partial gain, people decide to settle for something, which seems better than getting nothing. In a large-scale assessment, for example, an evaluator may agree to include different items on an agency's intake form in exchange for new data-entry procedures.

Problem solving means cooperative negotiation aimed at maximizing joint outcomes. Both self-interest and relationships with others matter. Whether fully realized or not, this is the case when individuals have long-term relationships with one another, such as at work, within community programs/organizations, or among family members. When people consider everyone's interests, they often can create integrative solutions so everyone benefits. Such results make everyone winners. For example, if evaluation data documented that a food bank was turning away neighborhood residents while serving people from other zip codes, integrative negotiation might lead to a new system that guaranteed local clients access and others either access or assistance in reaching nearby sources of free food.

Conflict is fraught with complexity, but conflict strategies theory—the dual-concerns model, with its equal and paradoxical priorities of maximizing self-interest and maintaining good working relationships—provides a helpful lens through which to assess it. When people force their way during a conflict ("My way or the highway") or when they withdraw to avoid the situation ("I won't talk about it"), little hope exists for constructive outcomes. In the context of evaluation practice, progress will surely suffer, if not totally stop.

Wise evaluators recognize that competence in successfully navigating conflict requires skill in using all five strategies. When principles or values matter deeply, it may be in one's best interest to stand respectful but firm (force) or to exit gracefully (withdraw) from unworkable situations. Doing so, however, may jeopardize future relationships with colleagues and, for external evaluators, future contracts. If people hope to work with others over time, finding ways to problem solve for mutual gain usually produces the most constructive outcomes and positive working relationships. Later in this chapter we will discuss specific competencies for doing this, but now we consider how mutual problem solving—also called **integrative negotiation** when dealing with conflict—is enhanced when people perceive their positive interdependence in achieving meaningful cooperative goals.

Constructive Conflict Resolution Theory

Deutsch's (1973, 2006) **constructive conflict resolution theory** is a second framework for thinking about interpersonal conflict. It illuminates the dynamics of conflict by describing and reliably predicting how cooperative versus competitive goals influence behaviors among individuals in conflict situations (see Exhibit 6.2). Conflict resolution theory originated from social interdependence theory (discussed in Chapter 3; see Deutsch, 1949a, 1949b, 2006; Johnson & Johnson, 1989, 2005a, 2009), and research on it suggests cooperative goals link individuals in positively interdependent relationships, creating situations in which people need one another to succeed. By contrast, competitive goals link individuals in negatively interdependent relationships, creating situations in which people can succeed or win only when others fail or lose. Constructive conflict resolution theory holds that underlying existing goal structures among individuals or groups in conflict situations (cooperative or competitive) influence interpersonal or intergroup interactions (promotive/responsive or oppositional/obstructive), which in turn determine the resolution of the conflict (constructive or destructive).

Simply put, individuals' responses to conflict tend to vary according to their degree of investment in one another's success. Mutual problem solving (similar to cooperative problem solving in the dual-concerns model) may occur when people perceive that each person's individual success depends on the success of the entire group, and vice versa. In a program evaluation, for example, if members of the data analysis team perceive that they truly need the unique perspectives and skills of all team members to complete the job successfully, as when the skills of both quantitative and qualitative experts are required, it makes more sense to engage in problem-solving behavior when conflicts arise. However, if success is defined competitively, as when a special privilege or monetary bonus will be awarded to the person in the group who completes his or her data analysis task first, those involved will be unlikely to engage

Exhibit 6.2   Constructive Conflict Resolution Theory (see Deutsch, 1973)

Cooperative (characterized by positive interdependence)	*Promotive/ Responsive* (problem solving for mutual benefit)	*Constructive* (win–win)
Goal Structure	**Interaction**	**Outcome**
Competitive (characterized by negative interdependence)	*Oppositional/ Obstructive* (concession seeking for exclusive benefit)	*Destructive* (win–lose)

SOURCE: From Stevahn and King (2005, p. 419).

constructively if interpersonal conflicts occur. Relationships matter, and cooperative goals or tasks that require mutual commitment and support for everyone's success tend to develop caring relationships, even if only instrumental, that lead to constructive interactions and outcomes.

Experimental and correlational research conducted over many decades indicates that goals structured cooperatively (vs. competitively) result in friendlier and more trusting attitudes among individuals, increased sensitivity to common interests, more open and honest communication of relevant information, and greater responsiveness to one another's needs (Deutsch, 1973, 2006). These qualities are essential for dealing with conflict constructively. Knowing how goal structures affect human interaction enables evaluators to better analyze situational contexts of organizations and programs, especially noticing cooperative and competitive activities and intentionally structuring positive interdependence into evaluation tasks when working with others. Knowledge of goal structures also provides grounding for realistic action; evaluators who attempt to facilitate problem solving in competitive contexts will likely fail as individuals vie for personal gain at others' expense.

SKILLS FOR CONSTRUCTIVE CONFLICT RESOLUTION

Theoretical frameworks are helpful for decision making and reflection in conflict situations, but successful action requires skills. Two critical skill sets highlight the evaluator's ability to (a) structure cooperative goals and tasks in evaluation practice and (b) negotiate for mutual gain when conflict occurs. Mastering these skills requires training, practice, reflection, and refinement. Here we outline key practical components.

Structure Cooperative Goals

Cooperative contexts set the stage for managing conflicts constructively. One of the most important skills for establishing such environments, therefore, is the ability to structure positive interdependence into social situations, including evaluation tasks. Doing so builds the capacity for productive working relationships grounded in a sense of trust and commitment. Such relationships tend to motivate participants to problem solve disagreements in mutually satisfying ways rather than pursuing less productive responses when conflict occurs. Where such relationships are lacking, the evaluator's challenge increases, and he must add trust building to the "to-do" list. Although the frequency of interaction among participants varies in any given evaluation (potentially more continuous for those actively involved throughout), each interaction provides an opportunity for examining how existing goals are structured among people and for creating conditions that nurture and support cooperative foundations.

You will recall that IEP is the intentional act of engaging people in making decisions, taking action, and reflecting while conducting an evaluation study. Cooperative goals and relationships tend to underpin successful efforts. People often assume—sometimes mistakenly—that individuals will naturally collaborate when gathered to work on a project. Why wouldn't they? But whether this collaboration occurs largely depends on how individuals perceive the goal and what is needed to accomplish it. If goal accomplishment is structured so everyone must contribute ideas, effort, skills, experience, and resources to complete the job successfully, then collaboration is more likely. Motivation to interact cooperatively and support one another in carrying out a task also tends to increase when everyone knows rewards will be mutual and apportioned fairly—that is, everyone on the team will receive a desired bonus or perk for success or no one will be rewarded if the group falls short of its goal. Structuring positive interdependence into interactive purposes and basic inquiry tasks (see Chapter 5, Exhibits 5.2 and 5.3) helps create such a culture of mutuality in evaluation studies. In fact, evaluators can think of positive interdependence as a tool for structuring engagement in ways that will require collaborative interaction for success, thereby nurturing cooperative relationships.

Positive interdependence can be structured into almost any group task, including evaluation activities. Whether framing or designing a study with program staff, collecting or analyzing data with colleagues, interpreting findings with organizational leaders, crafting recommendations with an advisory group, or reporting results to sponsors, evaluators often become facilitators of interaction among those involved. The key is to arrange tasks so everyone's contributions will be perceived as interconnected and necessary for success. The evaluator should start by establishing and emphasizing a common goal—for example, to understand comprehensively the interests of program leaders, staff, clients, and funders; to reach consensus on one set of evaluation questions that address the interests of multiple stakeholders; to agree on a strategic yet feasible sampling strategy representative of the larger population; or to develop one set of data-derived recommendations viable for taking action—then arrange procedures, materials, roles, and incentives in ways that foster coordinated efforts. The evaluator can designate separate yet interconnected roles/jobs, supply shared sets of materials/resources, and provide team rewards/celebrations for successful accomplishment of mutual goals. Arrangements such as these highlight the interdependence among participants, providing incentive for them to engage with one another in ways that will produce effective teamwork. For example, evaluators working with a non-profit agency examining a newly created leadership training program might develop five distinct roles for those on the evaluation advisory committee: manager/task coordinator, survey manager, interview manager, data analyst, and report developer. Although everyone will work together on all tasks, each person will have specific and interconnected responsibilities for getting the evaluation done.

More than half the 13 interactive strategies presented in Chapter 5 structurally establish strong or moderately strong positive interdependence among participants (see Exhibit 6.3). The distinguishing factor is the extent to which an activity requires cooperative interaction from everyone to achieve its aims or whether individuals working alone can successfully complete the activity. Although the strategies with slight positive interdependence may be less influential in building perceptions of "I need you and you need me" among participants, when used to evoke disclosure of personally meaningful perspectives, past experiences, or unique characteristics, those strategies can also stir interest, motivate involvement, and engage people in ways that create a positive social environment—the type of environment that seeks and honors all voices, which is needed for constructive conflict.

Positive interdependence in interactive strategies can almost always be strengthened by emphasizing the need for total involvement (making full participation the common goal for shared success), celebrating constructive participation with joint rewards (special refreshments for everyone), building in sequences for input (person-by-person contributions), arranging small groups to process results (mutually discuss and agree on what the input means), keeping groups small (it's hard to get left out of a pair), and rotating roles (taking turns recording input, managing group materials, or presenting the final team product). The point is that by consistently using strategies that highlight people's connectedness and common interests, evaluators help establish the types of cooperative relationships conducive to managing conflicts constructively when they occur. Like enriched soil that enables seeds to weather an occasionally harsh environment and flourish, relationships will be more likely to grow through conflict in healthy ways if a supportive social infrastructure exists for doing so.

Using strategies in evaluation practice that nurture cooperative relationships and build interpersonal trust is part of creating that infrastructure. In one

Exhibit 6.3   Interactive Strategies and Positive Interdependence

Positive Interdependence	Interactive Strategies (presented in Chapter 5)	Ways to Increase Positive Interdependence
Strong	4. Cooperative Interviews 8. Jigsaw 9. Graffiti/Carousel 10. Concept Formation 11. Cooperative Rank Order	Clearly articulate the common goal. Keep groups small (two or three people). Assign different but needed roles to all group members; emphasize interconnectedness for success. Arrange a sequence of interlocking steps such as rotating roles. Subdivide materials and tasks that will need to be recombined/reconnected to complete the whole. Designate a distinct workspace for each team. Provide desired or fun mutual rewards/incentives for team success. Brainstorm what teammates have in common as a "getting-to-know-you" warm-up prior to jointly working on evaluation tasks.
Moderate	3. Choosing Corners 5. Round-Robin Check-In 7. Data Dialogue	State that the mutual goal is for everyone to contribute; define success as everyone offering an idea, perspective, or comment. *Choosing Corners:* Participants pair up with one other person in their corner (pairs interact within each corner to maximize participation). *Check-In:* Systematically seek input person by person adjacent around the room or form small groups for clockwise round-robin input. *Data Dialogue:* Keep groups small (three or four people); use clockwise round-robin for contributions; rotate the role of scribe among group members.
Slight	1. Voicing Variables 2. Voicing Viewpoints/Beliefs 6. Making Metaphors 12. Fist to Five 13. Dot Votes/Bar Graphs	Frame the mutual goal as everyone contributing; define success as total participation; emphasize the need for all voices, perceptions, viewpoints. Emphasize how all input will be used in synthesis or analysis activities that follow. Form small groups of two or three people; instruct these groups to discuss and reach agreement on the meaning of the input. Focus on drawing mutual conclusions following individualistic input.

SOURCE: © 2010 Laurie Stevahn.

large social service agency, for example, members of the "Evaluation Platoon" (so named to make it more exciting than a committee) routinely engaged small subgroups to get tasks done and the larger group in discussions of progress, rotating the role of leader to build internal evaluation capacity for the organization and celebrating the completion of every step of their many evaluation tasks. With visible envy, other staff members began to comment on how much fun Platoon members seemed to be having. Platoon membership eventually expanded to include anyone interested in participating.

Negotiate for Mutual Gain

Individuals or groups must negotiate to resolve disagreements. The interactive process of negotiation, however, may have as its base either competitive or cooperative relations—or combinations of both. As described previously, different goal orientations tend to affect interactions and outcomes. Competitive situations fuel *distributive negotiations* in which disputants try to maximize personal outcomes at the expense of others. As with forcing in the dual-concerns model, people put themselves or their group's interests first; they are out to win. Numerous strategies and tactics for negotiating competitively exist and have been widely published (see Johnson & Johnson, 2009; Lewicki, Saunders, & Barry, 2010; Pruitt & Carnevale, 1993). The interactions in such settings often become win–lose battles as each side tries to defeat the other by coercing concessions.

Consider, for example, the sad conclusion of a community center's evaluation of its youth programming. Interview and survey data from longtime community members led the Evaluation Steering Committee to discuss a recommendation to reinstate the center's Cub Scout troop, once a vital source of outdoor experiences and leadership training for neighborhood boys. Although the national policy of the Boy Scouts of America prohibited the involvement of gay leaders, the local Scout council policy, at odds with the national, was openly inclusive. Nevertheless, two members of the committee, active in GLBT (gay, lesbian, bisexual, and transgender) circles, reacted emotionally. Without consulting the evaluator or any of the center's leaders, they wrote and widely broadcast copies of a harshly worded e-mail message condemning the evaluation process as anti-inclusion and a direct attack against GLBT center members. At their request, a spokesperson for a local antidiscrimination group got involved, demanding to know why the community center was moving to support a noninclusive organization. Efforts to engage the two committee members in conversation about the situation and their actions were unsuccessful; they were unwilling to entertain the possibility of what they considered a hateful recommendation.

Needless to say, the evaluation process halted, and, given the mistrust and enmity the actions of the two had fostered, the group was unable to develop recommendations and complete the study.

By contrast, cooperative situations fuel *integrative negotiations* in which people seek to understand one another's underlying interests and maximize everyone's outcomes. These negotiations engage disputants in mutual problem solving for joint benefits (like cooperative problem solving in the dual-concerns model). Successful cooperative negotiations typically require the following skills and steps (see Brett, 2007; Fisher, Ury, & Patton, 1991; Johnson, 1967; Johnson & Johnson, 2005b, 2009; Lewicki et al., 2010; Stevahn & King, 2005):

- Expressing cooperative intentions
- Mutually defining the conflict
- Stating wants
- Expressing feelings
- Explaining underlying reasons/interests
- Reversing perspectives to communicate understanding
- Generating multiple integrative solutions that attend to all interests
- Reaching agreement on a mutual solution
- Processing the effectiveness of the problem solving

The importance of developing expertise in integrative negotiation, along with other relevant interpersonal skills such as communication, group facilitation, group processing, teamwork/collaboration, and intercultural competence (see Stevahn, King, Ghere, & Minnema, 2005), becomes clear as we realize two things: (a) Conflicts are unavoidable when interacting with others, and (b) they can have value when resolved constructively. For example, conflicts can signal the need for changes in policies or practices, result in creative solutions that increase everyone's well-being, lead to greater productivity and achievement, strengthen trust, enhance caring, reinforce commitment, and boost confidence in resolving issues skillfully (Johnson & Johnson, 2009). Evaluators can influence such outcomes by mastering the skills of integrative negotiation and using them intentionally. Imagine what might happen when the head of an organization wants to shorten the timeline of an evaluation to ensure that its results can be included in a sizeable foundation grant submission. Exhibit 6.4 provides a scenario depicting what the steps of integrative negotiation might sound like in this situation.

Exhibit 6.4   Integrative Negotiation Scenario: "Speed It Up!"

Steps	Evaluator	Program Director
1. *Confront the conflict* and express cooperative intentions.	"Thanks for meeting with me today. I'd like to talk with you about the new evaluation timeline you requested yesterday. I'm concerned the truncated schedule puts the evaluation at risk. I care about making this evaluation work for all of us, and I'm hopeful we can problem solve this situation together."	"Of course; let's talk. I have some concerns, too."
2. *State what you want.*	"I want to conduct a high-quality evaluation that produces credible results useful for future decision making."	"I want the results of this evaluation sooner to be eligible to apply for a large foundation grant."
3. *Express how you feel.*	"I feel stressed. I'm unsure whether I can collect and analyze all the data in time. I'm afraid this new timeline will affect the quality of the results and blemish my integrity as an evaluator."	"I'm anxious because we just got notice of an opportunity to qualify for a sizeable amount of additional funding, provided we can show that the program is making a positive impact. I'm under a lot of pressure to expand program services, which will require a bigger budget."
4. *Explain your reasons.*	"The new timeline will necessitate eliminating the collection of some data. If shortcuts in this evaluation produce questionable results—because of inadequate or unrepresentative data sources—my reputation may be tarnished. My livelihood depends on future clients trusting I can produce credible and actionable findings. Integrity is huge for me; it's my name on the final report, and I take responsibility for what's in it. I also rely on my good reputation as an evaluator for obtaining future work. I don't want to lose that."	"My job depends on how well the program serves our clients and on the number of clients served. I need to find additional funds to be able to meet annual targets that increase each year. The opportunity to apply for a long-term grant of this magnitude may not come again for a long time. The grant requires recent data on program effectiveness. Moving the schedule up is imperative for being able to apply—and my boss has made it clear that applying is a must."

(Continued)

Exhibit 6.4 (Continued)

Steps	Evaluator	Program Director
5. *Reverse perspectives* by communicating your understanding of the other person's wants, feelings, reasons.	"I understand you want to secure additional funds that could significantly increase the services provided by your program. The stakes are high, and you want to act quickly before this great opportunity passes. You're also feeling pressure from your boss; you're trying to comply."	"You're experiencing anxiety about the possibility of ending up with unusable results. Your integrity is on the line; you feel responsible to ensure a credible process, and you're worried about whether you will be able to secure future evaluation contracts if that is compromised."
6. *Generate solutions* that benefit everyone.	A. "We could use the data dialogue strategy instead of conducting individual interviews." B. "We could hold off on interviewing and instead finish the survey, report those results immediately, then complete the remainder of the evaluation according to the original timeline."	C. "We could assign additional program staff to help with data collection and analysis." D. "We could secure another professional evaluator to assist." E. "We could hire a temp to prepare the data tables and type the final report."
7. *Mutually agree* on one solution.	"Let's focus on the survey first; it should provide credible evidence on program impact. I also will welcome some assistance with preparing this interim report."	"Sounds good. I'll ask my personal assistant to help. I can use the survey results now for the grant application, then look forward to the entire evaluation report when due."

SOURCE: © 2010 Laurie Stevahn.

CONFLICT COMPETENCIES FOR EVALUATORS

Philosopher John Dewey once noted, "Conflict is the gadfly of thought." Indeed, conflict can quickly open our eyes to interpersonal and political tensions that hold the potential to affect an evaluation. Understanding conflict theories and developing conflict competencies, therefore, can equip evaluators with tools to think about conflict and increase their ability to address it. First, with an eye for conflict, they can better analyze the social context of organizations or programs contemplating or conducting evaluation studies. Second, they can better identify people's responses to conflict and devise appropriate ways to deal with these behaviors. Third, when conflict occurs, they can facilitate and participate in resolving it constructively. Fourth, they can establish project, program, or organizational norms for managing conflict by structuring tasks that promote cooperative relationships. Fifth, they can better reflect on their own reactions and responses in conflict situations. In the pages that follow, we briefly elaborate on each of these.

Analyze the Social Context

Equipped with a conceptual understanding of conflict and skills for managing it constructively, evaluators can effectively analyze the conflict landscape of an organization or program. Just as analyzing the political context helps an evaluator decide if conducting a study will be feasible, examining the nature, frequency, and patterns of cooperation and conflict within the organization or program also reveals valuable information. Both external evaluators (who serve as outside sources to organizations/programs) and internal evaluators (who work full-time in an organization or program) can benefit from habitually asking questions about (a) existing goal structures within the evaluation setting, (b) the breadth and depth of cooperative interaction among individuals in that setting, and (c) how those individuals respond to conflict. Questions to guide such analyses follow, along with Exhibit 6.5, which holistically describes what evaluators might observe in cooperative versus competitive (and/or individualistic) evaluation settings.

Goal Structures

What types of goal structures predominantly exist within the organization or program? When and where do people work cooperatively, competitively, or individually? To what extent does the organization or program value cooperative efforts and mutual problem solving? How does the organization or program encourage, support, and reward such efforts? What are the mutual goals to which everyone is committed? To what extent is mutual problem solving a way of life? What rules, routines, and norms support cooperative interaction and constructive conflict resolution?

Cooperative Interaction

What tasks within the organization or program require people to coordinate their ideas, resources, and energy to be successful? Do cooperative tasks have well-defined mutual goals? Are teams rewarded for success? What types of incentives make individuals want to work together? How do individuals benefit from working together? What motivates cooperative behavior within the organization or program? What types of tangible incentives or rewards exist for collaborative work? How do people coordinate their efforts? Do the physical work space and arrangement of desks, tables, or other furniture promote or block cooperative interaction?

Conflict Situations

What types of conflicts occur in the organization or program? How do people respond? Do they predominantly force, withdraw, smooth, compromise, or problem solve? What communication patterns unfold in conflict situations? To what extent do people hold positive attitudes toward resolving conflict? Do individuals express cooperative intentions for mutual problem solving when conflicts occur? Do leaders model and use constructive conflict procedures?

Exhibit 6.5   Analyzing the Social Context of the Evaluation Setting

Analysis	Organization A: Cooperative	Organization B: Competitive/Individualistic
Goal Structures	• The mission statement includes/ emphasizes teamwork, mutual commitment to shared goals, cooperative processes and outcomes, and constructive conflict resolution. • Cooperative values are evident in the organization's motto, tagline, logo/ symbols, wall displays, websites, newsletters, and so on. • The organizational chart shows collaborative interaction among divisions, departments, work units; interdivisional or interdepartmental projects are common. • Physical work space promotes teamwork; desks are clustered (or face one another) in one room; designated collective work space is centrally located, inviting, and regularly used; "open-door" policies prevail. • Staff meetings include interpersonal and/ or small-group interaction, team reports, and shared facilitation; input is elicited from organizational members, and discussion is encouraged.	• The mission statement does not include/ emphasize collaboration to "get the job done"; mainly focuses on products/ services provided to clients; emphasizes individualistic efforts or competitive practices for success. • The organization's motto, tagline, logo/ symbols, wall displays, websites, newsletters, and so on focus on products/ services to clients or highlight competitive (or individualistic) efforts/values; references to teamwork are absent. • The organizational chart shows divisions/departments as separate entities that do not intersect/interact. • Physical work space isolates individuals; workers complete tasks in cubicles or in separate rooms; "closed-door" policies exist; common meeting spaces do not exist. • Staff meetings are conducted by one person who provides information; theater-style seating; little (if any) interaction (most involves seeking clarification from the presenter).

Analysis	Organization A: Cooperative	Organization B: Competitive/Individualistic
	• Policies, procedures, rules, and routines place a high priority on team projects, cooperative interaction, and shared decision making; rewards are shared (e.g., team bonuses, celebrations, or perks for achieving common goals). • Promotions are linked to successful teamwork and group problem solving. • The organization's strategic plan focuses on collaborative initiatives/efforts; budgets provide resources for collaborative projects and support teamwork.	• Policies, procedures, rules, and routines place a high priority on individual performance, especially in comparison to others (trophy cases highlight the "employee of the month," top sales associate, most productive worker, best innovative idea, and so forth). • Promotions or pay raises are linked to individual performance/accomplishment and/or to outperforming others (competitive achievements).
Cooperative Interaction	• Organizational members regularly and positively work together on tasks, and enjoy it. • Daily work schedules involve numerous meetings/gatherings for collective work or decision making. • People feel safe interacting and trust one another; people willingly and regularly seek and share knowledge, information, resources, and needed skills within team projects or across divisions, departments, or work units. • People express that they value teamwork, give numerous examples of how this happens in the workplace, and talk about how they benefit from collaboration. • A social/interpersonal climate of caring exists; colleagues promote mutual success.	• Most work assignments/jobs are individualistic or competitive; organizational members rarely (if ever) interact with one another to complete tasks. • Daily work schedules reflect individualistic or competitive efforts; each individual works separately and apart from others; little interpersonal interaction occurs. • A climate of distrust (or fear) characterizes the workplace; people do not ask for help or assistance; people do not share ideas or resources with one another. • People express that they value independent work and/or are motivated by competition for personal advancement or rewards.
Conflict Situations	• People view conflicts as a normal part of life and embrace policies and procedures for constructively and routinely managing them. • The organization provides conflict training, and everyone is expected to participate; common conflict policies, knowledge, language, and procedures exist within the organization.	• People view conflicts as something negative to be eliminated from life. • People predominantly force (to win) or withdraw (to avoid) conflicts. • The organization does not provide conflict training, nor are policies in place for managing conflict in healthy ways; people are on their own when it comes to dealing with conflict.

(Continued)

Exhibit 6.5 (Continued)

Analysis	Organization A: Cooperative	Organization B: Competitive/Individualistic
	• Mechanisms are built into "how we do business around here" for regularly expressing concerns and resolving differences mutually; all meetings routinely devote time to people airing concerns, considering alternative points of view, and problem solving together. • People use language that reveals a desire for mutually agreeable solutions to conflicts or disagreements. • People listen carefully to others' points of view (interests, desires, feelings, reasons) and communicate understanding. • Leaders model the way by showing others what constructive conflict looks and sounds like by using integrative negotiation and mediating conflicts among organizational members; leaders consistently engage in social perspective taking to understand diverse points of view (whether or not in conflict). • People trust one another's best intentions by first seeking clarification when disagreements, conflicts, or tensions arise (rather than assuming the worst). • People confront conflict/disagreements/ tensions in ways that maintain the dignity of everyone and lead to mutual problem solving. • People recognize that conflict (despite its discomfort) can be a positive catalyst for learning, improvement, and change. • External professional mediators are hired to facilitate constructive conflict resolution if serious and/or intense conflicts surface.	• Mechanisms and/or procedures do not exist for expressing concerns or dealing with disagreements/tensions constructively. • People immediately blame others in conflict situations; people "point fingers" at one another, which fuels continued anger/hostility and further escalates the conflict. • Anger is volatile; people openly raise their voices, yell at one another, or storm out of the room when experiencing conflict. • Individuals (or groups) in conflict each try to get their own way by getting others to make concessions ("give in" to demands). • "Turf wars" are frequent within the organization. • Organization members never (or rarely) see leaders using or modeling constructive conflict resolution skills; instead, leaders deal with conflicts privately in ways unknown; leaders consistently arbitrate (rather than mediate) conflicts among organizational members or groups. • Assumptions go unnamed; rumors or speculations abound; misinformation and/or misunderstandings are frequent. • People do not feel safe sharing wants, feelings, or reasons in conflict situations; people are not honest when sharing for fear personal information divulged will be used against them. • When conflict occurs, people stay silent.

SOURCE: © 2005 Laurie Stevahn & Jean A. King.

Recognize Conflict Behaviors

Evaluation activities can create conflicts for people even when they willingly participate. Whether simply responding to given information or actually working together to complete evaluation tasks, meetings can become a stage for drama—with individuals promoting their personal agendas or ranting about pet peeves. Because much communication takes place outside of scheduled meetings, incidents apart from meetings can also stir conflict as people chat about concerns in the lunchroom, circulate e-mail or text messages, or hold TGIF (thank goodness it's Friday) discussions after hours. In the real world of practice, individuals can work actively to deflect, slow, or sabotage evaluation progress, especially in large, multisite organizations where communication is challenging, at best, given geographic and/or social distance.

Evaluators can use the five conflict strategies in the dual-concerns model (see Exhibit 6.1) to analyze conflicts that surface during evaluation projects. Awareness of these approaches to conflict can help evaluators, as well as program staff and participants, devise appropriate responses, remembering that any of the five may be best depending on circumstances. Because one of the approaches, cooperative problem solving, facilitates positive interaction, it is typically the most constructive for dealing with interpersonal issues. It is also the approach most often pursued by individuals who want to engage one another in ways that clarify alternative perspectives to create mutually beneficial solutions. Consider, however, the other four approaches: forcing, withdrawing, smoothing, or compromising.

Forcing

The act of forcing focuses on accomplishing a personal goal at the risk of alienating people and destroying long-term relationships. Examples of forcing in evaluation practice include the following:

- The strong individual who dominates group interactions, including people with positional power (the boss, the team leader) and people with domineering personalities and abrasive interpersonal styles
- The person who generates and thrives on conflict, the naysayer, she who doesn't want to negotiate, he who opposes the action item (doesn't want resources to go to that), and that unhappy individual who lives with a negative attitude

- The person who never comes to meetings on time and disrupts what is going on by arriving loudly well after the announced start time (as if to say, "Look at me!")
- The person who hates any type of warm-up activity perceived as too "touchy-feely" and asks openly, "When do we link arms and sing 'Kumbaya'?"
- The person who needs to feel important in the group and always explains the multiple activities going on in his or her world ("Behold, I am busy!")
- The person who attends meetings sporadically or misses meetings in a random pattern so he or she never knows what is going on and has to be updated by those who do attend

Recognizing when people are seeking personal goals (getting their way, feeling important, being in control, dodging the process) allows evaluators to refocus efforts on the broader goals of the evaluation and on relationships that will be necessary for successful accomplishment. Sometimes this means meeting force with force by having someone in authority articulate norms and hold people accountable for altering their behavior. Other times it means labeling the forcing behavior so those practicing it can see its consequences and choose to change. In some cases it means ignoring the behavior but keeping a watchful eye on the situation and standing ready to intervene if destructive behavior escalates. Truly, such interventions may be more art than science. However, all evaluators can systematically focus attention on both the evaluation's overall purpose and the interpersonal relationships required for success, especially, as in work situations, when those involved are in long-term relationships with one another.

Withdrawing

If people withdraw from evaluation processes, it is difficult to move forward. Forms of withdrawing include the following:

- The person who intentionally misses every meeting, despite a requirement or expectation to attend
- The person whose body shows up but who doesn't pay attention, choosing instead to talk, text or tweet, surf the Internet, knit, read a magazine, or do something else unrelated to the discussion or the task at hand
- The quiet person who doesn't readily participate out loud in the meeting, perhaps because of a style preference, a personality trait, a cultural norm, or discomfort in the situation

Withdrawing neither achieves evaluation goals nor builds relationships. Evaluators can deal with the first two issues (those who don't show up or who do and don't participate) by letting individuals know the effects of their actions, expecting change, and encouraging compliance. People in the third category (the quiet types who seem withdrawn) present a different challenge. If they are genuinely shy or if their culture rewards silence and silent attendance, they may *appear* to be withdrawing when, in fact, they are mentally focused and engaged yet outwardly behaving in ways ingrained or comfortable. The evaluator in that case must first recognize this and then structure activities that allow everyone opportunities to participate without threatening individuals for whom meaningful involvement doesn't involve speaking publicly. The interactive strategies presented in Chapter 5 illustrate how to invite meaningful and comfortable involvement from everyone. To give one example, *Strategy 4: Cooperative Interviews* creates specific roles for every person and gives each an equal opportunity to speak in a small (and presumably less threatening) group.

Smoothing

Every organization needs people who build relationships and make others feel good about themselves and ongoing activities. They are the people who regularly bring snacks, acknowledge birthdays, write encouraging notes, and provide support during times of personal crises. Such behaviors, however, may put an evaluation at risk, if smoothing overrides substantive work that must be accomplished for success. Smoothers can derail evaluation processes. Consider these smoothing behaviors:

- The person who, having survived multiple new initiatives ("This, too, shall pass"), supports the status quo, firmly believing "it ain't broken" so why ruffle the feathers of coworkers who are friends?
- The person who avoids meaningful interaction like the plague by giggling, making jokes that detract from the issue at hand, chatting during meetings, or agreeing with anything simply to agree, thinking this is what it takes to gain approval from others
- The person who can't say no to any request ("Of course I'll help you!") but also becomes unproductive by being overcommitted, overextended, and overwhelmed

Again, when you observe these behaviors, you can label them and let people see the likely effects of their actions. You can also structure situations to encourage and support more productive behavior. For example, you can convene coworkers who are friends to discuss past disappointments with fleeting initiatives and examine the mechanisms built into this evaluation that support meaningful long-term application. You can establish and adhere to agreed-on behavior norms at meetings. You might develop and enforce workload policies to prevent overload and exhaustion. You can work with people in ways likely to make the evaluation more personally relevant—that is, help people better understand and buy into the purpose of the evaluation and its benefits from a personal perspective.

Compromising

In situations where cooperative negotiation is impossible for whatever reasons, compromise may be the most positive option evaluators can pursue. It is important to remember that, unlike the other response categories, the compromiser is at least partly willing to work toward the stated goals and to maintain relationships. Nevertheless, two kinds of compromisers may prove problematic:

- The compromiser with a tit-for-tat mentality ("If you get five, then I get five, too")
- The person who sincerely asks, "What's in it for me?" and will engage in the process only if he or she perceives an outcome of meaningful personal value

The two previous suggestions for dealing with smoothers apply here as well: Label the behavior and expect change, or engage with the individual to create a personal connection to the evaluation and its benefits. Building positive commitment may foster increased ownership of the process. Because these problematic responses seem to hold a competitive edge, it may also be helpful to remind such individuals that this is not a give-or-take contest.

These responses to obstructive behaviors and variations thereof point to the continuing challenges evaluators and program staff face in evaluation practice. Individuals may force during a meeting and then withdraw afterward if they don't get their way. Inveterate smoothers may find it impossible to move beyond muffins and warm fuzzies, knowing meaningful work will necessarily engage divergent points of view and disagreements among participants. Veteran employees who have watched innovations come and go will need some reason to believe the process and results of this evaluation are really going to enhance their lives and improve the organization. Evaluators, as well as others involved, can support constructive interactions by structuring evaluation activities for cooperative interdependence and holding individuals accountable for their roles and needed contributions. Evaluators can also teach and use integrative negotiation for mutual problem solving to manage conflicts in ways that constructively advance evaluation efforts.

Facilitate Mutual Problem Solving

Numerous factors affect conflict situations. One is the nature of the issues themselves (see Deutsch, 1973). Those that tap into deeply ingrained values (e.g., ideals, principles, ideologies) and beliefs (e.g., religious, philosophical, moral) are more challenging to resolve than those that deal with control over resources (e.g., money, space, time) or preferences (e.g., dim lights in the office, healthy snacks at meetings, a relaxed dress code on Fridays). Other factors include power relations (low vs. high), people's abilities to manage anger and control emotions, levels of trust and suspicion, ethnic and/or cultural differences/considerations, and intergroup conflicts (involving multiple parties or coalitions) versus interpersonal conflicts (concerning two or only a few individuals).

Regardless of these factors, those leading evaluation efforts can systematically guide interactions toward mutual problem solving and integrative solutions. This can take the form of actually using constructive skills when personally facing conflicts, mediating the conflicts of others, or teaching the skills of conflict management to others when appropriate. Consider this real-world evaluation conflict successfully resolved by using these skills. A foundation program officer who had commissioned an extensive evaluation called and demanded that his evaluators meet with him immediately, that day. When they arrived at his office, he spoke sternly, questioning their objectivity and attacking the study they had designed in collaboration with the fundees. Taken aback, the evaluators worked to understand the conflict. Over the course of the conversation, it became clear the program officer's intent was a summative impact evaluation of several newly funded programs. He viewed the evaluators' efforts to teach him the inappropriateness of such a study as biased—an effort to protect staff whose developing programs were weak. Thanks to integrative negotiation, the program officer and evaluators came to a solution that provided the infrastructure for an eventual impact study while gathering formative information to shape the new programs. They also established a cooperative process for addressing additional conflicts that might arise.

As the previous example shows, the actions of people can contribute to influencing the various pathways conflict will take—whether constructive or destructive—although, given the complexity of conflict, intervening actions by evaluators or evaluation participants cannot in every case guarantee success. Evaluators can, however, always keep constructive conflict in mind, intentionally and systematically working toward that aim.

Create Cooperative Norms

Evaluators can help create organizational, program, or project norms for constructive conflict resolution by structuring cooperative interaction among participants. Pragmatically, this entails repeatedly incorporating positive interdependence into evaluation interactions and tasks. Systematically applying the interactive strategies presented in Chapter 5—especially those with strong positive interdependence—is a practical way to take action. The cooperative relationships likely to develop not only promote stakeholder commitment to the evaluation; they also help build organizational infrastructure that grounds and supports problem-solving negotiation when conflicts occur.

Know Thyself

Understanding conflict theories enables evaluators to better reflect on their own reactions and responses to conflict. We all have different triggers, tolerances, and thresholds in conflict situations. Thinking about personal response patterns in relation to conflict strategies theory, for example, may help individuals become more strategic in responding. It pays to pick and choose battles, as well as how to engage in them. Evaluators can systematically choose when to problem solve, compromise, smooth, withdraw, or force by weighing dual concerns to determine the importance of each—attaining goals and maintaining positive working relationships. Better understanding these possibilities paves the way for dealing with conflicts intentionally rather than haphazardly.

APPLYING INTERACTIVE EVALUATION PRACTICE PRINCIPLES TO MANAGING CONFLICT CONSTRUCTIVELY

The English language contains multiple terms for conflict: *dispute, dissension, disagreement, controversy, strife, friction, dissonance, argument,* and *discord,* among others (Stevahn & King, 2005). These words speak of its common occurrence in human experience. People who are unable or who refuse to engage in dialogue, casting their competing values only in shades of black and white, will never find mutual solutions. Although conflicts typically are complex, the theories presented in this chapter, along with skills that promote positive outcomes, are supported by an abundance of empirical evidence. As Exhibit 6.6 documents, the seven IEP principles provide ideas for structuring participation that will successfully address eventual conflicts and ideas for resolving them when they do occur. Conflicts are inevitable in evaluation practice and especially

Exhibit 6.6   Applying IEP Principles to Managing Conflict Constructively

IEP Principle	Applied to Managing Conflict Constructively
1. Get personal.	• Study the personal conflict styles of evaluation participants, especially primary intended users. Know how they are likely to respond to conflict. Know your own personal reactions to conflict as well. • Establish cooperative interpersonal relationships *before* conflict occurs; people are more willing to work toward mutual solutions with friends.
2. Structure interaction.	• Be systematic in creating positive interdependence and establishing cooperative goal structures throughout the evaluation process; this sets the stage for constructive conflict interactions. • Work with your primary intended users to create cooperative interactive norms for the evaluation and, as possible and appropriate, within the organization for the constructive resolution of conflict. • Facilitate mutual problem solving when conflicts arise. Teach people to name the conflicts they experience and apply the steps of integrative negotiation to resolve them constructively—don't leave conflict resolution to happenstance.
3. Examine context.	• Pay attention to the features of the evaluation context that are important to resolving conflicts, such as goal structures, cooperative interaction, and conflict strategies used for resolution. • Recognize conflict behaviors in the evaluation context and confront them appropriately; notice patterns of forcing, withdrawing, smoothing, compromising, and problem solving.
4. Consider politics.	• Be aware that political agendas can be at the root of conflict that occurs in evaluation practice; be vigilant in seeking to understand the diverse interests and perspectives of stakeholders. • Work thoughtfully within the organization's political context to inform key leaders and encourage their support for a successful evaluation study, which includes constructively managing conflict.

(Continued)

Exhibit 6.6   (Continued)

IEP Principle	Applied to Managing Conflict Constructively
5. Expect conflict.	• Know what conflict looks like; recognize when it occurs. • Never be surprised when conflict occurs in evaluation practice; be surprised if it doesn't! • Work to establish cooperative relationships, teach participants the skills of integrative negotiation, and facilitate mutual problem solving.
6. Respect culture.	• Understand that cultural differences may lead to conflicts during evaluations; pay attention to them. • Be aware that different cultures may respond differently to conflict; allow people the freedom to do so. • Recognize cultural/ethnic values, customs, norms, or traditions that support (or frustrate) constructive conflict.
7. Take time.	• Devote time to resolving conflicts constructively. • Recognize that intense conflicts concerning deeply rooted value differences or diverse philosophical beliefs typically demand much more time than do other types of conflicts. • Choose your battles thoughtfully—you have only 24 hours each day, and your life is filled with competing priorities. Do take time to work through those conflicts that matter the most for the success of the evaluation. • Timing matters; deal with conflicts in timely ways when they arise—don't let conflicts fester, escalate, or become toxic by not taking the time to deal with important issues. • Make the time to reflect systematically on the evaluation process and to analyze any conflicts that have occurred. Learn from them.

SOURCE: © 2010 Jean A. King & Laurie Stevahn.

so when studies seek eventual change, but fortunately we now understand conflict in ways unthought of 100 years ago.

What, then, are realistic expectations for evaluators in conflict situations? We believe they can (a) recognize and expect that conflicts will occur, (b) assess organization and program contexts to determine the extent to which cooperative relationships exist among individuals and where cooperative goal structures are needed, (c) observe how individuals respond to conflict, (d) use appropriate conflict strategies and negotiation skills to keep evaluation implementations on track, (e) constantly reflect on personal approaches to conflict, and (f) practice the skills of constructive conflict resolution. Throughout, evaluators must remember that social context is crucial. Attempting to use integrative negotiation in a competitive context will be frustrating at best and, based on consistent research evidence, likely doomed to fail. If, for example, managers are competing for limited funds and an evaluator is hired to provide "hard data" to decide which program will be cut, it is highly unlikely people will gleefully join in the evaluation process. Basically, success in managing conflict will be enhanced when evaluators and organizational leaders work to change program infrastructure and governing policies from competitive/individualistic to cooperative. The role of the evaluator is to recognize the impact of social structures and relationships and work to make them cooperative. Taking the time to do so is well worth it, supporting positive interaction even in challenging situations.

CHAPTER REVIEW

Evaluators should not be surprised when people bring different and often incompatible agendas and perspectives to evaluation settings. Instead, they should recognize that "to be alive is to be in conflict" (Tjosvold & Johnson, 1989, p. 1). In fact, managing conflict constructively can be critical to conducting successful evaluation studies. This chapter presented theories, frameworks, and skills evaluators can use to influence positive conflict.

1. Resolving conflict begins by recognizing that it exists. Conflict is classically defined as a situation in which one's personal goals get blocked by the activities of others (Deutsch, 1973, 2006).

2. Two theories provide insights into the dynamics of conflict: *conflict strategies theory* (Johnson & Johnson, 2009) and *constructive conflict resolution theory* (Deutsch, 1973, 2006).

3. *Conflict strategies theory* highlights dual concerns people face in conflict (achieving goals and maintaining positive relationships) from which five responses emerge: forcing, withdrawing, smoothing, compromising, and problem solving. These become lenses through which evaluators can analyze the evaluation context, reflect on strategies for action, and then act strategically to move the evaluation forward.

4. *Constructive conflict resolution theory* reliably predicts that goal structures (cooperative or competitive) influence interactions (promotive/responsive or oppositional/obstructive), which, in turn, determine outcomes (constructive or destructive). Evaluators, therefore, should strive to establish the cooperative infrastructure that underpins constructive conflict by incorporating positive interdependence into evaluation tasks whenever appropriate and possible.

5. Evaluators can set the groundwork for constructive conflict in evaluation by mastering two critical skill sets. The first involves structuring cooperative goals into

evaluation tasks. The second involves negotiating integratively to create mutually beneficial outcomes for everyone involved.

6. Thoughtful evaluators will intentionally use conflict competencies to (a) analyze the evaluation context for structures that affect social interaction, (b) recognize conflict behaviors, (c) facilitate mutual problem solving through integrative negotiation, (d) create cooperative norms by structuring shared goals into evaluation work, and (e) know and manage personal proclivities in conflict situations.

7. Although the complexity of conflict never renders guarantees, evaluators and organizational leaders can realistically influence people's experiences with conflict in evaluation by mastering and applying theories and skills that promote constructive interactions and outcomes.

7

CREATING A VIABLE INTERACTIVE EVALUATION PROCESS

Chapter Preview

- Review foundations for creating a viable interactive evaluation process
- Identify five components that influence the viability of interactive evaluation practice (IEP)
- Prescribe up-front planning and actions that evaluators can take to attend to each component
- Describe how to use an interactive evaluation process to build evaluation capacity within programs and organizations
- Explain the importance of ongoing assessment and adjustment of the interactive evaluation process
- Apply the IEP principles to creating a viable interactive evaluation process

INTRODUCTION

Imagine a charmed evaluation. The clients understand the evaluation process and happily arrange sessions with key stakeholders to frame issues and questions. No one feels threatened; participants are open to multiple possibilities and eager to attend multiple meetings. They easily agree on a focus and approach. Resources flow. The evaluators develop high-quality instruments, and data collection proceeds without a hitch—focus groups are oversubscribed, survey response rates top 95%, and the database effortlessly yields consistent and complete data. People clamor to be interviewed. Supported enthusiastically by potential users, analysis and interpretation are straightforward, and the interactions around reporting lead to detailed action plans and questions requiring additional evaluation. A new study begins.

Alas. The real world is a messy place. If only evaluations could all run so smoothly! The reality of evaluation practice is often a far cry from the dream sequence detailed above. Many clients know little about program evaluation, and, owing to previous negative experiences, what they do know may frighten them. Asked to help frame an evaluation study, some people will become defensive or nervous or just plain obnoxious, worried about how the ultimate outcomes will affect them personally. Funding is rarely sufficient to cover the Cadillac design that would make an evaluator proud, and data collection often creates multiple opportunities for mayhem—from bad items that confuse respondents, to such low survey response rates that the data are unusable, to poor attendance at focus groups despite repeated reminders and expensive incentives. Even after all the data are gathered and reports prepared, things can still go awry; a key user may take one finding out of context to use for political gain or the evaluation may be buried amidst competing factions in an organizational conflict. Harry Potter has no magic wand to guarantee an evaluation will run smoothly.

The fact that evaluations are fraught with such perils highlights the importance of using the skills of interactive evaluation practice (IEP) to develop and sustain a feasible process for every evaluation. Active engagement of on-site participants may not be necessary or appropriate in every evaluation (e.g., external accountability studies). But the interpersonal factor reminds us that evaluators both create and manage the interpersonal dynamics that make evaluations possible and inform their outcomes. What research has taught us about evaluation use points to the importance of involving clients and other important stakeholders, and social interdependence theory provides guidance for facilitating that involvement, fostering ongoing cooperation during the study. Playing three roles—decision maker, actor, and reflective practitioner—the evaluator engages people in meaningful conversations, structures interactions that participants join in over the course of a study, and thoughtfully addresses conflict head-on.

This chapter advocates up-front planning and ongoing monitoring, when appropriate, to develop a workable and meaningful interactive evaluation process. First we identify components that influence the process, then provide a variety of templates useful for establishing mechanisms likely to promote success. Next we focus on building evaluation capacity throughout the process, a broader commitment in programs and organizations seeking to conduct their own evaluations. We then discuss why and how evaluators working to support a worthwhile evaluation process should conduct ongoing assessment of the process itself. Systematically paying attention to indicators that reveal all is going well—or that something may be going wrong—and responding to them can be instrumental to keeping an evaluation on track. We conclude this chapter by discussing how the IEP principles introduced in Chapter 3 apply to creating and sustaining a viable interactive process for evaluation studies.

PLANNING A VIABLE INTERACTIVE EVALUATION PROCESS

Although planning never guarantees success, evaluators should consider and plan for certain components to the extent possible and appropriate. Such components can influence successful IEP as a study unfolds. Five components to consider are (a) the context/setting of the evaluation, (b) cultural characteristics, (c) whom to involve, (d) logistical concerns, and (e) various aspects of communication. The sections that follow detail how evaluators can promote and maintain an effective evaluation process by addressing these five components up-front and by revisiting them throughout the evaluation. As we proceed, however, keep in mind that although advance planning for these components can be helpful, getting stuck in planning tends to be unproductive. In fact, research on organization development and change indicates that devoting too much time or energy to mapping concrete pathways at the beginning of an endeavor actually tends to block success in the long run (e.g., see Fullan, 2006; Reeves, 2006, 2009). Instead, jumping in earlier rather than later enables learning from doing that, in the end, often proves more helpful by allowing evaluators to discover what needs fine-tuning, to adjust practice, and to sharpen focus for greater success along the way. So, do preplan, but know that the real power of the tools, templates, and suggestions presented here ultimately will come from *applying* them early toward creating practical processes that can lead to successful evaluation studies.

Context/Setting

First, knowing the evaluation context and setting well is imperative because that is the environment in which the study will take place. Environmental factors, especially well-established routines and norms, tend to influence human behavior and interactions greatly in nearly all social situations—in families, social clubs, educational institutions, service agencies, businesses, legislative bodies, religious organizations, and the like. That is why the initial evaluation conversations discussed in Chapter 4 so predominantly focus on learning about the evaluation context and setting. These dimensions are grounding factors that *will* affect the course of program evaluations in one way or another. Knowing these factors and leveraging them toward a successful evaluation process must be a primary concern in the planning stages, in addition to constantly revisiting and addressing contextual factors throughout.

Template 1 provides a general list of contextual factors relevant to programs and organizations that evaluators can and should address up front.

Template 1 Evaluation Context/Setting Worksheet: Organizational Dimensions of Culture

Name of the program/organization:	
Background Information	**Evaluator Notes** (record key information)
Mission/vision/values of the program/organization (purpose for existing)	
History of the program/organization (year founded, by whom, reasons, major milestones and/ or transitions, years of growth/decline/reorganization, reputation, etc.)	
Site/location of the program/organization (single to multiple; geographically near or far from one another; hub/headquarters or satellite/field status)	
Size/scale of the program/organization (e.g., local, regional, national, international; number of programs, managers/leaders, employees/volunteers, people served—small to large)	
Structure of the program/organization (hierarchical flow chart showing divisions, departments, units and interrelationships among them; personnel roles/titles/responsibilities—i.e., who reports to whom— and turnover information; standing governance committees and advisory boards; ad hoc commissions or task forces with special assignments)	
Norms/routines characteristic of the program/organization (predominant attitudes, customs, traditions, practices relevant to a host of factors including employment/hiring/ inclusiveness, turnover patterns, commitment, opportunities for advancement, ethnicity/race, gender, sexual orientation, accommodations for people with disabilities, etc.—also see Template 2)	
Logic models of the program/organization (people's assumptions/beliefs about attributes that influence effectiveness; cause-and-effect theories of action for program/organization processes and/or outcomes)	
Budget/funding for the program/organization (stable/ongoing; client fees; government or foundation grants; heavily or slightly influenced by current market conditions; etc.)	

Name of the program/organization:	
Background Information	Evaluator Notes (record key information)
Content/field of the program/organization (education, business, health, government, nonprofit, social service, etc.)	
Wider environment in which the program/organization exists (social, political, economic, cultural factors at large, etc.)	
Other relevant factors unique to the program/organization (that will influence interactive processes in evaluation practice)	

SOURCE: © 2010 Laurie Stevahn & Jean A. King.

Designed as a worksheet, this template focuses evaluators on background information useful for planning how best to facilitate interactive processes in each unique evaluation situation. We briefly discuss each factor below.

- *Mission/vision/values.* This is why the program/organization exists—its reason for being. In well-functioning programs/organizations, this drives all other decisions and activities. To what extent are the mission, vision, and values known, embraced, and enacted by program staff and organization members? How is the content/substance of each likely to support (or impede) effective interactive processes during an evaluation study?

- *History.* You may be familiar with Shakespeare's well-known adage: "What's past is prologue." What characterizes the program's past? What memorable highlights (or lowlights) are part of an organization's story? A context that has a steady history of stability, effectiveness, and collaboration may be more inclined to support future successful interactive evaluation processes than those with histories of constant upheaval, dysfunctional operations, or acrimonious rivalries among members or divisions.

- *Site/location.* Where is the program/organization located—at a single site or in multiple geographic settings? If in several, are these near one another (more localized within a community) or widespread (across countries or continents)? Will the evaluation focus on one site only, or on many? What are the implications for traveling to various locations (short or long distances) or electronic capabilities for connecting and interacting? Recognizing these particulars up front can help evaluators design workable systems for interactive processes.

- *Size/scale.* The size and/or scale of the program/organization will affect numerous aspects of an evaluation, including the feasibility of certain processes. Smaller settings may be more conducive to more inclusive and interactive evaluation designs, whereas larger settings, including multisite settings, may present greater challenges to creating sustainable interactive processes. In fact, size and scale may delimit from the beginning the extent to which an evaluation can be interactive in the collaborative sense (see Exhibit 2.3 in Chapter 2), and evaluators—whether internal or external to the organization—should realistically assess this when beginning a study.

- *Structure.* How is the program organized? What role does it play within the larger organization? Who participates in the organization? What are its demographics? What hierarchies exist, and who reports to whom? Are divisions/departments loosely or tightly coupled with management and/or one another? How autonomous are programs, units, and/or managers in their functions? Organizational charts can be helpful for showing various work units and their interrelationships, as can be talking with key individuals or groups within the organization. Also remember to obtain information about employee and/or volunteer turnover—i.e., whether the work force tends to be more or less stable over time. The long- or short-term tenure of organizational leaders and staff can greatly affect interactive evaluation processes for better or worse.

- *Norms/routines.* If structure is the body of the program/organization, then norms and routines are its pulse. These are the repeated actions and ingrained systems that basically define the day-to-day activities that are the organization's lifeblood. They reflect the customs, traditions, and commonly held assumptions about the organization—and how to navigate through them—that play out in daily operations. Closely associated with the norms/routines that define the organization's culture are the social–cultural dimensions of its people, whose life stories, traditions, experiences, and perspectives meaningfully enter into the mix. These more demographically oriented factors—dealing with the identities and diversities of people—influence the organizational norms and routines that develop within an organization and point to the importance of evaluator cultural competence, further elaborated in the pages that follow.

- *Logic models.* These are people's theories of action relevant to program/organization effectiveness (Chen, 2005; Donaldson, 2007; Frechtling, 2007; Funnell & Rogers, 2011; Patton, 2012). What assumptions do people in the organization hold about causes and effects of actions, operations, and outcomes? Knowing these may be insightful not only for shaping evaluations but also for learning about perceived and/or existing patterns of interaction that may be useful (or not) for facilitating evaluation processes.

- *Budget/funding.* Knowing how the program/organization is funded, or at least the evaluation budget, should assist the evaluator in figuring out whether funds will be sufficient to conduct the type of evaluation desired or to support interaction. Useful information includes whether budgets/funds are from sure/stable versus soft/unpredictable sources, time-bound grants versus ongoing client fees, and long-standing and well-supported annual fundraising events versus "one-shot" money makers. It also pays to know who controls the budget. Those with the authority to make budget decisions—either directly or indirectly—will also influence the resources, support structures, and processes feasible in any evaluation study.

- *Content/field.* Consider the overall content/field of the program/organization because it, too, is a grounding aspect of context and setting. Education, business, health, government, nonprofit, and other sectors—each of these fields has its own sets of major purposes, bases of knowledge, professional standards, lexicons/vocabularies for communicating, and shared understandings. These influence accepted norms and practices—e.g., whether lecturing versus collaborating normally takes precedence for dealing with information—which, in turn, can affect the extent to which interactive evaluation processes will be possible in any given setting. Language matters in evaluation, and understanding its effects in given contexts can help evaluators develop a process appropriate to the program (Hopson, 2000).

- *Wider environment.* The external environment in which the program/organization is situated cannot be ignored. Like it or not, social, political, economic, and cultural factors—along with community values, customs, traditions, and histories—play an influential role, even if indirectly. Pay attention to these factors because they can (and do) affect processes and procedures that organizations or programs embrace—whether willfully, as when the zeitgeist of the times influences the decentralization of organizational governance by promoting employee-involved decision making, or not, as when a natural disaster unexpectedly creates emotional havoc and material hardship, straining financial resources for years thereafter, compelling those in charge to shift priorities in ways that reduce or eliminate certain practices.

- *Other relevant factors.* Finally, you should always be on the lookout for other unique factors important to understanding the context and setting of the program/organization—especially those that may influence the viability of interactive evaluation processes. We offer the Template 1 worksheet as a place to start, knowing additions and adaptations will occur when you prepare for each distinct evaluation.

Although internal evaluators may have an advantage over those who are external when it comes to knowing about context and setting, both can benefit by recognizing readily available ways to (a) obtain, revisit, or review such information; (b) systematically consult easy-to-access information; and (c) pursue harder-to-get information when the "value added" will be worth it for planning interactive evaluation processes. For example, evaluators can

- engage in the type of evaluation conversations discussed in Chapter 4 with leaders, staff, and clients whose input may prove invaluable for thinking about interactive processes to support successful evaluation efforts;
- routinely access website homepage information posted by the program/ organization, especially noting mission/vision/values and when the website was last updated;
- pick up brochures, newsletters, and other announcements available in lobbies or hallways to clients or the public;
- conduct a **windshield survey**, if possible and appropriate, i.e., driving through neighborhoods in advance to get a sense of programs' local settings; and
- if feasible, visit program sites to observe firsthand their locations, environments, surroundings, and physical structures.

Evaluators might also consider pursuing information that, although useful for planning, may be more difficult (because of privacy or confidentiality issues) or time-consuming (because of labor-intensive activities) to obtain. These items may include the organizational chart, strategic plans, budget information, and staff characteristics such as turnover rates. Finally, it is important to use common sense and good judgment when seeking context information—and always strive to establish positive relations and trust when acquiring information. Make decisions about what to ask for, how to ask, and how hard to push for information in light of maintaining the positive interpersonal relationships that, in the end, may play a role in the ongoing interactive processes that will carry the evaluation to a successful conclusion.

Culture

The second factor likely to affect interaction is culture. Clearly, context and culture overlap. Although culture is part of the evaluation context—a big part to be sure—we separately focus on this dimension to emphasize its special role in foundational considerations that will influence establishing and maintaining interactive processes. First, let's examine two perspectives on culture, both of which pertain to evaluation. One perspective comes from the literatures on organization development and leadership/management for change. This perspective tends to define culture as the existing roles, relationships, responsibilities, and common practices that characterize an organization or program. Consider, for example, each of the following definitions of organizational culture, described by well-respected experts in the field:

- "The interwoven pattern of beliefs, values, practices, and artifacts that defines for members who they are and how they are to do things" (Bolman & Deal, 2003, p. 243)
- "A pattern of shared basic assumptions that a group learned as it solved its problems of external adaptation and integration, that has worked well enough to be considered valid and therefore to be taught to new members as the correct way to perceive, think and feel in relation to those problems" (Schein, 1992, p. 12)
- "The way we do things around here" (Deal & Kennedy, 1982, p. 4)

These definitions of culture essentially describe the norms/routines aspect of context and setting discussed in the previous section. People within the organization or program engage in familiar and accepted patterns of interaction to get the job done—whatever that job may be.

Another perspective on culture comes from the literatures on diversity, critical theory, social justice, and multicultural/intercultural education, all of which focus more pointedly on aspects of identity, pluralism, power, privilege, and equity. Definitions of culture that highlight these qualities make plain their prominence in grounding the human condition, which necessarily enters into evaluation practice. The American Evaluation Association (AEA, 2011), for example, defines **culture** as

the shared experiences of people, including their languages, values, customs, beliefs, and mores. It also includes worldviews, ways of knowing, and ways of communicating. Culturally significant factors encompass, but are not limited to, race/ethnicity, religion, social class, language, disability, sexual orientation, age, and gender. Contextual dimensions such as geographic region and socioeconomic circumstance are also essential to shaping culture. (p. 2)

This perspective on culture within organizations or programs underpins the importance of evaluators developing cultural competence. It is all too easy for those who grew up as members of society's dominant culture to perceive situations primarily through that lens, thereby excluding or dismissing—even if unintentionally—the valued experiences, histories, traditions, and viewpoints of those from other cultural groups whose perspectives illuminate the greater whole in more nuanced and textured ways.

Even language reflects one's cultural orientation. For example, calling a December vacation "Christmas break" ignores the fact that many people don't celebrate this holiday. Or using the phrase "homeless people" emphasizes their homeless condition rather than the qualities that identify them as individuals. Better to say "people who are homeless." It's about putting people first (American Psychological Association, 2010). Patton (2012) advises us to remember that

> respecting and honoring culture is a significant dimension of effective stakeholder involvement and group facilitation. . . . Culture is personal. Everyone who comes to the evaluation table brings culture with them. To ignore it is to disrespect those present. (p. 53)

Becoming culturally competent does not involve checking items off a list as "done" or "mission accomplished." It is not achievable once and for all time, like a lifetime license. Instead, it is the realization that developing cultural competence is a lifelong and intentional journey—we would argue largely experiential—through which an evaluator grows to appreciate more broadly and deeply people's diverse life histories and how their social–cultural group experiences have shaped their values, concerns, and realities. It is a cumulative process over time in which the evaluator makes a conscious commitment to engage in continuous learning to appreciate ever more fully what it means to be part of any diverse cultural group.

And it is a two-way process that involves looking inward as well as outward, becoming ever more aware of one's own culture and how it influences assumptions, beliefs, behaviors, and ways of constructing meaning in the world. The AEA (2011) *Public Statement on Cultural Competence in Evaluation,* shown in Exhibit 7.1, helps us all better understand the various dimensions of cultural awareness and respect for diversity, and why that matters in evaluation practice.

Undoubtedly, both perspectives on culture—the customs, traditions, conventions that characterize the organization/program itself *and* the demographics, identities, diversities of the people who work for and/or are served by the

Exhibit 7.1 Cultural Competence

AEA Public Statement on Cultural Competence in Evaluation

Cultural competence is not a state at which one arrives; rather, it is a process of learning, unlearning, and relearning. It is a sensibility cultivated throughout a lifetime. Cultural competence requires awareness of self, reflection on one's own cultural position, awareness of others' positions, and the ability to interact genuinely and respectfully with others. Culturally competent evaluators refrain from assuming they fully understand the perspectives of stakeholders whose backgrounds differ from their own. Cultural competence is defined in relation to a specific context or location, such as geography, nationality, and history. Competence in one context is no assurance of competence in another. The culturally competent evaluator (or evaluation team) must have specific knowledge of the people and place in which the evaluation is being conducted—including local history and culturally determined mores, values and ways of knowing.

SOURCE: AEA (2011, p. 3). Used with permission.

organization/program—intersect and help shape the processes and outcomes of the organization. These existing processes and outcomes will also interact and affect the conduct of a program evaluation study. For example, communication patterns and the content or substance especially valued, histories and experiences of particular ethnic groups, what is deemed respectful and dignifying, and so on, all will be part of enacting the various tasks needed in a study, particularly those that require interaction and, therefore, matter for IEP (e.g., consider the basic inquiry tasks described in Chapter 2).

We have already presented a template that evaluators can use to focus more closely on addressing the organizational dimensions of culture, i.e., Template 1 in the previous section. Template 2 can be used as a worksheet to focus more directly on the demographic dimensions of culture—the social identities, diversities, and differing worldviews of those in the evaluation context, and what these will mean for interactive processes throughout an evaluation. What cultural factors will open pathways to viable evaluation processes? Which factors can become vehicles for doing the work of evaluation? When evaluators recognize what matters to people from a social–cultural perspective, they may be better able to align evaluation tasks with such factors to enhance progress and/or creatively deal with challenges to pave the way for processes that will support evaluation efforts.

Culturally competent evaluators will strive to become aware of the identity/diversity dimensions of those in the organization (to the extent possible),

Template 2   Cultural Awareness Worksheet: Demographic Dimensions of Culture

Name of the program/organization:	
Cultural Considerations (relevant to identity, diversity, perceptions, values)	**Evaluator Notes** (record insights and understandings)
Demographic identities/groups relevant to the program/ organization (e.g., race/ethnicity, language, religion, social class, disability, sexual orientation, age, gender, immigrants, refugees, veterans, etc.)	
Institutional and community demographic information (statistics relevant to members, clients, and other pertinent stakeholders)	
Ethnic backgrounds (ethnicities/lineages represented—e.g., American Indian, African, Latino/a, Japanese, Korean, Chinese, Pacific Islander, Caucasian European, Arab, etc.; in the United States these family ancestry designations may apply to American- or foreign-born individuals and citizens or immigrants/refugees)	
Languages spoken (first languages; second languages; multiple languages; oral traditions; literacy proficiencies; alternative forms of communication, such as sign language in the Deaf community or visual images/symbols in societies that do not rely on an alphabet, etc.)	
Histories/experiences shared at large among distinct groups of people (e.g., power, privilege, oppression, marginalization, inclusion/exclusion, struggles, opportunities, and so on)	
Other relevant cultural factors (unique to the program/organization or setting/ environment)	

SOURCE: © 2010 Laurie Stevahn & Jean A. King.

anticipate how those dimensions will intertwine with evaluation processes, and plan options at the onset for responsibly and respectfully taking action— knowing adjustments will be necessary as the project unfolds. Culturally competent evaluators will also be aware of how their own backgrounds, experiences, and identities shape personal assumptions, attitudes, preconceptions, use of language, and other factors relevant to diversity, power, privilege, and influence—all of which can, and probably will, affect interactions in any evaluation study. SenGupta, Hopson, and Thompson-Robinson (2004) advise evaluators to "practice constant self-examination of values, assumptions, and cultural contexts" (p. 13). In short, social–cultural awareness goes both ways. Evaluators should enter evaluations with eyes wide open: "Know thyself" and "know thy context/setting." The Template 2 worksheet can be used to reflect on both.

Involvement

Chapter 5 briefly presented a rationale for approaching evaluation practice interactively by addressing *why, where,* and *when* such work makes sense, along with *how* to facilitate specific strategies to make it happen (see Exhibit 5.1). The third factor that affects interactive evaluation relates to *who* is involved in the process.

Thinking about involvement starts with a series of questions. With whom should evaluators strategize to create and sustain useful processes throughout an evaluation study? Who—besides the evaluator—will be instrumental to continued progress during implementation? Which types of organizational arrangements will help keep it all going? Realistically, many factors can and should be considered when deciding which people to involve and how to make their involvement possible—and those factors will vary across diverse circumstances. Nevertheless, general guidelines and templates useful for making such choices can be provided, which we do here. We especially focus on establishing committees, populating those committees, and analyzing the attitudes and aptitudes of those involved.

Although for the most part we present the following guidelines step-by-step, remember that in actual practice designating useful evaluation committees, determining members, and attending to their needs will likely play out much more iteratively because every decision will be somewhat linked to and influence all others. Therefore, establishing and populating committees may well require several rounds of adjusting and balancing in the planning stages, just as analyzing participants' attitudes and aptitudes will likely result in adjustments over time to address their changing needs. In all decision making, however, remember to be *inclusive* and *strategic*. Inclusive (broad) participation—whether involving people in providing input on proposed plans, actually doing the work of evaluation, or making meaning of results—builds capacity for embracing and using findings. Strategic (intentional) involvement further recognizes that individuals in pivotal positions—especially key leaders and those who control resources in the organization—and those who bring positive attitudes and the skills to perform well will be essential to successful evaluation processes.

Establish Committees

First, revisit the purpose/focus of the evaluation study and what this means for participation. Refer to the interpersonal participation quotient framework to determine whether the study will primarily be evaluator-directed, collaborative, or self-directed by those in a particular program (see Chapter 2, Exhibit 2.3). With this in mind, determine the extent to which establishing or designating committees to involve individuals will be helpful or necessary. In all likelihood, collaborative evaluations especially will rely on committees to conduct various tasks; however, even evaluator-directed studies can benefit from periodic input or feedback from appropriate organizational groups, such as divisions, departments, or leadership teams that eventually will be asked to implement recommendations. In any case, refer to the organizational chart to determine which structures already exist and the extent to which each has broad representation on important factors relevant to context, setting, and culture (see Templates 1 and 2). Next consider if additional committees would be helpful and appropriate. Don't create unnecessary infrastructure that risks becoming too complicated to implement—intricate plans on paper don't always work in practice—but do consider how each of the following may constructively contribute to the success of the overall evaluation effort.

- *Evaluation advisory board*—meets periodically with the evaluator to provide up-front input on the organizational context, program concerns, or evaluation plans; receives updates on evaluation progress; suggests ways to deal with challenges or conflicts that arise; and so on, but does not actually participate in conducting the study
- *Evaluation steering committee*—develops, shapes, and/or conducts the overall evaluation project from start to finish in conjunction with the evaluator
- *Data collection team*—obtains data according to the plan (e.g., conducts focus groups, administers surveys, carries out interviews, etc.)
- *Data analysis team*—analyzes the data and reports results to those who will interpret findings
- *Recommendation board*—makes results-based commendations and recommendations for program policy and/or practice

Also think about the optimal size of each committee. Keep groups small enough to get the job done—i.e., manageable numbers for meaningful communication, interaction, and mutual decision making—yet large enough for appropriate representation across important organizational factors pertaining to context, setting, and culture. An evaluation advisory board and/or steering committee (5–10 people) almost certainly will be needed either to counsel or work with the evaluator throughout the entire endeavor. Perhaps a long-standing organizational policy committee, made up of the CEO and every departmental leader, will take on this role. On the other hand, circumstances may require a newly formed advisory or steering committee with exclusive evaluation responsibilities that will disband at the conclusion of the study. Either way, the committee guiding the entire endeavor will need to determine whether to commission groups—such as short-term task forces or ad hoc teams—with data collection, analysis, or recommendation responsibilities at appropriate junctures along the way or whether to manage all aspects itself, working with the evaluator to decide which tasks the evaluator should complete when various tasks need special expertise.

Before moving on, we again caution against too many committees, which could add unnecessary bureaucratic layers and problematic red tape that may slow or obstruct the evaluation process. We do, however, suggest considering if additional groups would promote wider participation leading to broader commitment to eventually using the evaluation results and the extent to which those groups should overlap. The purpose of each committee should be clearly articulated and interconnections among functions clearly explicated so participants can understand their roles in the evaluation effort and maximize contributions toward successfully carrying out various tasks. Effective decision making here requires recognizing the value of widespread participation across stakeholders to promote ownership of the process and its outcomes while simultaneously maintaining a streamlined structure for enacting the process—a delicate dance, indeed.

Populate Committees

Many of the considerations relevant to planning evaluation committees also apply to determining who should serve on them. Again, we suggest revisiting information about the evaluation context, setting, and culture (see Templates 1 and 2) in light of the focus and/or purposes of the evaluation study—and what that means for ensuring representation on various committees. We also continue to encourage evaluators to think about being *inclusive* and *strategic*. Research on the use of evaluation results (discussed at length in Chapter 3) points to the importance of the inclusive and strategic involvement of stakeholders, especially the primary intended users in the organization or program being evaluated. If use is essentially about change—which evaluations for instrumental or process use most certainly are—then *inclusive* involvement ultimately recognizes the value of including as many individuals as possible toward promoting collective action. In short, meaningfully involving individuals in evaluation makes change more likely. In small organizations, it may be possible to include everyone (or most) in all (or some) of the tasks of evaluation. In most cases, however, some form of representative participation will be necessary, especially when evaluations take place in mid- to large-sized and/or multisite organizations.

Furthermore, *strategic* involvement recognizes that some people will be vital to success, such as certain leaders in the organizational hierarchy (CEOs, superintendents, division managers, department heads, program directors, unit leaders, etc.) who must be on board because they occupy positions of authority. Those who approve the allocation of resources should also be involved because they literally can bring any evaluation process to a halt by enacting counterproductive policies, failing to champion needed efforts, or denying access to necessary resources.

With the tenets of being inclusive and strategic in mind, determine whom to involve in committees by first consulting the organizational map or chart that depicts overall structure, or constructing one if it doesn't exist. Look at individuals who occupy leadership positions on the chart and then identify others (regardless of position) who will be integral to a successful evaluation process. The latter are those well respected by colleagues who possess the expertise and skills necessary for supporting the tasks of evaluation or for championing processes. These individuals may be frontrunners in evaluation efforts or possibly opponents; both should participate in initial efforts toward creating a productive process. Cross-sectional representation of all stakeholders and organizational units may also be important to the eventual success of any change effort.

Next, for each committee, create a worksheet listing helpful criteria for determining membership, such as the example shown in Template 3. The pattern of check marks across the criteria/boxes will visually reveal patterns of representation helpful in making final decisions. As noted earlier, important considerations include the size of the organization or program (small to large), whether it is single or multisite, its operational structure (hierarchical or flat), its funding sources, how leaders/managers/supervisors view their roles (authoritative, democratic, collaborative), who the gatekeepers are in the organization (Alkin, 2011, p. 44), and so on. Finally, although not specifically designated in column format on the worksheet, consider overall possible selections in light of cultural identity/diversity and

Template 3 Evaluation Steering Committee Worksheet

> **Directions:**
>
> A. Keep the steering committee *size* manageable (5–10 people)—write names of potential participants.
>
> B. Plan appropriate representation.
>   - Review the structure of the evaluation context (organizational chart).
>   - Consider *sites/locations* (single or multiple)—write those represented.
>   - Consider *departments/units* (subdivisions)—write those represented.
>
> C. Consider a range of *roles* (diverse perspectives)—check boxes that apply.
>
> D. Involve people over a continuum of *tenure* (established and new members)—check boxes that apply.
>
> E. Consider the *expertise* various individuals will bring to evaluation tasks—check boxes that apply.
>
> F. Ensure appropriate social–cultural factors are considered and addressed in final decisions.

Name	Site/Department		Role				Tenure		Expertise					
	Site/location	Department/unit	Leader/director	Staff/service provider	Client/service recipient	Other stakeholders	New	Established	Evaluation	Change facilitation	Interpersonal skill	Communication	Intercultural skill	Technology
1.														
2.														
3.														
4.														
5.														
6.														
7.														
8.														
9.														
10.														

SOURCE: Stevahn and King (2010, Figure 2.1).

appropriate representation. A university, for example, whose mission focuses on acquiring a culturally diverse faculty to serve a multicultural student body most certainly should include people representing different ethnicities, along with other appropriate constructs of diversity, on evaluation committees assessing the effectiveness of various programs or operations.

Analyze Attitude and Aptitude

Every organization has individuals with unique attitudes and aptitudes that influence their involvement throughout the evaluation process. Thinking about people's attitudes toward participating (willing or not) and aptitudes for completing the work (skills/abilities or lack thereof) can help evaluators create a viable evaluation process. When crossed, these two variables result in the four potential outcomes shown in Exhibit 7.2 and a range of possible responses, shown in Exhibit 7.3.

Exhibit 7.2   Individual Attitude/Aptitude Matrix

Attitude \ Aptitude		Able to do the work?	
		Yes	No
Willing to do the work?	Yes	1. Willing and able	2. Willing but unable
	No	3. Unwilling but able	4. Unwilling and unable

SOURCE: Stevahn and King (2010, Table 5.1).

Exhibit 7.3   Responses to Attitude/Aptitude Challenges

Classification	Example	How to Respond
1. Willing and able	Good citizen	• Watch for burnout.
	Control freak or martyr	• Monitor progress. • Find additional support if needed. • Provide individual coaching.

Classification	Example	How to Respond
2. Willing but unable	Positive incompetent (truly unable)	• Provide targeted training, coaching, and mentoring. • Remove for damage control. • Reassign to a doable task.
	Person on leave (temporarily unable)	• Reassign responsibilities. • Add short-term resources.
3. Unwilling but able	Negative obstructionist (negative attitude and against evaluation)	• Use conflict-management skills (cooperative negotiation, then force).
	Thoughtful opponent (positive attitude but against evaluation)	• Use conflict-management skills (cooperative negotiation and compromise).
	Passive aggressor	• Create mechanisms to document and track evaluation activities over time.
4. Unwilling and unable	Hostile incompetent	• Limit involvement. • Remove for damage control.

SOURCE: Stevahn and King (2010, Table 5.2).

The Willing and Able. The first category encompasses those who have both the will and the skills to participate fully in evaluation activities. This is the group instrumental in implementing the evaluation plan. Even so, the potential exists for problems, such as those who never say never and end up saddled with too much work. These intrepid contributors want to do everything, perhaps for control, by default, or due to martyr-like personalities. Ever the good citizens, they leap into the organizational vacuum the evaluation process may create. Yet this can be problematic if others become jealous when doers receive perks, such as release time or extra resources for engaging in evaluation activities, or if they keep their distance for fear extra tasks may be added to workloads. An educator once captured this tension by labeling those who constantly took on tasks as "élite lepers." Some thought the doers received too many privileges; others avoided them like the plague.

Because these are the people who get the job done, evaluators should use them throughout the evaluation. For overdoers who step in to control every evaluation activity or enjoy being organizational martyrs, monitoring progress is important. If a person is truly becoming overwhelmed, relief should be available through additional resources or limiting the task. If individuals are responsible for components of the study, one-on-one coaching may help them focus on actions to move the evaluation forward efficiently or on how best to manage time for doing so. Watch for symptoms of burnout—emotional exhaustion, missed deadlines, frequent illness, increased absenteeism, growing pessimism. If you observe these, consider reconfiguring roles and responsibilities before evaluation participants become frustrated, get sick, or abandon their tasks.

The Willing but Unable. In conducting an evaluation, evaluators must attend to those who, for whatever reason, are not able to contribute productively. Not acknowledging this fact puts an unfair burden on those who can do the job. There are at least two kinds of individuals in this category: people who are unable to contribute to the work (truly underqualified, incompetent, or dead wood drawing a paycheck) and people who are on leave (officially or not) owing to illness or other personal issues. Enthusiastic incompetence is perhaps the scariest of all. Inappropriate actions may substantially block an evaluation process.

For the people who are truly unable to participate meaningfully in the evaluation, solutions include training to develop needed skills, one-on-one coaching to increase competence, or individual mentoring to support their work. In participant-directed studies, removing or reassigning people to other tasks may become necessary if the evaluation can't be completed with existing personnel. Altering responsibilities and adding short-term resources are additional options. For example, when the executive director of a small not-for-profit organization needed chemotherapy that resulted in good days when she could work and bad ones when she had to stay home, the board hired a part-time manager to continue work on an evaluation for the 3 months the director underwent treatment.

The Unwilling but Able. There are potentially three types of individuals here, the first being those with inappropriate attitudes. These are the obstructionists, saboteurs, and rumor mongers who purposefully work to destroy the evaluation process. Also included is any leader who elects to delegate evaluation tasks and chooses not to play an active role. This may stymie the evaluation process through omission rather than commission. The second type consists of well-intentioned people who hold conflicting values or don't buy into the proposed study, actively fighting it because they think it is a bad idea. The third type contains capable individuals who appear willing and assume evaluation tasks but never complete them. They say, "Yes, yes," but don't deliver on promises. Like passive or passive-aggressive behavior, not following through on evaluation tasks can easily knock the process off course over time if progress is not tracked carefully.

What can an evaluator do with the unwilling but able? For those people able to work on the evaluation but blocking it either by not buying into the evaluation plan or intentionally setting out to sabotage it, conflict-management skills, such as those discussed in Chapter 6, become useful. Positive people who don't buy in must have a way to express concerns and stay engaged constructively. Integrative negotiation to clarify disagreements and understandings can result in improved evaluations and an increased commitment to move forward. If consensus isn't possible, then compromise may lead to participation with good will. Obstructionists with sharply negative attitudes may require a more direct approach. Negotiation may make sense as a first step, but if obstructers are not interested in maintaining good working relationships, you may have to force compliance by firmly stating expectations for the evaluation as well as consequences for not complying—a risky move since a common response to forcing is withdrawal. Although the demands of various situations require different versions of conflict management, systematically identifying and addressing conflict can be a powerful way to keep evaluation plans on track.

Passive aggressors can also hold up an evaluation, as others must wait for them to complete their part of the effort. Evaluation plans must somehow provide accountability for promised actions by documenting activities. One person may agree to become the monitor, noting what transpires at each meeting and then bringing up main points the next time the group convenes. An easily accessed and complete archive of carefully dated meeting minutes enables systematic tracking of progress. Posting an evaluation plan and timetable also makes decisions and next steps visible so people can be held accountable for their tasks. Ignoring inaction or a lack of progress may demoralize those who are trying to implement the study, only making matters worse.

The Unwilling and Unable. Talk about a double threat. These are the purposeful naysayers who couple a bad attitude with a lack of skills. In an ideal world, they would lose their jobs before they had the chance to poison evaluation activities or ruin them through incompetence, but, as we have noted, the world is a messy place where this may not happen.

The hostile incompetent presents a true challenge by being unwilling and unable to participate in evaluation activities. How can an evaluator work with people who not only have negative attitudes but couldn't do the required tasks even if they wanted to? Facing up to these individuals is sobering and requires extensive involvement of primary intended users. One possibility is to limit the involvement of the unwilling and unable. Another, possible only with support from the client and organizational leaders, is to block their participation. Chapter 8 provides additional ideas for addressing unwilling evaluation participants. But negative potential notwithstanding, evaluators should remember that *not* attending to these individuals may put an evaluation at grave risk.

Here is the point. An array of attitudes and aptitudes exists within any organization. Some may block the evaluation process. People respond in multiple ways to mandates and requests for participation, whether such directives entail small or dramatic commitment. There may (or may not) be conscious motivation for behaviors that detract from the evaluation. Individuals sometimes don't recognize their own negative attitudes or incompetent behaviors, and even though it isn't necessarily intended, such lack of awareness may affect the process. The more intentional the "can't," "won't," and "don't-do-it" behaviors, the more challenging the job of evaluators. Fortunately, we have presented ways you can begin to address individual attitudes and aptitudes that affect the evaluation process. You should not expect to succeed in eliciting high-quality involvement from every person in an organization, but that is the ultimate goal and you can take steps to move in that direction.

Regardless of how you analyze people's behaviors—using the dual-concerns conflict strategies model in Chapter 6, the individual attitude/aptitude matrix presented here (see Exhibits 7.2 and 7.3), or perhaps some other framework (such as personality or style preference inventories)—the importance of attending to the human details of involvement during the evaluation process cannot be overstated. People's opinions, feelings, and reactions matter. To ignore them is to risk a failed study.

Logistics

The fourth factor, logistics, deals with establishing consistent expectations/ procedures/routines, scheduling meetings, creating and using templates, organizing materials, and determining who will manage these items once established. Particulars include keeping and updating a calendar, arranging committee meetings, preparing agendas, documenting tasks, providing needed resources, organizing and storing materials, supplying technology, arranging and maintaining clerical and technical support, and so forth. These are the concrete components that help keep evaluations running smoothly and contribute to the viability of interactive processes. Such concerns may be especially important for collaborative studies designed to involve an array of stakeholders in the process (see Chapter 2, Exhibit 2.3).

We classify logistical concerns into five broad sets of actions. First, determine which evaluation processes can (and should) be standardized. Second, develop forms and templates to enact those processes. Third, focus on factors associated with meetings. Fourth, establish systems for organizing, storing, and accessing various documents and resources used to conduct evaluation studies. Fifth, if necessary, decide who will manage these logistical concerns and include those people in the planning. We elaborate on each of these in the sections that follow.

Establish Consistent Expectations, Procedures, and Routines

Start by thinking about activities that will be repeated throughout an evaluation study. For example, an evaluation steering committee will convene regularly, address an agenda, target tasks and timelines, create plans for conducting the evaluation, store and access relevant documents and resources, and so on. Once identified, establish routines and agreed-on procedures for managing these logistics—realizing that adjustments may be necessary to address unforeseen problems or new circumstances that occur along the way. Preplanning common sets of expectations and user-friendly procedures helps establish norms for consistency, which can be instrumental to the success of ongoing interactive processes. For example, how logistics are managed can facilitate or frustrate involvement, increase or decrease individual commitment to the process, and enhance or complicate problem solving. Familiar, smoothly running processes also help reduce uncertainty, apprehension, or anxiety that participants may bring to the evaluation from stressful or ineffective past experiences. We therefore encourage evaluators to deal with logistics up front by (a) identifying what can be standardized, (b) establishing set expectations and procedures that can be carried out routinely, and (c) reinforcing those norms by recording, distributing, reviewing frequently, and revising as necessary the agreed-on procedures.

Focus on Meetings

Next think about how best to schedule meetings. Setting a routine schedule good for all members of a committee (rather than scheduling irregularly or one meeting at a time) can enhance attendance by allowing participants to manage their individual calendars better. For example, a committee may consistently meet from 10:00 AM to 11:30 AM the first and third Wednesday of every month. In single-site situations (or with electronic conferencing capabilities across multiple sites), it may be advantageous to meet more frequently for shorter periods of time to foster greater ongoing communication. If possible, use a consistent location that is easily accessible and most convenient for all committee members. Also, systematically send out meeting reminders the week before as well as the day before. Finally, remember the creature comforts of meetings—refreshments, comfortable furniture/chairs, uplifting or inspiring (rather than drab/dull) surroundings, and the like—and, if you can, consistently provide these. Overall, successfully dealing with meeting logistics requires setting regular meetings at the same convenient and easily accessible location, in settings conducive to productivity, with food and other desirable comforts that contribute to a positive experience.

Create and Use Templates

Next, anticipate the types of procedural forms and documents that will be used frequently throughout the evaluation process. Certain tasks will be ongoing or repeated. Create templates for these to streamline recordkeeping and communication. Such documents include meeting agendas and minutes (see Template 4), "to-do" lists (see Template 5), and reflection or feedback forms (see Template 6). These templates—or ones like them created by evaluators for specific contexts—become common tools that orient committees toward tasks, provide normative structures for accomplishment, and promote consistent ways of communicating.

Organize Systems for Dealing With Documents

Preplan a system for organizing, storing, and accessing the documents and resources that will be generated and need to be consulted during the evaluation. Common expectations and jointly understood procedures will help avoid chaos that can quickly emerge when individuals on one or more committees are making their own unique contributions to the evaluation process. At the individual level, provide all committee members with templates and documents, either in preformatted electronic files or in tabbed notebooks that participants bring to all meetings, along with access to shared electronic sites/folders/files that contain these materials. At the project level, consider who will be responsible for maintaining files and/or archives (electronic and paper copies), what classification schemes will be easiest for labeling and storing documents, and who will have access to materials. A helpful system will standardize procedures to prevent ambiguity and pave the way for smooth operations. It also will affect communication networks and information management, both of which can make or break a viable evaluation process.

Template 4 Meeting Agenda

	Meeting date: *Year-Month-Day*
Organization Name Mission Statement	

Committee Name

Date: _____

Time: _____

Place: _____

Committee Members
("X" indicates those present)

☐ Name: _____ ☐ Name: _____ ☐ Name: _____

☐ Name: _____ ☐ Name: _____ ☐ Name: _____

☐ Name: _____ ☐ Name: _____ ☐ Name: _____

Agenda Items	Action Minutes
1. Check in (welcome, warm up, connect, report/discuss reflections from previous meeting, review/revisit/adjust working norms)	Topic/input
2. Review/correct/approve minutes from previous meeting	Corrections/approved
3. Review/finalize current agenda	Input/revisions
4. Review/update "to-do" list	A. Issue/item: B. Input/discussion: C. Decision/rationale:
5. Review/update other standing issues/items (list and number each in the same order at each meeting)	A. Issue/item: B. Input/discussion: C. Decision/rationale:
6. Parking lot items	A. Issue/item: B. Input/discussion: C. Decision/rationale:
7. Closure (reflections, pluses/wishes, lessons learned)	Collect/summarize

SOURCE: Stevahn and King (2010, Figure 2.2).

Template 5 "To-Do" List

			Meeting date: *Year-Month-Day*
	Committee Name **"To-Do" List** Date: _____		
Task (description)	**Who** (person responsible)	**Target Date** (for completion)	**Current Status** (progress/ completed)
1.			
2.			
3.			
4.			
5.			
6.			
7.			
8.			
9.			

SOURCE: Stevahn and King (2010, Figure 2.3).

Template 6 Meeting Reflections

Meeting Reflections Date: _____		
Pluses What did you like, appreciate, value?	**Wishes** What do you wish had been different?	**Questions** What questions remain? Ask them!
Thanks for your input!		

SOURCE: Stevahn and King (2010, Figure 2.4).

Determine Who Will Manage Logistics

Finally, decide whether one person or several will manage logistics, and name them. Responsibilities may include maintaining the calendar and meeting schedules, reserving meeting rooms and ordering refreshments, providing agendas and "to-do" lists, attending to technology needs, and so forth. If several people fulfill these roles, we suggest someone be the designated point person responsible for coordination. In deciding specifically who should manage logistics, consider personal skills, styles, and strengths of potential candidates. The ability to organize systematically, follow up consistently, attend to details, keep accurate records, and work with others supportively is instrumental; without these, the likelihood of success is reduced.

Communication

Communication is a fifth factor likely to influence the evaluation process. Many believe, with good reason, that the overall effectiveness of an organization or program has as much to do with its communication standards and networks as with anything else. In short, the existing culture of communication (those daily interactions that embody "how we work here") defines and characterizes a program/organization in substantive ways—something akin to "you are what you eat." In a perfect world, open, honest, responsive, respectful, culturally competent, and continuous communication would allow everyone—leaders and managers, service providers and support staff, clients and other stakeholders—to engage constructively in evaluation activities. However, as we keep saying, the real world is a messy place. Communication issues and/or difficulties are frequently at the heart of organizational woes, program troubles, or system snags. This creates a tremendous challenge for interactive evaluation processes that predominantly rely on effective communication and collaboration. Less-than-effective communication (which may already exist) will frustrate efforts and threaten, if not totally sabotage, success. Consider the following examples:

- Spotty attendance at department head meetings results in inconsistent patterns of data collection because not all leaders have been present to receive important directions, nor have they discussed them with others in attempts to learn and understand.
- The program director consistently sends out so many e-mail memos every day—many of which do not directly relate to evaluation responsibilities or functions—that service providers experience e-mail fatigue, often

ignoring or deleting messages, resulting in calamities when a key communication that does apply gets overlooked.

- Trying to get an appointment with key leaders for face-to-face evaluation problem solving is nearly impossible, leaving issues and emotions unsettled for weeks, which, in turn, results in low morale about the evaluation process and its potential to change the organization.

Each of these situations reveals problems with communication, perhaps symptomatic of those that existed within the organization prior to the evaluation. Clear and timely communication may help prevent such complications, along with the frustration and ill will that often result. Although changing communication patterns doesn't happen overnight, evaluators can take steps to head off disasters. Establishing agreed-on communication protocols at the start of an evaluation and vigilantly adhering to them throughout can begin to transform problematic patterns, as can consistently facilitating the types of interactive strategies presented in Chapter 5 that intentionally strive to build positive interdependence and cooperative relationships for enhanced communication among evaluation participants. We suggest that evaluators target six areas for communication protocols.

Communication Within Evaluation Committees

All committees engaged in the work of evaluation should establish, use, and monitor the effectiveness of a set of working norms or ground rules for communication among members. As a beginning, we suggest those listed in Template 7. Invite committee members to add others deemed important for maintaining

Template 7   Sample Working Norms

> **Working Norms**
>
> - Seek all voices; involve everyone.
> - Listen respectfully; communicate understanding.
> - Explore alternatives; don't jump to conclusions.
> - Raise issues constructively; engage in positive problem solving.
> - Appreciate each person's unique histories, perspectives, talents, skills.
> - Assume confidentiality; what's discussed in the meeting stays in the meeting.
> - Mutually agree on information to be shared with others outside of the meeting.
> - Other norms generated by participants . . .

SOURCE: Stevahn and King (2010, Figure 2.8).

effective communication and positive interpersonal relations. Post the list at each meeting and periodically reflect on what is working well and what needs adjusting. Also consider designating someone on the committee to be responsible for regularly engaging participants in following up on effectiveness. In fact, revisiting norms could be the first or last item routinely included in every meeting agenda to ensure follow-up will occur.

Communication Among Evaluation Committees

If multiple committees have been established, determining general guidelines for communications among them will be helpful. How will information be shared? Perhaps committee chairs (or a designated committee member) will provide updates systematically to other evaluation committees via an agreed-on method such as electronic postings or hard-copy summaries. It may be prudent to determine if all committee members simultaneously receive information/decisions or if committee chairs first receive communications and then forward those messages to committee members. The fewer evaluation committees, the greater the potential for more manageable communication. This may be an important factor in determining how many committees to establish. Remember the KISS principle: Keep it short and simple. Adding layers to already existing bureaucracy may be counterproductive and heighten frustration, thereby easily detracting from efforts to foster and support positive interpersonal relationships required for interactive evaluation processes.

Communication Beyond Evaluation Committees

Sometimes committees should share information with others not directly conducting evaluation activities. These may include various administrative hierarchies within the organization, departments or units, service providers across programs or divisions, clients or program/service recipients, governing or advisory boards, evaluation or program funders, other branches of the organization in multisite situations, the community/society at large, or other stakeholders. Those spearheading evaluation efforts should develop policies, guidelines, and procedures for such communications. For example, will the chair of the evaluation steering committee or some other designated participant be responsible for communicating information? Will there be opportunities for steering committee members to consider and/or provide feedback on written communications before release to wider audiences? What avenues for responding should those who receive information use? Planning procedures for these and other concerns related to communicating with groups not directly responsible for evaluation tasks should help create and sustain the types of interactive processes that will promote success.

Electronic Communication

Electronics can provide numerous advantages when it comes to communication. Evaluators and those on evaluation committees can share information among themselves and with organizational staff and other stakeholders rapidly, efficiently, and inexpensively. They can also obtain input easily and quickly—whether from a few or many via e-mail or electronic user-friendly surveys. Online chats, threaded discussions, video streams, and other interactive technology make connections more accessible than ever. However, these advantages also come with potential pitfalls, such as when everyone does not have appropriate hardware, software, or online access; e-mail overload becomes all consuming; new software or application updates make it difficult to access old files or merge new ones; individuals name files or folders differently, which complicates storage and retrieval; and so on. Just like other forms of communication, it is wise to establish guidelines for electronic interaction at the onset of a study to pave the way for smooth processes that will support effective work throughout.

Electronic protocol might include (a) agreeing to use certain electronic platforms or networking systems, (b) consistently naming folders/files (by date, title, committee name, person responsible, or other agreed-on options), (c) posting items on shared directories (meeting agendas and minutes, "to-do" lists, draft documents, or other information), (d) responding to e-mail messages (reply to sender only, reply to all, reply using an electronic mailing list), and (e) deciding when to use e-mail versus face-to-face communication (such as for short concrete messages, agenda distribution prior to meetings, and simple feedback rather than complex substantive communications). Discussing multifaceted, emotionally charged, or political issues face-to-face (rather than electronically) tends to foster the type of productive dialogue necessary in complex situations. Face-to-face interaction enables greater in-depth exploration of ideas, immediate opportunities to clarify and check for understanding, sensitivity to personal perspectives, attention to cultural nuances, and use of nonverbal cues (facial expressions, body postures, hand gestures)—all of which affect how individuals make sense of messages sent and received. When in-person conversations are not possible, as may be the case in multisite evaluations, then talking via telephone, live-stream video, or some other voice/visual conferencing option can be a helpful substitute.

Information Management

Managing information somewhat overlaps with the various aspects of communication noted above, as well as with the logistical concern of organizing systems for dealing with documents. Here the focus is more specifically on archiving documents and records for use in future evaluation studies. Evaluation processes produce documentation valuable for future studies. Every evaluation, therefore, presents an opportunity to ensure that an audit trail is in place and easy for others to follow. Each evaluation develops its own history; recording it serves numerous purposes. Documentation is useful for reflecting on actions and refining processes, reinforcing a culture of data-based decision making, promoting evaluation capacity building (ECB), bringing newcomers on board or stakeholders not directly involved in committee work up to speed, providing concrete evidence of what transpired if questions about procedure or accuracy arise, and so on. Consider three tips for information management.

1. *Put documentation in order every step of the way.* This may include collecting and organizing items such as (a) a chronological timetable of the various steps taken to conduct the evaluation; (b) records of committees, participants, meeting minutes, issues/decisions/rationales, and so on; (c) sampling procedures; (d) data collection methods and instruments; (e) raw data files; (f) data analysis strategies; (g) findings; (h) recommendations and priority decisions; (i) "lessons learned" and other written reflections on evaluation procedures and processes; and (j) other pertinent forms or materials. The goal is to tell the story of the evaluation and its processes so a detailed record exists for future or ongoing practice. An accessible, organized archive becomes an organizational learning tool that promotes ECB, enabling those involved to further develop the skills of gathering and using data to address questions of importance to the organization. Don't move on without creating the paper and/or electronic trail that others can consult, reflect on, and learn from.

2. *Systematically facilitate conversations about lessons learned.* Revisit and review collected documents to reflect on procedures and forms, database management, use of resources, project decisions, and so on. Involve evaluation participants in discussions on "What worked well?" "What did not?" "What refinements would be helpful for future projects?" These conversations throughout an evaluation generate an invaluable record of "do" and "don't" considerations—some of which can immediately be put into practice. Remember that dealing with problems is part of growth; you can't learn without them. Documenting difficulties helps

ensure what we learn from problems is not lost but, instead, integrated into ongoing efforts toward greater effectiveness. This also becomes an important part of metaevaluation, which entails evaluating the entire study at its completion both for accountability and learning purposes—that is, to assess quality and improve future practice.

3. *Decide how to label folders and files for storing/archiving documents.* Create a table of contents or tracking sheet that lists such information. Maintain electronic and paper copies of documents and determine where they will be housed (specific offices, central vs. secluded locations, protected vs. open environments, locked cabinets or password-protected files vs. shared storage options). Determine who has access to stored documents. Discuss confidentiality issues along with ethical, legal, political, or situational circumstances that might influence choices, and then make thoughtful and ethical decisions. Appoint someone with expert organizational skills to summarize protocols, collect documents, and manage files.

Confidentiality

Finally, think carefully about confidentiality. Trust is a necessary component for positive interaction; without it people won't risk sharing their ideas and experiences or investing their energy and resources. Transparency can foster trust, but it also can work against confidentiality; so it is important to appreciate the tension between confidentiality and transparency. Agree on what information, documents, and files must be kept confidential and what can be freely shared. Doing so will not guarantee smooth sailing but may help avert or diminish the negative effects that conflicts over confidentiality could bring. This becomes especially important for those who have access to raw data (e.g., members of a data collection team, those responsible for data entry, anyone involved in data analysis). Be clear and firm regarding data confidentiality. Just as one's reputation can be damaged in an instant, trust can be broken in a heartbeat; rebuilding can take a lifetime.

Communication is a major concern in nearly all human endeavors, and IEP is no exception. Although dealing with all aspects of communication goes beyond the scope of this text, gearing up for viable interactive evaluation processes requires paying attention to the communication issues noted above. We do not suggest trying to micromanage every aspect of communication throughout evaluations. That would be absurd, impossible, and unhelpful. However, we do advocate developing systematic routines and guidelines for communication at the start of evaluation projects—and revisiting and refining them as the evaluation progresses—to enhance, support, and sustain the interactive components likely to underpin effective practice.

BUILDING EVALUATION CAPACITY THROUGH INTERACTIVE PROCESSES

In thinking about creating a viable interactive evaluation process, it is appropriate to revisit the concept of ECB presented in Chapter 2, knowing that some evaluators seek to build the capacity of organizations in or with which they work to conduct evaluations routinely. ECB emerged as a distinct practice around the turn of the 21st century. In making ECB the theme of the 2000 annual meeting of the AEA, President Laura Leviton highlighted the potential of a new practice through which organizations can systematically increase their capacity to conduct program evaluations over time. Stockdill, Baizerman, and Compton (2002) define the role of the ECB practitioner as "bringing about and sustaining a state of affairs in which quality program evaluation and its appropriate uses are ordinary and ongoing practices within and/or between one or more organizations/programs/sites" (p. 8). The rationale for this work is multifaceted.

- *Building positive relationships through the evaluation process.* Participating in ECB activities may increase stakeholder involvement and buy-in, help people move past their fear of evaluation, build community support, decrease the marginalization of groups that don't routinely evaluate, and develop trust between levels of the organizational hierarchy.
- *Increasing program documentation and evidence.* The ECB process can be a tool for learning about and documenting what happens in an organization, which can provide evidence for funding and potentially demonstrate its value to outsiders.
- *Improving internal evaluation processes.* ECB can become a long-term solution to the high price of external evaluators while simultaneously allowing program staff to evaluate routinely, longitudinally, and in depth.
- *Improving practice.* Regardless of what an organization seeks to accomplish, engagement in ongoing evaluation efforts can lead to a better understanding of its culture, processes, and systems, which in turn can lead to increased effectiveness and efficiency as well as to an increased sense of professionalism.

Although the rationale and potential benefits are evident, given ECB's short history, the "hows" are less so. Pejsa (2011) writes, "In summarizing the empirical literature on ECB, one thing is clear—there is no definitive way to go about ECB work in organizations, and researchers have not attempted to design one sure path, model, or theory" (p. 46). Highlighting the complexity of ECB, Preskill and Boyle (2008) present a multidisciplinary model that includes two separate parallel circles under the heading "organizational learning capacity"— one labeled "evaluation knowledge, skills, and attitudes" (contains 10 actions or activities) and one labeled "sustainable evaluation practice" (gives eight outcomes of ECB, e.g., continuous learning about evaluation and evaluation frameworks and processes). The circles are connected by a two-headed arrow labeled "transfer of learning" and four areas that support the process: leadership, culture, systems and structures, and communication. With so many variables involved, building evaluation capacity—the "how"—remains a challenge.

We take a straightforward approach to ECB. If capacity building is a goal, then people need to be involved in doing the work of evaluation to learn, refine, and internalize the knowledge, skills, and dispositions required for effective practice. This can happen only when they participate in meaningful processes that support successful evaluation efforts. How can this occur? Volkov and King (2007) offer a research-based checklist for ECB that can help interactive evaluators structure capacity building activities. This checklist has three sections:

- *Organizational Context:* Be aware of the internal and external organizational context, power hierarchies, administrative culture, and decision-making processes.
- *Resources:* Make evaluation resources available and use them.
- *ECB Structures:* Purposefully create structures . . . that enable the development of evaluation capacity. (pp. 1–3)

We will discuss each in turn, noting that you can use many of the suggestions for planning a successful interactive evaluation process discussed previously in this chapter to build evaluation capacity.

Organizational Context

As evaluators work to build evaluation capacity, they need to pay attention to two aspects of an organization's context.

ECB-Friendly Internal Organizational Context

First, they should actively cultivate an internal context conducive to ECB. Determining if and to what extent the internal environment is supportive of change can mark an important beginning. Therefore, ensure that key leaders of the organization both support and take responsibility for the process itself and for recruiting evaluation champions who will support activities that can lead to additional support. A positive activity for encouraging engagement is to work purposefully to increase people's interest in and demand for evaluation information. This can be accomplished by organizing opportunities to socialize around evaluation activities during the work day—for example, by discussing a study's results during lunch or by having people develop a survey collaboratively. If people are going to use data to make decisions, it is important that they own the responsibility for those decisions; ECB can fall short if people are unable to use the results of their studies.

Support From the External Environment

Second, as noted earlier in this chapter, ECB practitioners, like all evaluators, should strive to understand and—to the extent possible—take advantage of a program/organization's external environment. This includes identifying external mandates or accountability requirements and then integrating them into ECB efforts. People are often more willing to learn about evaluation if they can complete a task they know must be done. Another tack is to see in what ways the external environment is supportive of data-based change—for example, if accreditation agencies, professional communities, or other external stakeholders provide support for conducting or using evaluation—and then using that impetus to build organizational support for evaluation.

Resources

Another area evaluators need to consider in ECB efforts concerns two types of resources that will support ongoing evaluation activities.

Access to Evaluation Resources

First, it is critical to secure continuing sources of support for program evaluation in the organization. This includes a line item in the budget with explicit, dedicated funding for program evaluation activities to ensure long-term fiscal support from the board or administration. It also includes having basic resources such as copying, equipment for data collection and analysis, computers and software, and so on to support evaluation activities. Additional resources may be required to provide adequate time and opportunities to collaborate on evaluation activities, including, when possible, being together physically in an environment free from interruptions. Some entrepreneurial evaluators have developed revenue-generating strategies to support program evaluation in their organizations—for example, by providing expert training for a fee, serving as evaluation consultants to other organizations for pay, or selling copies of specialized data collection instruments.

Sources of Organizational Support for Evaluation

Second, ECB practitioners should work to provide access to high-quality evaluation resources. This includes providing easy access to relevant research that contains "best-practice" content both for evaluation in general and for evaluation in program-specific content (e.g., health, education, visitor studies, etc.), as well as examples of exemplary evaluation descriptions and reports. The advent of search engines such as Google and Bing has made this task extremely manageable in sites that have Internet connection. Access to resources also includes ensuring the availability of sufficient information on how to find existing evaluation resources (e.g., websites, professional organizations, and, as appropriate, evaluation consultants). In addition, providing high-quality resources may mean modeling first-rate evaluation practice so people can see what that looks like, engaging staff in activities with the intent to teach them evaluation processes, and ultimately coaching people as they work on their own studies. Internal evaluators can plan these activities as part of their practice; external evaluators need to be hired to do so.

ECB Structures

This structural area is perhaps the most important because here ECB practitioners can intentionally create an infrastructure to support the long-term development of evaluation capacity. This infrastructure has four components.

Long-Term Plan for ECB

First, a purposeful, long-term ECB plan for the organization provides a blueprint for constructing a system of ongoing evaluation. The written plan, which should be revisited frequently to assess progress, should include the following elements: (a) a viable conception of evaluation for the organization; (b) an ECB oversight group to initiate, monitor, and advance evaluation processes continually; (c) a plan to integrate evaluation processes purposefully into organizational policies and procedures; and (d) a strategy for conducting and using evaluations that applies professional evaluation frameworks, guidelines, and standards. To ensure that capacity is increasing and the evaluation function growing, capacity building activities should be routinely evaluated and the plan updated accordingly.

Infrastructure to Support the Evaluation Process

A second structural component is the infrastructure to support specific elements of the evaluation process and related communication systems. There need to be organizational structures that will facilitate routine evaluation activities such as framing evaluation questions; conducting needs assessments; designing evaluations; and collecting, analyzing, and interpreting data. Someone needs to take responsibility for facilitating the ongoing development and assessment of these evaluation processes and for building individuals' readiness and skills to implement activities. Two critical systems—an internal reporting/monitoring/tracking system and an effective communication system with the capacity to explain evaluation processes and disseminate findings to stakeholder groups—will help ensure that, once built, the evaluation capacity will be sustainable.

Purposeful Socialization Into the Evaluation Process

Third, by introducing and attending to purposeful socialization into the organization's evaluation process, ECB practitioners systematically develop staff members knowledgeable about evaluation. During their orientations, new hires learn about how the organization does evaluation; longtime employees have regular opportunities to discuss program evaluation with their colleagues. It is important to establish clear expectations for people's evaluation roles and to provide sufficient time during the work day for these activities so no one feels punished for having to participate. When possible, incentives for participation, including extra pay, release time, an opportunity to engage meaningfully with peers, and even special refreshments, can inspire people to join the evaluation process.

Purposeful socialization also includes either providing or making available learning opportunities related to program evaluation. These can be university courses, professional development sessions such as conferences or training institutes, or individual coaching on evaluation competencies. One straightforward and often cost-effective way to promote and facilitate people's learning evaluation is by involving them in meaningful ways in evaluation planning and implementation, where they will learn evaluation by doing one. "The experience of being involved in an evaluation . . . for those actually involved, can have a lasting impact on how they think, on their openness to reality testing, and on how they view the things they do" (Patton, 2012, p. 142). Finally, an important part of evaluation socialization is modeling a willingness to be evaluated. Ensuring that evaluations and the ECB process itself are routinely and visibly evaluated demonstrates to people a willingness to walk the evaluation talk.

Peer Learning Structures

The fourth and final infrastructure component relates to the third, i.e., purposeful socialization. Peer learning structures create a place where people can be socialized to the organization's approach to evaluation—where they can build trust, both interpersonal and organizational, and support one another interdependently in the evaluation process. Ongoing learning activities through which people interact around evaluation processes and results can help people learn the evaluation process, as will incorporating a feedback mechanism in the decision-making process and an effective communication system. An additional way to encourage peer learning is through opportunities for both individual and group reflection on evaluation—for example, data-based discussions of successes, challenges, and failures in the organization.

Taken together, the components of this ECB checklist provide a set of possible tasks for developing evaluation capacity in an organization. These, combined with the information in this chapter for developing and sustaining a viable evaluation process, may help spread this new practice or reaffirm existing practice.

ASSESSING EVALUATION PROCESSES TO ENHANCE VIABILITY

Continuously assessing evaluation processes—especially those that are interactive—and systematically documenting progress can be instrumental to keeping evaluations on track. In short, assessing throughout allows evaluators to enhance the positive and attend to the negative more immediately. Even documenting simple aspects of the process, such as who attends evaluation committee meetings, may help evaluators and participants reinforce what is working or catch potential problems early on. For example, recording consistent attendance at advisory board meetings that include community members who requested child care helps the evaluator determine that providing such care is well worth the cost and should be maintained throughout the evaluation effort. In contrast, imagine realizing well into an evaluation study that a key leader holding the purse strings to the program being evaluated consistently arrives late to meetings or does not show up at all. Planning to keep attendance at the onset may have illuminated this pattern of troubling behavior earlier in the study when a discussion with that leader would have been helpful to learn about misgivings regarding certain aspects of the evaluation—all of which could have been problem solved as the initial stages of the study were under way.

There are at least three ways to focus the assessment of evaluation processes, as shown in Exhibit 7.4. *Formative* assessments ask, "How are we doing?"—specifically to improve processes (commonly referred to as *monitoring* in the world of government and large-scale international evaluations). *Summative* assessments ask, "How did we do?"—specifically to make final judgments ("go" or "no-go" decisions). *Reflective* assessments ask, "What did we learn?"—specifically to illuminate lessons garnered from experience (what is known now that was not known before).

Exhibit 7.4 Assessing Evaluation Processes

Assessment Focus	Evaluation Timeline	Evaluative Terms
How are we doing?	During, throughout the evaluation	Monitoring, formative
How did we do?	After, at the end of the evaluation	Summative
What did we learn?	Throughout, but especially at the end	Reflective

SOURCE: Stevahn and King (2010, Table 6.1).

While all these may be useful to creating and sustaining viable processes for the interactive work that makes up an evaluation study, we especially note the importance of gathering ongoing input to reveal signs that the process is going well or that something may be going wrong and, therefore, needs to be addressed. Patton (2008) advises evaluators to be "active-reactive-interactive-adaptive":

The phrase is meant to be both descriptive and prescriptive. It describes how real-world decision making actually unfolds—act, react, interact, and adapt. Yet it is prescriptive in alerting evaluators to consciously and deliberately act, react, interact, and adapt to increase their effectiveness in working with intended users. (p. 207)

Patton's (2008, p. 209) "adaptive cycle" highlights the fact that in evaluation negotiations throughout the course of a study, evaluators need to monitor and adjust their actions to address situations as they develop.

Numerous methods exist for assessing evaluation processes. Here we suggest two ways to think about planning for such assessment. Exhibit 7.5 offers a variety of concrete actions for seeking input relevant to each type of assessment focus. Exhibit 7.6 revisits the evaluator's dozen of interactive strategies first presented in Chapter 5 and indicates which are especially useful for each type of assessment focus. These various methods (such as routinely facilitating discussions at the end of committee meetings or administering simple feedback forms) and strategies (such as *Strategy 4: Cooperative Interviews, Strategy 5: Round-Robin Check-In, Strategy 7: Data Dialogue, Strategy 9: Graffiti/Carousel,* and so on) can be applied broadly across diverse evaluation contexts, settings, cultures, and purposes. They also lend themselves to incorporating any of the following sentence starters that may be appropriate:

- Evaluation processes that have been especially helpful so far are . . .
- Evaluation processes that have been most challenging and/or problematic are . . .
- The evaluation steering committee worked best when . . .
- The evaluation steering committee struggled most when . . .
- Data collection worked well when . . .
- Data collection was problematic when . . .
- Resources that especially helped during the evaluation were . . .
- Resources we didn't have but needed during the evaluation were . . .
- I felt especially motivated to tackle evaluation tasks when . . .
- Being involved in evaluation felt like a burden when . . .
- Communication worked best when . . .
- Communication was problematic when . . .
- I felt supported during the evaluation when . . .
- I struggled with the evaluation when . . .
- What I've learned from involvement in the evaluation is . . .
- Useful advice for those conducting future evaluations ("do" and "don't") includes . . .

Finally, as noted in the previous section, a large part of ECB is about process. Therefore, consistently assessing how well various processes are going—especially those that rely on effective interaction for success—becomes

Exhibit 7.5   Methods for Collecting Information on Evaluation Processes

Assessment Focus	Methods for Collecting Information
How are we doing?	• Interview the clients/primary intended users regularly to assess progress and situations that arise that may affect the evaluation. • Make one person responsible for compiling all materials related to the evaluation, creating a record for periodic review. • Hold routine reflection sessions (formal and informal) where people discuss specific details of the evaluation implementation, what's going well, what the challenges are, and what might be changed to improve the process. • Hand out simple feedback forms that are routinely completed by participants in evaluation activities and then compiled and reviewed by the evaluators and/or the evaluation steering committee. • Send a brief online survey to evaluation participants at different points in the process to elicit their ideas about how things are going and what changes might be needed.
How did we do?	• Hold informal debriefings with participants to critique evaluation processes and outcomes. • Conduct individual interviews with key members of the organization. • Conduct group interviews with members of different groups who participated in the process. • Send a feedback survey to all participants. • Hire an outside expert to conduct a formal audit.
What did we learn from the evaluation process?	• Make one person responsible for compiling all materials related to the evaluation and create an official archive for future efforts. • Hold formal reflection sessions for people to frame the lessons learned from their participation in the evaluation. • Refine these lessons in a discussion with others who took part. • Formally anticipate what the "lessons learned" will mean for future evaluation efforts by creating a written list of possible actions.

SOURCE: Stevahn and King (2010, Table 6.5).

important to maintaining a workable study. Input on topics such as those illustrated in the sentence starters above (recorded, archived, and accessible for future use) contribute to the types of ECB (e.g., see Compton, Baizerman, & Stockdill, 2002), process use (e.g., see Cousins, 2007; Patton, 2008), and systems learning (e.g., see Preskill & Torres, 1999; Senge, 2006) that underpin ongoing improvement in effective programs and organizations.

Exhibit 7.6   Interactive Strategies for Assessing/Monitoring Evaluation Processes

Interactive Strategies	How are we doing? Formative	How did we do? Summative	What did we learn? Reflective
1. Voicing Variables	X		
2. Voicing Viewpoints/Beliefs			
3. Choosing Corners	X	X	
4. Cooperative Interviews	X	X	X
5. Round-Robin Check-In	X	X	X
6. Making Metaphors	X	X	
7. Data Dialogue	X	X	X
8. Jigsaw			
9. Graffiti/Carousel	X	X	X
10. Concept Formation/Cluster Maps	X	X	X
11. Cooperative Rank Order	X		
12. Fist to Five	X	X	
13. Dot Votes/Bar Graphs	X	X	

SOURCE: Stevahn and King (2010, Table 6.6).

NOTE: See Chapter 5 for facilitation directions and sample materials.

APPLYING INTERACTIVE EVALUATION PRACTICE PRINCIPLES TO CREATING A VIABLE INTERACTIVE EVALUATION PROCESS

The seven IEP principles provide a game plan for developing and sustaining a viable interactive evaluation process. Exhibit 7.7 highlights how evaluators can keep these principles in mind throughout. In planning and implementing any evaluation, evaluators should strive to involve people in personally meaningful ways and purposefully structure interactions that engage them in evaluation activities. Attending to both the personal and the interpersonal factors, including

Exhibit 7.7 IEP Principles Applied to Creating a Viable Interactive Evaluation Process

IEP Principle	Applied to Creating a Viable Interactive Evaluation Process
1. Get personal.	• Directly focus on people's contextual and cultural identities and what this means for communicating throughout the evaluation and for helping people make personal meaning of the process and outcomes. • Arrange logistics in ways that support people's personal needs during the evaluation; pay particular attention to individuals' attitudes and aptitudes. • Focus on the personal aspects of involvement.
2. Structure interaction.	• Pay attention to the structural components of involvement, logistics, and communication that will move the evaluation forward. • Be sure the interactions facilitated are inclusive, strategic, and culturally appropriate. • When building evaluation capacity, structure interactions to teach people evaluation skills.
3. Examine context.	• Work to understand both the organizational and social–cultural contexts of the evaluation setting. • Make decisions about how to create a viable evaluation process in light of contextual information.
4. Consider politics.	• Recognize that resources help underpin the viability of the evaluation process; political factors may affect how resources are allocated. • Identify people in the program/organization who have power, and be sure to involve them in appropriate ways.
5. Expect conflict.	• Analyze the program/organizational context for potential conflict. • Embed constructive conflict processes into evaluation activities in advance. • Develop a conflict-positive attitude; conflict can be a catalyst for positive change.
6. Respect culture.	• Honor the varieties of cultural perspectives and experiences people bring to the evaluation process. • Capitalize on the unique cultural characteristics of participants that can enrich evaluation practice. • Know that developing cultural competence is a lifelong learning process for evaluators; make a commitment to it.
7. Take time.	• It takes time to prepare for logistics and to involve people meaningfully in the evaluation process; make sure you provide sufficient time. • Develop realistic timelines for the evaluation that attend to interactive process concerns. • Recognize that the evaluation process almost always pushes against established timelines; be ready to make adjustments.

SOURCE: © 2010 Jean A. King & Laurie Stevahn.

organizational and individuals' cultures, can enable evaluators to create a meaningful evaluation process uniquely designed for that time and place. Understanding context becomes critical because what makes sense in one situation, for example, where staff work cooperatively, may not succeed in another, where individuals vie for a manager's attention. Awareness of situational politics and the conflict that almost always emerges in evaluation settings will help evaluators know when they need to alter initial plans in light of developments on-site. Evaluating the evaluation from beginning to end may help evaluators identify needed changes in time to do something about them. As always, the "take-time" principle reminds us that, although there are typically timelines that constrain an evaluator's work, a rushed evaluation can be a risky endeavor.

CHAPTER REVIEW

This chapter described what evaluators can do to create a viable and sustainable interactive evaluation process. Because evaluations are always subject to multiple challenges, it is important to be thoughtful and systematic in planning from beginning to end.

1. To the extent feasible and appropriate, evaluators should pay attention to five components that can influence successful interactive evaluation practice both at the beginning of a study and as it unfolds: (a) the context/setting of the evaluation, (b) cultural considerations, (c) people to involve, (d) logistical concerns, and (e) various aspects of communication.

2. A sizeable number of contextual factors can influence an evaluation study, including the program/organization's (a) mission/vision/values, (b) history, (c) site/location, (d) size/scale, (e) structure, (f) norms/routines, (g) logic models, (h) budget/funding, (i) content/field, (j) wider environment, and (k) other relevant factors. Evaluators should reflect on each of these when planning a viable interactive evaluation process.

3. Attending to two broad cultural perspectives can also help an evaluator when planning a study. One perspective, grounded in the literatures on organization development and leadership/management for change, tends to define culture as the existing roles, relationships, responsibilities, and common practices that characterize a program/organization. The other, grounded in the literatures on diversity, critical theory, multicultural/intercultural education, and social justice, focuses more pointedly on aspects of identity, pluralism, power, privilege, and equity. Each perspective can help evaluators think about and attend to cultural

dimensions of the study that may influence people's experiences and the evaluation's process and outcomes.

4. Evaluators need to identify the committee structures that can effectively engage people in an interactive evaluation, identify the individuals who will serve on committees, and think carefully about the aptitudes and attitudes of participants for maximum effectiveness.

5. Logistical concerns can be divided into five broad sets of actions: (a) determining which evaluation processes can (and should) be standardized; (b) focusing on factors associated with meetings; (c) developing forms and templates to carry out those processes; (d) establishing systems for organizing, storing, and accessing various documents and resources; and (e) deciding who will manage logistical concerns and including them in planning for the evaluation.

6. Establishing standardized communication protocols at the beginning of an evaluation and adhering to them can help evaluations stay on track. Evaluators can target six areas for communication protocols: (a) communication within evaluation committees, (b) communication among evaluation committees, (c) communication beyond evaluation committees, (d) electronic communication, (e) information management, and (f) confidentiality.

7. Evaluators who want to build evaluation capacity in an organization should attend to context and resource issues and work to establish an evaluation capacity building (ECB) infrastructure, including (a) a long-term, written plan for ECB; (b) the infrastructure necessary to conduct quality evaluations; (c) purposeful socialization into the evaluation process; and (d) peer learning structures.

8. Assessing evaluation processes on an ongoing basis and systematically documenting progress can be instrumental to keeping evaluations on track. Evaluators will do well to evaluate themselves.

8

DEALING WITH THE UNEXPECTED IN PROGRAM EVALUATION

When Bad Things Happen to Good Evaluators

Chapter Preview

- Remind evaluators that they cannot control every aspect of an evaluation
- Detail the unexpected possibilities affecting evaluations that are largely beyond evaluators' control and possible responses to them
- Discuss in general what interactive evaluators can do to respond to the unexpected
- Distinguish between the ways internal and external evaluators can address the unexpected
- Consider how to resolve trade-offs in evaluation decision making
- Apply the interactive evaluation practice principles to dealing with the unexpected in program evaluation

INTRODUCTION

There is a famous moment in the movie *Apollo 13* when Tom Hanks's character, Jim Lovell, realizes that a key piece of equipment on the spacecraft has failed and says, in the calmest of voices, "Houston, we have a problem." Would that every person confronted with an unexpected challenge could remain equally unruffled. Some evaluators, less able to maintain their composure, wonder why challenging events appear to be part and parcel of the evaluation process. After all, the process is hard enough without throwing in monkey wrenches. As one of the decision makers interviewed for Patton's classic study on evaluation use noted, "Evaluation isn't a birthday party, so people aren't looking for surprises" (Patton, 2012, p. 330). Is it the fault of evaluators that over time they must learn to *expect* the unexpected?

Think for a moment of the many reasons someone might resist an evaluation process. When asked to participate, people tend to ask two questions about program evaluations: How will this affect me or my job personally? and What's in it for me? Some people lack evaluation skills, worried about crafting high-quality survey items or conducting complex statistical analyses on large data sets. Others think any form of evaluation is a waste of time, believing their program is doing just fine, thank you; they are uninterested in framing questions about its success or exploring its cost-effectiveness. Some are afraid of what the study's conclusions might suggest or of the negative potential of organizational change. Others are simply exhausted, burned out by the many responsibilities they are shouldering in an era of reduced budgets. Unfortunately, far too many people can detail negative experiences with previous evaluations. Now multiply these considerations times the number of people involved in any evaluation study, and it is easy to see the many particulars an evaluator or even an evaluation team may miss or misunderstand. Add in the complexity of the organizational environments—both external and internal—in which the study will take place, the countless details involved in designing and implementing an evaluation study, along with the evaluator's personal issues, and the potential for the unexpected becomes clear. There are simply many things an evaluator cannot nail down before or even during the process.

If there were an evaluator's Serenity Prayer, it might read (with apologies to Reinhold Niebuhr):

> Grant me the serenity
>
> to accept the things I cannot control;
>
> courage to control the things I can;
>
> and wisdom to know the difference.

Chapter 7 discussed the various ways courageous evaluators can control and manage (or at least influence) the many moving parts of an evaluation process. There *are* actions that build interactive evaluation practice (IEP), and the evaluator is in charge of them. The better the preparation for and oversight of a study, the more an evaluator can feel in control or at least be aware and have the opportunity to shape events as they develop. But even the best-laid evaluation plans are apt to face repeated challenges, some of them of the evaluator's own making—we hate it when that happens—and others the result of the environment, personal reactions, or something related to the process. Evaluators must learn to accept such "uncontrollia" as an inevitable feature of program evaluation and gain the wisdom to distinguish between what they do and do not have power over. As the adapted Serenity Prayer suggests, that is the true wisdom that can lead evaluators to a calmer perspective even as the unpredicted erupts around them.

Someone may be thinking—and rightly so—that the unexpected is not always bad. Imagine that a program director finds extra money to support the evaluation process, a new analyst is hired who can work magic with an existing database, or a custodian finds a dusty box of data long thought lost. True, these would be unexpected but beneficial events. So is getting a large inheritance from a relative you've never heard of. But in most cases, the unexpected throws evaluators a curveball that leads to a swing and a potential miss. Whatever happens, evaluators focused on the interactive evaluation process still need to make decisions, act, and reflect, applying the IEP principles to respond to whatever situations hand them.

This chapter details many of these unexpected possibilities and provides ideas on how to deal with them. Think of it as a resource, a compilation of potential problems with ideas for how an evaluator might respond. It cannot be a detailed "how-to," both because of space limitations and because, in truth, every evaluation situation is unique and nuanced; cookbook solutions are inappropriate. As experience teaches us, solutions really do depend on the specifics of a given situation. The chapter accordingly begins with a discussion of the limits of evaluation practice. This is followed by a description of what can go wrong in evaluations and brief suggestions of what interactive evaluators might do when such things happen. The description is divided into four categories: environmental issues, client/user issues, evaluation process/results issues, and evaluator issues. The next section summarizes these many details and adds general thoughts on what to do about the unexpected, followed by a discussion of how internal and external evaluators can handle these situations. We then discuss ways to resolve the inevitable trade-offs in evaluation decision making. The chapter concludes by noting how the IEP principles introduced in Chapter 3 apply to dealing with the unexpected in program evaluation.

THE LIMITS OF EVALUATION PRACTICE

Most people believe that evaluators are powerful. Staff members routinely get nervous when an evaluator enters their world, worried—often without reason—that they may be held accountable for professional failings or, worse yet, lose their jobs. Psychological researchers even study the subspecialty of **extreme evaluation anxiety** (Donaldson, Gooler, & Scriven, 2002), or what Patton

(2008, p. 47) jokingly calls, in its initial stages, **pre-evaluation stress syndrome**. In actuality, evaluators' so-called power is bounded, typically a function of their relationships with those who hold positional authority. As the moon reflects the sun, an evaluator reflects the power of another.

- For internal evaluators, placement in the organizational hierarchy in all likelihood determines the primary intended users with whom they will interact over time. The closer an evaluator's position to the top of the organizational chart, the more likely she will interact with key leaders who hold the power to effect major change. Even there, however, she does not personally make the decisions. Evaluators are commonly in staff, not line, relationships, so they seek to influence those with the power to shape evaluations and use their findings meaningfully. Placement further down the hierarchy, which requires working through others to reach those leaders, may further limit the evaluator's potential influence.

- For external evaluators, the roles of the individuals who are clients and primary intended users—those who commission studies and work with evaluators over the course of an inquiry—affect their power. As is true of internal evaluators, working with top leadership increases the likelihood that others will perceive reflected power. But external evaluators are not actors in the organization that hires them; they cannot make decisions resulting in change. At best they can influence others to do so by encouraging their clients to understand and use the evaluation's results. An external evaluator's power is in the eye of the beholder.

Whether internal or external, then, evaluators do not directly wield power that may lead to job loss, radical (or even minor) changes, or other consequences participants fear. Regardless of their setting, evaluators will ideally have influence over events (relational power), but only in unusual cases will they have authority (positional power).

As a result, there are many things evaluators are unable to control during the course of an evaluation, and you are well advised to remember that. People may think evaluators have power. They certainly do bear the power of social science research methods—a powerful tool in Western society—and they typically get to interact with those in the setting who *do* hold power. But, as this chapter will demonstrate, there is a lengthy list of items that even the most skilled evaluators can do little but react to. Let's face it: Things happen, and an evaluator may sometimes feel as though he is experiencing the perfect storm of constraints as one detail of a study after another goes amiss, threatening to sink the metaphoric evaluation ship. Exhibit 8.1 gives a brief example of the unexpected for every stage of the basic inquiry tasks, documenting that the unexpected can occur throughout the evaluation process. The unexpected can also occur at every point along the evaluation capacity building continuum and while using the interactive participation quotient as a frame, whether the evaluator is directing the study, collaborating on it, or coaching others. IEP involves complex interpersonal processes. It is challenging, messy, and at times unpredictable work, and oftentimes there are no easy answers to situations that may

Exhibit 8.1   Examples of the Unexpected for Each of the Basic Inquiry Tasks

Basic Inquiry Task	Examples of the Unexpected
Framing questions	There are two primary intended users, but they can't agree on the key issues to study in the evaluation. There is insufficient funding to address the many questions each has, and one leader threatens to quit the evaluation altogether.
Determining appropriate design	The client insists on the so-called gold standard, conducting a randomized-control-trial evaluation, despite the fact that the potential sample is too small and denying treatment to some clients as part of the randomization would be unethical.
Sampling	To make sure minority participants are represented adequately in the data, the evaluator wants to oversample that group. The client objects and accuses the evaluator of wanting to bias the results in favor of one group.
Collecting data	Having been forced to take part in many community studies, members of a local community refuse to complete the 75-item survey a government funder requires. Program staff are panicked and ask the evaluator for help in making them fill it out.
Analyzing data	Because the client wants detailed descriptions of program activities, the evaluator makes a plan to collect qualitative data but, thanks to an enthusiastic staff member, ends up with far more data than the plan called for. There is insufficient time to analyze everything collected.
Interpreting results	One member of a collaborative evaluation team takes it upon himself to interpret the results of a sensitive evaluation using critical race theory. Many participants feel put down or threatened by his interpretation, which highlights their role in sustaining oppression.
Reporting/ disseminating	The key actor who commissioned and championed the evaluation leaves for a new job, and the evaluator cannot find anyone else who cares to receive or discuss the findings.

SOURCE: © 2010 Jean A. King & Laurie Stevahn.

appear to arise out of nowhere. An unskilled evaluator may not figure out what happened until well after the fact. Is it fortunate that hindsight is 20/20?

The difficulty inherent in dealing with the unexpected is that people prefer easy answers, explicit directives to solve problematic issues: *If* this occurs, *then* respond in this way and all will be well. But, as mentioned earlier, in reality every case is unique. Context, individual players, the specific evaluation, and even the evaluators involved create nuances that make lockstep, one-size-fits-all solutions impossible. Our answer is to provide detailed lists of what we call potential woes, highlight what evaluators can look for, and then outline possible actions that could help address the situation. Although there are never guarantees for a quick fix or a perfect resolution, a variety of potentially successful actions for dealing with the unexpected can help evaluators proceed when they face challenging circumstances.

WHAT CAN GO WRONG DURING A PROGRAM EVALUATION?

Plenty. Mary Tyler Moore once quipped, "Worrying is a necessary part of life." For an evaluator, worrying is not only necessary but essential. Inevitably, the unexpected will occur, often disrupting the best intentions and designs. What are the worst things that can happen during an evaluation? Such dark ideas live in evaluators' nightmares. A tsunami, an earthquake, a fire, or a tornado wipes out an organization's offices and all existing documentation. War breaks out, and a key evaluation champion is called to active duty. A vital program leader is diagnosed with a virulent illness, resigns with only a week's notice, or drops dead at his desk. Program administrators are arrested for recurrent fraud. Data are lost or nonexistent because someone forgot to collect them. Thankfully, the unexpected is rarely so dramatic.

Exhibit 8.2 summarizes a set of potential evaluator woes that might benefit from the use of interactive evaluation skills—high-quality conversation, structured interaction, and conflict management—to move forward. Applying the evaluation commonplaces mentioned in Chapter 4, the woes are divided into four broad categories: environmental issues, client/user issues, evaluation process/results issues, and evaluator issues. Each category is divided into themes, and each theme into specific examples. Are these examples inclusive of every single thing that could ever go wrong in an evaluation? Of course not. Innovative snafus seem to be one of the ongoing aspects of evaluation practice; even long-time evaluators experience original challenges. As Patton (2012) puts it in discussing simulation work to prepare for data collection, "Bottom line: *Expect the*

Exhibit 8.2 Potential Evaluator Woes: Categories and Themes

Category	Themes
Environmental issues (see Exhibit 8.3)	External environment
	Internal program environment
Client/user issues (see Exhibit 8.4)	Internal leadership for the evaluation
	Internal support for the evaluation
	Individual responses to the evaluation process
Evaluation process/results issues (see Exhibit 8.5)	Implementation problems
	Technical problems
Evaluator issues (see Exhibit 8.6)	Personal problems
	Professional skills
	Interpersonal issues

SOURCE: © 2010 Jean A. King & Laurie Stevahn.

unexpected. Be prepared for contingencies" (p. 318; emphasis in original). So the examples include a wide range of practice-based possibilities that can alert evaluators to the variety of minefields lurking in evaluation settings.

For each of the four categories, we will first describe the themes and examples and then provide an exhibit (Exhibits 8.3–8.6) that presents a list of signs to watch for in each of the specific examples that would alert evaluators to the presence of this potential woe, followed by a set of ideas for handling such a situation. As much as possible, we have made the specific examples self-explanatory. It is not our intent to fully explicate each of them; such descriptions, in fact, could be the content of another entire book. Instead, for each category, we will give a scenario that highlights one of the woeful examples and a solution that gets the evaluation back on track, noting that other solutions can work in much the same way and acknowledging that, depending on the circumstances, evaluators can solve problems using different pathways.

Environmental Issues

Exhibit 8.3 presents a list of things to watch for related to environmental issues and a set of ideas for managing such negative possibilities. Potential environmental woes fall into two themes: external environment and internal program environment.

Exhibit 8.3 Environmental Issues: Potential Evaluator Woes and Responses

Environmental Issues	Things to Watch For	Ideas for Managing
External environment		
"Big-picture" external environment	• Staff unable to report to work or laid off • Organization unable to function routinely • Expected resources unavailable to support programs	• Be systematic in observing the "big picture"; don't become so engrossed in daily functioning that you ignore this perspective. • Establish a professional network that will keep you in the loop as events take place or situations develop.
External program environment	• Legislation or other documents affect programming, require changes • Expected resources unavailable to support programs • Organization forced to change due to reduced funding • Staff laid off or leave for other jobs	
Internal program environment		
Corrupt program (Patton, 2008, p. 214)	• Staff engaged in illegal or unethical activities • Budget documents manipulated • Key organizational leaders block the evaluation or avoid participation	• Pursue confirmatory information actively if you suspect that inappropriate activities are occurring. • Confer with a trusted colleague about how to handle the situation. • Report to appropriate superiors and/or authorities as soon as you are aware of illegal activities. • Withdraw from the evaluation if necessary.
Controversial program (Patton, 2008, p. 214)	• Media coverage, both positive and negative • Involvement of political figures, both positive and negative • Protests at program sites • Widespread interest in the evaluation	• If possible, establish a cooperative goal structure for the evaluation (see Chapter 6). • Create mechanisms to document and track evaluation activities over time. • Engage in constructive conflict management as issues arise (see Chapter 6).

(Continued)

Exhibit 8.3   (Continued)

Environmental Issues	Things to Watch For	Ideas for Managing
Highly visible program (Patton, 2008, p. 214)	• Media coverage, both positive and negative • Involvement of political figures, largely positive • Widespread interest in the evaluation	• Work with your client on a public relations plan for the evaluation findings, including presentation materials and written reports. • Create mechanisms to document and track evaluation activities over time. • Be sure all publicly available materials related to the evaluation are of high quality and clearly communicate key messages. • If appropriate, work with a media expert to handle reporters and other individuals interested in receiving and using the results.
Highly volatile program environment (Patton, 2008, p. 214)	• "Rapid change in context, issues, and focus" (p. 214) • Organization subsumed by another larger one • Physical move from one space to another • Continuous changes during the course of the evaluation • Staff stressed trying to keep up with and react/respond to the environment	• Keep your eyes open and your "feelers" out so you become aware of potential conflict or controversy as quickly as possible and address it appropriately. • Carefully monitor those with the power to affect the program and its evaluation; if they are your clients/users, work with them to make sense of the program environment over time. • Create mechanisms to document and track evaluation activities over time. • Consider using a developmental approach with an emergent design for the evaluation (see Patton, 2011). • Remain flexible as the evaluation process moves ahead.

Environmental Issues	Things to Watch For	Ideas for Managing
Underfunded program	• Staff overwhelmed with program responsibilities and lack time to participate meaningfully in the evaluation • Continuing search for additional funding takes away from program and evaluation activities • Minimal or no budget for evaluation	• Be sure sufficient funding is available to conduct a viable evaluation. • Highlight budgetary and cost issues in the evaluation, especially if underfunding is of concern to primary intended users.
Dysfunctional program	• Ongoing conflicts between/among leadership and staff • Competitive goal structure (winners and losers with every decision) • Failure to attend to key issues related to successful program implementation • Evaluation as scapegoat for other problems	• Strive to ensure the program's dysfunction does not negatively affect the evaluation's design or implementation. • Use the utilization-focused evaluation initial activities (Patton, 2012, pp. 20–21) or similar activities to encourage people's participation and increase their interest in the evaluation. • Interview key positional and opinion leaders to engage them in the evaluation process and identify constraints to active engagement. • If feasible, develop an interactive, participatory process to engage people positively (see Chapter 5). • Create mechanisms to document and track evaluation activities over time. • Engage in conflict management as issues arise (see Chapter 6).

SOURCE: © 2010 Jean A. King & Laurie Stevahn.

The *external environment* is further divided into two examples: the "big-picture" external environment and the external program environment. The first addresses large-scale external issues such as natural disasters, armed conflicts, and economic downturns, all of which will unavoidably alter people's lives and wreak havoc with evaluations. The second identifies external forces that will affect the program (e.g., budget cuts or reallocations, government shut-downs, changes in legislation or funder requests, or new national standards).

Equally important, the *internal program environment* includes six examples: a corrupt program, where people are actually breaking the law; a controversial program, one surrounded by unending *Sturm und Drang* (storm and stress); a highly visible program, in which staff must manage appearances; a highly volatile program environment, where rapid change holds the potential to disrupt activities; an underfunded program, which puts money constantly on people's minds; and a dysfunctional program, where ongoing tension and conflict hold the potential to destroy program and evaluation alike.

Environmental Scenario

An evaluator was hired after year 1 of a 3-year National Science Foundation–funded collaboration that included faculty from a college's teacher education program and several nearby school districts. The project goal was to improve the teaching of science by providing high-quality professional development and follow-up coaching to elementary school teachers. One of the college's deans supervised the project, but the daily management and much of the instruction fell to a newly hired assistant professor, who was a gifted instructor but not equally gifted with budget and other bureaucratic details.

The evaluator listened in dismay in an initial meeting with the dean who hired her as he complained about this professor's poor attention to detail and the many missteps in the first year of implementation, including a workshop canceled because of mistaken assumptions about teacher availability. Her first meeting with the professor brought equal discomfort as he, too, grumbled—the dean saw this grant as a feather in his cap and was already taking credit for its success to the college's leadership, even though he provided minimal support in managing complicated grant details across multiple sites. As a relative newcomer to the college, the professor felt overwhelmed with the responsibility for both arranging and teaching workshops and the day-to-day functioning of the grant. He admitted he was sadly behind on the paperwork that would get the teachers their stipends. Several had e-mailed him to find out if there was a problem, and he was embarrassed to tell them it was his fault. One of the district superintendents had even contacted him to complain.

After those meetings, alarms went off in the evaluator's head. Here were signs of a dysfunctional program: obvious tension between the two leaders, what might be a competitive tendency on the dean's part, and small but important grant details not attended to in a timely manner. This was a surprise, as the program had received positive press in the community, which is why she had applied to conduct its evaluation in the first place. Besides, in addition to complaints, she had heard many positive details in each of the initial interviews. Her primary concern now was to make sure the evaluation was not negatively affected by the program's dysfunction, so she went back over her notes from the meetings with the dean and the professor to highlight and summarize their individual concerns, developing a list of potential issues for the study. As soon as possible, she arranged a meeting of the evaluation's primary intended users, which included the dean and the professor but also the members of the grant's advisory group who had oversight responsibility.

The tone of that meeting was purposefully open and constructive. The evaluator integrated exercises she had learned at a training session, asking those present to discuss their images of evaluation, to develop project-specific criteria and standards, and interactively to generate a list of possible evaluation questions. The meeting went well, and by the end of the session the dean, the professor, and representatives from the college departments and school districts had discussed a range of issues, including the challenge of one person assigned the dual tasks of grant instruction and management. People clearly appreciated the chance to surface issues that had been bothering them and said so. The advisory group agreed to participate in a monthly update to monitor the evaluation's progress and help with ongoing decisions regarding the evaluation design, data collection, and eventual interpretation and reporting.

After that session, the evaluator typed the meeting content from the numerous flip-chart sheets that had covered the walls and circulated them to those who had attended, asking for clarification on a few items. She then asked to meet with the dean and professor together to review the notes and discuss plans for the study in preparation for the first update. At that meeting she was alert to signs of strain between the two, ready to engage in conflict management to build commitment both to their working relationship and to the evaluation process. But the tone of the meeting suggested the two were now working more collaboratively by constructively discussing program issues, and the evaluator sensed the evaluation process could move forward.

Client/User Issues

The second set of potential issues relates to clients and users. Exhibit 8.4 details a list of things to watch for in dealing with clients and the companion set of ideas for managing user-related problems. Issues related to clients/users fall into three themes: internal leadership for the evaluation, internal support for the evaluation, and individual responses to the evaluation process.

Exhibit 8.4   Client/User Issues: Potential Evaluator Woes and Responses

Client/User Issues	Things to Watch For	Ideas for Managing
Internal leadership for the evaluation		
Key positional leaders are uninterested or unwilling to support/ participate in evaluation activities or to use the results	• Leaders or their staff don't return phone calls or reply to e-mails or texts • Meetings with leaders difficult to arrange or routinely canceled/ moved • Leaders unwilling to attend key evaluation events or sign supportive materials when asked • Lack of leadership's public support for evaluation • Lack of engagement in discussion of evaluation results • Decision making not visibly connected to evaluation results	• Use the utilization-focused evaluation initial activities (Patton, 2012, pp. 20–21) or similar activities to encourage their participation. • Find someone who can serve as a liaison to key leaders, helping you communicate more effectively. • Interview them to engage them at least minimally in the evaluation process. • Ask them to agree to participate in limited but important ways that will facilitate the evaluation process. • Find a way to keep them in the loop as the evaluation process evolves.
Newly hired leaders demand changes in an existing evaluation plan/ process	• New leaders or their staff don't return phone calls or reply to e-mails or texts • Meetings with new leaders difficult to arrange or routinely canceled/moved • New leaders uninterested in becoming familiar with existing plans or evaluation processes • New leaders bring their specific approach to evaluation and a willingness to force it on others • Changes are made to the evaluation without the evaluator's knowledge • Lack of new leadership's public support for existing evaluation plan/process	• Meet as quickly as possible with the new leaders to discuss the evaluation plan/process/ system. • Explain the existing evaluation plan/process/system and its rationale. • Use current staff to facilitate a conversation with the new leaders. • Check the evaluation contract to see how flexible its requirements are. • If necessary, agree to changes following a thoughtful review of how they will affect the existing design and budget.

Client/User Issues	Things to Watch For	Ideas for Managing
Clients/intended users make impossible requests	• Timelines shorter than the appropriate evaluation process requires • Clients want the "truth" about the program's ability to result *directly* in desired change • Insufficient resources available to answer the client's evaluation questions meaningfully • Requests that would violate evaluation ethics (e.g., data suppression, confidentiality, rights of human subjects)	• If possible, modify the impossible requests and integrate a version of them into the existing evaluation plan. • Explain clearly what can be done within the existing time and budgetary constraints. • Stand firm when a request is truly impossible; do not agree to work miracles or perform the undoable. • Use constructive conflict-management skills if necessary (see Chapter 6).
Clients/intended users repeatedly change evaluation requirements	• Repeated requests to change the evaluation plan or its implementation • Lack of commitment or follow-through on existing evaluation plans • Program staff frustrated that the evaluation keeps changing	• Establish a clear timeline for the evaluation (what must be done by what dates) and stick to it. • Over time, teach the clients/intended users the negative effects of repeated changes on the evaluation process. • Do not agree to any major change without a thoughtful review of how it will affect the existing design and budget.
Key evaluation advocate/supporter leaves the organization, creating a vacuum of support	• The evaluation advocate/supporter leaves without working on transition of evaluation responsibilities • People don't return phone calls or reply to e-mails or texts • Meetings with staff difficult to arrange or routinely canceled/moved • Staff delay or no longer engage in evaluation activities	• Always develop multiple primary intended users/supporters (Patton, 2012, p. 78). • Ask the person who is departing to identify other advocates and to pass them the evaluation baton explicitly before leaving. • Identify likely successors and work with them to sustain support for the evaluation.
Internal support for the evaluation		
General lack of support for the evaluation process	• People don't return phone calls or reply to e-mails or texts	• Use the utilization-focused evaluation initial activities (Patton, 2012, pp. 20–21) or

(Continued)

Exhibit 8.4 (Continued)

Client/User Issues	Things to Watch For	Ideas for Managing
	• Individual meetings difficult to arrange or routinely canceled/moved • Advisory group meetings are not scheduled or are unproductive • Data collection made challenging (e.g., staff won't review draft instruments, sample not provided when requested, evaluators not told about opportunities to collect data with a group, etc.) • Existing data not provided in a timely manner • People feel free to confront/challenge the evaluator in unhelpful ways	similar activities to encourage people's participation and increase their interest in the evaluation. • Interview key positional and opinion leaders to engage them in the evaluation process and identify constraints to active engagement. • If feasible, develop an interactive, participatory process to engage people positively. • Create incentives (e.g., opportunities for meaningful discussion, release time, stipends) for participation.
Political issues overwhelm the evaluation so the process breaks down entirely	• Ongoing conflict within the organization and between the evaluator and leadership and staff • People feel free to confront the evaluator • Evaluation as scapegoat for other problems • Inability to attend to key issues related to successful implementation of the evaluation	• Identify the conflicts that have led to the impasse and engage in constructive conflict management. • Work with a positional leader to make the best of the situation and determine if the evaluation can move forward.
Miscommunication/rumors	• Inaccurate e-mails copied or blind copied to many • Contentious meetings where people express concerns (accurate or not) about the evaluation process • People sidebarring the evaluator with personal concerns about the evaluation • People feel free to confront the evaluator in volatile, destructive, or inappropriate ways	• Before the study begins, create an explicit plan for communication about the evaluation process and its results and use it. • Address miscommunication head-on; communicate key messages and correct misinformation as it emerges. • Work with primary intended users to communicate individually with key people or those who may be spreading rumors.

Client/User Issues	Things to Watch For	Ideas for Managing
Individual responses to the evaluation process		
The concerned—people who feel threatened by the evaluation process	• Lack of evaluation knowledge and skills • Anxiety about involvement in the evaluation • Requests for detailed information about the evaluation process	• Work to understand people's perspectives, whether or not you agree with them. • Use the initial activities of utilization-focused evaluation (Patton, 2012, pp. 20–21) or similar activities to encourage people's participation and show them the value of their engagement in the evaluation process ("what's in it for them"). • Provide targeted training, coaching, and mentoring. • Hold routine reflection sessions so people can process the evaluation as it occurs.
The complacent—people who engage in evaluation only because they are required to (Patton, 2012, p. 16)	• Disinterest in or devaluing of evaluation or refusal to take it seriously • An unwillingness to attend evaluation meetings • Requests for minimum requirements (how to complete the evaluation with minimal effort or engagement) • Minimal or perfunctory attention when engaged in evaluation-related tasks	• Use key informants/connectors to speak for others and raise issues that may concern the complacent. • Accept the fact that some people will not jump on the evaluation bandwagon. • Create incentives (e.g., opportunities for meaningful discussion, release time, stipends) for participation. • Engage in constructive conflict-management techniques if people's attitudes negatively affect the evaluation process • Refer to the attitude/aptitude matrix and possible responses (see Chapter 7).
The culturally different—people from cultures new to evaluation	• Reluctance to engage in the evaluation • Lack of program evaluation knowledge and skills • Traditional cultural responses that may preclude participation or negative feedback	• Learn about the cultural groups that will be part of the evaluation, identifying issues the evaluator must attend to. • Be aware of personal cultural blinders.

(Continued)

Exhibit 8.4   (Continued)

Client/User Issues	Things to Watch For	Ideas for Managing
		• Incorporate a variety of different perspectives into the evaluation. • Create a mechanism through which community members can provide rapid feedback about evaluation concerns. • If culturally appropriate, meet with leaders or elders of the community to explain the evaluation process and likely outcomes and to ask for their support and involvement. • If fitting, develop a culturally appropriate final report and present it to community leaders.
The culturally biased—people who have outright prejudice against certain groups (Patton, 2008, p. 214)	• Racial or ethnic slurs • Inappropriate "humor" at the expense of a culturally different group • Cultural disconnects evident at meetings (e.g., people sit separately, don't speak with one another, use contentious language)	• If possible, use the evaluation process to educate prejudiced individuals. • Make key evaluation participants aware of the bias, your discomfort with it, and the expectation that it will stop. • If necessary, withdraw from the evaluation.
The incompetent—people who are happy to help with the evaluation but lack the knowledge and skills to do so (Stevahn & King, 2010, pp. 120–122)	• Repeated questions on how to complete a task ("I'm not sure how to proceed . . .") • Uncompleted tasks or tasks that are simply abandoned • Assigned tasks are done poorly or incorrectly	• Identify such individuals early on and carefully monitor their evaluation-related interactions. • Assign individuals to tasks they are capable of completing successfully. • If necessary, limit their active work on the evaluation (damage control). • Use constructive conflict-management skills if necessary. • Consider the "willing" and "able" dimensions of attitude and aptitude, and take appropriate steps to respond.

Client/User Issues	Things to Watch For	Ideas for Managing
The gatekeepers—people who seek to control the evaluation by guarding access to others or to information/data (Alkin, 2011, p. 44)	• Evident turf or control issues ("I will decide what evaluators will get when") • Playing the role of protector ("Staff are already too busy . . .") • Requirement that evaluators contact them before proceeding at every step during the process • Reluctance to schedule meetings with appropriate people	• Identify such individuals early on and monitor their evaluation-related interactions. • Have a positional leader work with the gatekeeper to keep the evaluation process flowing. • Use constructive conflict-management skills when necessary.
The forcers—people who force their personal agendas onto the evaluation	• Evident turf or control issues ("My way or the highway") • Unwillingness to engage in back-and-forth dialogue • Apparent disinterest in thinking openly about evaluation issues or topics	• Identify such individuals early on and monitor their evaluation-related interactions. • If appropriate, integrate people's personal agenda items into the evaluation's purpose and questions; if not, explain why the study will not address these items. • Use constructive conflict-management skills when necessary.
The resisters—people who refuse to facilitate the evaluation process or work against the evaluation, either passively or actively	• Nonresponse to requests for scheduling meetings • Nonresponse to requests for existing data or for arranging data collection • Nonattendance at meetings • Agreeing to do something and then failing to follow through • Negative comments and body language during meetings • Rumors and behind-the-scenes negative talk	• Identify such individuals early on and monitor their evaluation-related interactions. • Use the initial activities of utilization-focused evaluation (Patton, 2012, pp. 20-21) or similar activities to encourage their participation and show them the value of engagement in the evaluation process ("what's in it for them"). • If possible, ask a positional leader to manage these people's behavior over time. • Engage in damage control if they distort the evaluation process or misuse its results. • If necessary and possible, remove hostile participants from the evaluation process. • Use conflict-management skills when necessary.
The politicos—people who use the evaluation process and its results for political gain (Patton, 2012, pp. 17–18)	• Visible engagement in the evaluation process for political gain ("Behold me evaluating") • Use or manipulation of evaluation results in public writing or appearances that highlight an individual	

SOURCE: © 2010 Jean A. King & Laurie Stevahn.

Internal leadership for the evaluation involves five examples: key positional leaders who are uninterested or unwilling to support/participate in evaluation activities or to use the results, newly hired leaders who demand changes in an existing evaluation plan/process, clients/intended users who make impossible requests, clients/intended users who repeatedly change evaluation requirements, and a key evaluation advocate/support who leaves the organization.

Internal support for the evaluation includes three examples: general lack of support for the evaluation process, political issues that overwhelm the evaluation so the process breaks down entirely, and miscommunication or rumors.

Individual responses to the evaluation process encompass at least these nine examples, although, given the variety of people in this world, there are surely many more:

1. The concerned, people who feel threatened by the evaluation process and are truly anxious about participating in it.

2. The complacent, people who engage in evaluation only because they are required to (Patton, 2012, p. 16). These individuals may have the skills necessary to participate, but they are unwilling to join the process unless required to do so.

3. The culturally different, people from cultures new to the Western concept of program evaluation whose own cultures may lack a similar concept or discourage making negative statements about programs publicly.

4. The culturally biased, people who are outright prejudiced against certain groups or lack understanding and respect, whether or not they openly express it (Patton, 2008, p. 214).

5. The incompetent, people who are willing to help with the evaluation but lack the knowledge and skills to do so effectively (Stevahn & King, 2010, pp. 120–122).

6. The gatekeepers, people who seek to control the evaluation by guarding access to others or to information/data—for example, by requiring their approval to provide existing data or schedule interviews (Alkin, 2011, p. 44).

7. The forcers, people who force their personal agendas onto the evaluation and use the power they have to assert their authority or block actions they perceive as negative.

8. The resisters, a large and diverse category of people who refuse to facilitate the evaluation process or who work against the evaluation, either passively or actively. This group also includes naysayers, cynics, and the offended

(Patton, 2012, p. 17). Morell (2010, p. 148) identifies two potential sources of resistance to evaluation—professional belief and clinical judgment—but some people may resist for more personal reasons.

9. The politicos, people who use the evaluation process and its results—or don't use them—for political gain (Patton, 2012, pp. 17–18).

One of the ideas for managing a potential woe included several times in the exhibits is to "use the initial activities of utilization-focused evaluation." Taken from Chapter 1 of *The Essentials of Utilization-Focused Evaluation* (Patton, 2012, pp. 20–21), these are 10 exercises a utilization-focused evalua-tor can use to "assess and facilitate stakeholder and program readiness for utilization-focused evaluation":

- Conducting an informal baseline assessment of evaluation use in the organization
- Developing people's baseline associations with and perceptions of the word *evaluate*
- Creating a positive vision for evaluation by discussing what a useful pro-cess would look like
- Assessing incentives for and barriers to reality testing and evaluation use in participants' own program culture
- Engendering a commitment to reality testing by asking people if they are willing to look at what is actually happening in their program
- Grounding any specific evaluation in the professional standards of evalu-ation utility, feasibility, propriety, and accuracy
- Establishing project-specific evaluation norms and standards
- Engaging in a discussion of good ideas that haven't worked out in prac-tice to demonstrate evaluative thinking
- Generating evaluation metaphors and analogies (see Chapter 5, Strategy 6)
- Generating questions for the evaluation

Client/User Scenario

The newly appointed manager of the unit within the State Department of Natural Resources that handles hunting and fishing licenses began to review the unit's existing data and ongoing evaluations. As the first person of color appointed to this position, he was eager to resolve the ongoing conflicts he knew existed with the state's minority communities. Almost as an annual rit-ual, the local media prepared stories about members of American Indian tribes who were exercising their treaty rights to fish in certain waters or about

Hmong hunters whose values and customs clashed with state laws regulating activities in the wild. He scheduled a meeting with the department's internal evaluator, the person responsible for the department's monitoring process.

This longtime employee, who was not a person of color, explained that the resources required in terms of staff and money to monitor policies and activities in the state—let alone evaluate how they were working—far exceeded those available in the departmental budget. Cutting him off, his new boss explained in no uncertain terms that he was unimpressed by the minimal data available and that the evaluator needed to design a study that would engage community members, including representatives from all the state's tribal governments, Hmong community elders, and leaders from other cultural groups in the state who fished or hunted, to determine their perceptions of the department and how it could better address their concerns. He wasn't interested in the evaluator's "whining" about the existing process. The internal evaluator felt as though he had been slapped.

Having worked in the unit for years, he fully understood the new leader was adding an emphasis that had never been part of previous managers' concerns. He also knew that, although he was sympathetic and even interested in conducting the study, he personally lacked the skills, experience, and confidence to engage the American Indian and Hmong communities on this potentially controversial topic. Checking with other local evaluators, he repeatedly heard one consultant's name as the person who could do this job; she was an evaluator of color with extensive experience in and a positive reputation for conducting evaluations in these two communities. The evaluator scheduled a meeting with his new boss to make a pitch for hiring this external evaluator for what was clearly an important study, and the manager agreed to pay for the contract. The evaluator hired her, and the three met to lay out thoughts for a participatory evaluation process. She was excited to begin, knowing the manager was behind the study and the internal evaluator understood the need for an inclusive, culturally sensitive process.

Her connections in the local communities of color enabled her fairly quickly to identify leaders who would be strong participants in this study. Several agreed to help her understand the issues as they saw them and to recruit other representatives from their communities. To her dismay, her recruiting experience in the state department was almost exactly the opposite. When she contacted department staff to engage them in the evaluation, no one returned her e-mails or calls, making it difficult to connect. The person responsible for preparing the existing data for her review met with her but proceeded to present a litany of reasons why this task was an overwhelming and unwelcome challenge. Seeing her in the office, one person who happened to be her neighbor confided that others in the department took offense at having to participate in what they saw as a potentially biased and unfair review of their activities when they were already overworked and underfunded.

The external evaluator immediately contacted the internal evaluator and set a meeting with him and the unit head. In neutral terms she detailed what had happened in recruiting participants and what she understood as potential roadblocks in the department. The internal evaluator was not surprised; the manager was angry. Setting aside negative feelings, the three came up with plans to get the evaluation off to a solid start.

The internal evaluator agreed to interview the departmental staff individually or in small groups—their choice—to understand more fully their perspectives, colleague to colleague, on key issues as the study began. These would be summarized without attribution.

The department head agreed to discuss his strong commitment to the evaluation at the next staff meeting. He also would encourage voluntary participation by providing incentives for his staff, including time during the work day to attend evaluation sessions off-site, support from temporary staff to handle all evaluation-related data compilation, and an opportunity to travel to the professional conference of their choice upon completion of the study.

The external evaluator agreed to do two things. First, collaborating with the internal evaluator, she would conduct a series of short evaluation training sessions for the staff, during which the new leader could incorporate his vision for increasing the department's evaluation capacity. Second, based on all the grounding information, she would design an inclusive evaluation process to engage both community members and staff in significant discussion of an important topic. Throughout, she agreed to focus on individual participants' reactions to the process and work to engage them meaningfully.

Evaluation Process/Results Issues

Exhibit 8.5 highlights the third set of potential woes—what evaluators should watch for regarding the evaluation process or its results—and identifies potential ideas for managing those situations. Because the evaluator is the technical expert in these areas, these lists could be far longer. Examples here focus on the overarching issues that may directly affect interpersonal relationships, including technical concerns truly out of the evaluator's control and the self-created mistakes over which evaluators lose sleep. Issues related to the evaluation process or its results fall into two themes: implementation problems and technical problems.

Exhibit 8.5   Evaluation Process/Results Issues: Potential Evaluator Woes and Responses

Evaluation Process/Results Issues	Things to Watch For	Ideas for Managing
Implementation problems		
Limited resources to conduct the desired evaluation	• Promising too much with the financial resources available • Continuing requests to expand the scope of the evaluation without corresponding increases in funding • Competition with program activities for funding	• Be sure sufficient funding is available to conduct a viable evaluation. • Be clear about what a proposed evaluation can and cannot afford to do. • Budget evaluation activities in detail to make sure the promised activities can be effectively completed. • Negotiate the budget for any changes in the evaluation plan, either adding additional funding or eliminating tasks previously agreed to. • Think creatively about how to conduct a shoestring-style evaluation using the few resources available. • Explain that evaluations can result in increased efficiency, hence saving money for use in the program. • Seek additional support for the evaluation.
Unrealistic timelines/ impossible demands, including changes in the evaluation's scope	• External timelines or requirements that constrain the evaluation in challenging ways • Clients who communicate changes in the evaluation after plans have been finalized • Clients who make informal requests on the fly that result in additional (unfunded) work	• Take primary responsibility for the evaluation plan and related timelines and communicate this to the clients/ primary intended users. • Design the evaluation within the existing constraints of the situation, promising only what can realistically be completed. • Document ongoing evaluation activities so clients see how their money is being spent. • Do not agree to work miracles or perform the impossible (e.g., causal attribution if that is not possible); explain what you are able to do within the existing time and finances. • Do not agree to any major change without a thoughtful review of how it will affect the existing plan and budget.

Evaluation Process/Results Issues	Things to Watch For	Ideas for Managing
Evaluation attacked (Patton, 2008, p. 214)	• Special meetings called to criticize the evaluation in public forums • Negative comments or attacks at meetings • Negative media attention • Withholding of evaluation funding	• Create mechanisms to document and track evaluation activities carefully and routinely over time. • Engage with a credible individual in the setting who has the power to manage the conflict over the evaluation. • Work to ensure the evaluator and the evaluation process/results remain credible. • "[Stay] focused on evidence and conclusions" (p. 214).
Propriety concerns beyond the evaluator's control	• Data that should be confidential but are not • Human subjects requirements not followed • Misuse of results	• Inform the client immediately when evaluation ethics have been violated. • Address the consequences of each such situation individually, including reporting concerns to authority figures if necessary. • Meet or speak individually with people involved to be sure they understand the concern and what should happen in the future.
Exclusion or minimal involvement of important stakeholders in the evaluation process	• Groups that are not "at the table" for evaluation discussions yet have a key stake in the program • Structures that provide minimal opportunities for input from important stakeholders • Efforts by those who feel excluded to become engaged in the process • Lack of understanding that this is an important issue	• Consult with primary intended users to identify all necessary stakeholders and ensure their involvement (Patton, 2012). • Engage every important stakeholder group in some way, minimally interviewing people to be sure relevant issues and concerns are included in the evaluation planning process. • If necessary, manage the conflict about why certain stakeholders have been excluded.
Technical problems		
Technical problems within the evaluator's control (mistakes)	• Data collected fail to answer every evaluation question • Inappropriate comparison group selected	• Acknowledge when mistakes are made. • Solve any problems as quickly as possible and address any consequences of the errors.

(Continued)

Exhibit 8.5 (Continued)

Evaluation Process/Results Issues	Things to Watch For	Ideas for Managing
	• Incorrect statistical analyses used (e.g., data violate requirements for use of an analysis) • Incorrect assumptions about availability of data (Morell, 2010) • Evaluation plan is brittle (i.e., has little flexibility) and conditions change, making it untenable (Morell, 2010) • Instruments are complex and unable to adapt to local circumstances	
Technical problems beyond the evaluator's control	• Inadequate sample provided by sponsoring organization • Comparison group unavailable after it was promised • Inaccurate or incomplete existing data provided • A data problem discovered too late to do anything about it (Morell, 2010) • Inaccurate "report" released by staff	• Inform the client when such problems arise. • Make the best of the situation by providing corrections, addressing any consequences of the errors, and clearly explaining what happened in any reports. • Leverage lessons learned into future planning.

SOURCE: © 2010 Jean A. King & Laurie Stevahn.

There are many possible *implementation problems* related to any evaluation, but the five examples included here can be especially problematic: limited resources to conduct the desired evaluation; unrealistic timelines/impossible demands, including changes in the evaluation's scope; an attack on the evaluation (Patton, 2008, p. 214); propriety concerns beyond the evaluator's control; and the exclusion or minimal involvement of important stakeholders in the evaluation process. *Technical problems* are of two types: those within the evaluator's control and those beyond it.

Evaluation Process/Results Scenario

When the award letter arrived, the grant writer for the coalition of community clinics was incredibly proud. Staff members and directors were elated. Their collaborative association of relatively small clinics had received a sizeable federal grant to deliver HIV/AIDS-prevention/"safe sex" services for local youth, which was a relief because infection rates for teenagers in the community had increased dramatically in recent years. The grant required a hefty commitment to evaluation, so with the help of a staff member who had handled such grants in the past, the project director developed a request for proposals for the study.

The evaluation team that was eventually hired had an impressive set of credentials; the evaluators had conducted many large-scale public health evaluations and understood the importance of interacting with the community. However, the evaluators, who knew the community well, chose not to engage local leaders in designing the study since they had not budgeted for such involvement and believed it wasn't necessary because the funder's requirements made the design constraints explicit. Program staff also thought this was fine since, to their minds, the evaluation was merely a requirement of the grant and their previous experience suggested evaluation was an unpleasant process best handled at a distance. Besides, regardless of its results, they had a 3-year funding commitment.

The eventual evaluation plan, designed to meet the grant's requirements, was thorough and rigorous, using baseline data available from the clinics and comparison-group data from a large nearby clinic that was not part of the collaboration. It was the lead evaluator's strong personal ties to that clinic, where his wife was a high-level administrator, that enabled them to get the comparison data; she easily convinced her boss to sign on. The staff launched the program to great fanfare across the collaboration's multiple clinics, and project activities began.

One problem surfaced when the evaluation team started to compile the baseline data. The project head had assured them the existing data were available from the participating clinics' databases, but this was only partly true. For one thing, they learned some of the existing data were missing or incomplete, but of more concern was the fact that each clinic had its own database, often on different platforms, several of which were antiquated. This did not allow for easy data collection. One evaluator was assigned to work on this unanticipated challenge, and, after a time-consuming process, she was eventually successful in compiling the minimal data that did exist, but this evaluator decided they were not useable. Because of this limitation, she identified a source of secondary data—a comprehensive state HIV/AIDS database—that would allow the team to discuss baseline conditions in the community prior to the project's beginning. However, costly or not, she recommended collecting new baseline data, and the team agreed. The time needed to complete this work slowed progress and added to the evaluation's cost.

That challenge paled in comparison with the second problem: the community's reaction to the baseline data collection. One father who had been asked to sign a consent form for his teenage son to complete the survey challenged the head of its sponsoring clinic, asking why children in this community were being asked about their sexual activity and why they were being used as guinea pigs for "some ivory tower research study." A natural connector, that parent called other parents, and soon the director of that clinic had received a number of calls protesting the clinic's involvement in the project. The discontent spread to parents in other participating clinics, and parents demanded to see the survey their children would be asked to fill out and any other instruments that would be used in the study. Staff began to fear the evaluation requirements would scuttle project activities before they were even fully under way. Worse yet for the evaluation team, a third problem emerged. Eager to avoid the controversy, the head of the comparison-group clinic pulled his clinic out of the study. In an instant the comparison group had vanished.

At this point the lead evaluator, who lived in the community, worked quickly with project staff to organize an open meeting and invited leaders, parents, potential participants, and staff from all participating clinics to discuss both the project and its evaluation. Attendance was impressive; the community center gym was packed with concerned parents and people representing each of the community clinics in the area. The project staff and evaluators had prepared extensively. They made presentations of state data documenting the changing HIV/AIDS status for the community's youth, the rationale for the project and its associated activities, and the evaluation requirements and benefits from such a study. There were many questions back and forth, and the meeting continued until everyone had their say. Thankfully, the information, clearly presented and openly discussed, helped community members change their minds about the project. Some even agreed to help recruit teenagers to participate, and a small number of parents committed to helping the evaluators review and revise data collection instruments. Based on this meeting's results, the lead evaluator met with the head of the comparison-group clinic to discuss how that clinic could benefit from collecting baseline and follow-up data, paid for by the evaluation, in 3 years. Understanding the value of such high-quality data on an important topic, he agreed.

Evaluator Issues

Exhibit 8.6 lists the final set of potential woes related to evaluators themselves and catalogues possible responses. There are three themes: personal problems, professional skills, and interpersonal collaborative skills.

Exhibit 8.6   Evaluator Issues: Potential Evaluator Woes and Reponses

Evaluator Issues	Things to Watch For	Ideas for Managing
Personal problems		
Life challenges	• Personal illness or illness of a significant other • Death in the family • Personal relationship issues • Family stress (e.g., dealing with divorce, caring for older parents, raising children with serious challenges) • Overcommitment, too many irons in the fire	• Communicate openly with clients when personal situations affect the ability to complete evaluation activities. • Make arrangements to either reduce the workload or find replacements to take over. • Pay attention to possible work overload. • Take personal time and connect with important others.
Professional skills		
Lack of professional or technical skills	• Tasks that require skills the evaluator lacks • A new environment or content area	• Identify the skills necessary to complete evaluation tasks. • Put an evaluation team together that covers all the required skills. • Reflect on evaluator competencies periodically. • Create a professional development plan to increase personal skills in important areas.
Interpersonal issues		
Professional collaboration (Patton, 2008, p. 214)	• Interpersonal issues among team members (e.g., disagreements, arguments, lack of trust) • Need to build on individuals' skills and strengths	• Be clear about who is in charge of managing the evaluation process. • Assign roles that build on individual evaluators' strengths and comfort levels. • Structure positive interdependence into evaluation tasks. • Use constructive conflict-management skills when necessary. • Evaluate the collaborative process frequently enough to make changes as necessary.

SOURCE: © 2010 Jean A. King & Laurie Stevahn.

Evaluator Issues Scenario

The evaluation team for the sizeable foundation grant laughingly called itself the "Rainbow Coalition." The six members of the team, including an internal evaluator from the foundation acting as team leader, represented a balance of racial and ethnic groups, and the group kidded the team's sole male member that his job was to represent all of mankind. The team's diversity—both cultural and technical—was essential for exploring the complexity and nuances of foster care in a three-state area where troubled families frequently moved in search of better lives. Led by one state's charismatic and politically ambitious commissioner, a coalition of state, county, and city agency leadership from across the states had applied for funding to identify what was working well ("best practices") and then to develop a highly visible plan for improvement that could be publicly monitored. Political and ethical challenges abounded, but for once, the availability of sufficient funding provided an opportunity to conduct a technically sophisticated evaluation of both foster-care practice and the issues surrounding it.

During an evaluation team meeting halfway through the 2-year study, what began as a misunderstanding quickly escalated into an argument. One evaluator, White and female, remarked in passing that from her perspective the data suggested that the African American family structure functionally limited possibilities that African American children placed in foster care could have positive outcomes and a successful life trajectory. The African American evaluator's head swung around as he exclaimed, "I can't believe you said that! Really?" Taking offense at the comment, he went on to heatedly question the cultural sensitivity of his colleagues, saying that to prejudge the data was inappropriate and unethical. He left the room, slamming the door on the way out. The rest of the team sat, stunned, and looked at one another. "What just happened?" the foundation evaluator thought. "Where did that come from?"

Knowing the importance of the team members' successfully working together, she told the rest of the group to take a break and went in search of the evaluator who had stormed out. He was seated on a bench outside the office building, obviously upset but willing to talk. He explained that he was a product of the foster-care system and had pulled himself up by his bootstraps after an extremely difficult childhood that included several out-of-home placements and an eventual home with his grandmother, who had recently passed away. To hear a privileged person, team member or not, dismiss the many youth like him, to condemn them out of hand to failure, infuriated him. He had worked too hard to have her put him and others like him down so summarily. The team leader listened carefully, repeating his main points to make sure she understood his perspective and emotions. She explained that she suspected the affront was unintentional and asked if he would be willing to come back to the meeting room to resolve the evident conflict. Calmer now, he agreed.

Owing to a previous career of community work, this foundation evaluator had finely honed conflict resolution skills. The remaining members of the team were still taken aback—uncertain why the blowup had taken place—but with tears in her eyes, the woman who had made the offensive comment apologized to her colleague. The group then engaged in an integrative negotiation process in which they all participated, clarifying feelings and beliefs, expressing what each of them needed for the evaluation process to continue effectively, brainstorming ways to communicate personal concerns, and finally agreeing to a plan of action. The team, including the African American evaluator, knew the others had heard and understood their individual experiences, and they had a plan for moving forward. People's feelings were never again as relaxed or their affect as warm, but the evaluation was able to proceed.

Exhibits 8.3 through 8.6 include a variety of examples of the unexpected that can affect the evaluation process. There is undoubtedly overlap across the four categories, and many items may appropriately fit in more than one place. However, exact placement is not the point of these exhibits. Their purpose is to present the overarching themes and related examples and then to suggest that evaluators use them to engage in situation analysis when evaluations seem to be heading off course. With the exception of two headings in the evaluation process/results category (exclusion of important stakeholders and technical problems within the evaluator's control) and two in the evaluator category (lack of professional or technical skills and professional collaboration), evaluators are not responsible for and cannot hope to directly control the examples listed. But they can be watchful for the types of events that can negatively affect the evaluation process and those that even hold the potential to ruin it. Alert to negative possibilities, evaluators can act, using their influence to make the best of situations and, ideally, to improve them so a viable evaluation study can continue.

WHAT CAN INTERACTIVE EVALUATORS DO WHEN BAD THINGS HAPPEN?

An old saying claims that the best defense is a good offense, which is to say, in this case, creating an effective evaluation process and then attending to it thoughtfully over time may help evaluators avoid some of the challenges that can derail their studies. Would that it were as easy to do as it is to say. The previous section presented four exhibits with 134 things to watch for and

130 ideas for managing situations. Using the four broad categories to summarize the overarching ideas will help ensure the forest of the unexpected isn't lost among its many trees.

General Responses to Unexpected Issues

Environmental Issues

Understanding the details of a program's external and internal environments is the first step in doing something to address issues relevant to them. Evaluators should keep their eyes and ears open and not become insulated from the larger contexts in which they are conducting a study. In some cases external changes have the power to affect the evaluation process dramatically, for better or for worse. Ignoring these big-picture forces puts the evaluation at risk; quick response may keep actions on track. The same is true of changes to the internal program environment, where awareness of the negative landmarks related to six possibilities—corruption, controversy, visibility, volatility, underfunding, or dysfunction—may help evaluators address challenging situations.

Client/User Issues

Issues related to participants always hold the potential to affect the evaluation process, in some cases thwarting it altogether. In thinking about internal leadership and support for the evaluation as well as individual responses to it, evaluators should envision the power challenges large and small that may arise and respond accordingly. Even when leaders have good intentions, issues around power have a way of emerging in organizations. Two things are clear. First, an organization's top leaders can use their clout to support and move an evaluation forward. When people see or hear a strong statement of support from their leaders, like it or not, they may accept the evaluation's importance. Second, although this clout factor may be necessary, it is surely not sufficient to support an evaluation. When people inside an organization do not back an evaluation effort for whatever reasons, when internal politics overpower efforts to plan or conduct a study, or when rampant miscommunication— intentional or unintentional—permeates an environment, evaluators need to analyze the situation quickly, decide how to handle it, and then act.

Understanding people's individual responses to the evaluation process gives evaluators information to shape an appropriate reaction. The complacent participant, for example, differs in important ways from the forcer or the resister. Understanding this is important. The potential for misunderstanding always exists, especially if the evaluation's stakes are high. Sometimes cultural or language factors enter into the mix as diversity adds new perceptions, interpretations, or meanings. In addition, rumors may surface and create their own energy in organizations.

Evaluation Process/Results Issues

Numerous textbooks have been written on how to design and conduct evaluations, and this book in no way tries to compete with them. Certain components of the evaluation process and the use of its results, however, can directly lead to problems for evaluators and deserve highlighting. When conducting a study, evaluators may face five process/results situations of special concern: limited resources, impossible demands of many types, an attack on the evaluation either from within or outside, propriety concerns not of the evaluator's making, and the effects of excluding important stakeholders. There may also be technical problems, both those of the evaluator's making (aka mistakes) and those beyond her control.

Evaluator Issues

Evaluators are people, too. Three negative possibilities related to the evaluator herself may affect the evaluation process: personal problems, a lack of the professional or technical skills required for a given study, and the interpersonal challenges of professional collaboration. Each of these could require intervention to allow an evaluation to move forward.

Putting It All Together

Thinking about the specific possibilities of what can go wrong and responding to them as they occur is a way to deal with the unexpected incident by incident. The other and perhaps more important way, because it is more broadly applicable, is to apply the skills explicated in Chapters 4 through 7 consistently—asking questions, structuring interaction, resolving conflict, and creating viable evaluation processes. Evaluators need to be ever vigilant to the interpersonal dynamics that can alert them to the unexpected. They need to watch for clues that something is not going as planned. Several images spring to mind—keeping a finger on the situation's pulse, developing eyes in the back of your head, having a sixth sense, or growing professional antennae that can sense problems before they occur. As Patton (2012) puts it, "In 40 years I can't remember any evaluation plan that has unfolded exactly as planned. The point is to monitor how things are unfolding, get on top of problems early" (p. 326). Evaluators must, therefore, actively work to understand what is occurring as problems develop. Again, in the words of Patton: "Situation analysis is ongoing. It's not something you do once, congratulate yourself on nailing it, check it off as done, and move on, never to pass that way again" (p. 87).

Evaluation conversations (Chapter 4) and strategies for engaging people (Chapter 5) are tools to explore emergent interpersonal issues. Constructively managing interpersonal conflict (Chapter 6) may keep an evaluation on track. As noted earlier, evaluators need not shy away from confronting conflicts that occur in an evaluation setting. Naming and respectfully addressing conflict directly now may avert disaster later. Overall, the time to address a potential problem is when an internal alarm goes off and an evaluator senses something amiss. Chapter 7 presented ways to build a viable evaluation process, and returning to those ideas in times of stress may be worthwhile. Two actions discussed there may help with ongoing interpersonal awareness and situation analysis. To review, one possibility is to create a structured communication system for evaluation processes with feedback loops that will surface potential problems as they arise. Routinely touching base with clients allows evaluators to know about any concerns as they develop. A second possibility mentioned in Chapter 7 is to document the evaluation process systematically as it develops so there is a record to trace activities over time. Another option is to identify key informants who will let evaluators know what's happening, the opinion leaders in an organization who not only know what is really going on but understand the importance of letting the evaluator know and are willing to share. They may or may not be the primary intended users.

Multisite evaluations present evaluators special challenges because they involve groups of people in different sites around a city, state, country, or even in other parts of the world. The multisite evaluator typically engages central primary intended users and then interacts with individuals at project sites to implement the study. If there are potential challenges with single-site evaluations, imagine the possibilities for mishaps when engaging multiple sites. The goals of the large-scale program may not be completely aligned with projects funded under its aegis, and the overarching evaluation somehow has to take that into account. In some cases projects are mandated to participate in tightly controlled studies where project staff must administer standardized instruments or use common protocols regardless of how well they fit with local project activities. In other cases individual projects may be conducting their own evaluations prior to the launch of the larger study but, obliged to participate midstream, may be forced to alter their designs. In multisite settings, the evaluator essentially becomes a middle manager and serves as the interface between the evaluation sponsor (typically the funder) and local project staff. This role is critical to ensuring that both the sponsor's and the individual projects' concerns are clearly understood and problems resolved as they arise. Exhibit 8.7 contains advice from four experienced multisite evaluators—Catherine Callow-Heusser, Arlen Gullickson, Frances Lawrenz, and Iris Weiss—about handling this especially challenging role.

An additional approach to handling the unexpected comes from Morell (2010), who labels the unexpected **surprise** (we use the terms interchangeably). His book, *Evaluation in the Face of Uncertainty: Anticipating Surprise and Responding to the Inevitable,* presents a continuum of surprise ranging from the unforeseen—things that could have been known in advance—to the unforeseeable—things that no one could have determined in advance. His goal in writing the book, captured in its first chapter's title, is to move the field of program evaluation "From Firefighting to Systematic Action" (p. 1). Morell divides his nine potential solutions to surprise into three categories.

For situations at the foreseeable end of the continuum, the evaluator's goal is to minimize surprise through advanced planning, which is typically possible at the early stages of evaluation design. Morell (2010) identifies three solutions for such situations. First, he suggests using theories of many types (e.g., life cycle, free market behavior, system, program) to expand evaluators' thinking

---

Exhibit 8.7 Recommendations for Multisite Evaluation Practice

1. Retain control of decisions regarding both evaluation design and instrumentation, even as you involve people in multiple ways to build ownership.

2. Thoughtfully use the evaluation process and its outcomes as interventions to improve individual projects.

3. Provide support to the extent possible for project staff to complete evaluation tasks, both to ensure high-quality data and to increase project ownership of the evaluation.

4. Purposefully and openly serve as a buffer between the funder and project staff.

5. Take leadership in raising cultural issues for people's consideration during the planning and implementation of the program evaluation.

6. Design and conduct the best evaluations possible, documenting limitations and being fully aware of trade-offs and necessary compromises.

SOURCE: Adapted from King et al. (2011, p. 70).

about the program. This may include conducting a thought experiment involving consultation with trusted colleagues to generate possible theoretical frameworks and then several cycles of picking one at random, "performing the evaluation" (imagining what the evaluation would look like from that perspective), then moving to another. Doing this mental exercise may suggest possibilities not previously considered. Second, Morell recommends "exploiting past experience" in two ways: understanding and applying both process knowledge (political context, organizational growth, and research and development) and domain knowledge—i.e., "knowledge about the specific topic under investigation" (p. 61). Third, he proposes limiting an evaluation's time frame to minimize the possibility of surprise. "Limiting time frames is useful because as 'distance' between program and outcome is extended," he writes, "opportunity for unpredictable change increases" (p. 68).

Morell's (2010) second set of solutions applies to situations where surprise is less foreseeable. "The key [in these situations] is to use methods that will supply evaluators with as much lead time as possible about impending problems" (p. 81). He again provides three possibilities. First, evaluators can develop and build "leading indicators" using forecasting techniques. Second, they can build on existing monitoring processes and work to structure the evaluation to detect change. "Our goal, after all, is to anticipate events and to prepare for them, not to get hit over the head and then have to react" (p. 77). Third, evaluators can apply system-based logic modeling to expand awareness and understanding of the broad evaluation context.

The third set of solutions Morell (2010) describes applies in situations where surprise is truly unforeseeable. He terms the overall approach to such situations **agile evaluation**, "an integrated approach that considers the unique and common effect of data, design, and program theory" (p. 99). Rolling with the situational punches, an agile evaluator interactively manages these three components—data, design, and program theory—to handle unforeseeable surprise. In thinking about data, the agile evaluator must consider two issues: characteristics of the data and processes for data acquisition. He then determines what must be done to collect the best data possible given the situation. Agile methodology "either employs an analysis logic that can encompass a wide range of evaluation needs, or has an organizational structure that can be reconfigured to meet new needs, or both" (p. 87). Finally, working with key stakeholders, an agile evaluator can revisit and potentially retool program theory in light of the unforeseen surprise. Taken together, Morell's nine solutions provide another take on how to deal with the unexpected. The diverse nature of surprise points to the value of having multiple lenses through which to view it.

THE ROLE OF INTERNAL VERSUS EXTERNAL EVALUATORS IN ADDRESSING THE UNEXPECTED

Throughout an evaluation, evaluators engage in two tasks related to the unexpected: first, knowing it when they see it and then, if necessary, doing something about it. Regardless of their location in the organization, their credibility and their relationships with primary intended users are essential. However, their role as an internal or external evaluator can affect their response to the unexpected.

Internal Evaluators

Internal evaluation is known to have inherent strengths. At the most basic level Chen (2005) notes, "Internal evaluators certainly have one advantage over external evaluators: Their services are low-cost or even no-cost" (p. 146). They also possess insider knowledge, can support ongoing evaluation needs and build systems to collect data routinely, are able to communicate with stakeholders in a timely and ongoing manner, and are invested in the organization for which they work (King & Rohmer-Hirt, 2011; Love, 1991; Sonnichsen, 2000). As a result, internal evaluators can tackle the unexpected in distinct ways. Because they work in a given setting, they are likely to have detailed background knowledge—to be keenly aware of program environments, to know who among the leadership supports evaluation and where the evaluation champions sit, to have a sense of what internal support exists for evaluation, and to identify in advance people's likely responses to a proposed study (e.g., concerns, gatekeeping, resistance). They also have the possibility of long-term relationships with primary intended users, an extended time frame, and the opportunity to think about building evaluation capacity over time as the result of people's ongoing and routine participation in multiple studies. For example, in one school district, an internal evaluator chose one willing department to use as a model for developing evaluation capacity in the rest of the district. The department head, a dynamo who understood the potential evaluation held for her programs, became an evaluation cheerleader and collaborated enthusiastically to develop processes and materials that built her program staff's capacity to conduct evaluation annually. Staff who dragged their feet or were less than committed to the process quickly saw they needed to change their attitudes and get involved or move to another district.

Because of this special knowledge and these prospects, then, internal evaluators may be able to create processes to spot the unexpected quickly and then respond appropriately. For example, applying Morell's (2010) strategies for addressing surprise, they can work to decrease surprise by exploring multiple theories, taking advantage of process and content knowledge, and designing evaluations with limited time frames. They can build a system of indicators not just for one study but for the multiple studies for which they are responsible, and they can design every evaluation to anticipate possible challenges. They can routinely develop system-based logic models for use in different studies and can practice agile evaluation, again, because they live there and know the situation on the ground intimately.

Any system of internal evaluation has potential limitations, however. Internal evaluators must be aware of their possible lack of the specialized skills and expertise that certain evaluations may require and devise a way to either gain or import them. Any long-term relationships that are less than positive may prove difficult to improve. More important, internal evaluators must always worry about the perception of potential bias—an absence of objectivity, a potentially weakened willingness to criticize, and a lack of accountability.

Consider a county board meeting where an internal evaluator presented the results of a thoughtfully designed qualitative implementation study of a nutrition program designed to reduce childhood obesity. The study included data from group interviews with more than 200 social workers. The analysis was thorough and by the book, and the results clearly documented the social workers' overwhelming belief that the program was working miracles with the youth involved. One board member began his attack by calling the results "anecdotes" and countering that he had spoken with two staff members who emphatically said the program was a waste of time and money. Another questioned the analysis by someone inside the county agency, calling it biased and opaque. Another wondered why the evaluation was done in-house when the board clearly needed an objective assessment of the situation. The board voted to commission an external evaluation to get at the "truth" of the program's outcomes. This example suggests that, regardless of systems in place, internal evaluators need to engage in ongoing and purposeful situation analysis to identify those situations where the *perception* of bias holds the potential to influence users' reactions to evaluation processes or results.

External Evaluators

In contrast to internal evaluation, the strengths of external evaluation stem from the perceived objectivity of those from outside the organization. As Chen (2005) writes, "The need for external evaluators . . . is strongest when stakeholders have highly divergent interests and backgrounds. In the midst of competing interests, the external evaluator tends to strike staff members as neutral and credible" (p. 146). External evaluators are hired for their specialized skills and expertise, their outsider knowledge, and, because they aren't regular employees of the organization, their perceived willingness to "tell it like it is." Although they may be expensive, they have a specific job to complete and they work to do it in a timely manner.

Most external evaluators need to take a different approach to the unexpected than do internal evaluators. Although external evaluators have technical skills and personal awareness and can watch for the unexpected in those categories, they may be less familiar with the organizational context and the personal and power dynamics of the program environment. Skilled manipulators *can* fool everyone some of the time. The interpersonal factor is critically important to external evaluators' ability to spot possibly problematic situations in a timely manner. They need to have active relationships with individuals in the organization to gain grounding knowledge and a detailed sense of the environment as well as an understanding of which leaders and evaluation champions support the study and which individuals may have problems with the evaluation or feel threatened as it moves forward. External evaluators can gain this information in two ways: by spending time in the organization and by identifying people who are willing to become their eyes and ears and keep them informed about developments. In any case, external evaluators can seek to reduce surprise using the approaches Morell (2010) described. Also, as noted in Chapter 1, some external evaluators may have long-term contracts with a given program and continuing support from specific primary intended users, in which case they become more like internal evaluators and can think more broadly about extended time frames and the potential of building evaluation capacity.

The unexpected may add stress to evaluation schedules by requiring additional time, but both internal and external evaluators ignore it at their personal risk. For example, when a program officer for a large foundation realized 3 months before an important board meeting that the board chair wanted hard data on a program with sites in multiple states, she threw money at the problem and hired a national firm that could quickly mobilize a team of evaluators to conduct 2-day interviews at 20 sites. Unfortunately, in their rush to complete the study, these external evaluators, who were virtually parachuted into diverse and culturally distinct sites with little preparation and no time to connect with people, managed to offend key stakeholders—including staff, community leaders, and tribal elders—at several sites. Once aware of the study's limitations, board members did not accept its conclusions as reliable and ignored the rushed results. Better to have worked with the board chair to explain the danger of an impossibly short timeline and to have brainstormed other solutions that might have averted the unexpected consequences of the evaluation.

THINKING ABOUT INEVITABLE TRADE-OFFS IN EVALUATION DECISION MAKING

Having discussed the many things that can go wrong, this chapter—and Part II of this book—concludes with a discussion of how to resolve the inevitable trade-offs in evaluation decision making. Unlike the rest of the chapter, which emphasized decision making and acting, this section highlights the importance of reflection and provides heuristics that may be helpful when evaluators are faced with difficult situations. When something goes wrong, the "if only" response can generate feelings of frustration and sometimes even despair.

- If only the director had taken an active interest in the evaluation . . .
- If only we had known about the accreditation requirements when we began . . .
- If only more respondents had completed the follow-up survey . . .
- If only the internal in-fighting had been evident earlier in the process . . .

Hindsight may be 20/20, but, as experienced evaluators (and economists) well know, foresight never entirely is. Even when evaluators do everything thoughtfully and by the book throughout the evaluation process, the resulting evaluation may still prove problematic. Why is that?

One reason is there is never just one way to conduct the evaluation of a specific program; indeed, there are many ways to peel the evaluation onion, and professional evaluators will have multiple ideas for how to tackle projects. Alkin and Christie (2005) used this fact to study the approaches of four evaluators when they asked each to design a study of the same education program and received, not surprisingly, divergent results that included a capacity building study, a policy study, a theory-driven study, and a value-engaged study. The point is that evaluations will inevitably lead to a range of options and a series of trade-offs dependent on the immediate situation. Three heuristics may prove helpful in analyzing such trade-offs and deciding how to move forward: the "good, quick, cheap" restaurant-industry classic (Stevahn & King, 2010), the Program Evaluation Standards (Yarbrough, Shula, Hopson, & Caruthers, 2011), and evaluators' own personal commitments.

A first heuristic for assessing options emerged in the restaurant world, where money is often a concern and entrepreneurs routinely face survival choices. The story goes that a sign was posted on the wall in a family-owned, mom-and-pop café. It read:

- Good
- Quick
- Cheap

Pick two.

In other words, if customers wanted good food quickly, it would not be cheap. If they wanted good food that was inexpensive, it would not arrive quickly. And if they wanted inexpensive food quickly, it would not be good.

Representatives of the fast-food industry may question the validity of this heuristic for restaurateurs, but its application to evaluation settings, where quality, time, and cost lead to trade-offs, can be helpful. Assuming a study has to be good—which professional evaluators consider a given—it can be either quick or cheap but not both. For example, if a social advocacy organization hires an evaluator to provide feedback on whether or not to support an upcoming legislative initiative, she may rent a phone bank and hire a team of callers to compile the needed data quickly. Doing so would be good and quick, but it may not be cheap. By contrast, if the same organization wants feedback on a legislative initiative in the upcoming session, the evaluator may work with staff to conduct community dialogues over the course of several months. Doing so would be good and cheap but not quick. This is often one of the implications of moving toward a more participatory process on the right side of the interactive participation quotient. If existing resources for an evaluation are a problem, cost can sometimes be addressed with in-kind contributions. By giving up speed, an organization may maintain quality and feasibility.

The second heuristic highlights the Program Evaluation Standards (Yarbrough et al., 2011; see Appendix A), a powerful tool for identifying and discussing trade-offs with clients. Consider the five categories of standards—utility, feasibility, propriety, accuracy, and evaluation accountability—which together create a framework for highlighting evaluation choices. Individual standards can become helpful topics for conversation. For example, suppose a validated standardized inventory could measure something cheaply and technically well but the data wouldn't be useful to the primary intended users. Utility might trump accuracy. Suppose again that an instrument could measure something technically well but would be extremely expensive. Feasibility might trump accuracy. Or suppose an evaluator has access to extremely sensitive data about a vulnerable population.

Using the data would mean revealing people's identities. Propriety might trump accuracy. Given the intensive process that led to their most recent revision, the Program Evaluation Standards provide evaluators a useful set of categories for considering and then making choices between and among alternatives.

The third heuristic—evaluators revisiting their personal commitments—is readily available to evaluators at a moment's notice. All of us have personal boundaries, the limits that define what we can and cannot live with. The ultimate issue is at what point an evaluator should say, "This doesn't work for me." In some situations, that point is obvious. Suppose, for instance, an evaluator uncovers illegal activities (someone misappropriating money), a situation in which program participants are being physically abused (at a "tough-love" boot camp for teens), a case where a client accuses the evaluator of falsifying data or asks the evaluator to withhold damaging results—all real examples. In such cases, the evaluator's decision is clear. Something must be done, and the resulting actions will be challenging but necessary.

In other situations, the right path may be less readily apparent. Imagine that an independent evaluation consultant who makes his living from contracts has a sense that a company's environment is dysfunctional. People keep sidebarring him, wanting to tell their side of the situation in private conversations. They complain that one vice president in particular repeatedly develops plans without consulting staff and that "everyone is unhappy." The evaluator witnesses people being unkind to one another, making snide comments, cutting one another off, and even shouting in meetings. He tries to raise these issues in conversations with his client, who happens to be that very vice president, but is told the organization's culture is outside the scope of his work. What if he needs this contract and wants to continue with the study, despite his qualms that it may be difficult to implement an effective evaluation? How might he proceed?

This is where reflection on how the evaluation is progressing from a personal stance may prove helpful. Consider this imprecise decision rule. An evaluator will continue to work on a given evaluation only when the following are true:

1. The likelihood exists that someone will use the results of the study to some benefit.

2. The likelihood exists that the evaluator will be able to conduct what she believes to be a meaningful study.

3. There will be no violation of ethical principles.

4. The data collected will be worth using.

5. The evaluator will feel good about being held accountable for the evaluation.

Attentive readers will note that these five statements stem from the categories of the Program Evaluation Standards; they are grounded in the field's standards for high-quality evaluation. If evaluators can identify potential users and uses, design and conduct an evaluation that meets their personal—and the field's—standards of quality, navigate the ethics of the situation to their own satisfaction, and be willing to vouch personally for the entire process, then they may feel comfortable moving forward with the contract. If not, it is important to withdraw from the situation thoughtfully and with integrity. The way such situations are handled will forever be on the evaluator's professional record.

Every evaluator will confront the challenges of creating feasible interactive processes and of managing the unexpected. This personal heuristic may provide a way to consider that next step—making decisions—with the potential for decisions well made and personally acceptable. Practicing evaluators need to study the legalities and ethics of such situations, knowing when to withdraw or force. Contractual agreements may compound the difficulties, and they may feel that their hands are tied. It may be helpful, then, for evaluators to create support in advance—to "get personal" for themselves, developing professional networks so if the need to discuss a situation arises, they have trusted colleagues and a context to do so. As noted above, it is also important for evaluators to know their own boundaries and to respond when they feel pushed or uncomfortable.

APPLYING INTERACTIVE EVALUATION PRACTICE PRINCIPLES TO DEALING WITH THE UNEXPECTED IN PROGRAM EVALUATION

Morell (2010) writes, "The truth is that when we plan our evaluations we are looking into a future in which . . . chance events can change what seemed like a sure thing" (pp. 115–116). Regardless of the best-laid plans, evaluations rarely go exactly as planned—chance events or, worse, those orchestrated by a disloyal opposition intervene, and evaluators are well advised to anticipate such occurrences. Many people's natural reactions to the unexpected include anger, panic, blaming, dismay, or "fight or flight," but evaluators must react with a commitment to address whatever situation has arisen. The IEP principles in Exhibit 8.8 remind us what is important even in times of stress and conflict. Remember that people matter. Keeping primary intended users in the loop ensures their involvement in any resolution, while working to understand other key players may help make sense of an unexpected circumstance.

Structuring interactions for problem solving will ensure the unexpected does not go unattended. Context, politics, conflict, culture—all may prove key to both determining what went wrong and figuring out how to get a study back on track. Not surprisingly, this may require time not built into an evaluation's original schedule, but the benefit of addressing a problem in a timely manner far outweighs the value of adhering to a timeline that is no longer meaningful. Finally, although the idea is cloying, it is important to remember that problems really can be our friends and that good can come from bad things. Holding that thought may provide reassurance and a helpful perspective when handling the unexpected.

Exhibit 8.8   IEP Principles Applied to Dealing With the Unexpected in Program Evaluation

IEP Principle	Applied to Dealing With the Unexpected in Program Evaluation
1. Get personal.	• Anticipate the unique and unexpected issues that individuals may bring to any evaluation context. • Know your clients and primary intended users well to be able to respond to surprises in productive ways. • Analyze key individuals in the evaluation process to better understand diverse perspectives and what those might mean for the evaluation study. • Identify people in the program/organization who can help problem solve.
2. Structure interaction.	• Acknowledge the unexpected when it occurs, and structure interactions aimed at problem solving. • Realize that handling the unexpected often requires high-quality, face-to-face interactions. • Consider that both internal and external evaluators can structure interactions that build on the inherent strengths of their respective roles.
3. Examine context.	• Remember that evaluators can never know every detail about an evaluation context, even with the most thorough planning. • When things go wrong, consider aspects of the evaluation context that may be contributing to the problem or that may be helpful in its resolution.
4. Consider politics.	• Accept the fact that political factors may negatively affect an evaluation or even bring it to an abrupt halt. • Remember the clout factor in handling the unexpected; people who have power in the program/organization may be able to get the evaluation back on track. • Consider internal and external evaluator roles; either may assist or limit an evaluator's success in tackling unexpected issues.

IEP Principle	Applied to Dealing With the Unexpected in Program Evaluation
5. Expect conflict.	• Know that the unexpected and conflict often go hand in hand; be ready to apply conflict skills. • Take advantage of the benefits that conflict can bring; positive change often evolves from problematic situations.
6. Respect culture.	• When something goes wrong, consider and seek to understand aspects of culture that may be involved in the situation. • Be alert to people who may potentially insult the cultural identities of diverse others; be ready to confront them. • Acknowledge cultural insensitivities that unintentionally occur, and apologize; work to make the situation right.
7. Take time.	• Make time to recognize and address the unexpected; ignoring this risks the success of the evaluation. • Acknowledge the unique opportunities unexpected problems may bring if you take the time to leverage them for change.

SOURCE: © 2010 Jean A. King & Laurie Stevahn.

CHAPTER REVIEW

Because bad things will inevitably happen to good evaluators, this chapter began with a reminder that, in many cases, it is not their fault. There are some elements of evaluation interactions over which an evaluator has little control, and the unexpected can happen at any time during a study, regardless of the role the evaluator may play. Nevertheless, faced with the unexpected, evaluators do have options and choices.

1. Literally dozens of unexpected issues can affect an evaluation, divided among four broad categories: environmental issues, client/user issues, evaluation process/results issues, and evaluator issues. There are also possible actions that can address these unexpected situations. Given the unique and complex nature of evaluation settings, these are not "if–then" statements but, rather, ideas that may be adapted to specific cases.

2. In general, evaluators can take several actions to deal with the unexpected: (a) understand the details of a program's external and internal environment; (b) think about internal leadership and support for the evaluation, as well as individual responses to it; (c) address the special circumstances of limited resources, impossible demands, an attack on the evaluation, propriety concerns, the effects of excluding important stakeholders, and any mistakes; and (d) attend thoughtfully to personal problems, a lack of required professional skills, and the challenges of collaboration.

3. The interactive evaluation practice skill set can also help evaluators address the unexpected. Evaluation conversations (Chapter 4) and strategies for engaging people

(Chapter 5) can be tools to explore interpersonal issues. Constructively managing interpersonal conflict (Chapter 6) may keep an evaluation on track. Using techniques that build a workable interactive evaluation process (Chapter 7) and constantly returning to those ideas in times of trial may prove helpful.

4. Internal evaluators, who work long-term in an evaluation setting, have the potential to build on existing relationships to handle the unexpected more systematically over time; external evaluators new to a context also have options for thinking about the unexpected and should carefully consider the interpersonal factor to spot possibly problematic situations in a timely manner.

5. Three heuristics can be applied to analyzing trade-offs in evaluation decision making toward moving forward: (a) the "good, quick, cheap" restaurant-industry classic; (b) the Program Evaluation Standards (Yarbrough et al., 2011); and (c) an evaluator's own personal commitments.

6. Interactive evaluators should pay attention to interpersonal dynamics at all times, conducting continuous situation analysis and staying alert to potential problems. Thoughtful communication, ongoing relations with key contacts, and documentation of the evaluation process may be useful along with other techniques, including those for dealing with *surprise*—Morell's (2010) term for the unexpected.

PART III

TEACHING CASES FOR BRINGING INTERACTIVE EVALUATION PRACTICE TO LIFE

The three chapters that follow each tell an evaluation story and raise issues for your consideration. These case descriptions (and we use the terms *case, case study,* and *case description* interchangeably) provide an opportunity to critique someone else's evaluation practice—a far easier task than making decisions on the fly in a real study. The purpose of the chapters is to create an opportunity to observe people using the interpersonal skills and techniques discussed in Part II—asking questions, structuring interactions, addressing conflict, creating viable evaluation processes, and dealing with the unexpected. In the cases, some evaluators do a better job than others, and the challenge is to figure out who is doing well and who is not and then reflect on alternative solutions.

Although we hope the situations and programs appear realistic, they are not real. They are based in part on actual events, but we have mixed and matched, simplified, and altered contexts and details to make the examples more obvious and explicitly targeted for reflection on the evaluations' interactive components. The individual actors described are not real people, and their names are invented. In many ways, these cases are composites of our experiences over many years, and we've tried to portray the good, the bad, and the ugly since evaluation practice in all its complexity is inevitably messy. We could have written exercises highlighting other aspects of the cases (e.g., their technical accuracy, evaluation budget issues, or evaluator accountability), but that was not our intent. We could also have used real studies or different examples (e.g., a large-scale evaluation or a study focused on causal outcomes or on performance measurement), but again, our intent was to create situations based on practice where interpersonal dynamics were visibly at play. These cases are far from being exemplary evaluations. Their purpose is to provide examples of interactive evaluation practice for you to critique.

How are the chapters similar? Each case has the same structure: (a) introduction, (b) evaluation context, (c) cast of characters, then (d) three sections that parallel the conversation goals presented in Chapter 4. Reflection questions at three points in the case encourage you to stop and think about how the evaluation is proceeding, and then TIPS (a set of exercises to *think*, *interact*, *practice*, and *situate*) ask you to reflect more thoroughly on issues raised in the case (see Appendix E for a generic set of exercises that can be applied across all the cases). To be clear about our intent, each chapter ends with an exhibit that applies the interactive evaluation practice principles to the case.

How are the chapters different? First, there are three different contexts (a city agency and nongovernmental organization in Chapter 9, a school district in Chapter 10, and a social services agency in Chapter 11) and many different personalities involved in the evaluations, highlighting the interactive components of evaluation practice and building on the evaluator roles of decision maker, actor, and reflector. Second, there is one example from each zone of the interactive participation quotient (Chapter 9 is evaluator-directed, Chapter 10 is collaborative, and Chapter 11 is participant-directed). Third, the cases involve both external and internal evaluators (an external evaluator in Chapter 9, one of each in Chapter 10, and an internal evaluator coaching a staff member in Chapter 11).

One of the challenges of program evaluation is that it creates real-world consequences for those involved. Evaluators constantly make decisions in situations where multiple options are routine, each with the potential to lead to different actions and possible outcomes. This much is clear: It is far easier to give examples, discuss frameworks, and provide lists of what evaluators *should* do than to determine sound choices in practice, especially when time or resource constraints are factors. Thankfully, as the saying goes, no one is perfect, which is why pencils have erasers. Thoughtful evaluators with thorough knowledge of the interpersonal factor have at their command both pencils and erasers. They do all they can to create a functional evaluation process throughout—the pencil—then pay attention as time passes and unexpected things occur, and make midcourse corrections as necessary—the eraser. The evaluators in these case examples all try to conduct useful and interpersonally competent evaluations. It is now your job to evaluate the extent to which they succeeded and to think about how your reflection on these cases relates to your own interactive evaluation practice.

9

THE EVALUATOR IS IN CHARGE

Evaluating a Controversial Shelter Project

Chapter Preview

- Consider *interactive evaluation practice* (IEP) that entails an evaluator-directed study conducted by an external evaluation consultant
- Examine how *basic inquiry tasks* and the *evaluation capacity building* continuum shape decisions in this case
- Reflect on evaluation decisions and actions at various junctures
- Engage in a set of exercises—TIPS (*think, interact, practice, situate*)—at the end of the case description
- Apply the IEP principles to the evaluator-directed study in this case

---

INTRODUCTION

This chapter describes an evaluator-directed study that an external evaluator conducts in a politically charged environment. The evaluator's client, the head of a city agency, needs a study completed in a timely manner that people will perceive as fair and accurate. Unfortunately, an interpersonal conflict between two intended users, coupled with difficulty collecting data from an important group of stakeholders, makes the evaluator's job problematic. She sincerely hopes her primary intended users (PIUs) will use the results of the evaluation. The presenting situation is this: In response to the high number of people who are homeless but unable to find space in local shelters—single men and women, couples, and families with children—a city agency in a large metropolitan area has asked Homeway, a nonprofit advocacy organization that runs shelters for the homeless, to pilot a 3-month temporary tent-city shelter on public property.

If successful, such temporary shelters could increase the number of available shelter spaces.

The Tent City Home Project (TCHP) builds on a successful program that Homeway staff had previously developed in response to the constant over-crowding of the city's shelters. For a month at a time, large tents become residences for a group of individuals who are homeless, referred to in Tent City parlance as "guests." Working with faith communities in the area, each month Homeway cosponsors Tent City on the property of a church, temple, or mosque in an accessible location (on a bus line or near social services), moving the tent infrastructure from site to site so there are a consistent number of beds available routinely. The guests live under a strict set of rules and, through elected representatives on the Tent City Governing Council, direct and manage all aspects of the program. One distinguishing feature of the Tent City concept is that couples and families may live together, which is not true in many of the city's other shelters, which are gender specific. Another essential feature is educational outreach and advocacy. The faith community that sponsors the Tent City not only organizes support for that month (meals, clothing, health services, etc.) but develops a set of interactions (conversations, lectures, panels, etc.) to engage both Tent City guests and community members in discussing issues surrounding the plight of people who are homeless and the possibilities for long-term solutions.

TCHP marks the first time that a shelter will be opened on public land, as opposed to the private properties owned and insured by faith communities. The proposed site is the parking lot of one of the city's most popular parks. If this pilot is a success, there are three other public sites in different parts of the city where TCHP will move; each site will host TCHP a total of 3 months a year. Centrally located midcity, the pilot site is near a large private university with an enrollment of 25,000 in a middle-class residential neighborhood. The neighborhood's property values benefit from access to the park and a shopping district where business is finally picking up after declines linked to the financial woes of previous years. When TCHP is set up at the pilot site, a sizeable number of parking spaces will be occupied for as long as the shelter is open.

In contrast to the traditional Tent City format that is a true collaboration, Homeway staff will be responsible for all aspects of TCHP, soliciting businesses, nonprofit organizations, and nearby faith communities to provide the necessary support for 3 months along with organizing educational activities and interacting with the elected TCHP Governing Council to ensure smooth operations. Although the Tent City concept has been operationalized successfully for 6 years and this pilot project may lead to a new format for expansion, Homeway staff members are clear that any form of tent city is only a short-term, transitional option even though it may benefit both those who are homeless and those who learn about homelessness. It would be far better, to them, if stable affordable housing eliminated the need for temporary shelters altogether. Exhibit 9.1 outlines the grounding components of the TCHP evaluation.

Exhibit 9.1 "The Evaluator Is in Charge" Evaluation

Case Grounding Components	Description
Relationship of the evaluator to the organization	External
Interpersonal participation quotient zone (see Exhibit 2.3)	Evaluator-directed study
Evaluation capacity building continuum focus (see Exhibit 2.6)	Use of a single study's process or results
Object of the evaluation	Tent City Home Project
The presenting situation	The head of a large city agency hires an evaluator to study the outcomes of hosting a temporary homeless shelter on public property

THE EVALUATION CONTEXT

In this large urban center, overall reaction to the need for homeless shelters is split between two broad views. On the one hand, in an era of economic turmoil and high unemployment, many community members are genuinely saddened by the growing numbers of people who are homeless and the fact that shelters are filled to overflowing on a regular basis. Two statistics—that many of those staying in shelters are working but unable to find affordable housing for their families and that children make up more than half the city's homeless—have spurred a motivated group of advocates to go public in an effort to solve the problems of homelessness in the city. On the other hand, a small but ardent group of community members expresses a general lack of sympathy for those who are homeless, believing these are lazy individuals who are happy to live on the state's welfare support, which is among the highest in the country. When asked the solution to homelessness in the area, they quickly reply, "Tell those people to get off their butts and look for a job."

After a local newspaper published an article describing the proposed pilot, reactions reflected the divided nature of the community's overall beliefs. Even before the pilot began, letters to the editor both supported and decried TCHP. In cyberspace the advocates for the homeless blogged and tweeted enthusiastically about the pilot's potential. But in meetings of small- and large-business owners, the reaction to what they perceived as a highly controversial project was decidedly negative. Despite his wholehearted support for the pilot, in response to complaints from several constituents, city council member Brian Orman approached Gus Stein, the head of the city's Department of Social Services—TCHP's sponsoring agency—and proposed a formal evaluation of the effects, both positive and negative, of the TCHP pilot. He noted that the merchants in the area were especially worried about the effects of TCHP on their businesses, owing to the decreased number of parking spaces and the potential effect of the shelter on their customers' sense of security. People living in the neighborhood near the proposed TCHP were reportedly worried about security and safety, asking questions such as, Will petty crime and panhandling increase? Will children be able to walk to school safely? Will people be able to use the park without fear of personal harm? According to Orman, some neighbors were also concerned about the effect of TCHP on their long-term property values.

Given the controversial nature of TCHP, Stein knew an evaluation could be a good idea. The social services agency he headed was doing its best to address the needs of the city's population of people without stable housing, but funding to address homelessness was limited and, if anything, likely to decrease in coming years. Advocates were pushing for more permanent solutions, but in the meantime TCHP might efficiently increase the number of shelter beds. If the project could adequately address the concerns raised, he might have an additional short-term option available. Yet he remained ambivalent about the program evaluation. Could an evaluation really provide evidence supporting a decision whether or not to expand TCHP to other public sites in the city while keeping his political worries in check?

THE CAST OF CHARACTERS AS THE EVALUATION BEGAN

Evaluator Katharine McMahon submitted the winning response to the **request for qualifications (RFQ)**. Her successful experience evaluating social service projects made her a strong candidate, and she was pleased to get the job. In her preliminary planning, McMahon identified a lengthy list of stakeholders for this evaluation, but she knew fewer people would necessarily play critical roles in the study. She sensed that Gus Stein, the administrator who had signed her contract, was not entirely confident about the prospects for the study. He expressed concerns to her about two key actors: Homeway director Dawn

Phillips, whom he respected but feared had already decided the outcome of the evaluation (i.e., unless it hurt her staff or the guests, TCHP was a good idea), and Councilman Brian Orman, who, as a relatively new city official, wanted to be responsive to the concerns of his district's constituents. Exhibit 9.2 details the list of characters in this evaluation, along with their concerns and issues at the beginning of the study.

As additional preparation, McMahon reviewed materials about Homeway's earlier Tent City efforts on private property and spoke with an evaluator who

Exhibit 9.2   Selected Cast of Characters for "The Evaluator Is in Charge"

Evaluation Role	Name/Title	Concerns/Issues
External evaluator	Dr. Katharine McMahon	Dr. McMahon is a respected member of the city's evaluation professionals and wins the contract for this study with her response to the agency's RFQ. Familiar with issues related to homelessness in the city, she understands the importance of her status as an outsider to the political process and the need for an evaluation process and data people will see as unbiased.
Client/PIU	Gus Stein, head of the city Department of Social Services, which is sponsoring TCHP	Gus Stein has led his agency for more than a decade and in those years has become increasingly cynical about the work his staff performs. The one constant in his professional life is political actors, all of whom strive to look good. Although he knows the potential value of evaluation and has participated in many effective studies, given the choice he would not have created a formal process for TCHP. His gut will tell him whether or not this pilot works. Given the council member's request, however, he issued the RFQ.
PIU	Dawn Phillips, director of Homeway	People familiar with Dawn Phillips, who founded Homeway 25 years ago, always speak of her passion and commitment to the homeless. She is a force in the community, backed by a passionate group of staff and community advocates. She views program evaluation as a waste of time and money and believes the evaluation will squander precious resources that would be better spent on people. Dawn's view of Gus Stein is not highly positive, but she is pleased he asked Homeway to run the TCHP pilot.

(Continued)

Exhibit 9.2 (Continued)

Evaluation Role	Name/Title	Concerns/Issues
Important stakeholders	Members of the TCHP Governing Council	Supported by the lead Homeway staff member, the 10 elected members of the TCHP Governing Council take their oversight job seriously. It is their responsibility to ensure Homeway Tent City rules are followed at this new site, to raise and then resolve concerns their peers share with them, and to take an active part in the evaluation, even though the process is new to them.
	Brian Orman, city council member	Newly elected to the city council, Brian Orman is the ultimate political actor who understands the importance of pleasing his constituents but also has a strong sense that his job is to represent the powerless at City Hall since their voices are rarely heard in the council chambers. As a businessman, he is familiar with quality improvement processes that rely on data to inform decisions.
	TCHP/Homeway staff	Ms. Phillips is the director of Homeway and a community icon, but the five staff members assigned to establish and manage TCHP are responsible for all the details involved in running a shelter for 100 men, women, and children who have no other home. In addition to other tasks, this includes connecting with and managing participation from community groups, organizing and providing three meals a day, fund-raising, and supporting the Governing Council. Evaluation is the least of their worries.
Other stakeholders	TCHP guests	The group of eventual guests at TCHP includes several couples and families with young children as well as individuals, primarily men. Most of the TCHP guests have been without stable housing for a number of months and have moved with the Tent City from site to site. All are eager to have their own home as quickly as possible. Strict rules govern how tents are assigned and who has access to them. About half the adult guests have jobs and need to get up and ready with sufficient time to get to work in the morning.
	Area residents	Many residents living near the park where TCHP will be set up consider themselves urban pioneers. Some have renovated houses that might otherwise have been torn down, and most work hard to keep their houses, lawns, and gardens in good shape. With the downturn in the economy, many of the houses have lost considerable value

Evaluation Role	Name/Title	Concerns/Issues
		and some people hold mortgages larger than the value of their homes. They do not look favorably on the prospect of additional decline in property value owing to the placement of TCHP near their homes.
	Owners of nearby businesses	Owners with businesses near the TCHP location complained to Councilman Orman about what they see as the likely effect of fewer parking spaces and their customers' security concerns when the site is up and running. Some enthusiastically support the efforts of Homeway but would prefer the tent cities continue only on private property—and, preferably, in another neighborhood.
	Volunteers/ advocates for the homeless	Intrepid activists have been volunteering for a decade in the pursuit of affordable and stable public housing for city residents in need. These advocates for the homeless see the potential expansion of Homeway's Tent City efforts as good—the more available shelter beds, the better—but also as potentially bad since a short-term "fix" may slow efforts to create permanent housing. Many have training and experience in research or evaluation in one form or another and are fixtures on-site during the TCHP pilot.

had conducted a recent outcome evaluation that documented positive effects, including data on the Tent City Governing Council and lengthy quotations from appreciative guests. Living in the community, she had a sense of some of the issues, but she also went online to review newspaper and television coverage of the upcoming tent raising and studied the proposal for TCHP carefully. At last, she felt she understood the issues involved and began her evaluation.

THE EVALUATION PROCESS

Initial Decisions/Actions

From her work on other evaluations, Dr. McMahon understood well the importance of establishing positive relationships early on while simultaneously learning about her intended users' information needs and perceptions of program evaluation. Her client, Gus Stein, seemed open enough to the evaluation process. There were no formal requirements from an outside funder (since there was none), and he was clear about his need to learn about the viability of this new shelter option. Without hesitation he agreed to be her contact as the study proceeded. They decided she would touch base with him regularly to keep him informed about how things were going and to identify any potential logistical issues or political concerns. He told her his agency routinely collected data on all its homeless shelters and she could access whatever existing data she needed. Somewhat to her surprise, Stein identified the well-known head of Homeway as a second key intended user. He explained she was potentially a loose cannon who might react publicly if the pilot or its evaluation angered her for some reason. McMahon knew Dawn Phillips was famous for her passionate commitment to solving the problem of homelessness and for her quick temper when anyone disagreed with her. Given that reputation, McMahon sensed a relationship with her might be challenging.

In their initial meeting, Dawn Phillips, the head of Homeway, arrived late and out of breath. She could chat for only 15 minutes before rushing to another commitment. She explained that her experience with evaluation had always been as a last-minute addition to an already overwhelming programmatic to-do list and that she had little use for it. When McMahon asked her what she really wanted to know about TCHP, Phillips immediately raised two issues:

1. She wanted to see if this expansion, which relied entirely on her staff rather than on collaboration with another community group, could generate sufficient support for the entire month without overwhelming them.

2. She wanted to know if the TCHP guests felt they were treated with respect and dignity, worrying the city bureaucracy might somehow interfere with the traditional Tent City culture of caring. If the evaluator could include their voices in the study, she would feel much better about spending money on it.

Then, switching her cell phone on to make a call, she was off to her next meeting. McMahon realized that keeping Phillips in the loop—or getting her to respond to requests of any sort—might prove difficult. She asked Phillips's assistant for his contact information and arranged for him to be the liaison with his boss, who seemed constantly in motion.

Already, Katharine McMahon sensed the potential for interpersonal conflict between Gus Stein and Dawn Phillips, the two people who would most directly affect the course of the study. Gus Stein seemed pleasant enough, an agency bureaucrat trying to solve a difficult problem. Phillips's reputation as a powerful community leader made her a force to be reckoned with, and her insistent demand for additional support for people who found themselves homeless, well documented in the newspaper, put her in a possible adversarial role with Stein, the pragmatist looking to expand the number of beds available. Plus, the success of TCHP might delay longer-term solutions. McMahon certainly recognized the importance of giving voice to TCHP guests through the evaluation process, but who else's voice mattered? Even though Councilman Orman would not be a primary user of the evaluation results, she decided to meet with him briefly to confirm that the study would provide him what he needed, since he was the one who had commissioned it. He was more than happy to meet and confirmed he was most interested in the reactions of his constituents—the business owners and nearby residents.

Within a week, McMahon had a good sense of what her PIUs wanted to know. They needed information on the feasibility and impact of TCHP, both on the guests living in the new shelter and on the surrounding neighborhood—in other words, on the pilot project's short-term consequences, good and bad. Her next concern was how viable this agency setting would be for conducting the evaluation. In this regard McMahon was cautiously optimistic. Through good fortune or divine intervention (she thought), she was able to schedule a joint meeting with Stein and Phillips to discuss their thoughts on how they might eventually use the data she proposed to collect. She watched body language and reactions closely. Leaning into the conversation, both PIUs suggested ideas for the use of the evaluation, especially the potential negatives. It became clear that three types of results, in this order, would lead to the pilot's being declared a failure: (a) if the implementation failed (e.g., staff couldn't find sufficient resources to support TCHP for all 3 months, if fund-raising failed, if costs to the agency were too high, and if no one attended the educational events), (b) if TCHP guests had negative experiences in this new format (a key indicator for Phillips), and (c) if there were negative environmental consequences (e.g., neighborhood crime statistics went up, businesses were adversely affected, neighbors felt uncomfortable). McMahon was ready to design the evaluation.

REFLECTION BOX I

How Is This Evaluation Going?

1. Who did the evaluator determine would be PIUs of the evaluation results? Do you agree or disagree with the evaluator's determination? Explain.

2. What actions did the evaluator take to establish positive connections with the PIUs in this study? How successful were these actions? What additional conversations with the PIUs may have been helpful? Explain.

(Continued)

(Continued)

3. Were there other key stakeholders with whom the evaluator should have interacted during the initial stages of framing this study? With whom else would you have interacted? What might have been advantages in connecting with these other individuals? Explain.

4. Revisit Chapter 4, Exhibit 4.2. Review Conversation Goals 1 through 4, shown in the first column. In your judgment, how well did the evaluator accomplish these goals? Explain.

5. Revisit Chapter 7, Template 1 and Template 2. Apply these worksheets to this case. What does the evaluator clearly know and understand about the evaluation context of TCHP and the demographic dimensions of that program and the community in which it operates? What else does the evaluator need to know? Explain.

6. How might Dawn Phillips's deep concern for advocacy affect the evaluation in this case? What steps do you believe the evaluator should take to deal with this situation? Explain.

7. How might the evaluator constructively manage relationships among Gus Stein (head of the city agency sponsoring TCHP), Dawn Phillips (director of Homeway), and Brian Orman (city council member)? What are their respective issues? How might the evaluation fail if these issues and relationships go unattended?

Data Collection and Analysis Decisions/Actions

Despite elements of controversy, the TCHP evaluation was not an overly complex study. From her lengthy list of stakeholder concerns, Katharine McMahon developed two overarching evaluation questions:

1. How viable is TCHP as an alternative temporary shelter?

2. What are its short-term consequences, both positive and negative?

Measuring TCHP's viability required documentation of a number of variables, including its cost-effectiveness in comparison with the cost of other shelters, the feasibility of Homeway staff running it on their own, and the effectiveness of its associated outreach activities (e.g., opportunities for public education and engagement, volunteer opportunities, and positive interaction with the guests). Intended consequences included the increased number of beds for individuals who were homeless, increased knowledge and empowerment for people—volunteers and guests alike—who participated in TCHP, and positive interactions with community members. Unintended consequences included largely negative possibilities related to crime, litter, loitering, neighbors' perceived safety, decreased sales at nearby businesses, and decreased property values in the neighborhood, among others.

McMahon always considered the Program Evaluation Standards as she thought about evaluation design. How could she conduct a high-quality study given the constraints she sensed in this context? As was often the case, she suspected there might be trade-offs among certain standards. She decided to propose a descriptive study that would detail and document the TCHP process, coupled with an outcome study looking at the short-term effects of TCHP, knowing the negative consequences might be the most important to capture for her two PIUs. Relying on McMahon's expertise, both Gus Stein and Dawn Phillips agreed with the proposed approach. The evaluator next determined what data to collect and how, again checking with her PIUs and making the minor changes they suggested. Ultimately, she identified eight methods of data collection, shown in Exhibit 9.3. She carefully considered all eight one last time

Exhibit 9.3   Data Collection Methods, Samples, and Those Responsible

Data Collection Method	Sample	Those Responsible
1. Analysis of existing data	• Archival data (e.g., cost data, police records)	Evaluator
2. Interviews	• Key business leaders identified by Gus Stein, plus others they name • A random sample of TCHP guests	Evaluator
3. Data dialogues	• Business owners within a 10-block radius of TCHP	Evaluator
4. Written surveys	• All households within a 10-block radius of TCHP	Homeway staff/volunteers (evaluator)
5. Electronic surveys	• All TCHP/Homeway staff	Evaluator
6. Observations	• Informal on-site visits at different times of day and night	Evaluator
7. Group interview	• The TCHP Governing Council	Evaluator
8. Documentation	• Those attending Councilman Orman's TCHP community forum on homelessness	Evaluator

in light of the evaluation questions framing the study and felt good about her choices. Exhibit 9.4 summarizes the evaluation questions, the data McMahon needs to collect, and the methods she will use.

Exhibit 9.4   Summary of Evaluation Questions, Data Needed, and Data Collection Methods

Question	Data Needed	Data Collection Method
1. How viable is TCHP as an alternative temporary shelter? 2. What are its consequences, both positive and negative?	• Cost data • Police records • Perceptions of business leaders, TCHP guests/ Governing Council members, neighbors, TCHP/Homeway staff • Observations of TCHP	• Analysis of existing data • Individual and group interviews • Data dialogues • Written and electronic surveys • Observations • Documentation

1. *Analysis of existing data.* Fortunately for McMahon, the city's data system included cost data on the traditional shelters for the homeless and archival data on community effects (e.g., police records of loitering, assaults, and vandalism before, during, and after the original Tent City placements). After meeting with the agency's data expert to better understand what was available, she gave Gus Stein a list of the data she needed, and he agreed to have his staff compile it and send her an electronic file by the date she proposed.

2. *Individual interviews.* Undoubtedly thinking of Councilman Orman, Stein had emphasized to McMahon the importance of garnering the perceptions of business leaders in the area. She asked him to compile a rank-ordered list of the people to interview one-on-one and decided to use a snowball sampling technique through which those interviewees suggested additional people to interview. Stein gave her an initial list, which grew longer with each interview. She met interviewees at their businesses. Because Phillips had emphasized the importance of understanding the perceptions of TCHP guests, McMahon also conducted one-on-one interviews with 20 randomly selected individuals at TCHP across the 3 months. She knew from checking her sampling table that for a population of 100, she would need to interview 80 people to ensure a sufficiently meaningful sample, but that was not possible. A sample of

20 seemed large enough, even if it wasn't technically adequate. Both Stein and Phillips agreed, and they reviewed and edited the interview protocols before she began.

3. *Data dialogue sessions (see Chapter 5, Strategy 7).* Knowing she could not conduct individual interviews with every business owner in the area, McMahon decided to hold three open sessions (one early morning, one midday, one after hours) for those owners within 10 blocks of TCHP (Stein's suggested range) who had not been individually interviewed. The sessions would be held in a private room at a restaurant near TCHP and use an adaptation of the individual interview questions.

4. *Written surveys of neighbors.* Again using the 10-block radius, McMahon decided to collect data from people who lived in the neighborhoods near TCHP. To save on costs, she had planned to send an electronic survey to every household in that area, but in reviewing the plan, Dawn Phillips objected because some households lacked Internet access. She volunteered to have Homeway staff and advocacy volunteers hand deliver TCHP descriptive materials and surveys and, if possible, engage the neighbors in short conversations about the project. Since resources were becoming increasingly limited and Phillips felt strongly about the value of this task, McMahon agreed.

5. *Electronic surveys of TCHP/Homeway staff.* The evaluator knew the staff were key respondents since they bore the brunt of the pilot's setup and implementation. An electronic survey would be quick, confidential, and easy to analyze since the data would come pretyped.

6. *Observations of TCHP in action.* McMahon thought it was important to see what TCHP looked like in operation and to document this with field notes and informal photographs at different times of day and night. Pictures would be included in reports only if guests signed release forms. She dressed appropriately for these observations—no business suit or high heels.

7. *Group interview of the TCHP Governing Council.* To capture the voices of guests in leadership positions, McMahon decided to conduct a group interview of the TCHP Governing Council during the final week of the 3-month pilot.

8. *Documentation.* Unbeknownst to the evaluator, Councilman Orman organized a community forum at the TCHP site, inviting representatives from the print and electronic media, the mayor, other members of the city

council, key community leaders, and every other person he believed should be there to visit and interact with the guests. Homeway staff went along with his arrangements, hoping positive press would help make their case. McMahon learned about the event when she found a flier during an on-site observation and decided to attend and take notes on what people said.

Since McMahon was in charge of most of the data collection, the process proceeded relatively smoothly. There were just two problems, only one of which could be solved. First, although she had rushed to put together her request for data from Stein's office, his staff missed her deadline by 2 weeks. It took three increasingly persistent e-mails to Stein before the electronic file arrived. Second, good intentions notwithstanding, the neighborhood survey process simply didn't work. McMahon had prepared a sufficient number of surveys (the required number plus 30 extra) and delivered them to the Homeway staff member in charge of the hand-delivery process. Although a self-addressed, stamped envelope was included with each survey, neighbors were told they could also stop by TCHP to drop off their surveys; not a single person did so. After 2 weeks, only 16 surveys had come in the mail, a response rate so low McMahon realized she couldn't use the data. It was too late to change the process, and, even if there were time, there was no money to redo the survey. Unfortunately, this meant there were virtually no data from Councilman Orman's neighborhood constituents.

With time running out, Katharine McMahon turned to conducting the data analysis, a task she always enjoyed because she liked working with data.

1. *Analysis of existing data.* First, she looked at the cost of regular shelters (per bed) and compared it to that of the original Tent City located on faith communities' properties and then to TCHP. The numbers looked good. Then she compared existing archival data on crime-related variables pre-TCHP and post-TCHP, comparing the rates in other neighborhoods that hosted Tent Cities as well as those in the pilot neighborhood, and found no differences.

2. *Individual interviews.* Having paid to have the individual interviews with area business owners transcribed, she conducted a qualitative analysis of their perceptions and was stunned by their negativity on virtually all counts. Although many reported never having set foot on the TCHP site, they felt free to say it was bad—that their customers complained about litter, having to park far away, and feeling uncomfortable seeing "those

people." The interview data from the TCHP guests were far more positive. People were appreciative of the city's attempt to create an additional shelter option, although a few guests said the social experience at TCHP was less positive than at the other Tent Cities because staff were always busy and couldn't really take time to get to know them individually.

3. *Data dialogue sessions.* McMahon was less sure about what to do with the results of the data dialogue sessions with the other business owners. More than 150 had been invited, but only 37 participated in the three discussions. She had inadvertently scheduled one session on Rosh Hashanah, an important Jewish holiday, and decided to move it to another day. Those who did come had thanked her for the opportunity to speak their minds. Like their peers who had been interviewed individually, their perceptions were uniformly negative, but they provided far fewer details to support their claims. Their complaints were cast more as general issues about people who were homeless in our society. Were those data usable? She wondered what to do with them.

4. *Written surveys of neighbors.* Since the response rate was low, McMahon decided to exclude the neighbors' survey data. She did glance at those submitted and was surprised to see positive responses and a few enthusiastic open-ended comments—quite a contrast to the business owners' documented perspectives.

5. *Electronic surveys of TCHP/Homeway staff.* McMahon had a 100% response rate from the staff, perhaps thanks to the chocolate chip cookies she brought to the staff meeting where she introduced the survey. The results looked fairly positive. Staff noted glitches, but by and large their responses appeared to document the feasibility of TCHP. As she read through the data, she realized to her dismay that she hadn't gotten input from the sizeable number of volunteers and advocates who regularly came and went at the site. "I won't forget them next time," she thought to herself.

6. *Observations of TCHP in action.* In contrast to the negative perceptions, when reviewing her field notes and the photographs she'd taken, McMahon was struck by the pervasive spirit of the pilot—TCHP had created a smoothly running, respectful, kind, and gentle environment with a few creature comforts for the guests who were experiencing major stress in their lives. McMahon sensed the atmosphere was positive, but she was concerned about making claims that were too strong, especially since the formal guest interviews were not entirely positive. She wrote a

description that gave specific details about how TCHP looked in operation. Most guests had been pleased to sign release forms for their photographs since they wanted others to know about their positive feelings.

7. *Group interview of the TCHP Governing Council.* Her notes from the Governing Council's group interview corroborated the observations' positive vibes, but one bit of data pointed to a possible concern. In the original version of the Tent City on private property, Governing Council members explained how members of the communities of faith who collaborated with Homeway staff made Tent City guests feel truly welcome. The guests got to know the volunteers over the course of the month and appreciated their support. Apparently, that wasn't the case in this public space. Homeway staff, who managed the pilot, had neither the time nor the resources to connect with guests in this special way. Despite volunteer participation, that aspect of Tent City seemed to have been lost in the TCHP implementation.

8. *Documentation.* Analyzing notes from Councilman Orman's community forum was a challenge because McMahon had a hard time keeping up with the fast-flying comments, most of them negative even though TCHP guests were present and willing to respond to any issues raised. The community members dominated the discussion, leaving the guests little room to speak. She summarized the themes of the questions and answers as best she could.

When she was finished, Katharine McMahon had a thorough analysis of the TCHP data. Her next challenge was to make sense of it.

REFLECTION BOX II

How Is This Evaluation Going?

1. What were the final evaluation questions that guided this study? To what extent do you believe these adequately dealt with the concerns of the PIUs? Explain.

2. How might an evaluation steering committee composed of several TCHP/ Homeway staff have helped the evaluator plan for data collection and analysis? Would you have advised the evaluator to establish such a committee for input? Why or why not? Explain.

3. Revisit Chapter 5, Exhibit 5.3. Which one of these strategies did the evaluator use to collect data for this study? The evaluator chose not to employ any of the other strategies useful for collecting data. Was that a good choice? Explain your rationale. What other strategies might have been helpful in collecting data from various sources to address the evaluation questions adequately? How might you have used those?

4. What steps might the evaluator have taken to obtain the needed neighborhood data in timely and cost-effective ways? For example, might it have been feasible to request time at already scheduled community events or social gatherings to obtain such data, perhaps by quickly using the "fist to five" or "dot votes/bar graphs" methods (see Chapter 5, *Strategies 12* and *13*)? Brainstorm feasible options and explain which you would have pursued.

5. How important was it to obtain data from TCHP/Homeway volunteers? How might the evaluator have obtained those data? Brainstorm feasible options; also consider the evaluator's dozen of interactive strategies presented in Chapter 5. Explain your thinking.

6. What do you think about how the evaluator handled the surprise community forum organized by Councilman Orman? Should she have spoken with the councilman once she became aware of the event? What might have been the political effects of each of these choices? What would you have done in this situation in the best interests of the evaluation? Explain.

Data Interpretation and Reporting Decisions/Actions

Time was running short as the end of the pilot's 3 months approached. McMahon had experience interpreting data, but the challenge seemed to be the range of opinions on TCHP. She looked at the analysis of each type of data separately.

1. *Analysis of existing data.* The comparative cost data actually looked good. TCHP was a cost-effective option for the agency. The archival data also looked good, documenting that having a Tent City or TCHP in a neighborhood did not lead to an increase in crime or safety concerns. The rates before, during, and after the shelters' presence were virtually identical.

2. *Individual interviews.* The overarching themes from the business owner interviews were a list of reasons TCHP should not be allowed to continue. Their data detailed reasons for their strong opposition to the pilot; they honestly believed businesses had lost customers and their customers felt uneasy around TCHP. The guests' data painted a positive view of their experience, although they seemed to want more connection with Homeway staff.

3. *Data dialogue sessions.* Even though the number of participants was low, the themes from the data dialogues paralleled those of the individual interviews with business leaders. There seemed to be consistency from the business community, although the data dialogue data were fairly general and vague.

4. *Written surveys of neighbors.* McMahon winced as she wrote a statement explaining why she was unable to include the neighborhood survey data.

5. *Electronic surveys of TCHP/Homeway staff.* The interpretation of the staff surveys was straightforward since the staff by and large agreed that, with a few minor tweaks, the TCHP pilot was doable.

6. *Observations of TCHP in action.* How many times had she observed the shelter in action? Was that number of visits sufficient to make positive claims? She decided it was and she would include descriptions and photographs in reports.

7. *Group interview of the TCHP Governing Council.* The TCHP Governing Council represented TCHP's leaders—elected by their peers—but she had done just one interview with them. McMahon decided she would reference in passing the comment that TCHP was not as good an experience for guests who had experienced a Tent City elsewhere.

8. *Documentation.* What did the notes she had taken at the community forum mean? What did they add to the formal data she had collected? She decided to omit any of the content and mention only that Councilman Orman had sponsored such a forum.

At last, all the data were analyzed and interpreted, and McMahon triangulated her results. As often happens, the evaluation results were mixed, and, unfortunately, she did not have data from neighbors or from TCHP volunteers, even though they were important stakeholders in this process. What could she write in answering the evaluation questions?

1. *How viable is TCHP as an alternative temporary shelter?* Staff reported the new arrangement was workable, and the archival data suggested it was cost-effective and having TCHP in a neighborhood did not lead to increased crime. The observation descriptions of TCHP in action pointed to a generally positive experience for guests staying there.

2. *What are its consequences, both positive and negative?* McMahon thought the most important positive consequence was additional shelter spaces at a reasonable cost. The negative consequences included anger from area business leaders and the possibility that the new model might be less attentive to guests than were the earlier Tent Cities.

McMahon was relieved she could start writing the reports she and her two PIUs had agreed on: (a) a short ("executive") summary and PowerPoint of the evaluation process and its key findings for Gus Stein, Dawn Phillips, city council members, and the TCHP Governing Council, and (b) a formal report for the city agency's files.

Knowing the importance of keeping her intended users up to speed, McMahon scheduled a meeting with Gus Stein and Dawn Phillips to review a draft report of the findings to check that her interpretations made sense and to frame possible recommendations. Given their busy schedules, having them in a room together seemed like a victory. They both thanked her for having the draft ready in a timely manner and explained how eager they were to see the results and put them into action. Stein was clearly pleased with the answer to the first question but asked her where the data from the neighbors were to include in the answer to the second question. McMahon explained the problems with the written survey process and said she had done the best she could given the situation. "But what am I supposed to tell Brian Orman? The data from the business owners are weak, and you have no data from the neighbors. I can't support expanding this pilot without that information."

Phillips kept shaking her head and flipping through the report's pages. She, too, liked the answer to the first question since she really wanted the pilot to be a success, but she asked in a pointed manner why there weren't multiple quotations and anecdotes from the TCHP guests and the volunteers to answer the second question. "Didn't I explicitly request that their voices be part of this evaluation? Didn't we agree on that? I would love for this project to be a success, but I need to know guests are well treated. What evidence do you have of that?" Red-faced, McMahon could only explain her oversight in not including more interview data—she could certainly do that in the next version—and in failing to interview volunteers. She mentioned the negative comment she had heard during the group interview with the TCHP Governing Council. The room became extremely silent.

"So what do we do now?" asked Gus Stein. Phillips thought for a moment and then said, "I may not be happy with what the data say, and I wish they came together better, but I think we can figure something out. Let's look at what we know from the data." McMahon took a marker and, as Stein and Phillips called out ideas, wrote the following list under the heading "What We Know":

1. Homeway staff successfully supported the TCHP pilot

2. TCHP guests not unhappy, want more personal relations with staff

3. Community volunteers and advocates—don't know what they think

4. Local business community—negative perceptions but no dollar data to support or refute

5. Cost and safety data—all positive

6. People living in the neighborhood—don't know what they think

McMahon felt better. Perhaps there was a way to bring this all together.

REFLECTION BOX III

How Is This Evaluation Going?

1. Revisit Chapter 6, Exhibit 6.1. What interpersonal conflicts occurred during the evaluation? Did the individuals involved predominantly respond by forcing, withdrawing, smoothing, compromising, or problem solving? How effective were those various responses in dealing constructively with conflict? Explain.

2. Revisit Chapter 8, Exhibit 8.2. What unexpected events occurred during the evaluation that were beyond the evaluator's control? Which broad categories did these unforeseen problems seem to exemplify? How did the evaluator respond? How effective were these responses in keeping the evaluation on track?

3. To what extent did the evaluator understand the politics inherent in this evaluation study? Was the evaluator blindsided when it came to political considerations? Explain.

4. Do you agree with the evaluator's interpretations of the study's findings? Why or why not? What specific recommendations would you make based on the findings? Explain.

5. At the end of this case, what conflicts do you see emerging between the evaluator and the two PIUs? How might the evaluator constructively acknowledge and deal with these conflicts? What tools in Chapter 6 might the evaluator employ?

6. If you were the evaluator in this study, what would you have done differently in the evaluation? Specify and explain your reasoning.

CASE STUDY TIPS: THINK, INTERACT, PRACTICE, SITUATE

This section contains four sets of exercises for further engaging with this case study. The first set involves *thinking* individually about various aspects of the case's evaluator-directed study. The second set entails *interacting* in small groups (consisting of two, three, or four people) on collaborative tasks that involve critical analysis, reasoned discussion, and decision making. The third set prompts *practicing* in the real world by carrying out field-based exercises related to the case. The fourth set prompts *situating* personal lessons learned from this case within your own context as an evaluator.

CASE STUDY TIPS

Think

1. What are the strengths and limitations of this evaluation study? Draw a chart with two columns; label one "strengths" and the other "limitations," and then list specifics for each. What might the evaluator have done to prevent or avoid the limitations? Explain.

2. In your judgment, did this evaluator-directed study adequately address the evaluation questions? To what extent? Explain.

3. Systematically review the evaluator's various decisions and actions in this case study. Which actions do you believe contributed most (vs. least) to a viable

(Continued)

(Continued)

evaluation process? Which most contributed to producing credible/trustworthy (vs. implausible/untrustworthy) results? Which most enhanced (vs. diminished) use of the results?

4. Revisit the definition of interactive evaluation practice (IEP) and its grounding principles. In your judgment, how effectively did the evaluator facilitate IEP? How well did the evaluator use its principles to guide effective practice? Explain.

5. What interpersonal skills were especially important for the evaluator in this evaluator-directed study? How well did the evaluator apply those skills? What other competencies positively contributed to the evaluation process and product? Explain.

Interact

1. With a colleague, discuss your responses to each of the items above. Compare and contrast your thinking. Try to reach consensus on each item. Present and defend your collaborative conclusions to other groups that also engaged in this exercise. How did these discussions expand your understanding of evaluator-directed studies?

2. Consider the following statement: "The evaluator attended to issues of cultural competence in designing and facilitating the Homeway/TCHP evaluation." Discuss this statement by (a) forming a group of four, (b) assigning pairs within the group to either look for case evidence that supports this statement or refutes this statement, (c) present and listen carefully to the alternative arguments, (d) engage in open discussion to challenge arguments, (e) reverse perspectives, (f) drop advocacy of positions, (g) together consider all information that surfaced, and (h) reach consensus on the best reasoned response. Craft a team letter to the evaluator containing advice for dealing with cultural competence in this evaluation, especially as it pertains to people who are homeless and often marginalized in society.

3. At the end of the evaluation the evaluator and two PIUs generated a list, labeled "What We Know," toward crafting recommendations based on the study's findings. Role-play what happens next. In groups of three, determine who will be Katharine McMahon (the evaluator), Gus Stein (head of the agency sponsoring TCHP), and Dawn Phillips (director of Homeway). Consider what

you know about IEP and what matters as you play your role toward completing a useful evaluation.

4. Form groups of three and use *Strategy 4: Cooperative Interviews* (described in Chapter 5) to address the following question: "From your perspective, what was the best decision the evaluator, Katharine McMahon, made in this case study? Why? Explain." Use the "Interview Response Sheet" (presented in Chapter 5) to record responses and identify key group ideas (similarities/themes/insights) across responses.

5. In a larger group of 10 to 20 people, use *Strategy 6: Making Metaphors* (described in Chapter 5) to complete the following stem: *"A successful evaluator-directed evaluation study is like a...because..."* Next, use *Strategy 10: Concept Formation/Cluster Maps* (described in Chapter 5) to identify common qualities or characteristics across all the metaphor responses. How did this exercise deepen or expand your understanding of evaluator-directed studies? Explain.

Practice

1. Interview an evaluator who primarily conducts evaluator-directed studies (or someone within an organization or program who is responsible for evaluation projects). In what field does this evaluator primarily work—e.g., education, business, health, government, nonprofit, social services, etc.? What does this evaluator believe are the most important skill sets for successfully conducting evaluations in his or her context? To what extent do interpersonal skills play a critical role? What advice would this evaluator give to others conducting evaluator-directed studies?

2. Use the Internet to locate evaluation studies conducted on shelter projects, transitional housing programs, or social services for people who are homeless. Read one (or several), and take note of the evaluation questions that frame the study, types of issues that emerge, political considerations, samples, data, and conclusions. How are these the same as or different from those presented in this case study? What advice might you give those conducting future studies of this type? Explain.

3. Arrange to shadow, assist, or intern in an evaluator-directed study in an organization or program in your content area within the community. Observe various

(Continued)

(Continued)

components of the study. How do the basic inquiry tasks unfold? What are the framing questions of the evaluation? How were these determined? With whom does the evaluator stay in contact throughout the evaluation? How does the evaluator interact with various stakeholders? Which decisions and actions seem to facilitate constructive evaluation processes? What challenges surface, and how does the evaluator respond? How does the evaluator make decisions about data collection and analysis? Seek permission to participate in various components of the study whenever appropriate. Reflect on lessons learned each step of the way.

4. Prepare and facilitate a professional development training activity that presents the foundations of IEP from an evaluator-directed perspective. Involve participants in activities that illustrate the usefulness of the basic inquiry tasks, interpersonal participation quotient, and evaluation capacity building frameworks when interacting with evaluation clients, funders, and other stakeholders.

Situate

1. Reflect on an evaluator-directed study you recently conducted (or in which you are currently involved). Compare and contrast the issues you faced to those in this case study. Draw a Venn diagram to record the similarities and differences.

2. What aspects of this case particularly inform your current evaluation practice? Explain.

3. What skills do you possess that make you particularly well suited to conducting evaluator-directed studies? Refer to evaluation standards, guidelines, and/or competencies in self-assessing your strengths and determining additional professional development.

4. What helpful lessons did you learn from this case? What are your main takeaways? How will these enhance your future work as an evaluator?

CHAPTER REVIEW

As a professional evaluator with a constrained timeline—Tent City Home Project (TCHP) would function for only 3 months—Katharine McMahon knew she had to work quickly and thoughtfully. Once she signed the contract, her first concerns were to develop positive relationships with Gus Stein and Dawn Phillips, her primary intended users (PIUs); to learn what they wanted or needed to know, along with their perceptions of evaluation; and to examine the TCHP context both for potential evaluation pitfalls and for the eventual use of the data she would collect. Next she designed the study, deciding what data she needed and how to collect them, as well as what analyses made sense. Once she had the data in hand, she had to interpret what she had analyzed and develop two reports. At every step of the process, she consulted with her PIUs and reflected on how things were going. Her reflection on the interactive evaluation practice (IEP) principles, shown in Exhibit 9.5, highlighted places where she might make different decisions the next time around.

Exhibit 9.5   Applying IEP Principles to "The Evaluator Is in Charge" Evaluation

IEP Principle	Positive Application	Negative Application
1. Get personal.	• Identified PIUs and other important stakeholders • Involved PIUs in important decisions throughout the evaluation • Respected a PIU's busy schedule	• Failed to collect data from two important stakeholder groups: (a) neighbors and (b) community volunteers and advocates
2. Structure interaction.	• Held joint PIU meetings • Conducted multiple one-on-one interviews • Used data dialogues to increase the number of businesspeople who could participate in the evaluation	• Did not take advantage of TCHP site visits to collect data from volunteers and advocates
3. Examine context.	• Reviewed pertinent newspaper and television coverage before beginning • Used credible data from existing sources	• Failed to appreciate the importance of data from community participants (neighbors, volunteers, advocates)
4. Consider politics.	• Recognized the potential for politics to affect the evaluation • Sought to pay attention to Councilman Orman's concerns • Agreed to let TCHP staff deliver surveys in the neighborhood to please Phillips • Attended the community forum	• Failed to collect data from a stakeholder group that mattered to the councilman • Lost data as a result of the hand-delivered surveys

(Continued)

Exhibit 9.5 (Continued)

IEP Principle	Positive Application	Negative Application
5. Expect conflict.	• Recognized the potential conflict between Stein and Phillips and worked to respect their separate concerns	• May have precipitated a potential conflict at the conclusion of the evaluation between the evaluator and the two PIUs
6. Respect culture.	• Moved the date of a data dialogue session to avoid scheduling it on a culturally specific holiday • Wore appropriate attire when observing at TCHP	• Failed to get feedback from TCHP guests during the evaluation process
7. Take time.	• Designed a study she could conduct within the time available • Managed to get existing data within a reasonable time (made requests appropriately)	• Ran out of time to collect data from the neighbors

10

WE'RE IN THIS TOGETHER

Evaluating a Remedial Math Program

Chapter Preview

- Consider *interactive evaluation practice* (IEP) that entails a collaborative study conducted by an internal evaluator working in partnership with an external evaluation consultant
- Examine how *basic inquiry tasks* and the *evaluation capacity building* continuum shape decisions in this case
- Reflect on evaluation decisions and actions at various junctures
- Engage in a set of exercises—TIPS (*think, interact, practice, situate*)—at the end of the case description
- Apply the IEP principles to the collaborative study in this case

---

INTRODUCTION

In this chapter, an internal evaluator with numerous responsibilities enlists the help of an external evaluator to design and conduct a collaborative evaluation of an important program. The work of the sole internal evaluator in the school district centers on the efficient management of its extensive and highly visible mandated testing program that each year involves every student from grades 2 through 12. Beyond evaluations required for funding compliance, program evaluation is a rare commodity, but in this instance the superintendent has asked for one. Knowing the district well, the internal evaluator thinks such a process may prove helpful. Given the many actors who could potentially be interested in the topic, she believes an inclusive study may have the multiple benefits of increasing people's understanding of the issues surrounding the program, identifying ways to improve it, and introducing them to the practice of evaluative thinking.

The local newspaper publishes the district's scores on standardized math tests under banner headlines every summer. The scores, which started low, have stayed low. Poor results in the past several years have put three of the district's five elementary schools in jeopardy, as they have not met their adequate yearly progress targets. The press has highlighted this fact, questioning the reasons for the achievement decline in a community where citizens once took high-quality public education for granted. After each set of disheartening scores, the superintendent and the curriculum coordinator face increasing criticism from the school board, parents, and community members.

As a result, the district's remedial math programming has expanded dramatically in recent years. In an effort to increase student learning in mathematics, each of the district's elementary schools (Grades K–5) now has a resource room staffed by a specially trained math teacher. Students with the lowest test scores on the previous year's standardized math tests—roughly 60 children per school—receive targeted, small-group remedial math instruction using an evidence-based program called NumberNastics! (NN!). Borrowing from the term *gymnastics*, which aims to develop physically agile and healthy children, NN! aims to help children become nimble with numbers and achieve academically in math. In fact, the advertising materials explain, "It's like math gymnastics!" Students who participate in NN! are pulled from regular classes during music, art, or technology lessons to receive their supplemental math instruction. Researchers have repeatedly documented the value of NN!'s personalized activities in helping students who need remediation, in part because children genuinely enjoy them. Unfortunately, however, although the NN! program has been in operation for 3 years and is well liked by teachers and students, test scores have not improved. The NN! "coaches," as they are called, wonder if they have the right skills to help students whose math skills are well below grade level, although their nonspecialist peers appreciate having the NN! option for students who are struggling in regular math. Members of the school board have started to question the cost of a program that appears to yield few gains.

During one of their weekly meetings, the superintendent asks his internal evaluator if a formal evaluation might identify what is working with the NN! remediation and what should be changed. He explains that what he really wants to know is whether or not—or in what ways—NN! directly improves children's math test scores, since the effects have seemed minimal in the first 3 years. The evaluator, thinking about the likely value of a broader conversation about remedial math, achievement testing, and elementary student learning in the district, proposes a collaborative evaluation process that could inform a variety of people about the issues, engage them in conversations about what is working and what isn't, and then make recommendations to improve the program. The superintendent agrees with the proposed process. The evaluator asks him if it would be possible to hire an external evaluator to work with her on this study. A number of factors call for the involvement of an external evaluator—among them the internal evaluator's many responsibilities related to the testing program, her limited background in quantitative methods, and the need for this evaluation to be credible and to appear bias free. She fears if someone inside the district conducts the study, outsiders may not accept the results as "objective." The superintendent concurs and asks her to identify and negotiate with an external evaluator. They then begin to generate a list of possible participants in the collaborative evaluation process. Exhibit 10.1 outlines the grounding components of the NN! evaluation.

Exhibit 10.1   "We're in This Together" Evaluation

Case Grounding Components	Description
Relationship of the evaluator to the organization	One internal, one external
Interpersonal participation quotient zone (see Exhibit 2.3)	Collaborative study
Evaluation capacity building continuum focus (see Exhibit 2.6)	Evaluation capacity building
Object of the evaluation	NumberNastics!, a remedial elementary math program
The presenting situation	The superintendent requests an evaluation of the elementary remedial math program in a financially challenged district

THE EVALUATION CONTEXT

For decades this small-town school district has taken pride in its reputation for winning athletic teams and educational excellence. Not anymore. It now faces funding issues, as state support and business and property tax revenues have plummeted. The district has serious financial troubles and has gutted its central-office staff to a skeletal number of administrators, all of whom must perform several roles. Growing class sizes remind teachers of the earlier days of the one-room schoolhouse, and even the athletic program's budget has been cut. Everyone who works for the schools is worried about the community vote a year from now on a tax levy targeted to support remedial education programs and the technology and maintenance they require. In this environment, Sara Moore, the internal evaluator, knows meaningful program evaluation could be helpful, but the resources to support evaluation are simply not there. With increasing numbers of requirements, the district testing program has expanded in the past decade and now consumes every dollar available for evaluative activities.

On the whole, people in the community—civic leaders and followers alike—freely express concerns about the district's changing image. These concerns stem in part from three related issues. First, they relate to demographics. There are more students of color—the children of migrant workers who have settled in town and the children of immigrants and war refugees who are not English speakers and who frequently are preliterate in their native languages. These children regularly arrive at school and are expected to perform, but their life experiences in many cases affect their ability to achieve well on standardized tests written in English.

Second, concerns relate to declining test scores and the media focus on comparisons with the past and with other districts in the state. For some reason, the district's reading scores are solid, slightly higher than the state average and increasing, but the math scores are ruining the schools' reputations. Year after year, the results continue to decline, despite efforts to boost them. People have started to voice alarm. The culture of the district office is nonconfrontational, a legacy of the many years of success. Administrators aren't sure how to handle these increasingly public criticisms.

Third, and perhaps most important, concerns relate to the community's economic future. One of the members of the school board, Paddy Bayer, is a lifelong resident of the community, a mechanical engineer by training, and the current CEO of the town's flagship company. In that role, he champions the importance of mathematics education. He is outspoken in his continuing demand that the district attend to the needs of all children, especially those with weak skills in math. He can and routinely does (to his colleagues' and friends' dismay) deliver passionate speeches about the importance of math achievement for the future of the city and the country. He speaks from both knowledge and experience, as he is a member of a state oversight committee on science, technology, engineering, and math (STEM) education.

Lower levels of math achievement directly affect his business. In the past, high school graduates could easily find work at his company, the town's largest employer. But now company employment requires relatively sophisticated math and technology skills, and jobs are no longer guaranteed for local youth. The company's head of personnel recently told several students who had assumed they would follow their parents' footsteps in employment at the company that they were unemployable with their current levels of math skills. Where are local graduates going to work if they don't have the skills needed for 21st century employment (mathematics being first among them, in Bayer's opinion)? With the most recent release of scores—again a disappointment—he wonders what, if anything, can be done to improve future achievement.

There is additional tension in the community between two groups of local advocates. Working against the levy and, indeed, against the arc of history, one taxpayer group supports a return to the three Rs (reading, 'riting, and 'rithmetic) and the cost savings that would result. Simpler is better, in their opinion. They do not oppose NN!—it is, after all, math—but only as long as it requires no additional funding. An opposing group represents citizens who support fine arts education. They are concerned that the NN! focus on remediation in math means some children will never get to experience or learn fine arts content areas in school. In their opinion, depriving children of art and music instruction to drill on math skills may deprive them of the very experiences that could motivate them to try harder and do better in school.

THE CAST OF CHARACTERS AS THE EVALUATION BEGAN

With the go-ahead from Superintendent Olson—and his strict instructions to handle *all* details related to the evaluation—Moore contacted the district's curriculum coordinator, Rosa Ortiz, to ask her advice about whom to hire. Ortiz, like Moore, knew the circle of local evaluators and suggested Robert Wentworth because of his direct experience in math education and his volunteer work in the district. Moore thought he would be a great choice. Once Wentworth understood the project and negotiated his role and fee, he happily agreed to participate; he knew that math achievement was an important topic for the district, and he was a master facilitator of group interaction. On a warm summer morning Moore and Wentworth sat together in the district office to brainstorm a structure for the collaborative evaluation. To begin, Wentworth suggested a small planning committee consisting of the people likely to use the study's eventual results. They decided to invite five people. Four were district employees: Superintendent Olson, curriculum coordinator Ortiz, teachers' union president Posey FlyingEagle, and lead NN! teacher Owen Lindquist. The fifth was Paddy Bayer, who was both a school board member and a business leader.

As Wentworth was leaving the building, the superintendent happened to see him chatting with Moore. He knew Wentworth had an excellent professional reputation, and their daughters were in the same soccer league. Olson stopped him and explained that what he personally needed from this evaluation was proof NN! increased students' test scores. That would be essential information for him in his school board leadership role around math achievement. Wentworth started to explain the challenge of "proving" causation in evaluation studies, but Olson's assistant came out to tell the superintendent his next appointment had arrived. Olson left without hearing the limitations. Wentworth left wondering if the superintendent's comment might cause conflict down the road. As an evaluator who valued his reputation, he certainly did not want to face any ethical dilemmas related to data collection, analysis, or reporting at the study's conclusion. Exhibit 10.2 details the list of characters in this evaluation, along with their concerns and issues at the beginning of the study.

Exhibit 10.2 Selected Cast of Characters for "We're in This Together"

Evaluation Role	Name/Title	Concerns/Issues
External evaluator	Dr. Robert Wentworth	Wentworth is a former math teacher who became an educational evaluator after completing his doctorate in quantitative research methods and statistics. He now works at a small evaluation consulting firm and still finds time to volunteer at one of the district elementary schools, where he tutors children struggling in math.
Internal evaluator	Sara Moore	Moore became the head of the district's testing and evaluation office after serving as her school's testing coordinator for a number of years. She has a master's degree in educational leadership and has learned the basics of measurement and statistics her job requires. Although she has limited district resources for evaluation, she is happy to work with Wentworth, knowing that together they may plant the seed of evaluative thinking in the district.
Client/primary intended user (PIU)	Dr. Sam Olson, superintendent of schools	Olson's role as district leader has become increasingly difficult as the math test scores have declined. He understands the importance of improving achievement in the district, knowing he could lose his job if test scores don't improve. His doctoral dissertation focused on school change, and he is not afraid to make tough decisions, but he needs hard data about program effects to support his decisions.

Evaluation Role	Name/Title	Concerns/Issues
PIU	Patrick (Paddy) Bayer, school board member	Bayer is the CEO of the community's largest employer, a company that began locally and now manufactures products used around the world. He was educated in the city's schools and believes strongly they can still provide excellent math education. As a mechanical engineer, he is not afraid of numbers.
PIU	Rosa Ortiz, district curriculum coordinator	Although her job supports all curricula, Ortiz is especially partial to math curricula. With an MAT in mathematics from the state's flagship university, she is well versed in both math content and pedagogy. She found NN! after an extensive search of remedial programs and believes it is the right program for the district. Because she was a former high school teacher, some elementary teachers wonder if she knows best.
PIU	Posey FlyingEagle, president of the local teachers' union	Owing to financial constraints, the teachers' union has tried to cooperate with the district in recent years. FlyingEagle is a popular leader who supports union members in every way she can. She fights against cutting teaching positions, defends the jobs of those currently on staff, and does not shrink from confrontation.
PIU	Owen Lindquist, NN! lead teacher	Lindquist has the dual responsibility of teaching NN! in one elementary school and supervising four colleagues who teach it in the other schools. A relatively new teacher, he was an undergraduate math major and specialized in math instruction during his teacher training. He is less than excited to have an evaluation focus on his program, as everyone is working hard and doing the best they can.
Important stakeholders	Elementary teachers who teach regular math	Including struggling math learners with large numbers of other students makes lesson planning difficult because the remedial work necessary for the struggling students will bore those who are more advanced. With class sizes as large as they are, individualizing instruction seems like an impossible dream. These teachers are thankful their neediest students can receive high-quality, specialized math instruction.
	Elementary teachers who don't teach math	These teachers are divided in worrying about their future employment. Technology and physical education teachers know the state requires instruction in their content, so their jobs are secure. Fine arts teachers, who already have only minimal offerings, may lose their jobs if the district decides to focus more intently on the basics. This has led to some tension between teachers.

(Continued)

Exhibit 10.2   (Continued)

Evaluation Role	Name/Title	Concerns/Issues
Other stakeholders	Parents	The district's parents are a diverse group representing multiple ethnic groups, social classes, and life experiences. Virtually all of them want the best education possible for their children, including high-quality instruction that will prepare them for the world of work. Middle-class parents form the core of the elementary school parent–teacher organizations. The district makes special efforts to connect with parents who are recent immigrants and parents of children with special needs.
	Students	Students in the district reflect the diversity of their parents. Some come from families that have lived in the community for decades; others are newcomers. Those enrolled in NN! may appreciate the extra support, but missing regular classroom activities on a frequent basis is difficult.
	Back-to-basics taxpayer group	This is a relatively small group of citizens who want to return education to the "good old days" when reading, writing, and arithmetic dominated elementary schools. They are fine with the idea of focusing on a limited number of basic subjects and not offering a broad array of other subjects.
	Community advocates for the fine arts	These advocates, also a small group, are fighting to keep music and art curricula in the elementary school. In their opinion, giving weak math students a second dose of math instruction and forcing them to miss the fine arts is a terrible idea.

THE EVALUATION PROCESS

Initial Decisions/Actions

For this lone internal evaluator, working with an external consultant was a refreshing change of pace. There was positive buzz in the district about the collaborative evaluation process, and Moore was happy to team with Wentworth to bring the evaluation to life. They already knew the key actors and suspected what they might want from the evaluation. To confirm this, the evaluators gathered their planning committee of five PIUs as the school year began to discuss what they wanted to learn from the study and how they personally wanted to participate. During the conversation, it became obvious they had different ideas about the evaluation. The superintendent was absolutely clear: He had no time to be directly involved—the upcoming levy meant he was meeting with community leaders and groups virtually on a daily basis—but what he needed from the evaluation was robust information about how teachers could increase remedial math students' test scores and what that might cost. The board expected him to produce that information and an improvement plan. If NN! wasn't the answer, what was?

By contrast, the other four participants expressed a willingness to attend multiple meetings and were more open to participating in the study. For her part, curriculum coordinator Rosa Ortiz wanted an objective process that would enable many voices, both professional and community-based, to be heard. Just because NN! results to date had not demonstrated achievement increases didn't mean students weren't learning more math; after all, these were the weakest math students, far below grade level. Perhaps they were catching up but not quickly enough for No Child Left Behind (NCLB), or perhaps they had learning disabilities complicating their efforts. Research showed NN! was an excellent program, and she didn't want the proverbial baby thrown out with the bath water as a result of the evaluation.

Neither union president Posey FlyingEagle nor lead NN! teacher Owen Lindquist was overly excited about participating in the evaluation. FlyingEagle was always wary of collaborative processes, especially when they gave community members an opportunity to bad-mouth teachers. Lindquist saw his job as ensuring the quality of information about the program, and, like FlyingEagle, his major concern was protecting his colleagues who had taken special NN! trainings, worked hard to implement this challenging new program, and even conducted action research on it. He really thought they were outstanding. It would be easy for people outside the program to find flaws and criticize the implementation, and he wanted fair treatment. Lindquist, who knew the teachers well, had every confidence they would be more than willing to hear about ways to improve their instruction. These teachers truly wanted their students to learn math, and the evaluation needed to treat them with respect.

Board member Bayer agreed that the information the superintendent wanted would be helpful, and he certainly didn't disagree with a focus on the actual program in this specific setting. But he hoped people who took part in the evaluation would understand the broader picture of STEM education in the 21st century, with an emphasis on mathematics. They needed to put NN! in context. Once community members saw the importance of this learning for students' lifelong careers and the future of the country, not only might people vote for the levy, but they might identify other ways to reshape the schools for future success. The back-to-basics and fine arts advocates might finally see the overarching importance of STEM content. He volunteered to attend as many meetings as his schedule would allow to support what he saw as a significant evaluation.

The evaluators believed the stage was set for a productive collaborative process. Internal evaluator Moore joining forces with external evaluator Wentworth brought sufficient resources to the required activities. The initial framing conversation suggested the five people who would ultimately use the evaluation's results had a clear desire for data, and, discussing possible outcomes, they seemed committed to using the data to make changes. In planning next steps, the evaluators had to develop a process that would engage a larger group of people in conversations to frame the study's final questions, then determine how to collect, analyze, and interpret data en route to making recommendations. Throughout, people's interactions would teach them about the evaluation process, content related to this specific evaluation of NN!, and a bigger picture of STEM education.

REFLECTION BOX I

How Is This Evaluation Going?

1. In addition to the internal and external evaluators, who composed the initial small planning committee of people likely to use the study's results? What were their professional positions/roles? Should individuals representing other divisions/roles within the school district or community also have been invited to participate in this initial meeting? Why or why not? Explain.

2. Revisit Chapter 5, Exhibit 5.2. Which of these strategies (if any) might the evaluators have used to facilitate interaction at the small planning committee's first meeting? If you were an evaluator in this study, how would you have structured interaction among the PIUs who participated in the initial planning committee meeting? Specify and explain.

3. Revisit Chapter 7, Templates 1 through 7. Which of these most probably should have been discussed at the initial planning committee meeting for possible use in the study? Which of these templates do you believe are most critical for determining and/or planning future collaborative processes in this study? Explain.

4. Revisit Chapter 7, Exhibit 7.1. To what extent do you believe the evaluators are demonstrating cultural competence in the framing of this collaborative study? What steps would you suggest the evaluators take to attend to the cultural differences and perceptions of the various stakeholders in this study? Explain.

5. Based on what you know so far, what potential conflicts might develop among those who will be steering this evaluation—specifically, the two evaluators (Moore and Wentworth) and the five PIUs (Olson, Ortiz, FlyingEagle, Lindquist, and Bayer)? What are their respective issues? How might the evaluation fail if these issues go unattended? Explain.

6. What is your reaction to Superintendent Olson's comment indicating he needs proof that NN! increases student test scores? What thoughts and feelings might Robert Wentworth (the external evaluator) have experienced upon hearing this from Olson? What conflicts might this create as the study unfolds? Explain.

Data Collection and Analysis Decisions/Actions

The two evaluators knew the overall approach to this evaluation would be collaborative, but it fell to them to develop the specific evaluation activities and timeline. They decided to hold two longer meetings—one full-day and one half-day—that would include structured interaction among 50 or so carefully selected people: faculty, staff, administrators, parents, community representatives, and at least one board member (Bayer). They planned to hold one meeting early in the school year and the other in May. The first, daylong retreat would use interactive strategies to ground people, to generate an array of potential topics for the evaluation, and to frame which concerns the study would zero in on; the second retreat, although shorter, would use similar techniques to review data and make recommendations. Cross-checking an initial list of people they had developed, Moore and Wentworth asked their five PIUs to identify key representatives from the district and community. They balanced selections to ensure as much diversity as possible (racial/ethnic, class, gender, neighborhood, grade level, content area, advocacy, life experience, etc.); reviewed and finalized the list with Olson, Bayer, Ortiz, FlyingEagle, and Lindquist; and then wrote a letter over the superintendent's signature inviting people to the retreats. Roughly 40 of the 50 people asked made the commitment to attend the fall and spring meetings.

People may have arrived at the fall retreat with doubts about what would happen, but by the end of the afternoon, the group had gelled around topics in the district's math program that they wanted the evaluation to look at—and most had made new contacts, learned some things about elementary math, and experienced group interaction techniques they enjoyed. The evaluators used their time carefully during the day, beginning with a welcome and introduction by the superintendent, who gave his strong endorsement for the evaluation before leaving to attend another meeting. Moore and Wentworth had designed the day's activities to engage people with both substantive content and their personal beliefs and reactions (see Exhibit 10.3). Following the introductory

Exhibit 10.3 Fall Retreat Activities/Strategies, Purposes, and Details

Activity/Strategy	Purpose	Detail
Strategy 1: Voicing Variables	• To let people see who else is participating in the study • To have everyone learn something about one another in a nonthreatening way	Questions included how long people had lived in the community, who had children in the district and at what grade levels, where people were born, etc.
Strategy 2: Voicing Viewpoints/Beliefs	• To encourage people to think about their values and beliefs related to math achievement and STEM education more broadly	Participants responded (*strongly agree, agree, disagree, strongly disagree*) to three statements: 1. In elementary school, no single subject area is more important than math. 2. Children who perform below grade level on math achievement tests will face challenges throughout their lives. 3. The district should require that children who perform below grade level on math achievement tests focus all their energies on catching up.
Strategy 3: Choosing Corners	• To encourage people to interact about topics meaningful to the day's discussion	During the corner discussions, people chatted with others who held similar views, then heard different ideas from the other corners.

Activity/Strategy	Purpose	Detail
Grounding Content 1: STEM presentation	• To provide substantive content and grounding about the evaluation in a broad context	Paddy Bayer introduced a charismatic local professor who was able to discuss national education issues in an engaging manner. The professor placed the district's NN! situation in the broad context of math achievement over time and space. Many people took notes.
[Break]		
Strategy 4: Cooperative Interviews	• To remind people that everyone occasionally struggles in learning situations • To have people conduct a cooperative task successfully • To encourage people to get to know one another a bit better	People participated in cooperative interviews on the following topic: *Think of a time when you were having trouble learning something that you eventually overcame. What helped you eventually learn when you had been struggling?* They did a quick analysis of the commonalities across their answers.
Grounding Content 2: The district's elementary math program	• To provide substantive content and grounding about the specific object of the evaluation	Ortiz gave a short presentation on the current elementary math program, including the rationale for selecting NN! as its remedial component.
Strategy 7: Data Dialogue	• To document people's perceptions of the elementary math program • To encourage small-group conversations	The dialogue sheet had three columns related to the elementary math program: what is working, what isn't working, and possible topics for the evaluation. Small groups completed the sheets together, discussing their perceptions.
Strategy 10: Concept Formation/ Cluster Maps	• To capture the content of the data dialogues for the large group • To determine which ideas were the most common across small groups	The groups then analyzed the content of their data dialogue results, looking for the commonalities across the columns. They wrote their most important questions on half sheets of paper and posted them on the wall. Robert Wentworth then facilitated a discussion that grouped and named categories of similar questions.

(Continued)

Exhibit 10.3 (Continued)

Activity/Strategy	Purpose	Detail
Strategy 13: Dot Votes/ Bar Graphs	• To identify which questions participants perceived as most important for the study • To demonstrate the group's power to control the evaluation topics	Each person received three dots to place on the questions that were the most important for the evaluation from their perspective. They could put all dots on one question or divide them across several questions.
[Lunch]		
Grounding Content 3: • The details of NCLB • Review of 3 years of elementary reading and math test data	• To provide substantive content and grounding about the national context for the evaluation • To encourage small-group conversations • To give people practice in making sense of data	After Sara Moore gave the presentation, small groups completed a worksheet that asked specific questions about the data. People had to read the data tables and practice making sense of test data. The Q&A session with the two evaluators gave everyone a chance to explain how their analysis went, agree on common findings, and suggest additional questions for the evaluation.
Strategy 11: Cooperative Rank Order	• To prioritize which questions participants perceive as most important for the study • To understand the rationale for the rank order	Using the evaluation questions posted on the wall, people were asked to rank order the top five from the discussion, document reasons for their rank order, and write specific things the group wanted to know about each question.
Wrap-up, key messages, and evaluation	• To summarize the day's activities and learnings • To generate a list of key messages for distribution through district communication channels • To have participants evaluate their day's experiences	Robert Wentworth led this activity. First he reviewed the day's agenda, noting all that had been accomplished. Then he asked the group to call out the key messages about the collaborative evaluation for wide-scale distribution. Participants ended by completing the short "pluses/wishes" evaluation form.
[Adjourn]		

exercise, the structured interactions alternated between grounding content (STEM education; the district's elementary math program, including NN!; and math test results) and reflection and discussion about elementary math set in the larger perspective of STEM teaching and learning. By the time Wentworth facilitated the data dialogues, people had lots of ideas to discuss.

The midmorning data dialogues generated a list of what people believed to be good about the current math program (e.g., a well-known curriculum; extra help for children who needed it; hard-working, dedicated teachers; the staff development available) and what they found lacking (e.g., little coordination between the regular curriculum and NN!, the pullout structure of NN! that forced children to miss class activities, too few services for English-language learners who had trouble learning math in a language they didn't know, among others). FlyingEagle and Lindquist thought the exercise was fair since both good and bad were discussed equally. Analyzing these ideas, positive and negative, people next conducted a concept formation in small groups to identify the themes and then developed possible questions the evaluation might answer, written one per half sheet of paper, large enough for all to see. Volunteers taped them on one wall, where they hung like a patchwork. As facilitator, Wentworth helped the group review, cluster, and clarify the questions, and then the participants' dot voting identified these as the top five:

- Is NumberNastics! working?
- How does NumberNastics! affect other content areas?
- Are changing demographics affecting the math scores?
- Why aren't elementary math scores improving overall?
- Does the district's elementary math curriculum prepare kids for their futures?

Some people whose questions didn't make the final cut were annoyed or discouraged; others, such as Paddy Bayer, were pleased to see their issues featured in a question. Regardless, each question had an equal opportunity for approval, and people couldn't really complain; they basically perceived the process as fair, since everyone had a say in the matter.

Following lunch, the afternoon's activities began with purposeful evaluation capacity building as participants learned the details of the NCLB legislation and how to make sense of test score data. Working with the data in small groups, they answered a series of questions about the district's elementary math achievement in previous years and then took part in a Q&A session with the two evaluators that clarified issues about the NCLB requirements and the differential achievement of certain groups of children. The next activity asked participants to rank order the questions the group had developed earlier, and people had many reasons for the orders they proposed. At the end of the day the key messages summarized the interactive process and people's expectations for data collection and the eventual use of the data. Stopping by as the retreat wrapped up, Superintendent Olson thanked everyone for participating.

Sara Moore felt good about the initial retreat, and she confirmed with each of the PIUs that they did also. She and Robert Wentworth carefully compiled the background materials, documented the large-group debriefs and discussions, and typed up the questions, rationales, and key messages. Because they were professional evaluators, they rewrote the group's overarching questions to frame them in the language of evaluation:

1. To what extent is NumberNastics! helping children who are behind in math skills achieve at their grade level in math?

2. In what ways does the implementation of NumberNastics! remediation affect elementary school instruction in the district?

3. To what extent does the district's elementary math curriculum (i.e., the math curricula for regular, special education, and NN!) teach students 21st century skills?

Their next task was to determine how to collect and analyze data to answer these questions in time for the spring retreat. Exhibit 10.4 summarizes their data collection plan.

Exhibit 10.4 Data Collection Methods, Samples, and Those Responsible

Data Collection Method	Sample	Those Responsible
1. Analysis of existing data	• Test score data for children (those in NN!, those not in NN! from the district and nearby districts)	Internal evaluator (compile) External evaluator (analyze)
2. Document analysis	• Elementary math curriculum documents • STEM education documents and materials	External evaluator
3. Web-based surveys	• Faculty and staff • Parents • Students	Internal and external evaluators
4. Participatory data collection	• Faculty and staff • Parents	Internal and external evaluators

1. *Analysis of existing data.* The existing test data held crucial information about the effectiveness of NN! Moore knew she could easily compile the data for the past 5 years and then ask Wentworth to conduct a statistical analysis to determine the effect of NN! He suggested getting data from similar elementary schools that did not have remedial programs to create a comparison group, and she immediately e-mailed the test coordinators in two nearby districts with similar demographics to see if they would share their data. They agreed to send them with names removed.

2. *Document analysis.* With his knowledge of mathematics education, Wentworth was the perfect person to review and critique the elementary math curriculum materials, including those from regular education, special education, and NN! He also agreed to look at STEM education materials so he could frame his analysis in the larger national picture. Rosa Ortiz agreed to get him all the materials and then help him with the analysis if necessary.

3. *Web-based surveys.* The district routinely sent web-based surveys to faculty, staff, students, and parents—so it would be no trouble to send surveys as a part of this evaluation. The district custom was to send surveys to entire populations, rather than sampling and eliminating some people's opportunity to provide input. There would be plenty of data to analyze, although people without Internet access would be missed.

4. *Participatory data collection.* Because this study was partly about evaluation capacity and community building, Moore and Wentworth decided to hold unique data collection sessions at each building—one for elementary faculty and staff and one for elementary parents. These would begin with a round-robin check-in (*Strategy 5*) of people's most memorable elementary math experiences, then a graffiti/carousel (*Strategy 9*) on the following topics:

   a. What makes you most proud about our elementary math program?

   b. What worries you most about our elementary math program?

   c. If you could change one thing about our elementary math program, what would it be?

Small groups would then analyze the responses using concept formation/cluster maps (*Strategy 10*) and present the results to the group. Sara Moore, as facilitator, would lead a discussion, collect the results, and type them. Elementary teachers and staff would participate in this process during one of their professional-development workshop days; parents would take part during one of the monthly parent–teacher organization meetings at their schools. Exhibit 10.5 summarizes the evaluation questions, the data Moore and Wentworth needed to collect, and their proposed methods for collecting them.

With their data collection plan complete, the evaluators met to discuss an appropriate committee structure that would engage as many people as possible in the collaborative process during the year. The more, the better, they thought as they brainstormed seven possible committees in addition to the PIU planning group, which they renamed the Evaluation Steering Committee (see Exhibit 10.6). Each committee needed chairs and members. The PIUs became committee chairs, and Moore and Wentworth assigned everyone who attended the retreat to one of the committees. Sara Moore then went through the staff directory to identify other people to add, checking representation of the different grades and subject areas, including special education (teachers of students with both high and low abilities), Title I, and English-language learners (ELL), and of different roles, including parents, teachers, paraeducators, central office staff, and community leaders. Although fairly large, the resulting

Exhibit 10.5　Summary of Evaluation Questions, Data Needed, and Data Collection Methods

Evaluation Question	Data Needed	Data Collection Methods
1. To what extent is NumberNastics! helping children who are behind in math skills achieve at their grade level in math?	• Math achievement test results over time • Perceptions of faculty/staff, parents, and students	• Analysis of existing achievement test data • Web-based surveys
2. In what ways does the implementation of NumberNastics! remediation affect elementary school instruction in the district?	• Perceptions of faculty/staff, parents, and students	• Web-based surveys • Participatory data collection
3. To what extent does the district's elementary math curriculum teach students 21st century skills?	• The district's elementary math curriculum materials • STEM education materials • Perceptions of faculty/staff, parents, and students	• Analysis of district's elementary math curriculum and STEM materials • Web-based surveys • Participatory data collection

committees were truly inclusive and would facilitate multiple conversations across the district about this important evaluation.

Moore drafted a letter over the superintendent's signature inviting people to serve on the committees to which they were named, and most were willing. Once she knew who had agreed to be on which committees, she sent a committee purpose statement along with a list of names and e-mail addresses to each chair with instructions to begin work. She also sent a message to the members of the Survey Development Committee, which she was heading, to set their first meeting.

Unfortunately, the evaluators did not think about having chairs develop norms or operating procedures, nor did they try to coordinate the work of the many committees they had created. Once started, the committees functioned on their own, which led to confusion and, in some cases, irritation about the evaluation process, as the following examples demonstrate.

- Wanting to be all encompassing, most committee chairs copied the entire retreat list on e-mails, so some people were receiving multiple messages each week, many of which did not pertain to them.
- Although his committee was supposed to review only STEM education documents, Bayer started discussing the evaluation with people in the community, which caused embarrassment for members of the Community Liaison Committee when they asked to meet with the same individuals. In addition, during a committee meeting one of the members of the "Big Picture" Committee made a negative comment about the teachers' union in confidence that somehow got back to Posey FlyingEagle, who was furious.
- The Data Collection Committee got copies of the rough draft surveys, which had not been piloted, from the Survey Development Committee and had them loaded and ready to send in the electronic survey system before Moore realized what was happening. If the committee had not asked her for e-mail addresses, the unpiloted draft would have been administered with no opportunity for revisions.
- Committee chairs reportedly had trouble getting members to attend meetings. There was a lot going on in people's lives, and these evaluation committee meetings seemed to take low priority.

In light of these events, the evaluators quickly organized a meeting of the Evaluation Steering Committee, which hadn't met since the other committees began their tasks. The superintendent, who had led school change efforts in the past, proposed reorganizing the committee structure. Two committees— "Big Picture" and Survey Development—had already completed their tasks, so they could be retired. He then suggested creating two larger committees by combining the Steering and Evaluation Accountability Committees into one (calling it the NN! Evaluation Steering Committee, with Robert Wentworth as chair) and the Community Liaison and Reporting Committees into a second (calling it the Reporting Committee, with Posey FlyingEagle as chair). Exhibit 10.6 documents the initial committee structure and this more viable revision. Each of the new committees would have two functions, rather than one. He noted that data analysis didn't actually need a committee since the evaluators would prepare the data for group analysis at the spring retreat. Everyone agreed this would be a better structure, and Moore prepared a memo of clarification and reassignment for distribution to committee members. People whose committees were either done or dissolved could opt into the Reporting Committee.

Exhibit 10.6 Committee Structure for the NN! Collaborative Evaluation

Initial Committee Structure		
Committee Name	**Committee Purpose**	**Committee Leaders**
Evaluation Steering Committee (PIUs)	To manage and troubleshoot the collaborative evaluation from beginning (question framing) to end (report delivery)	Sara Moore Robert Wentworth
The "Big Picture" Committee	To compile and analyze documents and materials related to STEM education in the 21st century	Paddy Bayer
Community Liaison/ Data Committee	To gather feedback from the community and to answer questions about the evaluation process	Robert Wentworth
Survey Development Committee	To create, pilot, and finalize surveys for the evaluation	Sara Moore
Data Collection Committee	To oversee the administration and compilation of data	Rosa Ortiz
Data Analysis Committee	To administer and interpret the data once collected	Owen Lindquist
Reporting Committee	To document the evaluation process and develop reports for various audiences	Posey FlyingEagle
Evaluation Accountability Committee	To ensure the collaborative evaluation adheres to the highest professional standards of program evaluation	Sam Olson

Revised Committee Structure		
Committee Name	**Committee Purpose**	**Committee Leaders**
NN! Evaluation Steering Committee	• To manage and troubleshoot the collaborative evaluation from beginning (question framing) to end (report delivery) • To ensure the collaborative evaluation adheres to the highest professional standards of program evaluation	Robert Wentworth
Reporting Committee	• To gather feedback from the community and to answer questions about the evaluation process • To document the evaluation process and develop reports for various audiences	Posey FlyingEagle

Once the committee structure was resolved, data collection activities proceeded smoothly. Robert Wentworth analyzed standardized test data and the elementary math curriculum, including the NN! program and STEM education documents. Faculty and staff, parents, and students completed electronic surveys, and the relatively high response rates for faculty/staff and students (89% and 94%, respectively) brought smiles to the evaluators' faces. The parent response rate of 18% was worrisome but fairly typical. Moore sent out one last e-mail reminder with the survey attached and got a few more back, boosting the response rate to 21%.

For many people the participatory data collection led to animated conversations on a subject they believed was important. Sara Moore had a good time facilitating and took responsibility for typing up each set of flip-chart data as it became available. After the fact, she wondered whether she should have separated the parents of NN! children from other parents, but at the time that seemed intrusive; she didn't want to create discomfort for anyone. At one of the schools, an East African social worker attended the participatory session with six Somali mothers, none of whom spoke English fluently. While Moore ran the carousel for everyone else, the social worker completed the carousel activity with these mothers, translating the questions into Oromo, their native language, and then translating their answers and recording them on the flip-chart paper in English.

As the time for the second retreat came closer, she and Wentworth prepared all the data for group review and analysis.

1. *Analysis of existing data.* Wentworth's rigorous analysis of the test data showed that NN! students were improving, actually quite dramatically—results showed a statistically significant difference compared with both their schoolmates and comparable students in the other districts—but

their rate of improvement was slower than the established NCLB requirements. He noted that the extremely low scores of students who were recent immigrants decreased the NN! means, and he learned, to his surprise, that the law required these students to take the test in English after they had been in an American school for a year. He wondered if these scores were measuring their knowledge of English or of math—suspecting more the former than the latter. Another detail that leapt out of his analysis was that very few students in the district were scoring extremely high on the tests; in all the schools across all the grades, he could count the serious outliers on one hand. The means were surely satisfactory and students were clearly making progress, but Wentworth got the feeling that perhaps everyone, not just the remedial students, could score higher.

2. *Document analysis.* As an outsider, Wentworth brought impartial judgment to his analysis of the district curriculum. The more literature he read—taking advantage of the materials gathered by the now defunct "Big Picture" Committee—the more he could analyze the existing curriculum against the cutting edge criteria of high-quality STEM education. He prepared a chart to summarize how the regular math curriculum and NN! looked against these standards. In preparing materials for the retreat, he included content from the STEM research documents to frame the conversation more broadly, noting that in addition to higher math skills, students genuinely needed technology skills and the so-called soft skills (the ability to interact and collaborate with others) to succeed in the future world of work.

3. *Web-based surveys.* The high response rates for faculty and staff helped the evaluators feel good about their results. The theme across schools was that there was too much of an emphasis in the district on the basics (reading and math), leaving no time for spontaneous lessons, collaboration on interdisciplinary units or projects, or field trips—the creative activities that often motivated students to work harder. Many teachers also added open-ended comments about not changing any curricula anytime soon since there had been so many to learn in recent years. On the plus side, regular teachers reported they were working hard (some thought too hard), believed the regular curriculum was solid, and thought the NN! teachers were an incredible asset. NN! teachers made it clear that pullouts were a challenge to schedule, both logistically and emotionally—students hated to miss fun classes even if they liked the NN! activities.

The evaluators also analyzed the student survey results separately for NN! students and non-NN! students. Non-NN! students thought their regular math classes were okay. Like the NN! teachers, NN! students did not like to miss classes such as art, music, and technology and, reportedly, often found it confusing when they reentered class each day.

Given the low response rate to the parent survey, there was not a lot to write up for the retreat. The parents who did respond seemed fine with the regular math curriculum; they wondered if their children were being adequately prepared for the annual tests they had to take. One parent wrote a lengthy open-ended response about the lack of programming in the district for the gifted and talented. Another wondered about how elementary math related to eventual job skills. There were only five NN! parent responses, and they were all pleased with the program.

4. *Participatory data collection.* Faculty and staff at the five schools generated a lengthy list of what made them proud of the elementary math program, highlighting the research base undergirding both the regular curriculum and NN! The list of concerns included a major worry in addition to their concern about their inability to boost student achievement; they feared the district might change curricula again and not have the funding to provide adequate professional development. Both the regular and remedial math curricula were new within the past 3 years, as was the reading curriculum. ("No wonder the district doesn't have money!" Wentworth thought as he read this.) Apparently, the prospect of having to learn another set of materials and lessons was daunting. As for the single change they'd like to see, teachers had many ideas. One common response across schools was "no more changes, please!" Another was "no more pullouts; push in," suggesting support teachers be placed in classrooms (pushed in), rather than pulling children out to work separately with them.

The parents' discussions at the five schools also generated a list of what made them proud (e.g., the hands-on components, the emphasis on mathematical thinking *and* the basics, the caring teachers), of what worried them (e.g., their children's readiness for the annual tests, including the high-stakes graduation test they would eventually take; an overemphasis on test-taking skills rather than learning math), and of what they would change (e.g., helping the children do even better, providing extra tutoring after school, offering computer options). Moore included the Somali mothers' data with the rest. They were happy to have their children in math classes, worried about their being removed from their regular classes every day (many of their children were pulled out both for NN! and for the ELL program), and wondered if that could be changed. As Moore was putting the data together, it suddenly hit her how few parents of color had attended the parent–teacher organization meetings.

REFLECTION BOX II

How Is This Evaluation Going?

1. What were the final evaluation questions that guided this study? To what extent do you believe these adequately dealt with the concerns of (a) the PIUs, (b) other key stakeholders in the school district, and (c) the community? In framing the final evaluation questions, should the evaluators have paid more attention to the five PIUs (those who participated in the initial planning meeting)? Explain.

2. Do you believe the final evaluation questions as revised by the evaluators adequately capture the issues/concerns/questions generated by those who participated in the fall retreat? Do you think it was acceptable for the evaluators to fine-tune the evaluation questions after the fall retreat, using their own words to express the major concerns raised by retreat participants? Why or why not? Explain.

3. To what extent do you think participants in the fall retreat adequately represented a cross-section of the diverse populations within the school system and community? Why or why not? What other segments of the school and/or community populations (if any) might (or should) have been included in the fall retreat? Explain.

4. Review the strategies used during the fall retreat to accomplish the various purposes specified in Exhibit 10.3. Next, revisit Chapter 5, Exhibit 5.7. What other strategies may have been helpful in facilitating the retreat to accomplish its purposes? Which might you have considered, suggested, or employed? Explain.

5. What steps might the evaluators have taken to obtain parent data in cost-effective ways? For example, might it have been feasible to request time at already scheduled school, district, or community events to obtain such data, perhaps by using the data dialogue, graffiti/carousel, or dot votes/bar graphs methods (see Chapter 5, *Strategies 7, 9,* and *13*)? Brainstorm feasible options for obtaining input from an adequate sample of parents. Explain which option you ultimately would have pursued and why.

6. What do you think about how the evaluators determined the committee structures for this evaluation, as well as each committee's chair and participants? With the interactive evaluation practice (IEP) principles in mind (see Chapter 3, Exhibit 3.3), what do you suggest the evaluators should have done differently? What information in Chapter 7 would have helped the evaluators plan a smoother committee structure from the onset? Explain your thinking.

Data Interpretation and Reporting Decisions/Actions

As Sara Moore feared, fewer people attended the spring retreat than the fall, but the 30 who did come—including the superintendent—were truly committed to making sense of the data and deciding on a course of action for elementary math. The format for the half day was similar to that of the full-day fall retreat, engaging participants in several interactive strategies (see Exhibit 10.7).

Exhibit 10.7 Spring Retreat Activities/Strategies, Purposes, and Details

Activity/Strategy	Purpose	Detail
Strategy 6: Making Metaphors	• To give each person an opportunity to introduce him- or herself in a creative way • To see and analyze the images the program evokes	As people picked up their name tags, they were asked to choose 1 picture that represented their experience with the evaluation process thus far from about 100 pictures on a table. For introductions, people stood, gave their names and roles, explained why they chose the pictures they had, and then taped them on a long piece of butcher paper.
Strategy 8: Jigsaw	• To analyze and fully understand the data collected • To "represent" these data in an interpretive conversation	Each type of data was printed on a different-color paper. People were preassigned to a color group, balanced so each group had at least one person with strong data analysis skills. Data-alike groups spent 30 minutes reading their data, discussing what they meant, and developing data-based claims. Next, the evaluators created mixed-color-paper groups that included representatives from each of the earlier groups. For another 30 minutes, these new groups compared and contrasted the results of their first discussion, then generated claims supported by two or more types of data. Recorders wrote these claims on flip-chart paper, and Robert Wentworth reviewed these with the entire group.

(Continued)

Exhibit 10.7 (Continued)

Activity/Strategy	Purpose	Detail
Strategy 7: Data Dialogue	• To develop data-based recommendations for action	Groups of four or five wrote recommendations based on the claims generated at the end of the jigsaw. They posted the recommendations on flip-chart paper so everyone could see them.
[Break]		
Strategy 12: Fist to Five (using clickers)	• To finalize the recommendations • To prioritize the recommendations	During the break, Moore and Wentworth quickly typed the recommendations so they could be projected on a screen. They listed similar recommendations adjacent to one another. First the group consolidated similar recommendations into one to create a final list of recommendations, knowing these might later be further wordsmithed. Then the group used clickers to vote on these final recommendations to identify a priority order.
Wrap-up, key messages, and evaluation	• To summarize the day's activities and learnings • To generate a list of key messages for distribution through district communication channels • To have people evaluate their experience at this retreat and with the year's evaluation	Robert Wentworth again reviewed the day's agenda and asked people to reflect on their experiences. The group then called out and refined a set of key messages, which were typed and displayed on the screen. The final task for the day was to complete an evaluation form with two sections: one for the spring retreat and one for the overall evaluation process.
[Adjourn]		

The first jigsaw groups came to the following interpretation of the data:

1. *Analysis of existing data.* The group looking at the existing data reported that NN! was doing what it was supposed to—that is, helping the lowest elementary math students improve their achievement. They also noted, however, the unfortunate problem with the pace of the improvement. Looking at the scores of students who were enrolled in both NN! and

ELL classes, the group recognized—not surprisingly—a high correlation; students who lacked English skills were also having problems with math. Finally, thanks to a pointed question in the task assignment, the group wrote that few elementary students in the district were scoring at the highest test levels.

2. *Document analysis.* Wentworth's chart of criteria helped the group interpreting the math curriculum documents make a straightforward assessment of the regular and NN! curricula. Both fulfilled the criteria of high-quality STEM education, including related technology skills (which the NN! students missed due to the pullout) and requirements for students to solve problems collaboratively, although there was no direct instruction of soft (people) skills.

3. *Web-based surveys.* There was one group assigned to interpret the faculty and staff survey results, and, owing to the low response rate on the parent survey, another took on both the student and parent survey responses. The faculty and staff survey group identified pluses (e.g., people liked the curriculum they taught, whether NN! or regular; being able to send children for extra support was helpful) and minuses (e.g., no time for fun activities, challenges with pullout scheduling). The group assigned the student survey discussed the fact that NN! student perception was not highly positive and listed the students' concerns. They took a quick look at the parents' responses but didn't feel they had enough data to offer any interpretations to the larger group.

4. *Participatory data collection.* The group that interpreted the results from the faculty and staff participatory data was impressed by the consistency across schools. Everyone seemed worried about whether they could get the math scores to rise, even with what they believed to be excellent, research-based regular and remedial curricula. They also wanted to stay the course and not change curricula for a while. The theme of "no more pullouts; push in" suggested one way to solve (a) the problem of students missing special content and (b) the challenge of their reentering classes midstream.

   The parental participatory data group took the lists of what made parents proud and worried at face value. They appreciated the additional ideas such as providing extra tutoring after school or offering computer options for learning, and, knowing they didn't have sufficient data on this, they discussed the question of how children fared who had two pullouts (for both NN! and ELL programs).

People seemed engaged during the data dialogues and had no difficulty generating data-based recommendations. Moore was especially pleased with the clicker activity (see Exhibit 10.7), as the entire group could easily see the "votes" displayed electronically for the different recommendations. The evaluations for the morning and for the overall evaluation process were extremely positive.

At this point, it again fell to the evaluators to take the retreat results and prepare them for the evaluation's next steps. Moore and Wentworth started by writing answers to the three evaluation questions framed earlier. Based on the results, they rewrote one of the questions to reflect how the collaborative evaluation had evolved midstream.

1. *To what extent is NumberNastics! helping children who are behind in math skills achieve at their grade level in math?* The data suggested NN! was actually working well and helping students in the remedial classes increase their math achievement. The problem was with the *pace* of their improvement. The data also raised a question about the effects of double pullouts on students in the ELL program and a possible issue that children who might achieve at high levels were not doing so.

2. *In what ways does the focus on math achievement testing, including the implementation of NumberNastics! remediation, affect elementary instruction in the district?* According to the data, teachers wanted to keep the regular curriculum and NN! and not change others at this time. There was reported concern about the emphasis on math (and reading) instruction to the exclusion of other content or spontaneous activities and about the documented effects of pulling students out for NN! (i.e., hard to schedule, confusing to children, causing them to miss certain content).

3. *To what extent does the district's elementary math curriculum teach students 21st century skills?* The regular curriculum and NN! met the criteria of high-quality STEM education, so the math content and pedagogy appeared fine. One worry was that NN! students missed out on technology instruction, an important 21st century skill. Another was the lack of formal emphasis on soft skills for all elementary students.

Next the evaluators cleaned up the recommendations the retreat participants had generated and voted on. The vote placed them in this order, most to least important:

1. Keep the current math curricula (regular and NN!) in place for at least 2 more years.

2. Examine the experiences and math achievement of children enrolled in NN! who are also ELL.

3. Augment explicit training in technology and people skills for all students as part of their elementary math experience.

4. Study the possibility of creating inclusive classrooms where NN! and ELL teachers are "pushed in" to coteach with regular-education teachers.

5. Increase opportunities for gifted and talented students to learn high-level mathematics.

Posey FlyingEagle convened the Reporting Committee to review the final materials: a brief description of the evaluation process, the letters of invitation, the agendas from the fall and spring retreats, the data interpreted at the spring retreat, the summarized answers to the three evaluation questions, and the recommendations. They made minor changes to some of the wording and then started formatting a report for the board. Paddy Bayer was extremely helpful, reminding them to make it short, to the point, and data-based. The group decided to have Robert Wentworth and Rosa Ortiz give the presentation to the board. The superintendent wondered aloud if they could omit the negative findings, fearing any negative content might work against the levy. Noting that his concern about finances hadn't made the cut when questions were identified, he also wondered about the budgetary implications of the results.

REFLECTION BOX III

How Is This Evaluation Going?

1. To what extent did the evaluators understand the politics inherent in this collaborative study? Were the evaluators prudent when it came to political considerations? Did they deal effectively with the political issues that surfaced? Explain. In addition, how well do you think the evaluators dealt with the two special-interest groups—the back-to-basics and fine-arts folks? Defend your conclusions.

2. If you were the evaluator in this collaborative study, would you have been conflicted by the superintendent's comment about omitting negative data from the final report? How would you have reacted to this comment? Revisit Chapter 6, Exhibit 6.1. Which of these responses—forcing, withdrawing, smoothing,

(Continued)

(Continued)

compromising, or problem solving—(and in which order) might the evaluators have used to deal with the superintendent on this issue? Explain your reasoning. Use the integrative negotiation steps outlined in Chapter 6, Exhibit 6.4 to role-play what a problem-solving confrontation between Wentworth (the external evaluator) and Olson (the superintendent) might have sounded like.

3. Revisit Chapter 8, Exhibits 8.2 through 8.5, which elaborate a variety of potential evaluator woes. Which of the unexpected problems detailed in these exhibits occurred during this evaluation? How did the evaluators respond? How effective were their responses in keeping the evaluation on track? Explain.

4. Do you agree with this study's final results and recommendations? Why or why not? Was it appropriate to have Robert Wentworth (the external evaluator) and Rosa Ortiz (the district curriculum coordinator) present the final evaluation report to the Board of Education? Who else could have been considered to make the presentation? Explain.

5. How effective do you believe the collaborative approach was in this study? How successful was this study in accomplishing its evaluation capacity building goals? How could collaborative efforts and/or capacity building have been enhanced during the evaluation? Explain.

6. If you were a member of the evaluator team in this study, what might you have done differently in this evaluation? What types of conversations might you have pursued with the evaluators—Sara Moore (internal) and Robert Wentworth (external)—toward developing and implementing a smooth and successful collaborative evaluation process? Specify and explain your reasoning.

CASE STUDY TIPS: THINK, INTERACT, PRACTICE, SITUATE

This section contains four sets of exercises for further engaging with this case study. The first set involves *thinking* individually about various aspects of the case's collaborative study. The second set entails *interacting* in small groups (consisting of two, three, or four people) on collaborative tasks that involve critical analysis, reasoned discussion, and decision making. The third set prompts *practicing* in the real world by carrying out field-based exercises related to the case. The fourth set prompts *situating* personal lessons learned from this case within your own context as an evaluator.

CASE STUDY TIPS

Think

1. What are the strengths and limitations of this evaluation study? Draw a chart with two columns; label one "strengths" and the other "limitations," and then list specifics for each. What might the evaluators have done to prevent or avoid the limitations? Explain.

2. In your judgment, did this collaborative study adequately address the evaluation questions? To what extent? Explain.

3. Systematically review the evaluators' various decisions and actions in this case study. Which actions do you believe contributed most (vs. least) to a viable evaluation process? Which most contributed to producing credible/trustworthy (vs. implausible/untrustworthy) results? Which most enhanced (vs. diminished) use of the results?

4. Revisit the definition of IEP and its grounding principles. In your judgment, how effectively did the evaluators facilitate IEP in this study? How well did the evaluators use its principles to guide effective practice? Explain.

5. What interpersonal skills were especially important for the evaluators in this collaborative study? How well did each evaluator—Sara Moore (internal) and Robert Wentworth (external)—apply those skills? What other competencies did the evaluators display that contributed to the overall success of the evaluation process and product? Explain.

Interact

1. With a colleague, discuss your responses to each of the items above. Compare and contrast your thinking. Try to reach group consensus on each item. Present and defend your collaborative conclusions to other groups that also engaged in this exercise. How did these discussions expand your understanding of collaborative studies?

2. Imagine the conversation Sara Moore (internal evaluator) and Robert Wentworth (external evaluator) might have had at the onset of their partnership to review and/or clarify the evaluation context and culture. Role-play what that conversation may have sounded like by using Templates 1 and 2 in

(Continued)

(Continued)

Chapter 7 to guide the interaction. What information about context and culture is apparent? What additional information would be helpful? Consider what you know about IEP skills as you play your role. Ask observers to provide feedback on aspects of the role play that seemed especially helpful for moving the evaluation forward.

3. Use *Strategy 3: Choosing Corners* (described in Chapter 5) to reflect on the evaluation conversations that took place in this study. First, post each of the following response options in a separate corner of the room: (a) *strongly agree,* (b) *agree,* (c) *disagree,* (d) *strongly disagree.* Next revisit Chapter 4, Exhibit 4.3 and specifically focus on Conversation Goal 5. Choose the corner that best reflects your response to this statement: "The evaluators in this collaborative study effectively engaged stakeholders in conversations to determine how best to collect and analyze data." Be ready to discuss and defend your response with others who also choose your corner.

4. Near the end of the study, the two evaluators rewrote the second evaluation question based on the study's results to reflect how the collaborative evaluation had evolved midstream. Do you believe this was ethical? Discuss this issue by (a) forming a group of four, (b) assigning pairs within the group to either argue "yes" or "no" to the question of ethics, (c) present and listen carefully to the alternative arguments, (d) engage in open discussion to challenge arguments, (e) reverse perspectives, (f) drop advocacy of positions, (g) together consider all information that surfaced, and (h) reach consensus on the best-reasoned response. Based on your group's final conclusion, what advice would you have given the evaluators in this study as they were preparing the final results for the Reporting Committee? Explain.

5. In a larger group of 10 to 20 people, use *Strategy 6: Making Metaphors* (described in Chapter 5) to complete the following stem: ***"A successful collaborative evaluation study is like a . . . because . . ."*** Next, use *Strategy 10: Concept Formation/Cluster Maps* (described in Chapter 5) to identify common qualities or characteristics across all the metaphor responses. Finally, use *Strategy 11: Cooperative Rank Order* (described in Chapter 5) to sequence the various themes from most to least essential for successful collaborative evaluation practice. Provide reasons for rankings. What additional insights did this exercise reveal about collaborative evaluation studies? Explain.

Practice

1. Interview an evaluator who primarily conducts collaborative studies (or someone within an organization or program who is responsible for participatory projects). In what field does this evaluator primarily work—e.g., education, business, health, government, nonprofit, social services, etc.? What does this evaluator believe are the most important skill sets for successfully conducting evaluations in his or her context? To what extent do interpersonal skills play a critical role? What advice would this evaluator give to others conducting collaborative studies?

2. Suppose your boss (or supervisor) asks you to conduct a collaborative study on the effectiveness of a particular program in your organization. First, name and briefly describe the purposes, functions, and assumptions of that program. Second, use Exhibit 6.5 (in Chapter 6) to analyze the extent to which the evaluation setting is cooperative or competitive/individualistic. Based on your analysis, should you proceed? What is the likelihood for success? On what did you base your conclusion? Third, if you believe a collaborative study will be problematic from the onset but your boss insists on such a study, plan how you will resolve this conflict. Consider how you could use the integrative negotiation steps to engage your boss in constructive conflict resolution—use Exhibit 6.4 (in Chapter 6) to write a possible script. Role-play your script with a colleague or friend, and then debrief the interaction by noting what seemed to work well and what you might say/do differently the next time.

3. Arrange to participate in a collaborative study being conducted by an organization in your community. Note how the lead evaluator attends to the basic inquiry tasks in the study. Which of the tasks tend to be carried out more collaboratively than others? Revisit Chapter 5, Exhibit 5.4. What types of strategies does the evaluator use to engage participants in responding to set content, generating content, and/or organizing or sharing content? Note the various stakeholders who participate. To what extent do PIUs help frame the evaluation questions? How does the evaluator structure participatory committees? How effectively do these committees operate? Are there established working norms? Which norms appear to be working well, and which need revising? Which decisions and actions seem to facilitate constructive evaluation processes? What unexpected challenges surface during the evaluation,

(Continued)

(Continued)

and how does the evaluator respond? Reflect on the lessons you learn from participating in the study. Ask the lead evaluator what he/she learned from conducting the study.

4. Prepare and facilitate a professional-development training session that presents the foundations of IEP from a collaborative study perspective. Teach and involve participants in experiencing several of the evaluator's dozen of interactive strategies presented in Chapter 5, all of which support successful collaborative evaluation practice. Especially focus on those strategies you believe will be most beneficial to participants by considering their evaluation roles and contexts.

Situate

1. Reflect on a collaborative study you recently conducted (or in which you are currently involved). Compare and contrast the issues you faced to those in this case study. Draw a Venn diagram to record the similarities and differences.

2. What aspects of this case particularly inform your current evaluation practice? Explain.

3. What skills do you possess that make you particularly well suited to conduct collaborative studies? Refer to evaluation standards, guidelines, and/or competencies in self-assessing your strengths and determining where additional professional development would be helpful.

4. What helpful lessons did you learn from this case? What are your main takeaways? How will these enhance your future work as an evaluator?

CHAPTER REVIEW

As an internal evaluator with a rare opportunity to move beyond analyzing and reporting test scores, Sara Moore hired a well-regarded colleague, Robert Wentworth, to help facilitate the collaborative evaluation process. A longtime district employee, Moore had positive relationships with those who would participate; Wentworth already knew many of the likely participants, and his positive reputation preceded him. Once he was on board, the evaluators' two initial concerns were to figure out what their primary intended users (PIUs) and other evaluation participants wanted to know, along with how they felt about evaluation more generally, and to think about how the district and community context might affect the collaborative process. Their next task was to develop interactive evaluation activities that would engage a sizeable number of stakeholders in conversations across the course of the school year as the evaluation proceeded through its basic tasks: to frame issues and questions, to approve design and data collection instruments, to help with data analysis and interpretation, and to develop recommendations for action.

The two evaluators built repeated opportunities for individual and group reflection into the collaborative evaluation process to ensure that, whatever happened, the participants—whatever their roles in the district or community—could learn from the experience. And learn they did. Despite some procedural challenges, by early the following summer the process was finished, and district staff began to implement the data-based recommendations for change. Exhibit 10.8 summarizes the case's positive and negative applications of interactive evaluation practice (IEP) principles.

Exhibit 10.8   Applying the IEP Principles to the "We're in This Together" Evaluation

IEP Principle	Positive Application	Negative Application
1. Get personal.	• Identified PIUs and large numbers of people through the evaluation and data collection processes • Involved PIUs in important decisions throughout the evaluation	• Did not directly connect with parents or people of color (other than Rosa Ortiz) to ensure their meaningful involvement
2. Structure interaction.	• Created a committee structure that would engage many people • Used interactive strategies at the two retreats	• Failed to teach or remind committee chairs how to run an effective committee • Failed to manage communication effectively among committees during the initial evaluation process
3. Examine context.	• Designed an inclusive process appropriate to the district	• Did not include financial data, even though finances are a critical concern in the district

(Continued)

Exhibit 10.8 (Continued)

IEP Principle	Positive Application	Negative Application
4. Consider politics.	• Actively involved an influential board member in the evaluation process • Had the superintendent lend visible support to the evaluation at the retreats	• Ran the evaluation process separate from discussion of the levy
5. Expect conflict.	• Used an inclusive process with many opportunities for people to express and discuss their opinions • Restructured the committees when the initial structure didn't work	• Did not anticipate the conflict between committees that resulted from poor preparation and communication • Had to handle the superintendent's desire to omit data in the final report to the board
6. Respect culture.	• Followed the district tradition of administering surveys to everyone rather than sampling • Used the data from the Somali mothers	• Did not translate parent survey or participatory data collection materials into other languages • Noticed too late that few parents of color participated in the data collection
7. Take time.	• Hired an external evaluator to buy time for the evaluation • Designed a study that fit within the time available	• Initially created a committee process that demanded excessive time commitments from a number of people

11

SERVING AS AN EVALUATION COACH

Engaging Staff and Participants in Evaluating a Healthy Nutrition Program

---

Chapter Preview

- Consider *interactive evaluation practice* (IEP) that entails a participant-directed study conducted by program staff and participants coached by an internal evaluator
- Examine how *basic inquiry tasks* and the *evaluation capacity building* continuum shape decisions in this case
- Reflect on evaluation decisions and actions at various junctures
- Engage in a set of exercises—TIPS (*think, interact, practice, situate*)—at the end of the case description
- Apply the IEP principles to the participant-directed study in this case

---

INTRODUCTION

This case highlights the role of an internal evaluator as coach to program staff and clients evaluating a healthy nutrition program for recent immigrants and refugees. *Alimento Para el Pensamiento* (Food for Thought) has been in operation for 5 years. It began with grant funding as a program for Spanish-speaking immigrant and refugee women from Latin America. With additional funding, in the past 2 years it has expanded to incorporate women from different parts of the world, including East Africa and Southeast Asia. Staff wanted to keep the Spanish name for branding reasons. The program is popular in the neighborhood surrounding the social services center where it is offered, and non-Spanish speakers may well have heard about it. The program began in response to the fact that many food shelves in the area didn't provide culturally appropriate food, and women new to the country often found themselves with free items they didn't know how to use. These often ended up in the garbage, wasted. The program's creator thought it would make sense to teach people how to cook available American food, along with providing instruction in basic nutritional information they may not have learned in their formal education, if they had any. Many had not.

The program operates using a trainer-of-trainers model. Staff trainers teach participant trainers information about nutrition, diet, American foods, and cooking as well as how to deliver three standardized lessons on the content. With the expansion to include multiple cultures, participants are also learning about others' ethnic cooking. Although not required, the women frequently bring samples of their cultural specialties and often share recipes and ideas for low-cost, healthy meals. Unavoidably, as a result of the training the program creates community across the diverse groups of women.

When participants have finished their training, they are each responsible for organizing and leading three sessions with members of their community, either alone or with a partner from their cultural group and with support from program staff. The sessions teach basic nutrition, a balanced diet, and how to use American ingredients that may be new to people. The session content is as follows:

- Session 1. Principal Nutrients and Their Sources (the basic science of carbohydrates, proteins, and fats)
- Session 2. Eating for Health and Vitality (a comparison of the American diet with diets from other countries and basic information about American foods that promote health and good nutrition)
- Session 3. Designing and Cooking a Balanced American Diet (guidance on designing a nutritionally balanced diet using common American foods)

Each presentation includes quizzes before and after the content presentations and cooking activities that create healthy dishes using common American ingredients (provided by the program) so people who are used to their own culture's food can experience tastes that may be new to them. Because the sessions are targeted to one cultural group and taught by one or two members of that group in their native language, the hope is that participants will speak freely about nutritional issues they face as recent arrivals and get ideas from others about how to resolve any problems. Part of the program's intention is also to empower the women who become the teachers of their peers. They receive a small stipend for each community presentation and reportedly feel good about their newfound leadership role. Community participants seem to enjoy taking part in the three sessions, owing both to the content and to their interactive nature. The new foods always make for interesting conversation, comparisons, and an occasional laugh.

A social worker by training, the program's founding director and strongest proponent is interested in having the staff and participant trainers work together on its evaluation. This owes in large part to the agency's internal evaluator, who has worked to integrate evaluation into the fabric of every program. The director sees how the process might increase the program's impact by teaching evaluative thinking to both staff and participants in the training sessions. Her staff could eventually apply evaluation skills to other programs, and the training participants could apply the skills to other areas of their lives. Many of the women have come from oppressive authoritarian regimes where a party's or a political strongman's opinion is the only form of "evaluation" and men often dominate social interactions. Participation in an inclusive and openly democratic evaluation process may be a novel and energizing experience. Although the director doesn't know much about evaluation—until recently, evaluation in her mind meant compliance with funders' demands for accountability—she is enthusiastic about the process and hopes the evaluation results will bolster the program's chances of receiving further funding when its current support ends in a year. She definitely needs data to meet the formal requirements of her grant, but is also interested in data for improvement and possible capacity building. Exhibit 11.1 outlines the grounding components of the *Alimento* evaluation.

Exhibit 11.1   "Serving as an Evaluation Coach" Evaluation

Case Grounding Components	Description
Relationship of the evaluator to the organization	Internal
Interpersonal participation quotient zone (see Exhibit 2.3)	Participant-directed study
Evaluation capacity building (ECB) continuum focus (see Exhibit 2.6)	Organization development
Object of the evaluation	*Alimento Para el Pensamiento* (Food for Thought), a healthy nutrition program at a social service agency serving immigrants and refugees
The presenting situation	Community Family Services' internal evaluator plans to coach a team of staff and participants in evaluating *Alimento*

THE EVALUATION CONTEXT

With a long and distinguished history, Community Family Services (CFS) was a well-established social services organization located in a working-class section of an urban center. For more than 100 years, CFS had been a resource for immigrants and refugees from multiple countries. The specific groups arriving in town had changed over the years, but CFS's commitment to serving them well had not altered one bit from the time of its founding by a reform-minded settlement house advocate, a colleague of Jane Addams at Hull House. A celebration of Founder's Day reminded the community annually of its Progressive roots.

Working in partnership with an evaluation volunteer from a local university, agency staff over the past decade had built internal capacity to conduct evaluations as part of regular operating procedures. Stuart Benjamin was currently the agency's half-time internal evaluator, supported in part by general operating funds and in part by 5% of all grant funding; the other 50% of his job entailed teaching in the English-language learners (ELL) program, the job that had brought him to the agency 8 years earlier. An undergraduate English major, Benjamin did not have a degree in evaluation, but he had earned an evaluation certificate from a well-known professional development organization and continued to learn by keeping up with the literature, attending national conferences, and actively participating in his local evaluation association. When he got the chance to take on the role of internal evaluator, he jumped at it. Since he was ultimately responsible for all CFS evaluations, Benjamin participated at some level in every evaluation in the agency and often collaborated with Laura Cramer, the agency's talented grant writer who always included data in her proposals. He was working to teach staff to evaluate their own programs regularly as part of organization development and CFS's continuous improvement process.

With support from the agency's top administrators, program evaluation was now, at least in theory, part of every CFS program, from inception to termination. This commitment was evident across the agency. CFS president Eduardo Rodriguez consistently reinforced the message that evaluation was vitally important to program functioning. Throughout the year, a Board Evaluation Committee provided oversight, tracking program progress on a number of variables and ensuring that evaluation was routinely written into policies and procedures. A monthly dashboard (a summary of agency data on key indicators) reminded board and staff members alike how things were going. Every program manager took part in a mandatory monthly meeting led by Stuart Benjamin to receive ongoing training and discuss evaluation issues as they arose—thus learning evaluation by doing it. A single database, skillfully managed by a competent secretary, captured consistent data across all programs on standardized measures, enabling staff to provide data quickly on an as-needed basis. When new employees came on board, one of their first responsibilities was to attend an evaluation orientation, taught by Benjamin and several staff members who were eager contributors to evaluation processes. New hires who brought other work or their knitting on the assumption that this meeting demanded compliance rather than active participation quickly learned otherwise. Program evaluation was serious business at CFS.

The evaluation of *Alimento* was Stuart Benjamin's first effort at coaching a program manager to conduct a participant-directed study that engaged other staff and participants in framing and implementing evaluation activities. He believed everything was in place for the work. The agency had a well-defined system for data collection through surveys and group interviews, a group of people who could support the process if necessary, an effective communication system, and access to extensive evaluation resources both in a staff library and online.

THE CAST OF CHARACTERS AS THE EVALUATION BEGAN

Benjamin couldn't think of a better manager than Veronica Casanueva to be the volunteer for his first effort at evaluation coaching. The last team he had coached had been his son's third-grade baseball team, and coaching 8-year-old boys had to be harder than coaching program staff and community participants. Besides, Casanueva was a bundle of positive energy, especially when it came to "her baby," *Alimento*. Using the skills he had developed over years of teaching, Benjamin would be her evaluation instructor and help develop her evaluation skills as she led this study with his support. Skills or not, she was ready to go. His hope was that the group conducting the evaluation would become—he hated the jargon—an "evaluation learning community." The fact that three ELL students would be part of the team was especially exciting. The students who had volunteered were bright and committed to learning skills that would help them succeed in their new country. He was confident they would be wonderful apprentices.

There might be a bit of a challenge with the project, he thought, at least in relation to one top administrator in the agency. CFS president Eduardo Rodriguez supported all things evaluative, and he liked the idea of staff-directed formative evaluation, so he would undoubtedly be pleased with this effort. Board chair Myagrace Jones always spoke of the importance of empowering CFS clients, so she, too, should appreciate this new aspect of participant-directed evaluation. It was program vice president Hannah Greene who might be less enthusiastic.

When staff returned to work after day-a-week furloughs for the entire previous year due to budget problems, Greene knew how far behind they were because she knew how far behind she was personally. Spending time on a program evaluation meant they would have even less time for interaction with clients or other program development work. With regard to *Alimento,* she thought Casanueva favored it too much. It was only one of several programs Casanueva oversaw, but it was clearly her favorite, and she spent more time nurturing its participants than she was paid to. In looking for funding to support the program in the future, Greene knew she needed solid data about the program effects, including its cost, not heartwarming stories about what a good time participants had or what they thought the first time they ate rhubarb or jicama. To avoid offending Greene, Benjamin consulted with the grant writer, Laura Cramer, to determine what information she needed to write proposals for additional funding and assumed those were also Greene's information needs. Cramer didn't mention a need for financial data.

Benjamin knew other issues were likely to surface. He had heard some grumbling from his non-Latina students about the name of the program and some complaints about the mysterious process through which people were picked to become trainers. Word was that Latina participants had a better chance than did other participants. He wasn't sure how Casanueva would respond to hearing potentially challenging concerns. Exhibit 11.2 details the list of characters in this evaluation, along with their concerns and issues as the study began.

Exhibit 11.2   Selected Cast of Characters for "Serving as an Evaluation Coach"

Evaluation Role	Name/Title	Concerns/Issues
Internal evaluator	Stuart Benjamin	Benjamin is CFS's half-time internal evaluator, with responsibility for all program evaluations. Building on earlier work, he continues to increase the agency's evaluation capacity through ongoing activities. The evaluation of *Alimento* will be his first as an evaluation coach.
Primary intended user (PIU)	Dr. Hannah Greene, CFS vice president for programs	Greene understands the evaluation process and fully supports the agency's ECB efforts. What she needs is hard evidence that the program is achieving outcomes and would prefer that Benjamin conduct the evaluation himself. Given staff time commitments, she is concerned about using *Alimento* as the test case for participant-directed evaluation and wonders if she will get the data she needs.

Evaluation Role	Name/Title	Concerns/Issues
"Client"/PIU/ staff evaluator	Veronica Casanueva, director of *Alimento*	Director Casanueva founded this program and supports it enthusiastically. She has volunteered to lead the evaluation because it seems like a chance to document the good things her program achieves, and she looks forward to learning from the process. Her evaluation skills are minimal; she once took a course but knows no statistics, no qualitative methods, and admittedly is not a good writer. She does have great interpersonal skills and is well liked by staff and participants.
Staff evaluators	Amina Jibreel, *Alimento* staff	Jibreel immigrated to the United States from Somalia when she was a child and is a fluent English speaker but also able to communicate with her Somali clients in both Somali and Oromo. She is working on her undergraduate degree in education and plans to become an elementary school teacher in one of the local public school systems that serve Somali children.
	Michael Kowalski, *Alimento* staff	Born in the United States, Kowalski is working on a master's degree in public health at a local university. He speaks Spanish fluently. Based on his work at CFS, he is especially interested in the health and nutrition issues of recent immigrants. He took a course on program evaluation as part of his coursework and is excited to try out the process.
Participant evaluators	Nadifa Salaam, *Alimento* participant	Salaam's family lived in a refugee camp for more than 3 years before coming to the United States. She and her husband are both students in CFS ELL programs, and she enrolled in *Alimento* to learn about the different foods available in her new country. The mother of six has discovered she is an excellent presenter.
	Alecia Garcia, *Alimento* participant	A recent arrival from Costa Rica, Garcia was a nurse in her native country but lacks the credentials and English skills to continue that practice in the United States. She has studied English for 2 years at CFS but, as the mother of four young children with no family members nearby, often misses classes when one of them is sick.
	Kia Yang, *Alimento* participant	Yang is part of a close-knit Hmong community that arrived 2 years ago from a refugee camp in Thailand. She knew no English when she arrived but has been studying hard and making good progress. Participation in the program has strengthened her ambitions. She hopes to complete her GED and then enroll in a community college to become a teacher's aide. She has three young children.

(Continued)

Exhibit 11.2   (Continued)

Evaluation Role	Name/Title	Concerns/Issues
Important stakeholders	Eduardo Rodriguez, CFS president	Rodriguez is an evaluation champion. During his tenure as president, he has built the agency's evaluation infrastructure, including creating a part-time position for an internal evaluator. He wants CFS to be known for using data to build sustainable programs for the immigrant and refugee communities.
	Myagrace Jones, chair of the CFS Board of Directors	Jones is an outspoken advocate for CFS participants and wants to empower clients to succeed in the United States. This new participatory aspect of evaluation appeals to her. Articulate and well positioned in the African American community, she works for a local company and represents it on the board.
Other stakeholders	Laura Cramer, longtime agency grant writer	Cramer has been part of the CFS fabric for 35 years and has held many positions in the organization. As the "elder stateswoman," she is now the highly skilled grant writer, able to identify potential funding sources, meet competently with representatives from funding agencies, and then write high-quality proposals that are the source of ongoing support for agency programs. If or when she retires, she will be extremely difficult to replace.
	Sharon Nolan, chief clerical support for CFS	Nolan is responsible for managing the agency's database, including comprehensive data for all the agency programs. With her current workload, she would like to hire another person, but there is no funding to do so. She routinely gets frustrated by people's demands for data, often at the last minute.

THE EVALUATION PROCESS

Initial Decisions/Actions

Because Stuart Benjamin had worked in the agency for 8 years and still taught ELL classes half-time, he already had positive relationships with the key actors in the participant-directed evaluation. The same was true for Veronica Casanueva. Her relations with the staff and participants in *Alimento* were especially upbeat, and the tension between her and Hannah Greene didn't affect day-to-day program operations. In consultation with Benjamin, Casanueva identified five members for her evaluation team: two staff (Amina Jibreel and Michael Kowalski) and three outstanding participants (Nadifa Salaam, Alecia Garcia, and Kia Yang). Using funds from the program's evaluation budget, she was able to offer the three participant–trainer evaluators a small stipend for conducting the evaluation, and they appreciated the support. The staff members didn't require incentives since this work was technically part of their jobs, but Kowalski needed a project for one of his classes at the university and got permission to count this as an internship.

As the internal evaluator, Benjamin attended the initial evaluation team meetings and helped shape the conversation around what topics the study should address. For Casanueva, the PIUs were herself and the program staff, but Benjamin gently suggested that the team might want to consider what questions the vice president for programming would want answered. "But that's not the point of *this* evaluation," Casanueva responded. "This is *our* evaluation, and we'll look at what is important to *us*. Isn't that the idea?" Stuart Benjamin wasn't sure how to respond. On the one hand, Casanueva was right—this was a participant-directed evaluation, and they were the participants. On the other hand, this was the program evaluation for a sizeable grant from one of CFS's important funders, and the evaluation team really needed to consider key PIUs such as the funder, Greene, and members of the CFS board. There were issues in CFS's broader community context, including a sense of competition for services among different groups of immigrants and refugees. Government funding was consistently available for new arrivals, but when such funding ended, community members sometimes felt a loss of support. Members of immigrant groups who had lived in the community for many years, whose children were fully assimilated, wondered if they had roles in programs such as *Alimento* or questioned the extent to which CFS was committed to helping them on an ongoing basis.

The members of the evaluation team were clearly looking to Casanueva for her thoughts, and she wavered. Finally, the three participants—Salaam, Garcia, and Yang—noted that they represented specific cultural groups and they *were* the broader community. Jibreel and Kowalski said that they, too, had a pretty good sense of community issues because of their work with other CFS programs. At this point Benjamin reminded them that the grant had specific evaluation requirements, and he emphasized the importance of completing everything required in the funding document. The team agreed. They decided that by adhering to the requirements of the grant and answering their own additional questions, the evaluation would provide useful information to everyone who needed it.

What did they want to know? Clearly, they needed to document what the funder required, including the number of people served in the trainings and in the community sessions, the dates and places for both, the pre- and post-community-session quiz results, and so on. Jibreel observed they could use the participant satisfaction data they already had—evaluation forms from each training session and from the program's culmination, and the simple, language-appropriate quizzes attendees completed after community sessions. The three participant evaluators raised other questions: Had other participants learned as much as they had about nutrition and diet? Did the other trainers feel comfortable presenting to their communities? Did people from diverse cultures respond differently to the presentations? Kowalski wondered if people who attended the community sessions actually learned enough to change their home diets and cooking practices. Casanueva, now thinking about the broader community issues, thought it might be important to do a comparison of how the program worked in the three different communities. Maybe that comparison would suggest ways to strengthen program activities in a more fundable future iteration.

The evaluation team looked to Benjamin for next steps. Time was passing quickly—the new quarter's ELL classes were about to begin—and they definitely wanted to get going on instrument development and data collection. He told them he would meet with Veronica Casanueva and they would collaborate on a plan and timeline for the evaluation that the group could discuss at its next meeting.

REFLECTION BOX I

How Is This Evaluation Going?

1. What steps did those involved in this evaluation take to identify PIUs? Do you believe these steps were adequate? Why or why not? What might Stuart Benjamin (the internal evaluator coaching this participant-directed study) have done differently to ensure that concerns of PIUs were considered by the participants conducting this study? Explain.

2. Revisit Chapter 4, Exhibit 4.2. Review Conversation Goals 1 through 4, shown in the first column. In your judgment, how well did Stuart Benjamin (the internal evaluator coach) and Veronica Casanueva (initial leader of the participant-directed evaluation team) engage members of the evaluation team in conversations to accomplish these conversation goals? Who else (if anyone) do you think should have been included in these conversations? Explain.

3. Revisit Chapter 5, Exhibit 5.2. Which of these strategies (if any) might have been productively employed at the initial participant-directed evaluation team meeting? How might Stuart Benjamin (the internal evaluator) have coached Veronica Casanueva (initial leader of the participant evaluation team) in using the various interactive strategies during the meeting? Which do you believe could have been most fruitfully employed? Why? Explain.

4. Revisit Chapter 7, Templates 1 through 7. Which of these most probably should be used at each participant-directed evaluation team meeting throughout this study? Use *Strategy 10: Cooperative Rank Order* (described in Chapter 5) to sequence these seven templates from what you think is **most** to **least** essential for promoting success in this case study. Explain your reasoning.

5. Revisit Chapter 7, Exhibit 7.1. Based on what you know so far about the organization that houses CFS and the people participating in this study, how would you characterize the overall cultural competence in this evaluation setting? Do you think it is well developed, somewhat developed, or in need of development? On what did you base your assessment? What steps might you take to advance people's appreciation for, understanding of, and positive interaction with diverse others in this study? Explain.

6. What issues seem ripe for interpersonal conflict in this participant-directed evaluation study? To what extent do those involved in this study seem to be aware of the potential for conflict? Who (if anyone) has actually experienced conflict up to this point? Revisit Chapter 6 and review how to analyze an evaluation situation/setting with an eye for conflict. Apply that information to what has transpired so far in this participant-directed study. Explain.

7. How might Veronica Casanueva's role as the director of the *Alimento* program—plus her unwavering enthusiasm for the program—be problematic as she leads this participant-directed study? Do you think it is ethical (or wise) for Casanueva to lead this participant-directed evaluation? Why or why not? Explain.

Data Collection and Analysis Decisions/Actions

Shortly after that discussion, Casanueva met in Benjamin's office to discuss how the team would conduct its evaluation. Knowing he wanted to teach her about the evaluation process, Benjamin took out the notes from the brainstorming session. There were many possible issues and questions the study could address. Together they discussed what the evaluation had to include for the grant and what other topics would be most important to PIUs. Within 30 minutes they had agreed on three evaluation questions:

1. To what extent does *Alimento Para el Pensamiento* successfully teach its participant trainers nutrition content and presentation skills?

2. How well do community participants learn key content during the nutrition sessions led by those trained in the program?

3. To what extent does *Alimento Para el Pensamiento* effectively address the differing nutritional needs of CFS's immigrant communities?

Next they laid out a plan for the evaluation team to conduct the study. Knowing the grant report was due in roughly a year, they decided the team would meet for 2 hours immediately after training sessions every other week for the coming year (i.e., the next four quarters of ELL classes). Benjamin wrote down the steps of the evaluation process and coached Casanueva in planning backward as she developed a rough timeline for creating data collection instruments, collecting and analyzing data with a manageable schedule, interpreting the data, and preparing reports. Looking at the calendar, she saw that the Founder's Day celebration fell near the end of the year. It would be an ideal public event at which to present the evaluation results to community members. That became the key deadline for the evaluation. She could invite grant-funder staff to attend, and it would mark a meaningful end to the study.

And so the evaluation process began. At first Benjamin stayed in the background at team meetings. Even though he helped Casanueva prepare the content and agenda for each session, he knew she was a novice evaluator. Out of self-interest he attended to make sure things were going smoothly. He quickly realized it was a good thing he attended. Casanueva's enthusiasm for evaluation simply did not translate to an ability to lead the group effectively in the evaluation process. Too often, she deferred to Kowalski because he had taken an evaluation course, and he was happy to dominate the discussion. Jibreel and the participant evaluators did not speak unless called on. Worst of all, Casanueva occasionally gave incorrect answers on technical evaluation issues. Not wanting to take over, Benjamin didn't say anything at first during the sessions and gave her corrections during a debriefing at their next planning meeting. He moved from merely helping her prepare materials and started going over her evaluation presentations in advance, making sure she understood the tasks and answering the questions likely to arise. He encouraged her to notice when Kowalski talked too much and to call on someone else. Casanueva truly appreciated his coaching and seemed to get better week to week.

With Casanueva leading the process, the team members made decisions about how they would collect data. They decided on the following data collection methods (see Exhibit 11.3).

Exhibit 11.3 Data Collection Methods, Samples, and Those Responsible

Data Collection Method	Sample	Those Responsible
1. Analysis of existing data	• Existing data (program materials, including evaluation forms, check quizzes, and attendance records)	Database manager (compile, clean) Evaluation team (analyze) Internal evaluator (support)
2. Electronic and written surveys	• *Alimento* staff • All participant trainers • Community members at upcoming sessions	Evaluation team Internal evaluator (support)
3. Group interviews	• Invited participants (past 2 years)	Evaluation team Internal evaluator (support)

1. *Analysis of existing data.* As program director, Casanueva was happy the team could analyze the existing data they had discussed early on, including the number of people served in various ways, program materials, pre- and post-community-session quiz results, attendance records, and participant satisfaction data from training and community sessions' evaluation forms.

2. *Electronic and written surveys.* The evaluation team wanted everyone associated with the program to have an opportunity to provide input. There would be three surveys:

   a. An electronic staff survey that would go to everyone who had ever worked for *Alimento* (eight people in all).

   b. A written survey for participant trainers who completed the program (roughly 60 individuals), available in four languages (English, Hmong, Somali, and Spanish). The evaluation team decided to sponsor a reunion and skills update for all participant trainers and have people complete the survey there. The evaluation team would mail the survey with a self-addressed, stamped return envelope to those unable to attend that event.

   c. A written survey for attendees at community events, also available in four languages. The team understood that many women in the community might find completing the survey difficult and discussed ways to help them. They decided to administer the survey only during upcoming community sessions in the next two quarters when one of them could be present to assist people in filling it out.

3. *Group interviews.* Given the potential problem with getting enough surveys from community members, the evaluation team decided to hold one group interview at CFS for each of the three communities: Hmong, Latina, and Somali. They planned to invite participant trainers from the past 2 years to an afternoon session where they would be asked questions from two perspectives: that of participant trainer and that of community member. The three group interviews would be held off-site, two at culturally specific restaurants that had private rooms and one at a nearby church. The afternoon's activities would be a round-robin check-in, oral data dialogues, and then large-group discussion. The session would include child care and healthy American refreshments. As an incentive for attending, Casanueva decided to hold a drawing for a $25 gift card to a local food store.

Exhibit 11.4 summarizes the evaluation questions, the data the evaluation team needs to collect, and the data collection methods.

Exhibit 11.4 Summary of Evaluation Questions, Data Needed, and Data Collection Methods

Evaluation Question	Data Needed	Data Collection Methods
1. To what extent does *Alimento Para el Pensamiento* successfully teach its participant trainers nutrition content and presentation skills?	• Perceptions of learnings (staff and those trained)	• Electronic and written surveys
2. How well do community participants learn key content during the nutrition sessions led by those trained in the program?	• Results of pre- and post-session check quizzes • Perceptions of learning (those trained, participants)	• Analysis of existing data • Written surveys • Community-specific group interviews
3. To what extent does *Alimento Para el Pensamiento* effectively address the differing nutritional needs of CFS's immigrant communities?	• Attendance data • Perceptions of program outcomes (staff, those trained, participants)	• Analysis of existing data • Electronic and written surveys • Community-specific group interviews

Knowing they could get the existing data whenever they needed it, the team worked collectively at several meetings to develop and then translate the three surveys and the questions for the group interviews. At Casanueva's insistence, Benjamin took a more active instructional role during these work sessions than he had previously, explaining how to write sound survey items and the important features of a survey's graphic layout. The group discussed what would motivate people to complete their survey and how to make the survey process as smooth and meaningful as possible. The team asked Benjamin to help them make sure their survey and interview questions were of high quality, so, with their permission, he edited their drafts between meetings and then discussed why he made certain changes so they could learn from the process. It was definitely a win–win situation: Team members learned how to write better items, and Benjamin made sure the data collection instruments were technically strong.

As work progressed, the team had to deal with two problems. The first was the loss of a member. One of Yang's children was diagnosed with juvenile diabetes, and she no longer had the time needed to attend team meetings. The group was truly sorry to lose her, especially since she had agreed to be in charge of the survey database in Excel. The second problem related to the behavior of the team's two staff members. It was evident from the start that Kowalski tended to talk too much at the evaluation team meetings, perhaps because the evaluation was his internship project. Unfortunately, he didn't see the silencing effect this had on the participant evaluators. In addition, once the process began in earnest, Jibreel, who was already annoyed by Kowalski's routine domination, became concerned at the prospect of having participants evaluate her professional activities. It was one thing to have Benjamin or an external evaluator collect data, but having the participants she trained and supported in charge of evaluating her work simply seemed inappropriate. To make sure her perspective actively shaped the instruments, she became increasingly vocal at the meetings, even cutting Kowalski off once, to Benjamin's amazement. The three participant evaluators had even less opportunity to contribute ideas.

Benjamin asked Casanueva to meet with him and the two staff on the evaluation team, where he counseled them on the effect of their behaviors. If the participant evaluators consistently deferred to the staff, the participatory evaluation process had failed. Kowalski was surprised to learn that he talked too much and knew he had to change his behavior. At the meeting Jibreel had a chance to express her concerns about what this evaluation meant for her professionally and felt better having done so. The group of four discussed how Kowalski and Jibreel could listen more carefully and encourage equal participation from all team members.

The data collection began, with different members of the evaluation team assuming responsibility for the various components. After several months Benjamin realized that with Yang's departure, the analysis of existing data assignment had somehow slipped through the cracks. Someone else needed to pick up this time-consuming task. Benjamin went to see Sharon Nolan, the keeper of the CFS agency database, thinking she could help by getting the data compiled and ready for analysis. Unfortunately, his request came at a bad time for Nolan, as extensive quarterly reports were due to all managers within a week. When Benjamin explained what he needed, she snapped. "I don't have time to get that for you. And anyway I don't think it's appropriate for participants to have access to agency data. That's just not the way we do things around here!" Benjamin, who knew her reputation as data gatekeeper, firmly told her that "things around here" were changing and demanded that she prepare the data as soon as possible or he would report this situation to her manager. She agreed to do it but told him in no uncertain terms that she was not pleased with the task or his tone.

That crisis paled in comparison with what occurred the following week. With no warning, Veronica Casanueva announced that she was taking a job at another agency and gave 2 weeks' notice. The agency's information communication system—also known as the gossip tree—quickly detailed the harsh words she and Hannah Greene had had one evening a few months earlier behind closed doors. Casanueva was evidently not pleased with the outcome of that conversation and, unbeknownst to others, had started thinking about employment elsewhere. With her skill set and experience, she was routinely recruited by other agencies—many of whom paid more than CFS did—and when the next position came her way, she went for it. With vacation days to use up, Casanueva really had only 3 days in the office before her departure. The evaluation of *Alimento* was only one of many details she needed to wrap up. Kowalski had told her he could take on the evaluation team if that would help, but she didn't immediately agree.

Sensing the potential slippage in the situation, Benjamin scheduled a meeting with Casanueva to discuss next steps for the evaluation team once she left. They brainstormed multiple ideas, going back and forth, putting different thoughts together, and landed on the only solution they thought could work in the short term: to make Kowalski the lead in this evaluation, since he had volunteered and was already doing a lot of work as part of his internship. They were confident he could help the team finish the data collection and complete the remaining steps, and Benjamin would coach him on his tendency to dominate. Since the decision was internal to the participant-directed evaluation and the most important thing was to keep moving, Benjamin didn't check with program vice president Greene or CFS president Rodriguez before telling Kowalski the plan. Kowalski was pleased and happily agreed to take on the leadership role. It might be more work, but this was another evaluation competency he could add to his résumé. At Casanueva's going-away party he publicly thanked her for her confidence in him.

At the next evaluation team meeting, however, something had clearly changed. There was tension in the air, and the only voice heard was Kowalski's as he presented his plans for how to complete the evaluation on time. He pointedly grilled people on where they were with earlier tasks, assigned new jobs, and handed out materials. When someone asked a question or suggested a change, Kowalski dismissed it. He had spent a lot of time preparing and, to his mind, had thought of everything, which he explained in excruciating detail. The women—Jibreel and the two remaining participant evaluators—stopped trying to speak, but their expressions spoke volumes. They had no voice and did not feel happy about it. They kept looking at one another. Kowalski did not notice, but Benjamin did.

After the meeting, he asked Kowalski to come to his office—right away—and privately reviewed the notes he had taken showing how much the new evaluation team leader had talked, how he had cut off anyone who had a different idea, and the women's negative reactions. "But I was only trying to get the evaluation back on track. I didn't mean to take it over," he protested. Having read about cultural competence in his evaluation course, Kowalski knew this situation was unacceptable. Even if he hadn't meant to be, he was behaving in a stereotypical domineering way, and he really felt bad. After all, he thought he was helping and instead he had hurt the process. "What if we have another team meeting and let the group figure out who should be in charge?" he proposed. Benjamin thought that was a good idea—and it spoke a lot to Kowalski's good intentions.

Kowalski opened the next meeting with an apology, and then Benjamin facilitated an open discussion and saw to it that everyone participated. Once again, the energy level was high, and the eventual solution elevated participant evaluator Nadifa Salaam to the leadership role, with backup from Kowalski, Jibreel, and Benjamin. Having a participant evaluator as the lead and spokesperson highlighted the importance this team placed on involvement in the process. Salaam was extremely hardworking, and she clearly had leadership potential. She agreed to lead as long as everyone would support her. When CFS president Rodriguez and board chair Jones heard about this, they were pleased. Program vice president Hannah Greene suggested putting an article in the CFS newsletter.

The group moved on and finished the data analysis.

1. *Analysis of existing data.* There were three types of existing data: attendance records, evaluation forms, and the pre- and post-session quizzes community session attendees completed. The attendance and evaluation data for all 5 years of the program were surprisingly thorough, both for the training sessions and the community presentations.

    a. Training session attendance was consistently at maximum capacity, and for the past 3 years there had been a waiting list of individuals who wanted to become participant trainers. The post-session evaluation forms were consistently positive.

    b. Attendance at community presentations was less consistent. Attendance at presentations by Latina trainers was the highest (8 to 11 individuals), and attendance at the Somali trainers' sessions was routinely less (4 to 5 individuals). But because the sessions were designed to work for groups with as few as five people, the data suggested that all the community sessions had sufficient enrollment. Not one session had been canceled owing to low attendance.

    The community session quiz and evaluation data disappointed the team. There were many gaps and omissions. Some sessions had not even collected the forms, which should have been the responsibility of one of the trainers. The participant evaluators discussed what might have happened. From their own trainings, they knew some community members were unable to complete the quizzes and evaluation forms since they were preliterate in their native language or just learning to read. Maybe these data represented the participants who could read, and maybe the data problem related to literacy levels. They looked at the data in hand and saw clearly that people had higher scores on the post-session quiz, getting most of the answers correct, and seemed to have enjoyed the sessions.

2. *Electronic and written surveys.* The group analyzed the results of three different surveys.

    a. *Program staff.* The results for program staff (seven of eight responded) were universally positive. Staff felt good about program content and process, and several noted their sincere appreciation of Casanueva's passion, creativity, and commitment. In response to an open-ended item, a few made minor suggestions for improvement, but overall, they provided strong support for *Alimento*.

b. *Participant trainers.* The reunion and skills update for participant trainers had been a success, and 24 of the roughly 60 eligible to attend came and completed the survey. Only 13 of the remaining 36 individuals, who received their surveys in the mail, responded—for a total response rate of 37 (24 plus 13) out of 60, or 62%. The participant trainers were extremely supportive of *Alimento* content and overall experience but were reportedly less confident about the presentation skills they gained. More than half the responses—mostly from the non-Latina participants—questioned the program's Spanish name since the program was inclusive of several cultures. A majority also expressed a desire to expand the program; the small stipend meant the training counted as employment and could be included on a résumé. Many also suggested increasing the size of the stipend.

c. *Community members.* The team had decided to attend training sessions and ask community members in attendance (a total of 120 or so) to complete the survey. The data collection process didn't work well for three reasons: The survey was tacked on at the end of the session, people also had to fill out the post-session quiz and session evaluation form, and many had trouble with these writing tasks, even with help. The total number of completed surveys was 43. Nonetheless, there were responses from each of the cultural groups, and the evaluation team member who was fluent in that language translated the results. Although small in number, the results were positive. Women enjoyed attending the sessions, and many reported they were using what they learned in their cooking at home.

3. *Group interviews.* If high attendance was an indicator, the group interviews were a huge success. In fact, even Casanueva attended the Latina session, telling the group she just couldn't stay away; people were happy to include her. The results were extremely positive regarding meeting the educational needs of each community around diet and nutritional issues. Someone in each of the groups mentioned the potential benefit of cross-cultural community sessions as a way to connect women to people outside their home cultures. The culturally specific community sessions were fine, but some thought there might be value in adding opportunities for cross-cultural discussions and sharing.

At last the group completed the data analysis, and that was good because Founder's Day was drawing closer. They had plenty of evaluative content to work with but no cost data—the one thing program vice president Greene was waiting for.

REFLECTION BOX II

How Is This Evaluation Going?

1. What were the final evaluation questions that guided this study? To what extent do you believe these adequately dealt with the concerns of the PIUs? Explain.

2. Should others besides Stuart Benjamin (internal evaluator coach) and Veronica Casanueva (director of the program being evaluated and evaluation team lead) have participated in finalizing the evaluation questions that ultimately guided this study? Why or why not? If so, who? Explain.

3. Consider the conflict that occurred between Stuart Benjamin (the internal evaluator coach) and Sharon Nolan (who provided chief clerical support for CFS) when he unexpectedly asked her to help compile the data in preparation for analysis. Revisit Chapter 6, Exhibit 6.4 to write a script indicating how Benjamin and Nolan might have constructively problem solved this situation.

4. Revisit Chapter 7, Exhibit 7.5. Which of these methods do you think could/ should be applied in this participant-directed evaluation study? Why? How might doing so help keep this study on track? Explain. Select one method you believe would be especially helpful, and then explain in detail how to implement it in this study. What materials would be needed? Explain and provide examples.

5. What steps might Stuart Benjamin (internal evaluator coach) have taken at the onset to help the evaluation team in this study obtain the needed pre- and post-session quiz data from CFS program participants? How might you have obtained a more complete data set? Explain. Consider how *Strategy 12: Fist to Five* or *Strategy 13: Dot Votes* (described in Chapter 5) may have been used instead of the pre- and post-session quizzes to obtain information on what program participants learned. Describe how you would implement each of these alternatives.

6. What do you think about how Stuart Benjamin (internal evaluator coach) managed the conflict that erupted between Michael Kowalski and Amina Jibreel (*Alimento* program staff members and evaluation team participants)? Review the information presented in Chapter 6 on managing conflict constructively. How might you have intervened to help these two individuals resolve their conflict constructively? Specify the steps you would have taken. Explain your reasoning.

Data Interpretation and Reporting Decisions/Actions

Nadifa Salaam had never interpreted data before, so she suggested the evaluation team work together on the interpretation, setting aside two entire meetings to review the analyses. Founder's Day was in a few weeks, and the team felt pressured to complete their interpretation and prepare the report for the community. They needed to determine what exactly the data meant. When a weather emergency canceled one meeting, their timeline became even more challenging.

1. *Analysis of existing data.* The attendance data—sufficient numbers—suggested both the participant trainer and community presentation components of *Alimento* were working for all three cultural groups. The team wasn't sure what the pre- and post-session quiz or evaluation data meant since there were many gaps. The data they did have pointed to positive results, but what about the data they didn't have? They decided not to use the quiz and session evaluation data.

2. *Electronic and written surveys.* The staff survey data indicated strong support for the training activities. The participant-trainer data were also positive, although they raised three possible changes: (a) additional support for developing presentation skills, (b) the potential value of a more inclusive name, and (c) potential expansion of the trainings. The community session results, although limited, were like the outcomes of the other surveys in that they, too, were positive. In addition, they provided at least some evidence that women from all the groups were using what they learned at home.

3. *Group interviews (by community).* Like the survey results, the group interview data were highly positive about how the program was meeting the nutritional needs of the three communities. The team thought the idea of cross-cultural sessions was an interesting suggestion that would, in one way, build on the positive interactions of the participant trainers during training sessions.

Unfortunately, given busy schedules and missed meetings, the team didn't follow the timeline carefully enough, resulting in a rush to complete the study. When the team had finished reviewing and making sense of the different types of data, Benjamin suggested they go back, look across the results from the different methods, and see if they could now answer the original evaluation questions. They did so, with the following results:

1. *To what extent does* Alimento Para el Pensamiento *successfully teach its trainers nutrition content and presentation skills?* According to the data, people perceived that the program successfully taught the nutrition content but had somewhat less success teaching presentation skills.

2. *How well do community participants learn key content during the nutrition sessions led by those trained in the program?* The evaluation team was less confident about the answer to this question because the data were fairly limited. There was some evidence that community participants did learn content and use it in their homes, but the available data meant they could not say that with complete confidence.

3. *To what extent does* Alimento Para el Pensamiento *effectively address the differing nutritional needs of CFS's immigrant communities?* Looking at the question, the team realized they hadn't really collected data that directly answered it. The data suggested the program appeared to meet the needs of the immigrant communities overall, but there were no data about their *differing* needs. Salaam and Garcia felt confident the evaluation results showed the program was working in their communities, but perhaps the team could do another study of what each community's needs were and then see how *Alimento* might address any differing needs straightforwardly. Knowing he now had experienced (if novice) evaluators on the team, Benjamin thought another evaluation might be feasible.

In thinking about the data and their upcoming report, the group decided to include the following recommendations:

- *Alimento* staff should examine how they are teaching presentation skills and consider more effective methods or additional support to participants.
- The program's name should be changed to reflect the multicultural nature of the current participant trainers.
- CFS should consider expanding the program to serve more women.
- *Alimento* staff should collaborate with CFS ELL staff to develop more effective ways to collect information on the learning of community participants.
- The *Alimento* evaluation team should conduct a study to see how the program addresses the differing nutritional needs of CFS's immigrant communities.

Pressure truly increased, as the agency's Founder's Day event was literally around the corner and the results were not yet ready for presentation. The team had decided to present the study's results in three ways: (a) posters plus conversations at a community event, (b) an oral report to the CFS board, and (c) a summary for the funder that Laura Cramer, the CFS grant writer, could also use. Kowalski wrote a first draft of the poster content that the team edited, then Salaam and Garcia, with help from other native speakers, translated the content into their native languages. Salaam contacted Kia Yang, and she volunteered to prepare the Hmong translation. The head of the agency's computer lab helped Jibreel finalize the technical form for the four posters, and she had the posters printed and laminated at a nearby copy store.

For Founder's Day, Benjamin reserved a table for the evaluation team in the agency's lobby, and the staff and participant trainers decided to provide items that would attract people to the table—healthy food samples, a sign-up sheet for interest in cross-cultural cooking sessions, and slips as part of a contest to suggest a new, inclusive name for the program. The Founder's Day event was a great success. Participant trainers took turns sitting at the table, greeting people—including several board members and a representative from the foundation that had funded the program—handing out samples, and going over the evaluation in whatever language was appropriate. Salaam and Garcia beamed as they discussed aspects of the evaluation process and its results. Yang spent time at the table, too, and said she wanted to rejoin the team for the next study. Jibreel and Kowalski stayed in the background, answering questions only when asked by one of the participant evaluators.

The four posters were hanging on the wall at the next CFS board meeting, and board members reviewed the results before the formal meeting began. Salaam and Jibreel divided the oral presentation between them and then responded to questions. The board received the report gladly and discussed the implications of changing the program's name and broadening its focus. After the meeting, program vice president Hannah Greene asked Stuart Benjamin how much the program cost per participant and why the team hadn't included those data. He quickly responded that the evaluation team had focused on other issues but volunteered to get the cost data for Greene the following week, which he did. That same week, Kowalski prepared the summary for submission to the funder, including program cost data, and forwarded the report to Hannah Greene, who was responsible for submitting it since the agency had not yet replaced Veronica Casanueva. He also e-mailed a copy to Cramer to use in writing proposals, with the message to contact him or Benjamin if she had any questions.

REFLECTION BOX III

How Is This Evaluation Going?

1. Revisit Chapter 6, Exhibit 6.1. What interpersonal conflicts occurred during this participant-directed evaluation? Make a list. Did the individuals involved predominantly respond by forcing, withdrawing, smoothing, compromising, or problem solving? How effective were those various responses in dealing constructively with conflict? What steps could/should Stuart Benjamin (the internal evaluator who coached the evaluation team) have taken toward constructively dealing with these conflicts? Revisit Chapter 6, Exhibit 6.6 to determine actions that might have been helpful. Explain your reasoning.

2. What unforeseen problematic events occurred during this participant-directed evaluation? Make a list. Revisit Chapter 8, Exhibits 8.3 through 8.6. Which of the events on your list are similar to those noted in these exhibits? How did Stuart Benjamin (the internal evaluator coach) and whoever was leading the participant evaluation team at the time of each unexpected event respond? How effective were these responses in keeping the evaluation on track? How might you have handled each incident? Explain.

3. Revisit the cast of characters in this case, shown in Exhibit 11.2. Next, revisit Chapter 7, Exhibit 7.2. Based on the behaviors of the characters in this case, where do you believe each lies on the attitude/aptitude matrix? Why? Next, revisit Chapter 7, Exhibit 7.3. Use this to discuss actions Stuart Benjamin (the internal evaluator coach) might have taken to deal with the challenges that various individuals displayed during this evaluation. How might you have dealt with the individuals whose attitudes and/or aptitudes put this evaluation at risk? Explain.

4. Who seemed to have real power during this participant-directed evaluation study? Put differently, who was especially influential in this study? In what ways? Do you think the distribution of power in this study affected the evaluation process and/or product in either negative or positive ways? Specify and explain.

5. Do you agree with the evaluation team's interpretations of the study's findings? Why or why not? What specific recommendations would you make based on the findings? Explain.

6. If you were the evaluator coaching those conducting this participant-directed evaluation study, what would you have done differently? What might you have said or done to successfully guide the evaluation team in this case study? If you were a participant on the evaluation team in this study, what contributions might you have made toward forging a successful evaluation process and product? Specify and explain your reasoning.

CASE STUDY TIPS:
THINK, INTERACT, PRACTICE, SITUATE

This section contains four sets of exercises for further engaging with this case study. The first set involves *thinking* individually about various aspects of the case's participant-directed study. The second set entails *interacting* in small groups (consisting of two, three, or four people) on collaborative tasks that involve critical analysis, reasoned discussion, and decision making. The third set prompts *practicing* in the real world by carrying out field-based exercises related to the case. The fourth set prompts *situating* personal lessons learned from this case within your own context as an evaluator.

CASE STUDY TIPS

Think

1. What are the strengths and limitations of this evaluation study? Draw a chart with two columns; label one "strengths" and the other "limitations," and then list specifics for each. What might the internal evaluator who coached those conducting this study have done to prevent or avoid the limitations? Explain.

2. In your judgment, did this participant-directed study adequately address the evaluation questions? To what extent? Explain.

3. Systematically review the various decisions and actions in this case study of (a) the evaluator who coached those conducting the study, (b) the individuals designated as leads in this evaluation, and (c) the team of participants conducting the study. Which actions among these individuals do you believe contributed most (vs. least) to a viable evaluation process? Which actions most contributed to producing credible/trustworthy (vs. implausible/untrustworthy) results? Which most enhanced (vs. diminished) use of the results?

4. Revisit the definition of interactive evaluation practice (IEP) and its grounding principles. In your judgment, how effectively did the evaluator who coached those conducting this study facilitate IEP? How well did this evaluator as coach use its principles to guide effective participant-directed evaluation practice? Explain.

5. What interpersonal skills were especially important for the evaluator who coached those conducting this participant-directed study? Explain. Make a list of the individuals who were members of the evaluation team that actually

(Continued)

(Continued)

conducted this study. What interpersonal skills did each display that either helped or hindered the evaluation process and product? What other participant competencies promoted the success of this evaluation? What competencies did the participants seem to lack that would have been helpful to the evaluation effort? Explain.

Interact

1. With a colleague, discuss your responses to each of the items above. Compare and contrast your thinking. Try to reach group consensus on each item. Present and defend your collaborative conclusions to other groups that also engaged in this exercise. How did these discussions expand your understanding of participant-directed evaluation studies?

2. Form groups of three and use *Strategy 4: Cooperative Interviews* (described in Chapter 5) to address the following question: "Think of a time when you participated in a participant-directed or participant-involved evaluation designed as a self-study (e.g., for program improvement, accreditation, accountability, or some other reason). What worked well? What was frustrating? What types of unexpected incidents occurred during the evaluation project? What were the effects of these incidents on the evaluation project and/or on those participating? Explain." Use the "Interview Response Sheet" (presented in Chapter 5) to record responses and identify key group ideas (similarities/themes/insights) across all responses.

3. Read this case study once more. Make a list (in chronological order) of each participant-directed evaluation team meeting that took place and note the names of those who participated in each. Form groups to simulate each evaluation team meeting and assign each person in each group to portray one of the characters who participated in that meeting. Role-play what occurred during that meeting, and then revisit Chapter 7, Template 6. Complete this template to reflect on the meeting from the perspective of the character you played. Next, use *Strategy 5: Round-Robin Check-In* (see Chapter 5) to share the Reflection Sheets within each group, and then conduct a qualitative analysis of the input across all sheets. What major themes emerge? What outlier ideas or concerns surface? How might such information have been helpful to Benjamin (the internal evaluator coach) and whoever was leading the participant evaluation team meetings? Explain. Consider using Template 6 systematically in your own practice to help keep evaluation processes on track.

4. The broadly stated goals of this participant-directed study were to promote ongoing organization development for continuous improvement by involving program participants in learning evaluation skills, owning results, and making change. Do you believe this study accomplished these goals? Discuss this issue by (a) forming a group of four, (b) assigning pairs within the group to either argue "yes" or "no" to the question of goal accomplishment, (c) present and listen carefully to the alternative arguments, (d) engage in open discussion to challenge arguments, (e) reverse perspectives, (f) drop advocacy of positions, (g) together consider all information that surfaced, and (h) reach consensus on the best-reasoned response. Based on your group's final conclusion, what advice would you have given to those who framed this study relevant to successfully promoting organization development through participant-directed evaluations? Revisit Chapter 2, Exhibit 2.6. Based on your group's conclusion, which spot on the ECB continuum do you believe this evaluation best represents? Why? Explain your reasoning.

5. In a larger group of 10 to 20 people, use *Strategy 6: Making Metaphors* (described in Chapter 5) to complete the following stem: *"A successful participant-directed evaluation study is like... because..."* Next, use *Strategy 10: Concept Formation/Cluster Maps* (described in Chapter 5) to identify common qualities or characteristics across all the metaphor responses. How did this exercise deepen or expand your understanding of participant-directed studies? Explain.

Practice

1. If you are able to, attend an annual meeting of a major professional evaluation association such as the American Evaluation Association or Canadian Evaluation Society in North America, or others around the world. Identify conference sessions that specifically focus on participant-directed evaluations—e.g., sessions on empowerment evaluation, organizational learning, inclusive evaluation, transformative participatory evaluation, and the like. Notice the issues highlighted in these sessions relevant to successfully conducting such studies. Seek out and introduce yourself to an evaluator who primarily conducts participant-directed studies. What does this evaluator believe are the most important skill sets for successfully conducting participant-directed evaluations? To what extent do interpersonal skills play a critical role? What advice would this evaluator give to others conducting participant-directed studies? If you cannot actually attend a

(Continued)

(Continued)

conference, then access the conference program (often posted online) and search for sessions that deal with participant-directed evaluation practice. Revisit Chapter 2, Exhibit 2.4 for key descriptors that will be helpful to your search. Select and read several conference papers that deal with participant-directed evaluations. What seem to be the major issues, concerns, challenges, and benefits in this approach to evaluation? Explain.

2. Use the Internet (or access electronic databases) to locate resources on participant-directed evaluation studies. Organize these resources into two categories: (a) books, articles, or manuals designed to teach people how to conduct such studies, and (b) evaluation reports on participant-directed studies conducted in various contexts. Obtain two or three resources from each category. Look through these resources and note various issues highlighted, participatory structures implemented, questions framed, data collected and analyzed, and conclusions or recommendations. How are these the same as or different from issues presented in this case study? What advice might you give to those conducting participant-directed evaluation studies in the future? Explain.

3. Identify an organization, institution, or program in your community devoted to organization development for continuous improvement. Arrange to meet with various individuals who work in that organization/institution/program to discuss the role of evaluation in such efforts, the various ways individuals contribute to these efforts, committee structures used to facilitate processes, issues/challenges that arise, and perceived benefits of such practice. Especially find out how the basic inquiry tasks are tackled in the organization's participant-directed evaluation projects. Do internal evaluators coach program participants to conduct evaluation tasks, or are external evaluation consultants hired to train and coach participants? Which structures, decisions, and actions seem to facilitate constructive evaluation processes? What challenges surface, and how are those handled? What advice would those you speak with give others involved in participant-directed evaluation practice? Explain.

4. Prepare and facilitate a professional-development training session that presents the foundations of IEP from a participant-directed evaluation perspective. Focus on involvement for organization development. Teach and involve people in experiencing several of the evaluator's dozen of interactive strategies presented in Chapter 5, all of which support successful participant-directed evaluation practice. Especially focus on those strategies you believe

will be most beneficial to people in the session by considering their evaluation roles and contexts.

Situate

1. Reflect on a participant-directed study where you served as evaluation coach or participated as a member of the team conducting the study. Compare and contrast the issues you faced in your participant-directed study to those in this case study. Draw a Venn diagram to record similarities and differences.

2. What aspects of this case particularly inform your current evaluation practice? Explain.

3. What skills do you possess that make you particularly well suited to coach or conduct participant-directed studies? Refer to evaluation standards, guidelines, and/or competencies (see Appendices A through C) in self-assessing your strengths and in determining where additional professional development would be helpful.

4. What helpful lessons did you learn from this case? What are your main takeaways? How will these enhance your future work as an evaluator?

CHAPTER REVIEW

Stuart Benjamin's role as part-time internal evaluator included the task of building his agency's capacity to conduct program evaluations as an ongoing part of their functioning. Program by program, the agency was implementing a continuous improvement process. This study marked Benjamin's first effort at coaching a staff member in leading a team of nonevaluators—two staff and three program participants—to collect and analyze data on how to improve a program. His intent was to teach people the evaluation process by having them conduct an evaluation. The organizational infrastructure supported this learning by doing, and a program head with more enthusiasm than technical skills was happy to receive coaching as the process moved forward. When she left the agency for another job, the team suddenly found itself without a leader. After a misstep, the team reorganized and got back on track, ultimately completing the evaluation and presenting results and recommendations to the board and community participants. The case's positive and negative applications of interactive evaluation practice (IEP) principles are summarized in Exhibit 11.5.

Exhibit 11.5   Applying the IEP Principles to the "Serving as an Evaluation Coach" Evaluation

IEP Principle	Positive Application	Negative Application
1. Get personal.	• Supported the leader of the evaluation project for as long as she was present • Also provided support to the staff and participant evaluators throughout the process • Stepped in when Veronica Casanueva left so the other evaluators did not feel abandoned	• Ultimately failed to pay attention to an important PIU's information needs
2. Structure interaction.	• Collaborated to structure evaluation meetings and materials thoughtfully to teach novices evaluation skills • Adjusted the process when it became clear that Casanueva needed help	• Confronted Sharon Nolan negatively rather than purposefully shaping a successful interaction
3. Examine context.	• Knew the internal workings of the organization well • Thought about how the various communities the participants represented would affect the evaluation	• Failed initially to ground the evaluation in the broader community context
4. Consider politics.	• Understood the importance of Casanueva having a successful evaluation experience	• Identified a replacement for a staff member without checking with those who had administrative authority • Did not keep the program vice president in the loop
5. Expect conflict.	• Worked with Casanueva, Kowalski, and Jibreel constructively to resolve unequal participation issues that occurred at evaluation team meetings • Worked with Casanueva to ensure a smooth transition when she left CFS	• Created unnecessary conflict with Sharon Nolan • Didn't anticipate the conflict with the participant evaluators when Michael Kowalski took charge
6. Respect culture.	• Invited members of different communities to serve as participant evaluators • Noticed how the participants deferred to the staff and helped shape staff behavior in response • Focused on program results for three distinct communities	• Failed to see the implications of having Kowalski assume a leadership role
7. Take time.	• Developed a timeline to ensure the evaluation would be completed in a timely manner	• Didn't monitor the timeline carefully, resulting in a rush to complete data interpretation in time for presentation

EPILOGUE

The End—and a Beginning

We began this book by stating that to be human is to engage with the forces among people that lead to activity and change: interpersonal dynamics. We end by affirming that effective interpersonal dynamics are the key to successful interactive evaluation practice (IEP). As the definition of IEP suggests, the interpersonal factor has two components: an evaluator's ability to interact constructively with a variety of players to further the success of an evaluation study and to structure activities conducive to promoting mutual success among people who participate in the evaluation. We structured this book to teach and reinforce a set of skills and strategies for use in program evaluations.

- Part I introduced IEP—defining it, framing it, and grounding it in research.
- Part II presented five chapters of skills and strategies with adaptable materials for use across many types of program evaluations.
- Part III encouraged you to observe, then reflect on and discuss three distinct cases, practicing IEP by analyzing, critiquing, and applying the content; the "Situate" exercises at the end of the cases encouraged you to engage these ideas in your own practice.

In Chapter 1 we defined evaluation as a process of systematic inquiry to provide sound information about the characteristics, activities, or outcomes of a program or policy for a valued purpose. We believe that IEP enables evaluators to address people's valued purposes by ensuring they truly understand the context, the significant actors operating within it, and the concerns and issues most important to the study at hand. We also believe that IEP enables evaluators to provide sound information by attending to the human details that may affect the technical aspects of a study, from its framing to its final reports—whatever form those aspects take.

If, as *Outliers* (Gladwell, 2008) detailed, an expert is someone with 10,000 or more hours of experience, novice evaluators just starting to log professional hours and far short of the 10K mark may wonder how they can engage successfully with the many and varied interpersonal demands of an evaluation setting. Exhibit E.1 returns one final time to the IEP principles, raising one or two broad questions for each principle to keep in mind when engaging in IEP.

Exhibit E.1   Questions to Keep in Mind When Engaging in IEP

IEP Principle	Questions to Keep in Mind
1. Get personal.	What are the needs of the people with whom you are working (both the personal factor and interpersonal factor)?
2. Structure interaction.	What interactions and activities will work well or be productive with these specific individuals or groups?
3. Examine context.	What interactions and activities are appropriate and will work in this setting?
4. Consider politics.	What evidence is there that political factors are at work? What can you realistically do about them?
5. Expect conflict.	Where is conflict likely to emerge? How can situations be structured to reduce destructive conflict and support constructive conflict?
6. Respect culture.	What interactions and activities are appropriate and will work within the cultures present in the evaluation setting?
7. Take time.	What are reasonable time frames for important interactions and activities?

SOURCE: © 2010 Jean A. King & Laurie Stevahn.

In closing, let us also recommend five actions based on what we've learned from our practice over time. These ideas are woven through the content of this book's chapters but are included here as final thoughts. First, start every evaluation by fostering meaningful involvement—building the buy-in and trust of primary intended users, getting everyone on the same page, overcoming people's fear and evaluation anxiety, creating incentives to motivate involvement, nurturing an open environment, and so on. It is well worth any extra time it may take. Second, communicate clearly at every stage of the evaluation; in our experience it is extremely difficult to overcommunicate and ever risky to undercommunicate. Third, don't be shy about confronting conflict head-on. Power issues can quickly derail an evaluation, and it falls to the evaluator to structure interactions effectively—staying alert to potential conflict—and then to respond if and when things go awry. Fourth, be thoughtful about project management and the time required for interactions. Just as we know the standard answer to any evaluation question is, "It depends," the standard length of time any evaluation activity will take is, "Longer than we thought." Fifth, reflection is a must—i.e., make and take the time for reflection, both as you direct the evaluation process and once it is finished. We know well it is incredibly easy to get caught up in the rush of events, and it is hard to stop and reflect before you're on to the next task, the next study, or everything you put on hold to complete the evaluation. But as Yogi Berra once asked, "How can you hit and think at the same time?" At its best, IEP requires thoughtful reflection on the interpersonal interactions integral to every evaluation. We have never regretted taking time out to think.

The next chapters of the book are unwritten. They are those you will create by applying these ideas to your own evaluation practice. This is the end of our book but the beginning of your thoughtful application of these ideas, in all likelihood building on what you already know and do but with newfound ideas and support. The proof that IEP works, finally, will be found in mastering the interpersonal dynamics that are the lifeblood of successful evaluation studies.

GLOSSARY

Accountability: A program's responsibility to provide evidence it is using resources, implementing activities, and achieving desired outcomes in conformance with requirements

Action research: "The scientific process whereby in a given problem area, where one wishes to improve practice or personal understanding, inquiry is carried out by the practitioner" (McKernan, 1988, p. 174)

Agile evaluation: An integrated approach to evaluation "that considers the unique and common effect of data, design, and program theory" in situations where surprise is unforeseeable (Morell, 2010, p. 99)

Ascriptive evaluation: An evaluation where an evaluative judgment is made but use is no longer possible (e.g., historic events, programs that no longer exist)

Audience: The individuals or groups who receive evaluation reports

Basic inquiry tasks (BIT): The seven steps common to multiple forms of social inquiry (framing questions, determining an appropriate design, identifying samples or data sources, collecting data, analyzing data, interpreting results, and reporting and disseminating the findings)

Carrot-and-stick use: The mandated use of evaluation findings, e.g., having to implement a validated program to receive funding (also imposed use)

Clients: The people who negotiate with and hire an evaluator and typically help shape and monitor the evaluation study

Collaborative evaluation: A form of participatory evaluation in which the evaluator becomes a co-investigator with clients and others in a process of joint decision making and implementation

Communicative evaluation: A "complementary evaluation approach that may be used along with the primary methods of school accountability to provide a more comprehensive picture of a school environment" (Brooks-LaRaviere, Ryan, Miron, & Samuels, 2009, p. 372)

Community-based research (CBR): A "partnership of students, faculty, and community members who collaboratively engage in research with the purpose of solving a pressing community problem or effecting social change" (Strand, Maruloo, Cutforth, Stoecker, & Donohue, 2003, p. 3)

Compromising: A response to conflict in which a person uses give-and-take to create a 50/50 split when personal goals and relationships with others are both moderately important

Conceptual use: The use of evaluation findings to better understand a program or policy (also enlightenment)

Conflict: "A *conflict* exists whenever *incompatible* activities occur" (Deutsch, 1973, p. 10; emphasis in original)

Conflict strategies theory: The dual-concerns model for managing conflict that includes the equal and paradoxical priorities of maximizing self-interest and maintaining good working relationships

Constructive conflict resolution theory: A theory that illuminates the dynamics of conflict by describing and reliably predicting how cooperative versus competitive goals influence behaviors among individuals in conflict situations

Culture: "The shared experiences of people, including their languages, values, customs, beliefs, and mores. . . . [Culture] also includes worldviews, ways of knowing, and ways of communicating" (American Evaluation Association, 2011, p. 2)

Deliberative democratic evaluation: A form of participatory evaluation that meets three requirements: "inclusion of all relevant interests; the evaluation is dialogical . . . to identify the real interests of the relevant parties; and the evaluation is deliberative, in the sense that results are discussed by the relevant parties" (House & Howe, 2000, p. 5)

Developmental evaluation: "An approach to evaluation in innovative settings where goals are emergent and changing rather than predetermined and fixed" (Patton, 2008, p. 277); "developmental evaluation supports program and organizational development to guide adaptation to emergent and dynamic realities from a complex systems perspective" (p. 278)

Empowerment evaluation: A form of participatory evaluation that "aims to increase the likelihood that programs will achieve results by increasing the capacity of program stakeholders to plan, implement, and evaluate their programs" (Fetterman & Wandersman, 2005, p. 27); often refers to an evaluation process that fosters self-improvement for groups with little traditional power

Enlightenment: The use of evaluation findings to better understand a program or policy (also conceptual use); enlightenment may refer more broadly to influence in the field

Essential Competencies for Program Evaluators: A set of standardized knowledge, skills, and attitudes that program evaluators should possess (Stevahn, King, Ghere, & Minnema, 2005)

Essential Skills Series in Evaluation: The curriculum for program evaluator trainings endorsed by the Canadian Evaluation Society (1999)

Evaluation capacity building (ECB): The process of using an evaluation not only for its results but also for the explicit purpose of building people's capacity to evaluate again

Evaluation influence: "The capacity or power of persons or things to produce effects on others by intangible or indirect means" (Kirkhart, 2000, p. 7) (also leveraged use)

Evaluation participants: Individuals who take part in a program evaluation in one of two ways: (1) participating in making decisions about the evaluation or in implementing it, or (2) providing data in one form or another

Evaluation standards: Commonly agreed-on principles of professional practice in program evaluation; "the standards identify and define evaluation quality and guide evaluators and evaluation users in the pursuit of evaluation quality" (Yarbrough, Shula, Hopson, & Caruthers, 2011, p. xxii)

Evaluation use: The act of people employing the process or results of an evaluation study to do something (e.g., make a decision, change someone's mind, learn about evaluation)

Evaluator role: The part that an evaluator plays in a specific setting (e.g., insider or outsider, expert, judge, collaborator, etc.)

Evaluator-directed evaluation: A form of evaluation in which the evaluator designs, produces, and delivers the evaluation products with relatively minimal involvement from clients or primary intended users

External evaluator: An evaluator who is not a permanent employee, hired by an organization to conduct an evaluation (also called an independent or third-party evaluator)

Extreme evaluation anxiety: "Disproportionate or excessive evaluation-induced anxiety" (Donaldson, Gooler, & Scriven, 2002, p. 262)

Forcing: A response to conflict in which a person achieves personal goals at the expense of others

Formative evaluation: A type of evaluation conducted for program staff to provide information on how to improve the program

Guiding Principles for Evaluators: A set of principles grounding high-quality evaluation practice developed by the American Evaluation Association

Imposed use: The mandated use of evaluation findings, e.g., having to implement a validated program to receive funding (also carrot-and-stick use)

Inclusive evaluation: A form of evaluation that "involves a systematic investigation of the merit or worth of a program or system, for the purpose of reducing uncertainty in decision making, and to facilitate positive social change for the least advantaged" (Mertens, 1999, p. 5)

Instrumental use: The use of evaluation findings for making decisions

Integrative negotiation: A process that engages conflict disputants in mutual problem solving for joint benefits and through which people seek to understand each other's underlying interests and maximize everyone's outcomes

Interactive evaluation practice: The intentional act of engaging people in making decisions, taking action, and reflecting while conducting an evaluation study

Interactive evaluation strategies: Carefully designed plans of action for engaging stakeholders throughout evaluation studies that are applied to achieve specific goals

Internal evaluator: An employee hired to conduct evaluations of an organization's programs

Interpersonal dynamics: The forces between people that lead to activity and change

Interpersonal factor: The unique ability of an evaluator to do two things: (a) interact with people constructively throughout the framing and implementation of evaluation studies and (b) create activities and conditions conducive to positive interactions among evaluation participants

Interpersonal participation quotient (IPQ): A statement of the possible relationships between evaluator and evaluation participants that specifies varying degrees of evaluator and stakeholder involvement in making and enacting decisions throughout an evaluation study

Interpersonal validity: The extent to which an evaluator is able to relate meaningfully and effectively to individuals in the evaluation setting; "the soundness or trustworthiness of personal understandings emanating from personal interactions" (Kirkhart, 1995, p. 4)

Leveraged use: Another name for evaluation influence; an integrated understanding of evaluation's consequences

Logic model: A graphic representation of the chain of assumed relationships between a program's actions and its outcomes that may include inputs, activities, outputs, and short- and long-term outcomes; people's theories of action relevant to program/organization effectiveness

Organizational learning: A continuous process of growth and improvement that uses information or feedback about both processes and outcomes (i.e., evaluation findings) to make changes; is integrated with work activities and within the organization's infrastructure (e.g., its culture, systems and structures, leadership, and communication mechanisms); and invokes the alignment of values, attitudes, and perceptions among organizational members (Preskill & Torres, 1999)

Participant-directed evaluation: A form of participatory evaluation in which staff or program participants lead the evaluation process

Personal factor: "*The presence of an identifiable individual or group of people who personally care about the evaluation and the findings it generates*" (Patton, 2008, p. 66; emphasis in original)

Persuasive use: The use of evaluation findings to persuade others to hold a specific opinion

Political use: The use of evaluation findings to support a decision someone has already made or to persuade others to hold a specific opinion

Practical participatory evaluation (P-PE): A form of participatory evaluation based on the premise "that stakeholder participation will enhance evaluation relevance, ownership, and thus utilization" (Cousins & Whitmore, 1998, p. 6)

Pre-evaluation stress syndrome: Michael Quinn Patton's (2008, p. 47) tongue-in-cheek label for the signs and symptoms of the unpleasant psychological reaction of some people to the beginning of a program evaluation

Primary intended user: "Those *specific* stakeholders selected to work with the evaluator throughout the evaluation" (Patton, 2008, p. 72; emphasis in original)

Problem solving: A response to conflict that uses cooperative negotiation aimed at maximizing joint outcomes when both self-interest and relationships with others matter

Process use: The influence of the evaluation process on people and systems being evaluated

Program evaluation: A process of systematic inquiry to provide sound information about the characteristics, activities, or outcomes of a program or policy for a valued purpose

Program Evaluation Standards: The formal set of standards for program evaluation, now in its third edition (Yarbrough, Shula, Hopson, & Caruthers, 2011)

Program participants: Individuals who receive services from or take part in a program

Qualitative methods: Procedures for collecting data primarily in narrative rather than numerical form (words rather than numbers)

Quantitative methods: Procedures for collecting data primarily in numerical rather than narrative form (numbers rather than words)

Request for qualifications (RFQ): A notice, usually from an evaluation funder or sponsor, that describes a proposed evaluation project and invites interested evaluators to submit their credentials for consideration

Responsive evaluation: An evaluation approach in which the evaluator seeks to understand and address stakeholders' concerns and information needs; it is not necessarily a participatory approach

Smoothing: A response to conflict in which a person gives up personal goals to maintain positive relationships with others at the highest level possible

Social interdependence theory: A theory that specifies how individuals can be in relationship with each other (cooperatively or competitively), the type of interaction characteristic of each relationship (promotive or oppositional), and the likely subsequent outcome (mutually or exclusively beneficial)

Sponsors/funders: The people who provide resources to conduct an evaluation

Stakeholders: The individuals who have a vested interest in a program or its evaluation

Summative evaluation: A type of evaluation performed to determine whether the program has achieved its desired outcomes

Surprise: Morell's (2010, p. 1) term for the unexpected in program evaluation

Symbolic use: The use of the evaluation process or its findings as a symbol of a thoughtful process to support a decision or to persuade others to hold a specific opinion

Transdiscipline of evaluation: An autonomous discipline "concerned with the analysis and improvement of a[n evaluation] process that extends across the disciplines" (Scriven, 1994, p. 160)

Transformative participatory evaluation (T-PE): A "form of participatory evaluation that invokes participatory principles and actions in order to democratize social change" (Cousins & Whitmore, 1998, p. 7)

Utilization-focused evaluation: "Evaluation done for and with specific, intended primary users for specific, intended uses" (Patton, 2008, p. 37)

Value-engaged evaluation: "*A value-engaged approach to evaluation emphasizes responsiveness to the particularities of the context, inclusion of and engagement with multiple stakeholder perspectives and experiences, and attention to the social and relational dimensions of evaluation practice*" (Greene, 2005, p. 27; emphasis in original)

Valuing use: "Use of the core work of evaluation to place value on a program or policy; use of the totality of the evaluation, not solely its process and/or outcomes" (Ottoson & Martinez, 2010, p. 10)

Windshield survey: A data collection process that involves driving around a neighborhood and documenting what can be seen through the windshield

Withdrawing: A response to conflict in which an individual gives up on both personal goals and positive relationships with others, a natural response to forcing

Appendix A

The Program Evaluation Standards: A Guide for Evaluators and Evaluation Users (3rd Edition)

UTILITY STANDARDS

The utility standards are intended to increase the extent to which program stakeholders find evaluation processes and products valuable in meeting their needs.

U1 Evaluator Credibility Evaluations should be conducted by qualified people who establish and maintain credibility in the evaluation context.

U2 Attention to Stakeholders Evaluations should devote attention to the full range of individuals and groups invested in the program and affected by its evaluation.

U3 Negotiated Purposes Evaluation purposes should be identified and continually negotiated based on the needs of stakeholders.

U4 Explicit Values Evaluations should clarify and specify the individual and cultural values underpinning purposes, processes, and judgments.

U5 Relevant Information Evaluation information should serve the identified and emergent needs of stakeholders.

U6 Meaningful Processes and Products Evaluations should construct activities, descriptions, and judgments in ways that encourage participants to rediscover, reinterpret, or revise their understandings and behaviors.

U7 Timely and Appropriate Communicating and Reporting Evaluations should attend to the continuing information needs of their multiple audiences.

U8 Concern for Consequences and Influence Evaluations should promote responsible and adaptive use while guarding against unintended negative consequences and misuse.

FEASIBILITY STANDARDS

The feasibility standards are intended to increase evaluation effectiveness and efficiency.

F1 Project Management Evaluations should use effective project management strategies.

F2 Practical Procedures Evaluation procedures should be practical and responsive to the way the program operates.

F3 Contextual Viability Evaluations should recognize, monitor, and balance the cultural and political interests and needs of individuals and groups.

F4 Resource Use Evaluations should use resources effectively and efficiently.

PROPRIETY STANDARDS

The propriety standards support what is proper, fair, legal, right, and just in evaluations.

P1 Responsive and Inclusive Orientation Evaluations should be responsive to stakeholders and their communities.

P2 Formal Agreements Evaluation agreements should be negotiated to make obligations explicit and take into account the needs, expectations, and cultural contexts of clients and other stakeholders.

P3 Human Rights and Respect Evaluations should be designed and conducted to protect human and legal rights and maintain the dignity of participants and other stakeholders.

P4 Clarity and Fairness Evaluations should be understandable and fair in addressing stakeholder needs and purposes.

P5 Transparency and Disclosure Evaluations should provide complete descriptions of findings, limitations, and conclusions to all stakeholders, unless doing so would violate legal and propriety obligations.

P6 Conflicts of Interests Evaluations should openly and honestly identify and address real or perceived conflicts of interest that may compromise the evaluation.

P7 Fiscal Responsibility Evaluations should account for all expended resources and comply with sound fiscal procedures and processes.

ACCURACY STANDARDS

The accuracy standards are intended to increase the dependability and truthfulness of evaluation representations, propositions, and findings, especially those that support interpretations and judgments about quality.

A1 Justified Conclusions and Decisions Evaluation conclusions and decisions should be explicitly justified in the cultures and contexts where they have consequences.

A2 Valid Information Evaluation information should serve the intended purposes and support valid interpretations.

A3 Reliable Information Evaluation procedures should yield sufficiently dependable and consistent information for the intended uses.

A4 Explicit Program and Context Descriptions Evaluations should document programs and their contexts with appropriate detail and scope for the evaluation purposes.

A5 Information Management Evaluations should employ systematic information collection, review, verification, and storage methods.

A6 Sound Designs and Analyses Evaluations should employ technically adequate designs and analyses that are appropriate for the evaluation purposes.

A7 Explicit Evaluation Reasoning Evaluation reasoning leading from information and analyses to findings, interpretations, conclusions, and judgments should be clearly and completely documented.

A8 Communication and Reporting Evaluation communications should have adequate scope and guard against misconceptions, biases, distortions, and errors.

EVALUATION ACCOUNTABILITY STANDARDS

The evaluation accountability standards encourage adequate documentation of evaluations and a metaevaluative perspective focused on improvement and accountability for evaluation processes and products.

E1 Evaluation Documentation Evaluations should fully document their negotiated purposes and implemented designs, procedures, data, and outcomes.

E2 Internal Metaevaluation Evaluators should use these and other applicable standards to examine the accountability of the evaluation design, procedures employed, information collected, and outcomes.

E3 External Metaevaluation Program evaluation sponsors, clients, evaluators, and other stakeholders should encourage the conduct of external metaevaluations using these and other applicable standards.

SOURCE: Yarbrough, Shula, Hopson, and Caruthers (2011).

APPENDIX B

American Evaluation Association Guiding Principles for Evaluators

THE PRINCIPLES

A. Systematic Inquiry: Evaluators conduct systematic, data-based inquiries.

1. To ensure the accuracy and credibility of the evaluative information they produce, evaluators should adhere to the highest technical standards appropriate to the methods they use.

2. Evaluators should explore with the client the shortcomings and strengths both of the various evaluation questions and the various approaches that might be used for answering those questions.

3. Evaluators should communicate their methods and approaches accurately and in sufficient detail to allow others to understand, interpret, and critique their work. They should make clear the limitations of an evaluation and its results. Evaluators should discuss in a contextually appropriate way those values, assumptions, theories, methods, results, and analyses significantly affecting the interpretation of the evaluative findings. These statements apply to all aspects of the evaluation, from its initial conceptualization to the eventual use of findings.

B. Competence: Evaluators provide competent performance to stakeholders.

1. Evaluators should possess (or ensure that the evaluation team possesses) the education, abilities, skills, and experience appropriate to undertake the tasks proposed in the evaluation.

2. To ensure recognition, accurate interpretation, and respect for diversity, evaluators should ensure that the members of the evaluation team collectively

demonstrate cultural competence. Cultural competence would be reflected in evaluators seeking awareness of their own culturally based assumptions, their understanding of the worldviews of culturally different participants and stakeholders in the evaluation, and the use of appropriate evaluation strategies and skills in working with culturally different groups. Diversity may be in terms of race, ethnicity, gender, religion, socio-economics, or other factors pertinent to the evaluation context.

3. Evaluators should practice within the limits of their professional training and competence, and should decline to conduct evaluations that fall substantially outside those limits. When declining the commission or request is not feasible or appropriate, evaluators should make clear any significant limitations on the evaluation that might result. Evaluators should make every effort to gain the competence directly or through the assistance of others who possess the required expertise.

4. Evaluators should continually seek to maintain and improve their competencies, in order to provide the highest level of performance in their evaluations. This continuing professional development might include formal coursework and workshops, self-study, evaluations of one's own practice, and working with other evaluators to learn from their skills and expertise.

C. Integrity/Honesty: Evaluators display honesty and integrity in their own behavior, and attempt to ensure the honesty and integrity of the entire evaluation process.

1. Evaluators should negotiate honestly with clients and relevant stakeholders concerning the costs, tasks to be undertaken, limitations of methodology, scope of results likely to be obtained, and uses of data resulting from a specific evaluation. It is primarily the evaluator's responsibility to initiate discussion and clarification of these matters, not the client's.

2. Before accepting an evaluation assignment, evaluators should disclose any roles or relationships they have that might pose a conflict of interest (or appearance of a conflict) with their role as an evaluator. If they proceed with the evaluation, the conflict(s) should be clearly articulated in reports of the evaluation results.

3. Evaluators should record all changes made in the originally negotiated project plans, and the reasons why the changes were made. If those changes would significantly affect the scope and likely results of the evaluation, the evaluator should inform the client and other important stakeholders in a

timely fashion (barring good reason to the contrary, before proceeding with further work) of the changes and their likely impact.

4. Evaluators should be explicit about their own, their clients', and other stakeholders' interests and values concerning the conduct and outcomes of an evaluation.

5. Evaluators should not misrepresent their procedures, data, or findings. Within reasonable limits, they should attempt to prevent or correct misuse of their work by others.

6. If evaluators determine that certain procedures or activities are likely to produce misleading evaluative information or conclusions, they have the responsibility to communicate their concerns and the reasons for them. If discussions with the client do not resolve these concerns, the evaluator should decline to conduct the evaluation. If declining the assignment is unfeasible or inappropriate, the evaluator should consult colleagues or relevant stakeholders about other proper ways to proceed. (Options might include discussions at a higher level, a dissenting cover letter or appendix, or refusal to sign the final document.)

7. Evaluators should disclose all sources of financial support for an evaluation, and the source of the request for the evaluation.

D. Respect for People: Evaluators respect the security, dignity, and self-worth of respondents, program participants, clients, and other evaluation stakeholders.

1. Evaluators should seek a comprehensive understanding of the important contextual elements of the evaluation. Contextual factors that may influence the results of a study include geographic location, timing, political and social climate, economic conditions, and other relevant activities in progress at the same time.

2. Evaluators should abide by current professional ethics, standards, and regulations regarding risks, harms, and burdens that might befall those participating in the evaluation; regarding informed consent for participation in evaluation; and regarding informing participants and clients about the scope and limits of confidentiality.

3. Because justified negative or critical conclusions from an evaluation must be explicitly stated, evaluations sometimes produce results that harm client or stakeholder interests. Under this circumstance, evaluators should

seek to maximize the benefits and reduce any unnecessary harms that might occur, provided this will not compromise the integrity of the evaluation findings. Evaluators should carefully judge when the benefits from doing the evaluation or in performing certain evaluation procedures should be forgone because of the risks or harms. To the extent possible, these issues should be anticipated during the negotiation of the evaluation.

4. Knowing that evaluations may negatively affect the interests of some stakeholders, evaluators should conduct the evaluation and communicate its results in a way that clearly respects the stakeholders' dignity and self-worth.

5. Where feasible, evaluators should attempt to foster social equity in evaluation, so that those who give to the evaluation may benefit in return. For example, evaluators should seek to ensure that those who bear the burdens of contributing data and incurring any risks do so willingly, and that they have full knowledge of and opportunity to obtain any benefits of the evaluation. Program participants should be informed that their eligibility to receive services does not hinge on their participation in the evaluation.

6. Evaluators have the responsibility to understand and respect differences among participants, such as differences in their culture, religion, gender, disability, age, sexual orientation, and ethnicity, and to account for potential implications of these differences when planning, conducting, analyzing, and reporting evaluations.

E. Responsibilities for General and Public Welfare: Evaluators articulate and take into account the diversity of general and public interests and values that may be related to the evaluation.

1. When planning and reporting evaluations, evaluators should include relevant perspectives and interests of the full range of stakeholders.

2. Evaluators should consider not only the immediate operations and outcomes of whatever is being evaluated but also its broad assumptions, implications, and potential side effects.

3. Freedom of information is essential in a democracy. Evaluators should allow all relevant stakeholders access to evaluative information in forms that respect people and honor promises of confidentiality. Evaluators should actively disseminate information to stakeholders as resources allow. Communications that are tailored to a given stakeholder should

include all results that may bear on interests of that stakeholder and refer to any other tailored communications to other stakeholders. In all cases, evaluators should strive to present results clearly and simply so that clients and other stakeholders can easily understand the evaluation process and results.

4. Evaluators should maintain a balance between client needs and other needs. Evaluators necessarily have a special relationship with the client who funds or requests the evaluation. By virtue of that relationship, evaluators must strive to meet legitimate client needs whenever it is feasible and appropriate to do so. However, that relationship can also place evaluators in difficult dilemmas when client interests conflict with other interests, or when client interests conflict with the obligation of evaluators for systematic inquiry, competence, integrity, and respect for people. In these cases, evaluators should explicitly identify and discuss the conflicts with the client and relevant stakeholders, resolve them when possible, determine whether continued work on the evaluation is advisable if the conflicts cannot be resolved, and make clear any significant limitations on the evaluation that might result if the conflict is not resolved.

5. Evaluators have obligations that encompass the public interest and good. These obligations are especially important when evaluators are supported by publicly generated funds; but clear threats to the public good should never be ignored in any evaluation. Because the public interest and good are rarely the same as the interests of any particular group (including those of the client or funder), evaluators will usually have to go beyond analysis of particular stakeholder interests and consider the welfare of society as a whole.

SOURCE: American Evaluation Association (2004). Retrieved from http://www.eval.org/publications/guidingprinciples.asp. Used with permission.

APPENDIX C

Essential Competencies for Program Evaluators

1.0	Professional Practice
1.1	Applies professional evaluation standards
1.2	Acts ethically and strives for integrity and honesty in conducting evaluations
1.3	Conveys personal evaluation approaches and skills to potential clients
1.4	Respects clients, respondents, program participants, and other stakeholders
1.5	Considers the general and public welfare in evaluation practice
1.6	Contributes to the knowledge base of evaluation
2.0	Systematic Inquiry
2.1	Understands the knowledge base of evaluation (terms, concepts, theories, assumptions)
2.2	Knowledgeable about quantitative methods
2.3	Knowledgeable about qualitative methods
2.4	Knowledgeable about mixed methods
2.5	Conducts literature reviews
2.6	Specifies program theory
2.7	Frames evaluation questions
2.8	Develops evaluation designs
2.9	Identifies data sources
2.10	Collects data
2.11	Assesses validity of data

2.12	Assesses reliability of data
2.13	Analyzes data
2.14	Interprets data
2.15	Makes judgments
2.16	Develops recommendations
2.17	Provides rationales for decisions throughout the evaluation
2.18	Reports evaluation procedures and results
2.19	Notes strengths and limitations of the evaluation
2.20	Conducts meta-evaluations
3.0	**Situational Analysis**
3.1	Describes the program
3.2	Determines program evaluability
3.3	Identifies the interests of relevant stakeholders
3.4	Serves the information needs of intended users
3.5	Addresses conflicts
3.6	Examines the organizational context of the evaluation
3.7	Analyzes the political considerations relevant to the evaluation
3.8	Attends to issues of evaluation use
3.9	Attends to issues of organizational change
3.10	Respects the uniqueness of the evaluation site and client
3.11	Remains open to input from others
3.12	Modifies the study as needed
4.0	**Project Management**
4.1	Responds to requests for proposals
4.2	Negotiates with clients before the evaluation begins
4.3	Writes formal agreements
4.4	Communicates with clients throughout the evaluation process

4.5	Budgets an evaluation
4.6	Justifies cost given information needs
4.7	Identifies needed resources for evaluation, such as information, expertise, personnel, instruments
4.8	Uses appropriate technology
4.9	Supervises others involved in conducting the evaluation
4.10	Trains others involved in conducting the evaluation
4.11	Conducts the evaluation in a nondisruptive manner
4.12	Presents work in a timely manner
5.0	**Reflective Practice**
5.1	Aware of self as an evaluator (knowledge, skills, dispositions)
5.2	Reflects on personal evaluation practice (competencies and areas for growth)
5.3	Pursues professional development in evaluation
5.4	Pursues professional development in relevant content areas
5.5	Builds professional relationships to enhance evaluation practice
6.0	**Interpersonal Competence**
6.1	Uses written communication skills
6.2	Uses verbal/listening communication skills
6.3	Uses negotiation skills
6.4	Uses conflict resolution skills
6.5	Facilitates constructive interpersonal interaction (teamwork, group facilitation, processing)
6.6	Demonstrates cross-cultural competence

SOURCE: From Stevahn, King, Ghere, and Minnema (2005, pp. 49–51).

APPENDIX D

Interactive Evaluation Practice Principles Chapter Crosswalk

- Derived from theoretical foundations for interactive evaluation practice (IEP) in Chapter 3
- Applied across chapters in Part II: Skills and Strategies for Interactive Evaluation Practice

IEP Principle	What This Means
1. Get personal.	• Find people who care about the evaluation and its results, especially primary intended users. • Know your leaders; they make a difference. • Involve people in evaluation planning, decision making, and implementation to increase their commitment to using results.
Applied to	
Chapter 4 *Evaluation Conversations*	• Strategically engage primary intended users in evaluation conversations. Learn what matters to them; determine their priorities and agendas. • Pay attention to the ways in which people interact during evaluation conversations; identify personal interactive styles. • Be personally present in evaluation conversations; listen intently. • Strive to establish cooperative relationships in evaluation conversations.
Chapter 5 *Interactive Strategies*	• Strategically use interactive strategies with appropriate others to engage them personally and meaningfully in cooperative work for successful evaluation practice. • Recognize how positive interdependence is structured into the interactive strategies and its potential for fostering positive relations and building trust among those participating.
Chapter 6 *Managing Conflict Constructively*	• Study the personal conflict styles of evaluation participants, especially primary intended users. Know how they are likely to respond to conflict. Know your own personal reactions to conflict as well. • Establish cooperative interpersonal relationships *before* conflict occurs; people are more willing to work toward mutual solutions with friends.

Applied to	
Chapter 7 *Creating a Viable Interactive Evaluation Process*	• Directly focus on people's contextual and cultural identities and what this means for communicating throughout the evaluation and for helping people make personal meaning of the process and outcomes. • Arrange logistics in ways that support people's personal needs during the evaluation; pay particular attention to individuals' attitudes and aptitudes. • Focus on the personal aspects of involvement.
Chapter 8 *Dealing With the Unexpected in Program Evaluation*	• Anticipate the unique and unexpected issues that individuals may bring to any evaluation context. • Know your clients and primary intended users well to be able to respond to surprises in productive ways. • Analyze key individuals in the evaluation process to better understand diverse perspectives and what those might mean for the evaluation study. • Identify people in the program/organization who can help problem solve.

IEP Principle	What This Means
2. Structure interaction.	• Not all interactive participation is good; it may be helpful or not. • Goal structures influence whether interpersonal interaction will be constructive or destructive. • Structure positive interdependence for cooperative interaction likely to produce mutually beneficial outcomes and positive interpersonal relations.
Applied to	
Chapter 4 *Evaluation Conversations*	• Intentionally interact with appropriate others to seek answers to the overarching goals of evaluation conversations. • Be systematic about structuring positive interdependence among conversation participants, to the extent possible. • Interact with primary intended users to create cooperative norms for the evaluation and, as possible and appropriate, within the organization.
Chapter 5 *Interactive Strategies*	• Apply the evaluator's dozen of interactive strategies to structure productive interaction and participation in evaluation studies.
Chapter 6 *Managing Conflict Constructively*	• Be systematic in creating positive interdependence and establishing cooperative goal structures throughout the evaluation process; this sets the stage for constructive conflict interactions. • Work with your primary intended users to create cooperative interactive norms for the evaluation and, as possible and appropriate, within the organization for the constructive resolution of conflict. • Facilitate mutual problem solving when conflicts arise. Teach people to name the conflicts they experience and apply the steps of integrative negotiation to resolve them constructively—don't leave conflict resolution to happenstance.

(Continued)

(Continued)

Applied to	
Chapter 7 *Creating a Viable Interactive Evaluation Process*	• Pay attention to the structural components of involvement, logistics, and communication that will move the evaluation forward. • Be sure the interactions facilitated are inclusive, strategic, and culturally appropriate. • When building evaluation capacity, structure interactions to teach people evaluation skills.
Chapter 8 *Dealing With the Unexpected in Program Evaluation*	• Acknowledge the unexpected when it occurs, and structure interactions aimed at problem solving. • Realize that handling the unexpected often requires high-quality, face-to-face interactions. • Consider that both internal and external evaluators can structure interactions that build on the inherent strengths of their respective roles.

IEP Principle	What This Means
3. Examine context.	• Always analyze the evaluation context. • Know that mixed motives are always in play in social situations; cooperative people may have competitive motives. • Consider context from a variety of perspectives; both macro and micro views provide valuable information—consider the forest as well as its trees.
Applied to	
Chapter 4 *Evaluation Conversations*	• Engage in evaluation conversations with appropriate others to examine and better understand the context of the evaluation setting.
Chapter 5 *Interactive Strategies*	• Apply interactive strategies with appropriate others to examine the context and setting of the evaluation study for effective decision making.
Chapter 6 *Managing Conflict Constructively*	• Pay attention to the features of the evaluation context that are important to resolving conflicts, such as goal structures, cooperative interaction, and conflict strategies used for resolution. • Recognize conflict behaviors in the evaluation context and confront them appropriately; notice patterns of forcing, withdrawing, smoothing, compromising, and problem solving.
Chapter 7 *Creating a Viable Interactive Evaluation Process*	• Work to understand both the organizational and social–cultural contexts of the evaluation setting. • Make decisions about how to create a viable evaluation process in light of contextual information.
Chapter 8 *Dealing With the Unexpected in Program Evaluation*	• Remember that evaluators can never know every detail about an evaluation context, even with the most thorough planning. • When things go wrong, consider aspects of the evaluation context that may be contributing to the problem or that may be helpful in its resolution.

IEP Principle	What This Means
4. Consider politics.	• Understand that evaluation processes and results are not the only factors that inform decisions; political forces are also at play.
Applied to	
Chapter 4 *Evaluation Conversations*	• Engage in evaluation conversations with appropriate others to better understand political considerations, issues, and agendas that will likely affect the success of the evaluation study.
Chapter 5 *Interactive Strategies*	• Apply interactive strategies with appropriate others to examine the political landscape, anticipate challenges, and problem solve issues.
Chapter 6 *Managing Conflict Constructively*	• Be aware that political agendas can be at the root of conflict that occurs in evaluation practice; be vigilant in seeking to understand the diverse interests and perspectives of stakeholders. • Work thoughtfully within the organization's political context to inform key leaders and encourage their support for a successful evaluation study, which includes constructively managing conflict.
Chapter 7 *Creating a Viable Interactive Evaluation Process*	• Recognize that resources help underpin the viability of the evaluation process; political factors may affect how resources are allocated. • Identify people in the program/organization who have power, and be sure to involve them in appropriate ways.
Chapter 8 *Dealing With the Unexpected in Program Evaluation*	• Accept the fact that political factors may negatively affect an evaluation, or even bring it to an abrupt halt. • Remember the clout factor in handling the unexpected; people who have power in the program/organization may be able to get the evaluation back on track. • Consider internal and external evaluator roles; either may assist or limit an evaluator's success in tackling unexpected issues.

IEP Principle	What This Means
5. Expect conflict.	• Conflict is not inherently bad; recognize its virtue. • Conflict will occur; manage it constructively.
Applied to	
Chapter 4 *Evaluation Conversations*	• Know that each person will bring diverse interests and perspectives to evaluation conversations; listen carefully and communicate understanding. • Frame conflicts and disagreements that may emerge in evaluation conversations as mutual problems to be solved rather than as contests to be won.

(Continued)

(Continued)

Applied to	
Chapter 5 *Interactive Strategies*	• Systematically apply cooperative interactive strategies to establish the social foundation for dealing with conflict constructively when it occurs. • Recognize that cooperative interactive strategies invite diverse perspectives that may create tension; trust the power of positive interdependence for creating conditions for constructive outcomes. • Cooperation and conflict are not exclusive; although the interactive strategies purposely structure cooperation, individuals will bring divergent views to the process.
Chapter 6 *Managing Conflict Constructively*	• Know what conflict looks like; recognize when it occurs. • Never be surprised when conflict occurs in evaluation practice; be surprised if it doesn't! • Work to establish cooperative relationships, teach participants the skills of integrative negotiation, and facilitate mutual problem solving.
Chapter 7 *Creating a Viable Interactive Evaluation Process*	• Analyze the program/organizational context for potential conflict. • Embed constructive conflict processes into evaluation activities in advance. • Develop a conflict-positive attitude; conflict can be a catalyst for positive change.
Chapter 8 *Dealing With the Unexpected in Program Evaluation*	• Know that the unexpected and conflict often go hand in hand; be ready to apply conflict skills. • Take advantage of the benefits that conflict can bring; positive change often evolves from problematic situations.

IEP Principle	What This Means
6. Respect culture.	• Appreciate the power of culture; different cultural foundations greatly influence perspective. • Seek and engage multiple and diverse voices. • Value differences, clarify assumptions, and create mutual meaning.
Applied to	
Chapter 4 *Evaluation Conversations*	• Apply cultural competence and cross-cultural communication skills in evaluation conversations. • Attend to cultural values, customs, norms, or traditions for respectful and constructive communication. • Value voice and inclusion in evaluation conversations.

Applied to	
Chapter 5 Interactive Strategies	• Appreciate how cooperative interactive strategies structure inclusion, value all voices, and capitalize on diversity for optimal decision making. • Recognize cultural/ethnic values and/or norms that support (or frustrate) the underlying cooperative intent of the interactive strategies.
Chapter 6 Managing Conflict Constructively	• Understand that cultural differences may lead to conflicts during evaluations; pay attention to them. • Be aware that different cultures may respond differently to conflict; allow people the freedom to do so. • Recognize cultural/ethnic values, customs, norms, or traditions that support (or frustrate) constructive conflict.
Chapter 7 Creating a Viable Interactive Evaluation Process	• Honor the varieties of cultural perspectives and experiences people bring to the evaluation process. • Capitalize on the unique cultural characteristics of participants that can enrich evaluation practice. • Know that developing cultural competence is a lifelong learning process for evaluators; make a commitment to it.
Chapter 8 Dealing With the Unexpected in Program Evaluation	• When something goes wrong, consider and seek to understand aspects of culture that may be involved in the situation. • Be alert to people who may potentially insult the cultural identities of diverse others; be ready to confront them. • Acknowledge cultural insensitivities that unintentionally occur, and apologize; work to make the situation right.

IEP Principle	What This Means
7. Take time.	• Interpersonal processes take time; be ready to devote time to what matters for successful IEP. • Positive interpersonal relationships develop progressively; persevere. • Think of IEP as a journey that involves shared decision making and constructive conflict resolution; it's a step-by-step process that will likely provide new insights along the way.
Applied to	
Chapter 4 Evaluation Conversations	• Meaningful conversations take time; don't rush the process of obtaining important information that will be needed to shape an effective evaluation. • Systematically take time to reflect on what has been learned from evaluation conversations; use that information to determine future decisions and actions.

(Continued)

(Continued)

Applied to	
Chapter 5 Interactive Strategies	• Consider time needed to facilitate interactive strategies; some demand more time than others. Apply strategies thoughtfully in light of what each can accomplish and the time needed for success. • Recognize and appreciate the "strategy-versus-time" trade-off; interactive strategies may take time but can produce big payoffs for effective evaluation decision making, implementation, capacity building, and commitment to using results.
Chapter 6 Managing Conflict Constructively	• Devote time to resolving conflicts constructively. • Recognize that intense conflicts concerning deeply rooted value differences or diverse philosophical beliefs typically demand much more time than do other types of conflicts. • Choose your battles thoughtfully—you have only 24 hours each day and your life is filled with competing priorities. Do take time to work through those conflicts that matter the most for the success of the evaluation. • Timing matters; deal with conflicts in timely ways when they arise—don't let conflicts fester, escalate, or become toxic by not taking the time to deal with important issues. • Make the time to reflect systematically on the evaluation process and to analyze any conflicts that have occurred. Learn from them.
Chapter 7 Creating a Viable Interactive Evaluation Process	• It takes time to prepare for logistics and to involve people meaningfully in the evaluation process; make sure you provide sufficient time. • Develop realistic timelines for the evaluation that attend to interactive process concerns. • Recognize that the evaluation process almost always pushes against established timelines; be ready to make adjustments.
Chapter 8 Dealing With the Unexpected in Program Evaluation	• Make time to recognize and address the unexpected; ignoring this risks the success of the evaluation. • Acknowledge the unique opportunities unexpected problems may bring if you take the time to leverage them for change.

SOURCE: © 2010 Laurie Stevahn & Jean A. King.

APPENDIX E

Generic Exercises for Reflecting on Interactive Evaluation Practice Case Studies

Part III of this book contains case studies that illustrate what interactive evaluation practice (IEP) might look, sound, and feel like in real-world settings. Chapter 9 presents an evaluator-directed study, Chapter 10 a collaborative study, and Chapter 11 a participant-directed study. Although these cases are not meant to be perfect (because no evaluation ever is), they do illustrate various dimensions of IEP and how evaluators might make decisions, take action, and reflect to conduct effective studies. To expand the reflection questions and case study TIPS (*think, interact, practice, situate*) in the case chapters, here we present a generic set of IEP exercises that can be applied across all the cases. Each of the exercises (tasks) invites readers to revisit and use key exhibits and templates (tools) as the basis for reflection and discussion. These generic exercises, therefore, reinforce the major concepts, frameworks, principles, and skills that form the backbone of IEP. Each task ends by inviting you to think about how to use each tool to reflect on the interactive dimensions of your own evaluation practice.

As you pursue these exercises, plan to discuss your reflections with collaborative colleagues. Doing so can enrich and deepen your insights through grappling with the multiple perspectives likely to surface during the conversation. In fact, using the exhibits and templates to guide discussions with colleagues somewhat simulates what real practice can be—meaningful conversations with coevaluators, clients, and other participants on how to frame and conduct useful studies. Think about how you might actually use these concrete tools to ground interactions with evaluation stakeholders and participants as you conduct your own studies. Ultimately, coming to know and appreciate IEP means making it your own. We offer these generic exercises in that spirit.

Tools	Tasks
Revisit the following:	Focus on a case presented in Part III of this volume or on an evaluation study you have conducted to address these reflective questions:
Chapter 2 Exhibit 2.1	How were the seven *basic inquiry tasks* determined and implemented in the evaluation study? Who was involved in deciding each step? Who was involved in carrying out each step? What processes were used to carry out each step? To what extent did the evaluator(s) engage primary intended users in the process? How meaningful was the interaction between the evaluator(s) and primary intended users? What other stakeholders participated in each step of the study? How successful was the study overall? What were its strengths and limitations? Explain. Whether acting as an internal or external evaluator, how might you use Exhibit 2.1 to guide conversations with clients and/or participants in your own evaluation practice?
Chapter 2 Exhibit 2.3	Based on what you know about the evaluation, in the end, where would you place it on the *interpersonal participation quotient*? The cases presented in Chapters 9, 10, and 11 of this book were intended to be examples of evaluator-directed, collaborative, and participant-directed evaluations, respectively. In your judgment, did these studies unfold as intended or did the evaluator–participant mix seem to shift midstream? How so? What issues and actions affected the evaluator–participant mix as the study was implemented? Explain. Whether acting as an internal or external evaluator, how might you use Exhibit 2.3 to guide conversations with clients and/or participants regarding the evaluator–participant mix in your own evaluation practice?
Chapter 2 Exhibit 2.6	Based on what you know about the evaluation, in the end, where would you place it on the *evaluation capacity building* (ECB) continuum? The cases presented in Chapters 9, 10, and 11 of this book were initially framed, respectively, as creating capacity to (a) use the process and/or product results of a single study, (b) enhance evaluation skills of participants, and (c) sustain change for organization development. In your judgment, did each study accomplish its intended ECB purpose? Why or why not? Explain. Whether acting as an internal or external evaluator, how might you use Exhibit 2.6 to guide conversations about capacity building options when framing and/or monitoring evaluation studies you conduct in your own practice?
Chapter 3 Exhibit 3.1	Based on what you know about the organization, program, and setting of the evaluation, what type of *social interdependence* predominantly seems to exist? In other words, how do people socially interact to accomplish goals? Where do you see evidence of people striving to accomplish common goals by promoting one another's success for mutual benefit? Where do you see people striving to compete by exhibiting oppositional behaviors to achieve exclusive benefits? Where do you see evidence that interaction does not occur—people do not cooperate or compete but, rather, work alone to accomplish goals? At the beginning, what was the likelihood of IEP being successful in the evaluation setting given the observed patterns of social interaction? In the end, how

Tools	Tasks
	successful was IEP in the evaluation setting given the social interactions that occurred during the study? What steps might you take to strengthen positive interdependence for cooperative relations among those in the evaluation setting? Whether acting as an internal or external evaluator, how might you use Exhibit 3.1 to assess cooperative and competitive social relations in the evaluation settings of the studies you conduct?
Chapter 3 Exhibit 3.3	Based on what you know about the evaluation, how successfully did the evaluator(s) attend to the *principles for IEP?* How did the evaluator(s) apply each principle? Which principles need further attention? What steps could the evaluator(s) take to strengthen each principle? Explain. Whether acting as an internal or external evaluator, how might you use Exhibit 3.3 to guide your own evaluation practice—especially as you intentionally act to engage people in making decisions, taking action, and reflecting while conducting an evaluation study? Explain.
Chapter 4 Exhibit 4.2	Based on what you know about the evaluation, how successfully did the evaluator(s) accomplish the seven overarching *goals for evaluation conversations?* On what did you base your judgments? Explain. What issues arose? What pitfalls occurred? Conversation Goals 1 to 3 tend to occur before agreeing to conduct a study; Goals 4 to 6 tend to occur after agreeing to conduct the study and throughout; Goal 7 occurs both during and throughout the study. With a group of colleagues, assign various character roles, then simulate a segment of the evaluation by using the goals to guide conversation (the *conversation starters and sample questions* in Exhibit 4.3 may also be helpful). Whether acting as an internal or external evaluator, how might you use Exhibits 4.2 and 4.3 to keep evaluation conversations on track in your own practice? Explain.
Chapter 5 Exhibit 5.2	Based on what you know about the evaluation, which *interactive strategies* were used to conduct the study? In your judgment, were the strategies employed effectively? Which strategies were not used but might have been? For what purposes? Explain. Whether acting as an internal or external evaluator, how might you use Exhibit 5.2 (also see Exhibits 5.3 and 5.4) intentionally to engage people in making decisions, taking action, and reflecting while conducting an evaluation study? Describe how you would implement each strategy chosen. What materials would you need? Consider *strategy outcomes, advantages, disadvantages,* and *useful applications* (described in Exhibit 5.7) in making plans.
Chapter 6 Exhibit 6.1	What conflicts surfaced in the course of conducting the evaluation? Who was involved? Which *conflict strategies* did disputants use to deal with their conflict situations: *forcing, withdrawing, smoothing, compromising, problem solving?* In your judgment, how was each conflict finally resolved: constructively or destructively? Whether acting as an internal or external evaluator, how might

(Continued)

(Continued)

Tools	Tasks
	you use Exhibit 6.1 to assess how conflict is managed in the organizations/programs in which you are working? How might you use Exhibit 6.1 to guide your responses to conflict in your own evaluation practice?
Chapter 6 Exhibit 6.4	Focus on one conflict that occurred between or among individuals in the evaluation. Apply *integrative negotiation* to resolve the conflict constructively. Use Exhibit 6.4 as a guide to write a script for managing the conflict incident constructively. Role-play the scenario. Debrief by discussing how you felt and what you noticed during the role play. What seemed to be especially helpful during the negotiation toward reaching a mutually satisfying resolution? What might you do differently the next time to further enhance constructive conflict resolution? Whether acting as an internal or external evaluator, how might you use Exhibit 6.4 to practice responding to anticipated conflicts or to guide your responses when conflict erupts in your own evaluation practice?
Chapter 7 Template 1	What was evident up front about the *evaluation context/setting?* Use Template 1 as a worksheet to record what is known. What additional information would be helpful? How might the evaluator(s) obtain that information? Whether acting as an internal or external evaluator, how might you use Template 1 to gather information on the contexts/settings of evaluations in your own practice?
Chapter 7 Template 2	What was evident up front about the *cultural context* of the evaluation setting? Use Template 2 as a worksheet to record what is known. What additional information would be helpful? How might the evaluator(s) obtain that information? Whether acting as an internal or external evaluator, how might you use Template 2 to gather information on the cultural characteristics relevant to an evaluation study you are conducting?
Chapter 7 Template 3	Was the evaluation guided by an *evaluation steering committee?* If so, use Template 3 to list those on the committee and what you know about each. In your judgment, does there seem to be appropriate representation? What is the size of the committee? What advice would you give the evaluator about populating the committee? Whether acting as an internal or external evaluator, how might you use Template 3 to determine who should serve on an evaluation steering committee in a study you are conducting?
Chapter 7 Template 6	Did the evaluator(s) systematically obtain *meeting reflections* to assess and respond to participants' experiences throughout the evaluation? Where and how might Template 6 have been used throughout the evaluation? Explain. Whether acting as an internal or external evaluator, how might you repeatedly use Template 6 in your own practice to keep evaluations on track?
Chapter 7 Template 7	Did the evaluator(s) systematically establish and revisit *working norms* throughout the evaluation? What impact did the use of norms (or lack thereof) seem to have on the evaluation process? Where and how might Template 7 have been used throughout the evaluation? Explain. Whether acting as an internal or external evaluator, how might you use Template 7 in your own practice to keep the evaluation process on track?

Tools	Tasks
Chapter 7 Exhibit 7.1	Based on what you know about the evaluation, to what extent do you believe the evaluator(s) demonstrated *cultural competence?* What evaluation concerns, decisions, actions, interactions, and so on seemed to indicate cultural competence (or lack thereof)? What evidence (if any) suggested the evaluator(s) grew in cultural competence during the evaluation? In other words, what seemed to indicate that the evaluator(s) became more aware of (a) self and others culturally; (b) positions of power; or (c) cultural norms, values, and ways of knowing? How did the evaluator(s) use language in ways that demonstrated understanding of cultural diversity (or lack thereof)? Whether acting as an internal or external evaluator, how might you use Exhibit 7.1 to reflect on your own cultural competence in evaluation situations and to assess your own lifelong growth?
Chapter 7 Exhibit 7.2	Refer to the *cast of characters* in each of the case studies in this book (Exhibits 9.2, 10.2, and 11.2), or make a list of the people involved in an evaluation you are conducting. Use the *individual attitude/aptitude matrix* (Exhibit 7.2) to think about the contributions of each character. Who seems to be both willing and able to do the work of evaluation? How do those people enhance the evaluation process? Which of the individuals seems to impede the evaluation process by being unwilling or unable to do the work? Focus on one individual and brainstorm how to respond to that person's situation (also see Exhibit 7.3). Whether acting as an internal or external evaluator, how might you use Exhibits 7.2 and 7.3 to keep evaluation processes on track in your own practice?
Chapter 7 Exhibit 7.4	Where (if at all) did the evaluator(s) focus on *assessing evaluation processes* during, after, and throughout the study? Were informal or formal actions taken to conduct such assessments? How might such assessments have been built into the evaluation more systematically (also see Exhibits 7.5 and 7.6)? Whether acting as an internal or external evaluator, how might you use Exhibits 7.4 through 7.6 to assess evaluation processes to keep studies on track in your own practice?
Chapter 8 Exhibit 8.2	What unexpected negative incidents occurred during the evaluation over which the evaluator had no control? Make a list. Categorize each using the *potential evaluator woes* framework. Which surprise incidents seemed to stem from the (a) environment, (b) client/user, (c) evaluation process/results, or (d) evaluator? In your judgment, how effectively did the evaluator respond to each incident (also see Exhibits 8.3 through 8.6)? Whether acting as an internal or external evaluator, how might you use Exhibits 8.2 through 8.6 to (a) anticipate potential unexpected incidents in your own evaluation practice and (b) respond in effective ways to keep the evaluation on track?

SOURCE: © 2010 Laurie Stevahn & Jean A. King.

REFERENCES

Abma, T. A., & Stake, R. E. (2001). Stake's responsive evaluation: Core ideas and evolution. In J. C. Greene & T. A. Abma (Eds.), Responsive evaluation. *New Directions for Evaluation, 92,* 7–22.

Alkin, M. C. (1985). *A guide for evaluation decision makers.* Beverly Hills, CA: Sage.

Alkin, M. C. (2011). *Evaluation essentials from A to Z.* New York: Guilford Press.

Alkin, M. C., & Christie, C. A. (2005). Theorists' models in action. *New Directions for Evaluation, 106.*

Alkin, M. C., Daillak, R., & White, P. (1979). *Using evaluations: Does evaluation make a difference?* Beverly Hills, CA: Sage.

Alkin, M. C., & Taut, S. (2003). Understanding evaluation use. *Studies in Educational Evaluation, 29*(1), 1–12.

Altschuld, J. W., Engle, M., Cullen, C., Kim, I., & Macce, B. R. (1994). The 1994 directory of evaluation training programs. In J. W. Altschuld & M. Engle (Eds.), The preparation of professional evaluators: Issues, perspectives, and programs. *New Directions for Program Evaluation, 62,* 71–94.

American Evaluation Association. (1995). Guiding principles for evaluators. In W. R. Shadish, D. L. Newman, M. A. Scheirer, & C. Wye (Eds.), *Guiding principles for evaluators: New Directions for Program Evaluation, 66,* 19–26.

American Evaluation Association. (2004). *American Evaluation Association guiding principles for evaluators.* Retrieved from http://www.eval.org/publications/guidingprinciples.asp

American Evaluation Association. (2011). *Public statement on cultural competence in evaluation.* Fairhaven, MA: Author. Retrieved from www.eval.org

American Psychological Association. (2010). *Publication manual of the American Psychological Association* (6th ed.). Washington, DC: Author.

Arredondo, D. E., & Block. J. H. (1990). Recognizing the connections between thinking skills and mastery learning. *Educational Leadership, 47*(5), 4–10.

Ayers, T. D. (1987). Stakeholders as partners in evaluation: A stakeholder-collaborative approach. *Evaluation and Program Planning, 10,* 263–271.

Baizerman, M., Compton, D. W., & Stockdill, S. H. (2002). New directions for ECB. In D. W. Compton, M. Baizerman, & S. H. Stockdill (Eds.), The art, craft, and science of evaluation capacity building. *New Directions for Evaluation, 93,* 109–119.

Bamberger, M., Rugh, J., & Mabry, L. (2011). *RealWorld evaluation: Working under budget, time, data, and political constraints* (2nd ed.). Thousand Oaks, CA: Sage.

Bennett, B., & Rolheiser, C. (2001). *Beyond Monet: The artful science of instructional integration.* Toronto, ON: Bookation.

Block, J. H. (1980). Promoting excellence through mastery. *Theory Into Practice, 19*(1), 66–74.

Bloom, B. S. (1986a). Automaticity: The hands and feet of genius. *Educational Leadership, 43*(5), 70–77.

Bloom, B. S. (1986b). What we're learning about teaching and learning: A summary of recent research. *Principal, 66*(2), 6–10.

Bolman, L. G., & Deal, T. E. (2003). *Reframing organizations: Artistry, choice, and leadership* (3rd ed.). San Francisco: Jossey-Bass.

Brandon, P. R., & Singh, J. M. (2009). The strengths of the methodological warrants for the findings on research on program evaluation use. *American Journal of Evaluation, 30*(2), 123–157.

Brett, J. M. (2007). *Negotiating globally: How to negotiate deals, resolve disputes, and make decisions across cultural boundaries* (2nd ed.). San Francisco: Jossey-Bass.

Brooks-LaRaviere, M., Ryan, K., Miron, L., & Samuels, M. (2009). Broadening the educational evaluation lens with communicative evaluation. *Qualitative Inquiry, 15*(2), 372–396.

Campbell, B., & McGrath, A. L. (2011). Where the rubber hits the road: The development of usable middle-range evaluation theory. In M. M. Mark, S. I. Donaldson, & B. Campbell (Eds.), *Social psychology and evaluation* (pp. 346–371). New York: Guilford Press.

Canadian Evaluation Society. (1999). *Essential skills series*. Retrieved from http://www.evaluationcanada.ca

Chen, H.-T. (1990). *Theory-driven evaluation.* Newbury Park, CA: Sage.

Chen, H.-T. (2005). *Practical program evaluation.* Thousand Oaks, CA: Sage.

Christie, C. A. (2007). Reported influence of evaluation data on decision makers' actions: An empirical examination. *American Journal of Evaluation, 28*, 8–25.

Compton, D. W., Baizerman, M., & Stockdill, S. H. (Eds.). (2002). The art, craft, and science of evaluation capacity building. *New Directions for Evaluation, 93.*

Compton, D. W., Glover-Kudon, R., Smith, I. E., & Avery, M. E. (2002). Ongoing capacity building in the American Cancer Society (ACS) 1995–2001. In D. W. Compton, M. Baizerman, & S. H. Stockdill (Eds.), The art, craft, and science of evaluation capacity building. *New Directions for Evaluation, 93*, 47–61.

Cousins, J. B. (1996). Consequences of researcher involvement in participatory evaluation. *Studies in Educational Evaluation, 22*(1), 3–27.

Cousins, J. B. (Ed.). (2007). Process use in theory, research, and practice. *New Directions for Evaluation, 116.*

Cousins, J. B., Donohue, J. J., & Bloom, G. A. (1996). Collaborative evaluation in North America: Evaluators' self-reported opinions, practices, and consequences. *Evaluation Practice, 17*(3), 207–226.

Cousins, J. B., Goh, S. C., Clark, S., & Lee, L. E. (2004). Integrating evaluative inquiry into the organizational culture: A review and synthesis of the knowledge base. *Canadian Journal of Program Evaluation, 19*(2), 99–141.

Cousins, J. B., & Leithwood, K. A. (1986). Current empirical research in evaluation utilization. *Review of Educational Research, 56*(3), 331–364.

Cousins, J. B., & Whitmore, E. (1998). Framing participatory evaluation. In E. Whitmore (Ed.), Understanding and practicing participatory evaluation. *New Directions for Evaluation, 80*, 3–23.

Davidson, E. J. (2005). *Evaluation methodology basics: The nuts and bolts of sound evaluation.* Thousand Oaks, CA: Sage.

Deal, T. E., & Kennedy, A. A. (1982). *Corporate cultures.* Reading, MA: Addison-Wesley.

Deutsch, M. (1949a). An experimental study of the effects of cooperation and competition upon group processes. *Human Relations, 2*, 199–231.

Deutsch, M. (1949b). A theory of cooperation and competition. *Human Relations, 2*, 129–151.

Deutsch, M. (1973). *The resolution of conflict: Constructive and destructive processes.* New Haven, CT: Yale University Press.

Deutsch, M. (2006). Cooperation and competition. In M. Deutsch, P. T. Coleman, & E. C. Marcus (Eds.), *The handbook of conflict resolution: Theory and practice* (2nd ed.; pp. 23–42). San Francisco: Jossey-Bass.

Donaldson, S. I. (2007). *Program theory-driven evaluation science: Strategies and applications.* Mahwah, NJ: Lawrence Erlbaum.

Donaldson, S. I., Gooler, L. E., & Scriven, M. (2002). Strategies for managing evaluation anxiety: Toward a psychology of program evaluation. *American Journal of Evaluation, 23*(3), 261–273.

Fetterman, D. M. (2001). *Foundations of empowerment evaluation*. Thousand Oaks, CA: Sage.

Fetterman, D. M., & Wandersman, A. (Eds.). (2005). *Empowerment evaluation principles in practice*. New York: Guilford Press.

Fisher, R., Ury, W., & Patton, B. (1991). *Getting to yes: Negotiating agreement without giving in* (2nd ed.). New York: Penguin Books.

Fitzpatrick, J. L., Sanders, J. R., & Worthen, B. R. (2010). *Program evaluation: Alternative approaches and practical guidelines* (4th ed.). Boston: Pearson Education.

Fleischer, D. N., & Christie, C. A. (2009). Evaluation use: Results from a survey of U.S. American Evaluation Association members. *American Journal of Evaluation, 30*(2), 158–175.

Frechtling, J. A. (2007). *Logic modeling methods in program evaluation*. San Francisco: Jossey-Bass.

Fullan, M. (2001). *The new meaning of educational change* (3rd ed.). New York: Teachers College Press.

Fullan, M. (2006). *Turnaround leadership*. San Francisco: Jossey-Bass.

Funnell, S. C., & Rogers, P. J. (2011). *Purposeful program theory: Effective use of theories of change and logic models*. San Francisco: Jossey-Bass.

Gladwell, M. (2008). *Outliers: The story of success*. New York: Little, Brown.

Greene, J. C. (1987). Stakeholder participation in evaluation design: Is it worth the effort? *Evaluation and Program Planning, 10,* 379–394.

Greene, J. C. (1988). Stakeholder participation and utilization in program evaluation. *Evaluation Review, 12*(2), 91–116.

Greene, J. C. (2005). A value-engaged approach for evaluating the Bunche-Da Vinci Learning Academy. In M. C. Alkin & C. A. Christie (Eds.), Theorists' models in action. *New Directions for Evaluation, 106,* 27–45.

Henry, G. T., & Mark, M. M. (2003). Beyond use: Understanding evaluation's influence on attitudes and actions. *American Journal of Evaluation, 24,* 293–314.

Hofstetter, C. H., & Alkin, M. C. (2003). Evaluation use revisited. In T. Kellaghan & D. L. Stufflebeam (Eds.), *International handbook of educational evaluation* (pp. 197–222). Dordrecht: Kluwer Academic.

Hopson, R. K. (Ed.). (2000). How and why language matters in evaluation. *New Directions for Evaluation, 86.*

House, E. R., & Howe, K. R. (2000). Deliberative democratic evaluation. In K. E. Ryan & L. DeStefano (Eds.), Evaluation as a democratic process: Promoting inclusion, dialogue, and deliberation. *New Directions for Evaluation, 85,* 3–12.

Johnson, D. W. (1967). The use of role reversal in intergroup competition. *Journal of Personality and Social Psychology, 7,* 135–141.

Johnson, D. W., & Johnson, F. P. (2009). *Joining together: Group theory and group skills* (10th ed). Boston: Pearson Education Allyn & Bacon.

Johnson, D. W., & Johnson, R. T. (1989). *Cooperation and competition: Theory and research.* Edina, MN: Interaction Book Company.

Johnson, D. W., & Johnson, R. T. (2005a). New developments in social interdependence theory. *Genetic, Social, and General Psychology Monographs, 131*(4), 285–358.

Johnson, D. W., & Johnson, R. T. (2005b). *Teaching students to be peacemakers* (4th ed). Edina, MN: Interaction Book Company.

Johnson, D. W., Johnson, R. T., & Stevahn, L. (2011). Social interdependence and program evaluation. In M. M. Mark, S. I. Donaldson, & B. Campbell (Eds.), *Social psychology and evaluation* (pp. 288–317). New York: Guilford Press.

Johnson, J. B. (1998). Toward a theoretical model of evaluation utilization. *Evaluation and Program Planning, 21*(1), 93–110.

Johnson, K., Greenseid, L. O., Toal, S. A., King, J. A., Lawrenz, F., & Volkov, B. (2009). Research on evaluation use: A review of empirical literature from 1986–2005. *American Journal of Evaluation, 30*(3), 377–410.

Joyce, B., & Showers, B. (1988). *Student achievement through staff development.* White Plains, NY: Longman.

Joyce, B., Weil, M., & Calhoun, E. (2009). *Models of teaching* (8th ed.). Boston: Pearson Education Allyn & Bacon.

Kemmis, S., & McTaggart, R. (Eds.). (1988). *The action research planner* (3rd ed.). Geelong, Victoria, Australia: Deakin University Press.

King, J. A. (1988). Research on evaluation use and its implications for the improvement of evaluation research and practice. *Studies in Educational Evaluation, 14*, 285–299.

King, J. A. (2003). The challenge of studying evaluation theory. *New Directions for Evaluation, 97*, 57–67.

King, J. A., & Pechman, E. M. (1984). Pinning a wave to the shore: Conceptualizing school evaluation use. *Educational Evaluation and Policy Analysis, 6*(3), 241–251.

King, J. A., & Rohmer-Hirt, J. A. (2011). Internal evaluation in American public school districts: The importance of externally driven accountability mandates. In B. B. Volkov & M. E. Baron (Eds.), Internal evaluation in the 21st century. *New Directions for Evaluation, 132*, 73–86.

King, J. A., Ross, P. A., Callow-Heusser, C., Gullickson, A. R., Lawrenz, F., & Weiss, I. R. (2011). Reflecting on multisite evaluation practice. In J. A. King & F. Lawrenz (Eds.), Multisite evaluation practice: Lessons and reflections from four cases. *New Directions for Evaluation, 129*, 59–71.

King, J. A., & Stevahn, L. (2002). Three frameworks for considering evaluator role. In K. E. Ryan & T. A. Schwandt (Eds.), *Exploring evaluator role and identity* (pp. 1–16). Greenwich, CT: Information Age.

King, J. A., & Thompson, B. (1983). Research on school use of program evaluation: A literature review and research agenda. *Studies in Educational Evaluation, 9*, 5–21.

Kirkhart, K. E. (1995). 1994 conference theme: Evaluation and social justice seeking multicultural validity: A postcard from the road. *American Journal of Evaluation, 16*(1), 1–12.

Kirkhart, K. E. (2000). Reconceptualizing evaluation use: An integrated theory of influence. In V. Caracelli & H. Preskill (Eds.), The expanding scope of evaluation use. *New Directions for Evaluation, 88*, 5–23.

Krueger, R. A., & King, J. A. (1997). *Involving community members in focus groups.* Newbury Park, CA: Sage.

LaVelle, J. M., & Donaldson, S. I. (2010). University-based evaluation training programs in the United States 1980–2008: An empirical examination. *American Journal of Evaluation, 31*(1), 9–23.

Lewicki, R. J., Saunders, D. M., & Barry, B. (2010). *Negotiation* (6th ed.). Boston: McGraw-Hill.

Lewin, K. (1951). *Field theory in social science.* New York: Harper.

Love, A. J. (1991). *Internal evaluation: Building organizations from within.* Newbury Park, CA: Sage.

Mark, M. M. (2003). Toward a comprehensive view of the theory and practice of program and policy evaluation. In S. I. Donaldson & M. Scriven (Eds.), *Evaluating social programs and problems: Visions for the new millennium* (pp. 183–204). Mahwah, NJ: Lawrence Erlbaum.

Mark, M. M., Donaldson, S. I., & Campbell, B. (Eds.). (2011). *Social psychology and evaluation.* New York: Guilford Press.

Mark, M. M., & Henry, G. T. (2004). The mechanisms and outcomes of evaluation influence. *Evaluation, 10*(1), 35–57.

Mark, M. M., Henry, G. T., & Julnes, G. (2000). *Evaluation: An integrated framework for understanding, guiding, and improving policies and programs.* San Francisco: Jossey-Bass.

McDonald, B., Rogers, P., & Kefford, B. (2003). Teaching people to fish? Building the evaluation capacity of public sector organizations. *Evaluation, 9*(1), 5–25.

McKernan, J. (1988). The countenance of curriculum action research: Traditional, collaborative, and emancipatory-critical conceptions. *Journal of Curriculum and Supervision, 3*(3), 173–200.

Mertens, D. M. (1999). Inclusive evaluation: Implications of transformative theory for evaluation. *American Journal of Evaluation, 20*(1), 1–14.

Moors, A., & De Houwer, J. (2006). Automaticity: A theoretical and conceptual analysis. *Psychological Bulletin, 132*(2), 297–326.

Morell, J. A. (2010). *Evaluation in the face of uncertainty: Anticipating surprise and responding to the inevitable.* New York: Guilford Press.

O'Sullivan, R. G. (2004). *Practicing evaluation: A collaborative approach.* Thousand Oaks, CA: Sage.

Ottoson, J., & Martinez, D. (2010). *An ecological understanding of evaluation use.* Princeton, NJ: Robert Wood Johnson Foundation. Retrieved from http://www.rwjf.org/files/research/71148.ottoson.final.pdf

Patton, M. Q. (1978). *Utilization-focused evaluation.* Beverly Hills, CA: Sage.

Patton, M. Q. (1994). Developmental evaluation. *Evaluation Practice, 15*(3), 311–319.

Patton, M. Q. (1997). *Utilization-focused evaluation: The new century text* (3rd ed.). Thousand Oaks, CA: Sage.

Patton, M. Q. (2008). *Utilization-focused evaluation* (4th ed.). Thousand Oaks, CA: Sage.

Patton, M. Q. (2011). *Developmental evaluation: Applying complexity concepts to enhance innovation and use.* New York: Guilford Press.

Patton, M. Q. (2012). *Essentials of utilization-focused evaluation.* Thousand Oaks, CA: Sage.

Patton, M. Q., Grimes, P. S., Guthrie, K. M., Brennan, N. J., French, B. D., & Blyth, D. A. (1977). In search of impact: An analysis of the utilization of federal health evaluation research. In C. H. Weiss (Ed.), *Using social research in public policy making* (pp. 141–164). Lexington, MA: D. C. Heath.

Pejsa, L. J. (2011). *Improving evaluation in the nonprofit sector: The promise of evaluation capacity building for nonprofit social service organizations in an age of accountability.* Unpublished doctoral dissertation, University of Minnesota.

Posavac, E. J. (2011). *Program evaluation: Methods and case studies* (8th ed.). Boston: Prentice Hall.

Posavac, E. J., & Carey, R. G. (2006). *Program evaluation: Methods and case studies* (7th ed.). Boston: Prentice Hall.

Preskill, H., & Boyle, S. (2008). A multidimensional model of evaluation capacity building. *American Journal of Evaluation, 29,* 443–459.

Preskill, H., & Caracelli, V. (1997). Current and developing conceptions of use: Evaluation use TIG survey results. *Evaluation Practice, 18*(3), 209–225.

Preskill, H., & Russ-Eft, D. (2005). *Building evaluation capacity: 72 activities for teaching and training.* Thousand Oaks, CA: Sage.

Preskill, H., & Torres, R. T. (1999). *Evaluative inquiry for learning in organizations.* Thousand Oaks, CA: Sage.

Pruitt, D. G., & Carnevale, P. J. (1993). *Negotiation in social conflict.* Pacific Grove, CA: Brooks/Cole.

Reeves, D. B. (2006). *The learning leader: How to focus school improvement for better results.* Alexandria, VA: ASCD.

Reeves, D. B. (2009). *Leading change in your school: How to conquer myths, build commitment, and get results.* Alexandria, VA: ASCD.

Rodriguez-Campos, L. (2005). *Collaborative evaluations: A step-by-step model for the evaluator.* Tamarac, FL: Lumina Press.

Rossi, P. H., Lipsey, M. W., & Freeman, H. E. (2004). *Evaluation: A systematic approach* (7th ed.). Thousand Oaks, CA: Sage.

Russ-Eft, D., & Preskill, H. (2009). *Evaluation in organizations: A systematic approach to enhancing learning, performance and change* (2nd ed.). Boston: Perseus Books.

Ryan, K. E., & Schwandt, T. A. (Eds.). (2002). *Exploring evaluator role and identity.* Greenwich, CT: Information Age.

Schein, E. H. (1992). *Organizational culture and leadership* (2nd ed.). San Francisco: Jossey-Bass.

Scriven, M. (1967). The methodology of evaluation. In R. W. Tyler, R. Gagné, & M. Scriven (Eds.), *AERA monograph series on curriculum evaluation* (Vol. 1, pp. 39–83). Chicago: Rand McNally.

Scriven, M. (1991a). Beyond formative and summative evaluation. In M. W. McLaughlin & D. C. Phillips (Eds.), *Ninetieth yearbook of the National Society for the Study of Education, Part II. Evaluation and education: At quarter century* (pp. 19–64). Chicago: The University of Chicago Press.

Scriven, M. (1991b). *Evaluation thesaurus* (4th ed.). Newbury Park, CA: Sage.

Scriven, M. (1994). Evaluation as a discipline. *Studies in Educational Evaluation, 20,* 147–166.

Scriven M. (2003). Evaluation in the new millennium: The transdisciplinary vision. In S. I. Donaldson & M. Scriven (Eds.), *Evaluating social programs and problems: Visions for the new millennium* (pp. 19–41). Mahwah, NJ: Lawrence Erlbaum Associates.

Scriven, M. (2005). Book review: Empowerment evaluation principles in practice. *American Journal of Evaluation, 26,* 415–417.

Senge, P. M. (2006). *The fifth discipline: The art and practice of the learning organization* (Rev. ed.). New York: Doubleday.

SenGupta, S., Hopson, R., & Thompson-Robinson, M. (2004). Cultural competence in evaluation: An overview. In M. Thompson-Robinson, R. Hopson, & S. SenGupta (Eds.), In search of cultural competence in evaluation: Toward principles and practices. *New Directions for Evaluation, 102,* 5–19.

Shadish, W. R., Cook, T. D., & Leviton, L. C. (1991). *Foundations of program evaluation: Theories of practice.* Newbury Park, CA: Sage.

Shula, L. M., & Cousins, J. B. (1997). Evaluation use: Theory, research, and practice since 1986. *Evaluation Practice, 18*(3), 195–208.

Skolits, G. J., Morrow, J. A., & Burr, E. M. (2009). Reconceptualizing evaluator roles. *American Journal of Evaluation, 30*(3), 275–295.

Sonnichsen, R. C. (2000). *High impact internal evaluation: A practitioner's guide to evaluating and consulting inside organizations.* Thousand Oaks, CA: Sage.

Stake, R. E. (1975). To evaluate an arts program. In R. E. Stake (Ed.), *Evaluating the arts in education: A responsive approach* (pp. 13–31). Columbus, OH: Merrill.

Stevahn, L., & King, J. A. (2005). Managing conflict constructively in program evaluation. *Evaluation, 11*(4), 415–427.

Stevahn, L., & King, J. A. (2010). *Needs assessment phase III: Taking action for change.* Thousand Oaks, CA: Sage.

Stevahn, L., King, J. A., Ghere, G., & Minnema, J. (2005). Establishing essential competencies for program evaluators. *American Journal of Evaluation, 26*(1), 43–59.

Stockdill, S. H., Baizerman, M., & Compton, D. W. (2002). Toward a definition of the ECB process: A conversation with the ECB literature. In D. W. Compton, M. Baizerman, & S. H. Stockdill (Eds.), The art, craft, and science of evaluation capacity building. *New Directions for Evaluation, 93,* 7–25.

Strand, K., Maruloo, S., Cutforth, N., Stoecker, R., & Donohue, P. (2003). *Community-based research and higher education: Principles and practices.* San Francisco: Jossey-Bass.

Stufflebeam, D. L. (1999). *Evaluation contracts checklist.* Retrieved from www.wmich.edu/evalctr/checklists/

Stufflebeam, D. L., & Shinkfield, A. J. (2007). *Evaluation theories, models, and applications.* San Francisco: Jossey-Bass.

Tjosvold, D., & Johnson, D. W. (1989). Introduction. In D. Tjosvold & D. W. Johnson (Eds.), *Productive conflict management: Perspectives for organizations.* Minneapolis, MN: Team Media.

Trochim, W. (2008, November). *Evaluation policy and evaluation practice.* Plenary session presented at the annual meeting of the American Evaluation Association, Denver, CO.

van Gog, T., Ericsson, K. A., Rikers, R. M. J. P., & Paas, F. (2005). Instructional design for advanced learners: Establishing connections between the theoretical frameworks of cognitive load and deliberate practice. *Educational Technology Research and Development, 53*(3), 73–81.

Volkov, B. B., & King, J. A. (2007). *A checklist for building organizational evaluation capacity.* Retrieved from http://www.wmich.edu/evalctr/archive_checklists/ecb.pdf

Weiss, C. H. (1972). Utilization of evaluation: Toward comparative study. In C. H. Weiss (Ed.), *Evaluating action programs: Readings in social action and education.* Boston: Allyn & Bacon.

Weiss, C. H. (1998a). *Evaluation* (2nd ed.). Upper Saddle River, NJ: Prentice Hall.

Weiss, C. H. (1998b). Have we learned anything new about the use of evaluation? *American Journal of Evaluation, 19,* 21–33.

Weiss, C. H., Murphy-Graham, E., & Birkeland, S. (2005). An alternative route to policy influence: How evaluations affect D.A.R.E. *American Journal of Evaluation, 26,* 12–30.

Worthen, B. R., Sanders, J. R., & Fitzpatrick, J. L. (1997). *Program evaluation: Alternative approaches and practical guidelines* (2nd ed.). New York: Longman.

Yarbrough, D. B., Shula, L. M., Hopson, R. K., & Caruthers, F. A. (2011). *The program evaluation standards: A guide for evaluators and evaluation users* (3rd ed.). Thousand Oaks, CA: Sage.

Author Index

Subject Index

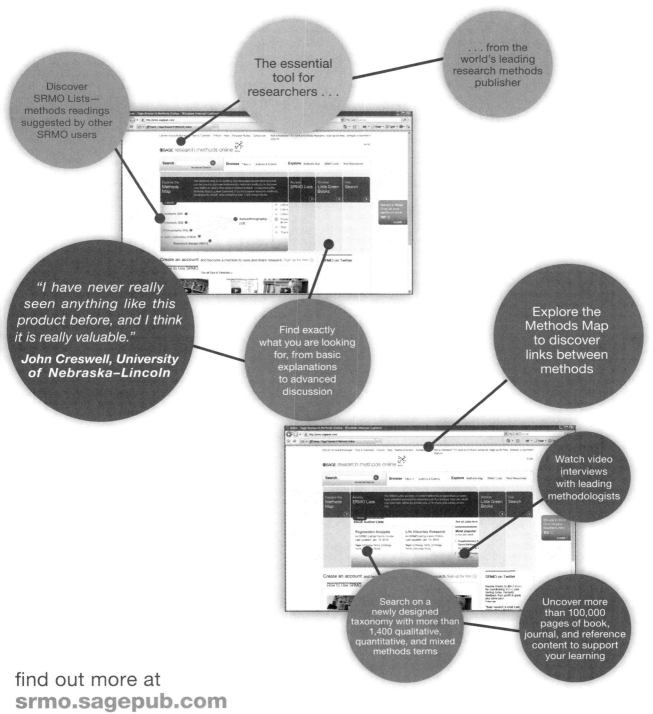